Along These Lines

Writing Paragraphs and Essays

Annotated Instructor's Edition

Along These Lines

Writing Paragraphs and Essays

Second Edition

John Sheridan Biays
Broward Community College

Carol Wershoven
Palm Beach Community College

Prentice Hall

Upper Saddle River, New Jersey 07458

Editor in Chief: Leah Jewell
Acquisitions Editor: Craig Campanella
Editorial Assistant: Joan Polk
AVP/Director of Production and Manufacturing: Barbara Kittle
Managing Editor: Mary Rottino
Production Editor: Joan E. Foley
Production Assistant: Elizabeth Best
Copyeditor: Kathryn Graehl
Prepress and Manufacturing Manager: Nick Sklitsis
Prepress and Manufacturing Buyer: Ben Smith
Marketing Director: Gina Sluss
Marketing Manager: Rachel Falk
Text Permissions Specialist: The Publisher's Domain
Image Permissions Coordinator: Charles Morris
Creative Design Director: Leslie Osher
Interior and Cover Designer: Anne DeMarinis
Cover Art: Piet Mondrian (1872–1944). *Tableau II*. Dutch. Superstock, Inc.
Development Editor in Chief: Susanna Lesan
Development Editor: Elizabeth Morgan

This book was set in 11/13 ITC Century Book by TSI Graphics and was printed and bound by
Courier Companies, Inc. Covers were printed by Phoenix Color Corp.

For permission to use copyrighted material, grateful acknowledgment
is made to the copyright holders listed on page 496, which is considered
an extension of this copyright page.

© 2001, 1998 by John Sheridan Biays and Carol Wershoven
Prentice-Hall, Inc./A Division of Pearson Education
Upper Saddle River, New Jersey 07458

Printed in the United States of America
10 9 8 7 6 5 4 3 2 1

ISBN 0-13-086993-7 (Annotated Instructor's Edition)
ISBN 0-13-086817-5 (Student Edition)

Prentice-Hall International (UK) Limited, *London*
Prentice-Hall of Australia Pty. Limited, *Sydney*
Prentice-Hall Canada Inc., *Toronto*
Prentice-Hall Hispanoamerica, S.A., *Mexico*
Prentice-Hall of India Private Limited, *New Delhi*
Prentice-Hall of Japan, Inc., *Tokyo*
Pearson Education Asia Pte. Ltd., *Singapore*
Editora Prentice-Hall do Brasil, Ltda., *Rio de Janeiro*

Contents

v

Narration   65

Process   91

CHAPTER 5
Comparison and Contrast   112

CHAPTER 6
Classification   140

CHAPTER 7   Definition   160

CHAPTER 8   Cause and Effect   182

Argument   206

Writing an Essay   231

CHAPTER 11   Writing from Reading   274

THE BOTTOM LINE Grammar for Writers   301

The Simple Sentence   306

Beyond the Simple Sentence: Coordination   320

Beyond the Simple Sentence: Subordination   332

CHAPTER 15 Avoiding Sentence Fragments   343

CHAPTER 16 Using Parallelism in Sentences   352

CHAPTER 17 Using Adjectives and Adverbs   360

CHAPTER 18 Correcting Problems with Modifiers   369

CHAPTER 19 Using Verbs Correctly   377

20 More on Verbs: Consistency and Voice   389

21 Making Subjects and Verbs Agree   401

22 Using Pronouns Correctly: Agreement and Reference   414

23 Using Pronouns Correctly: Consistency and Case   422

24 Punctuation   429

25 Spelling   445

26 Words That Sound Alike/Look Alike   454

27 Word Choice   468

28 Sentence Variety   473

Grammar for ESL Students   486

Preface

We are deeply grateful to the adopters and reviewers of the first edition of *Along These Lines*. This second edition, *Along These Lines: Writing Paragraphs and Essays*, has been refined and expanded in response to the encouraging reactions and practical suggestions from careful and generous reviewers. They appreciate the importance of combining individual and collaborative reinforcement in beginning writing classes.

THE WRITING CHAPTERS

We have retained what you liked most: the meticulous and intensive coverage of the writing process. This step-by-step coverage continues to trace the stages of writing, from generating ideas, to planning and focusing, to drafting and revising, to the final proofreading. The *lines* of the title refer to these stages, which are called **Thought Lines, Outlines, Rough Lines,** and **Final Lines** to serve as convenient prompts for each stage. Every writing chapter covering a rhetorical pattern takes the student through all the stages of writing, in detail.

These chapters remain filled with exercises and activities, both individual and collaborative, because we believe that basic writers are more motivated and learn more easily when they are *actively* involved with individual or collaborative tasks. In keeping with these beliefs and with the emphasis on process, this edition of *Along These Lines* offers instructors more choices than ever.

New Features

While the overwhelming response to the writing chapters was enthusiastic, some reviewers wanted more. Therefore, this edition of *Along These Lines* contains the following new features:
- A chapter on writing the definition paragraph, with complete coverage of the writing stages
- More exercises on topic sentences
- Additional exercises on comparison/contrast

Additional Features

Along These Lines continues to include these distinctive features:

- A lively, conversational tone, including question-and-answer formats and dialogues
- Not much "talk" about writing; instead, no more than two pages of print are without a chart, a box, a list, an example, or an exercise
- Small, simple clusters of information surrounded by white space rather than intimidating expanses of small print
- Boxed examples of the outline, draft, and final version of the writing assignment in each chapter
- Exercises throughout each chapter, not merely at the end, so each concept is reinforced as soon as it is introduced
- Exercises that are not merely fill-in-the-blanks, but collaborative ones that have students writing with peers, interviewing classmates, reacting to others' suggestions, and building on others' ideas
- Numerous writing topics and activities in each chapter, providing more flexibility for the instructor
- A peer review form in each chapter, so students can benefit from a classmate's reaction to their drafts

THE READING SECTIONS

New Features

Reacting to reviewers' suggestions, we have made these changes and additions to the reading sections:

- The chapter on "Writing from Reading" has been repositioned. It is now at the end of the writing chapters, so that it does not interrupt the flow of the writing instruction.
- A new section, "Writing the Essay Test," has been added.
- New readings, on such topics as high school and professional athletics, being bilingual, and reaching for the American Dream, have been added.
- The reading selections include more topics for writing a summary or answering a comprehension question.

Additional Features

Along These Lines continues to offer these features:

- A separate and detailed chapter on "Writing from Reading," explaining and illustrating the steps of prereading, reading, annotating, summarizing, and reacting (in writing) to another's ideas
- Vocabulary definitions for each reading selection
- Grouping of selections by rhetorical pattern
- Readings selected to appeal to working students, returning students, and students who are parents, spouses, and veterans. Selections focus on such topics as the workplace, getting an education, generational divisions and definitions, fitting in, or feeling left out
- Readings that are accessible to this student audience—thus many of the selections come from newspapers or magazines students would flip through at a newstand
- Topics for writing sparked by the content of the writing, designed to elicit thinking, not rote replication of a model

THE GRAMMAR CHAPTERS

New Features

- Thirty percent more exercises
- A chapter on adjectives and adverbs
- A chapter on spelling
- A chapter on sentence variety
- A chapter on words that sound alike/look alike
- A chapter on word choice
- An ESL appendix
- Expanded coverage of the uses of the apostrophe
- Expanded coverage of pronoun case in comparisons
- Expanded coverage of subject-verb agreement

Additional Features

Because reviewers especially praised the focus and the exercises of the grammar chapters, these chapters continue to include these features:

- Emphasis on the most important skills for college readiness
- Grammar concepts taught step-by-step, as in "Two Steps to Check for Fragments"

- Numerous exercises, including practice, editing, and collaborative exercises

This new edition of *Along These Lines: Writing Paragraphs and Essays* also retains its dual appeal: **both traditionalists and innovators will find something useful in the many activities, assignments, and exercises designed to get students thinking, reacting, and connecting ideas.** It stresses the planning stage of writing and proposes the outline as a useful tool. Instructors who feel uncomfortable with outlining may skim the outlining sections, preferring to spend more time on the extensive sections on generating ideas and on revision. The text is designed to be a menu: we recognize that every instructor knows what works best in his or her classroom. Our goal is to provide sufficient options to accommodate a diversity of teaching strategies and student populations.

Instructors will find *Along These Lines*, second edition, easy to use for several reasons:

- It has so many exercises, activities, assignments, and readings that teachers can pick what they like and adapt their choices to the needs of different class sections.
- The tear-out exercises reinforce every instructional concept and eliminate the pressure instructors face in preparing supplemental materials.
- The exercises provide an instant lesson plan for any class period or individualized work for students in a writing lab.

This book will appeal to instructors, but more importantly, it will work for students. *Along These Lines* has many distinctive features, but the book's most distinctive feature is our belief that a basic text does not have to be tedious, patronizing, or boring. In contrast, *Along These Lines* is written with the philosophy that an effective text should not only stimulate and motivate students, but it should also respect their individuality and their innate desire to learn and succeed.

ACKNOWLEDGMENTS

We have been extremely gratified and encouraged by the positive feedback from adopters of *Along These Lines*. This new edition also treats writing as an ongoing process, and we have maintained much of the collaborative nature of the text while significantly expanding the grammar coverage. Our refinements reflect the collective insight of conscientious reviewers, and we wish to thank the following professionals for their collegial support and practical suggestions:

Rita Delude	New Hampshire Community Technical College
Carin Halper	California State University at Fresno
Carlotta Hill	Oklahoma City Community College
Ken McLaurin	Central Piedmont Community College
Keflyn Reed	Bishop State Community College
Bonnie Ronson	Hillsborough Community College
Harvey Rubinstein	Hudson County Community College
Janet Seim	Mt. San Antonio College

Thanks also to Joan Polk, editorial assistant, for coordinating these constructive reviews and for always helping us find our way in Upper Saddle River.

We are also indebted to many individuals at Prentice Hall whose enthusiasm for out project never waned. Leah Jewell, editor in chief, graciously coordinated several meetings on our behalf; she helped us increase the scope of our book while maintaining our original vision. For the past year, Craig Campanella, English editor, kept in regular contact, responded promptly to our frantic e-mails, and gently broke the news about imminent deadlines. Despite his own full plate of projects, Craig treated us to some very fine cuisine as production dates loomed, and he always respected the time demands of our full-time jobs in the classroom. All authors should be fortunate enough to work with such a caring editor.

Additionally, we were fortunate to have Betty Morgan as our development editor. She shrewdly reshaped sections, reorganized exercise sequences, and provided us with an impressive blend of detailed critiques and compliments. She streamlined the revision process and made it more productive than we ever thought possible. We also benefitted from the superb copyediting talents of Kathryn Graehl. Her judicious edits, typesetting codes, and tactful notes helped shape a rather bulky manuscript into production-ready copy. Thanks also to Susanna Lesan for her help in keeping the project on schedule, to the late Bonnie Biller for her numerous insightful suggestions, and to The Publisher's Domain for painstaking efforts at tracking down copyright holders and securing necessary permissions.

We are most grateful to the talented design and production staffs at Prentice Hall. Based on just a few of our suggestions and design preferences, Anne DeMarinis, Nancy Wells, and Leslie Osher created an attractive, user-friendly design for this edition, and Joan Foley patiently guided us through the production/page proof process for both the student and instructor's annotated versions. Without Joan's thorough attention to detail and uncanny skill at cutting through clutter, we would still be lost in a maze of page proofs and reminder notes taped to our computer screens. Many thanks, Joan, for keeping it all straight for us.

Finally, we are profoundly grateful to our colleagues at Broward Community College and Palm Beach Community College for tolerating our puzzled looks and incessant mutterings as visions of missed deadlines danced in our heads. As our extended family, you always manage to keep us relatively sane. Thanks for your camaraderie and constant support along *all* lines.

John Sheridan Biays
Carol Wershoven

Supplements

Annotated Instructor's Edition. (0-13-086993-7) The *AIE* features the answers to all of the exercises and includes marginal annotations to enhance instruction. Written by John Biays and Carol Wershoven, these annotations are derived from their years of experience teaching developmental writing. "Teaching Tips" offer practical, proven ideas for getting the most out of each class session. They include specific activities to help students master the material. "Notes" provide chapter cross-references and suggestions for helping the class run more smoothly. "Discussion Questions" offer ideas on promoting class interaction. "Answers Will Vary" alert instructors to the questions that have a range of responses.

Instructor's Resource Manual. (0-13-089135-5) An additional free supplement for instructors, the *Instructor's Resource Manual* provides additional teaching strategies, additional collaborative exercises, sample syllabi, chapter summaries, and more.

Companion Website: http://www.prenhall.com/biays Free to students, the Companion Website is an interactive study resource for students. In includes Chapter Objectives, self-grading quizzes, essay-writing exercises, and web destinations for further study.

ALONG THESE LINES, Second Edition, The Online Course. Prentice Hall's new online developmental writing course offers you all the advantages of a custom-built program without the hassle of writing it from scratch. This course supports and augments the ALONG THESE LINES series by providing a complete array of writing concepts and exercises at your fingertips—to use just as it is presented *or* to be customized to fit your specific course syllabus.

Compatible with WebCT^{TM}, Blackboard, and eCollege platforms, ALONG THESE LINES Online includes the following features: Chapter Introductions, Lecture Notes, and Writing Workshops for each writing chapter; Quizzes that are auto-scored and recorded; Essay Questions; E-mail Accounts for each student and instructor; and Course Management.

To view a demonstration, go to <http://www.prenhall.com/cms>.

English on the Internet: A Critical Thinking Guide, 2001. This guide focuses on developing the critical thinking skills necessary to evaluate and use online sources effectively. The guide also provides a brief introduction to navigating the Internet, along with complete references related specifically to the English discipline and how to use the companion websites available for many Prentice Hall textbooks. This 96-page supplementary book is **free** to students when shrinkwrapped as a package *with any English title.*

To receive any of these supplements, contact your local Prentice Hall representative or call Faculty Services at 1-800-526-0485.

Writing in Stages
The Process Approach

INTRODUCTION

Learning by Doing

Writing is a skill, and like any skill, writing improves with practice. This book provides you the practice to improve your writing through several activities. Some activities can be done by yourself, some will ask you to work with a partner or a group, some can be done in the classroom, and some can be done at home. The important thing to remember is that *good writing takes practice:* you can learn to write well by writing.

Steps Make Writing Easier

Writing is easier if you *do not try to do too much at once.* Producing a piece of effective writing requires that you think, plan, draft, re-think, focus, revise, edit, and proofread. You can become frustrated if you try to do all these things at the same time.

To make the task of writing easier, *Along These Lines* breaks the process into stages. Throughout this book, the writing process is divided into the following four major parts:

Thought Lines

In this stage, you *think* about your topic, and you gather ideas. You *react* to your own ideas and add more ideas to your first thoughts. You can also *react* to other people's ideas as a way of generating your own writing material.

Outlines

In this stage, you begin to *plan* your writing. You examine your ideas and begin to *focus* them around one main idea. Planning involves combining, dividing, or even eliminating the ideas you started with. It involves more thinking about the point you want to make and the order of details that can best express your point.

Rough Lines

In this stage, the thinking and planning begin to shape themselves into a piece of writing. You complete a *draft* of your work, a rough version of the finished product. And then you think again as you examine the draft and check it. Checking it begins the process of *revision*, "fixing" the draft so that it takes the shape you want and expresses your ideas clearly.

1

Final Lines

In this stage, the final version of your writing gets one last careful *review*. When you prepare the final copy of your work, you *proofread* and concentrate on identifying and correcting any mistakes in spelling, mechanics, or punctuation you may have overlooked. This stage is the *final check* of your work to make your writing the best it can be.

These four stages in the writing process—*thought lines*, *outlines*, *rough lines*, and *final lines*—may overlap. You may be changing your plan (the outlines stage) even as you work on the rough draft of your paper; there is no rule that prevents you from moving back to an earlier stage. Thinking of writing as a series of stages helps you to see the process as a manageable task, for it helps you avoid doing everything at once and becoming overwhelmed by the challenge.

Throughout the chapters of this text, you will have many opportunities to become familiar with the four stages of effective writing. Working individually and with your classmates, you can become a better writer along *all* lines.

CHAPTER 1

Illustration

This section focuses on writing a paragraph. You may ask, "Why a paragraph? Why not something longer, like a two- or three-page paper?"

For one thing, all essays are a series of paragraphs. If you can write one good paragraph, you can write more than one. The **paragraph** is the basic building block of any essay. It is a group of sentences focusing on one idea or one point. Keep this concept in mind: *one idea to a paragraph.* Focusing on one idea or one point gives a paragraph **unity.** If you have a new point, start a new paragraph.

You may ask, "Doesn't this mean a paragraph will be short? How long should a paragraph be, anyway?" To convince a reader of one main point, you need to make it, then support it, develop it, explain it, and describe it. There will be shorter and longer paragraphs, but for now, you can assume your paragraph will be somewhere between seven and twelve sentences long.

This chapter will guide you through each stage of the writing process:

- Thought Lines—how to generate and develop ideas for your paragraph
- Outlines—how to organize your ideas
- Rough Lines—how to make and revise rough drafts
- Final Lines—how to edit and refine your ideas

Note: You can use these terms simply as convenient "cues" to help students stay focused on the basic stages of the writing process. As you review brainstorming, drafting, and revising steps, remind students that they can easily become frustrated if they try to do too many steps at the same time.

We give extra emphasis to the thought lines in this chapter, to give you that extra help in getting started that students need.

BEGINNING THE THOUGHT LINES

Suppose your instructor asks you to write a paragraph about clothes. You already know your **purpose,** to write a paragraph that makes some point about clothes. You have an **audience** since you are writing this paragraph for your instructor and classmates. Knowing your purpose and audience is important in writing effectively. Often, your purpose is to write a specific kind of paper for a class. But sometimes you may have to write for a different purpose or audience, such as writing instructions for a new employee, or a complaint letter to a company, or a short essay for a scholarship application.

Freewriting, Brainstorming, Keeping a Journal

Discussion Questions: Ask students why freewriting might seem awkward at first. Also, if they are "free" to write any thoughts they have on a subject, do they feel less pressure or more pressure than usual? (Responses should prove insightful about possible fears about writing.)

Once you have identified your audience and purpose, you can begin by finding some way to *think on paper*. You can use the techniques of freewriting, brainstorming, or keeping a journal to gather ideas.

Freewriting Give yourself fifteen minutes to write whatever comes into your mind on your subject. If your mind is a blank, write, "My mind's a blank. My mind's a blank," over and over until you think of something else. The main goal here is to *write without stopping*. Do not stop to tell yourself, "This is stupid," or "I can't use any of this in a paper." Do not stop to correct your spelling or punctuation. Just write. Let your ideas flow. Write *freely*. Here is an example:

Freewriting About Clothes

Clothes. Clothes make the man. I hate my clothes. Work clothes. Clothes shopping is a pain. Sizes never right. Fit wrong. Price of clothes is going up. People can't afford new clothes. Thrift shops. Uniforms. Military uniforms. Sports teams wear uniforms. Sports clothes. Everybody wears sweatshirts, running shoes, expensive sneakers. The Pump. Tee shirts. Mickey Mouse. Sports tees. Ads on tee shirts. Casual clothes. Sports clothes not just for sports.

TEACHING TIP: Tell students that brainstorming and question-and-answer sessions can be enjoyable when done in pairs or small groups. Alternating between collaborative and individual approaches to exercises in this text can lead to productive discussions about generating specific details.

Brainstorming **Brainstorming** is like freewriting because you write whatever comes into your head, but it is a little different because you can pause to *ask yourself questions* that will lead to new ideas. When you brainstorm alone, you "interview" yourself about a subject. You can also brainstorm and ask questions within a group.

If you are brainstorming about clothes, alone or with a partner or group, you might begin by listing ideas and then add to the ideas by asking and answering questions. Here's an example:

Brainstorming About Clothes

Clothes.
Clothes shopping.

What kind of clothes?
Work clothes. Sports clothes. Sports teams wear uniforms. Insignias of teams.

Who else wears uniforms?
The military wear uniforms. Some schools wear uniforms.

Are there special clothes for certain times and places?
The workplace requires certain clothes. Sports clothes—basketball, tennis, running shoes.
Casual clothes are for any time.

What's casual?
Shorts, sweats, jeans, sneakers, tee shirts.

When do you wear tee shirts?
Weekends, evenings. Some people wear casual clothes to work or to shop. Tee shirts are everywhere. All ages wear them. In all places.

If you feel like you are running out of ideas in brainstorming, try to form a question out of what you've just written. *Go where your questions and answers lead you.* For example, if you write "Some students wear school uniforms," you could form these questions:

> Which students? What kind of schools? What grades? Are school uniforms a good idea? Why? Why not?

You could also make a list of your brainstorming ideas, but remember to *do only one step at a time.*

Keeping a Journal A **journal** is a notebook of your personal writing, a notebook in which you write *regularly and often. It is not a diary, but it is a place to record your experiences, reactions, and observations.* In it, you can write about what you have done, heard, seen, read, or remembered. You can include sayings that you would like to remember, news clippings, snapshots—anything that you would like to recall or consider. A journal provides an enjoyable way to practice your writing, and it is a great source of ideas for writing.

If you were asked to write about clothes, you might look through entries in your journal, in search of ideas, and might see something like this:

Journal Entry About Clothes

I went to the mall yesterday to look for some good shoes. What a crowd! Some big sale was going on, and the stores were packed. Everybody was pushing and shoving. I just left. I'll go when it's not so crowded. I hate buying clothes and shoes. Wish I could just wear jeans and tee shirts all the time. But even then, the jeans have to have the right label, or you're looked down on. There are status labels on the tee shirts, too. Not to mention expensive athletic shoes.

Finding Specific Ideas

Whether you freewrite, brainstorm, or consult your journal, you end up with something on paper. Follow those first ideas; see where they can take you. You are looking for specific ideas, each of which can focus the general one you started with. At this point, you do not have to decide which specific idea you want to write about. You just want to *narrow your range* of ideas.

You might think, "Why should I narrow my ideas? Won't I have more to say if I keep my topic big?" But remember that a paragraph has one main idea; you want to state it clearly and use convincing details for support. If you try to write one paragraph on the broad topic of clothes, for example, you will probably make so many general statements that you will either say very little or bore your reader with big, sweeping statements. General ideas are big, broad ones. Specific ideas are smaller, narrower. If you scanned the freewriting example on clothes, you might underline many specific ideas as possible topics:

> Clothes. Clothes make the man. I hate my clothes. <u>Work clothes</u>. <u>Clothes shopping</u> is a pain. <u>Sizes</u> never right. Fit wrong. <u>Price</u> of clothes is going up. People can't afford new clothes. <u>Thrift shops</u>. <u>Uniforms</u>. <u>Military uniforms</u>. <u>Sports</u> teams wear <u>uniforms</u>. <u>Sports clothes</u>. Everybody wears <u>sweatshirts</u>. <u>Running shoes</u>, sneakers, <u>expensive sneakers</u>. The Pump. <u>Tee shirts</u>. Mickey Mouse. <u>Sports tees. Ads on tees. Casual clothes</u>. Sports clothes not just for sports.

Consider the underlined terms. Many of them are specific ideas about clothes. You could write a paragraph about one item or about several related items on the list.

Or you could make a list after brainstorming, and you could underline specific ideas about clothes:

clothes	clothes for a certain time
work clothes	clothes for a certain place
sports uniforms	clothes shopping
military uniforms	sports clothes
basketball clothes	team insignia
running shoes	school uniforms
casual clothes at work	tennis clothes
tee shirts everywhere	casual clothes
ages of people who wear tee shirts	

These specific ideas could lead you to a specific topic.

If you reviewed the journal entry on clothes, you would be able to underline many specific ideas:

I went to the mall yesterday to look for some good shoes. What a crowd! Some big sale was going on, and the stores were packed. Everybody was pushing and shoving. I just left. I'll go when it's not so crowded. I hate buying clothes and shoes. Wish I could just wear jeans and tee shirts all the time. But even then, the jeans have to have the right label, or you're looked down on. There are status labels on the tee shirts, too. Not to mention expensive athletic shoes.

Remember that if you follow the steps, they can lead you to specific ideas. Then, after you have a list of specific ideas, pick one and try to develop it by adding ideas.

Adding Details to an Idea

You can develop the one idea you picked in a number of ways:

1. *Check your list* for other ideas that seem to fit with the one you've picked.
2. *Brainstorm*—ask yourself more questions about your topic, and use the answers as detail.
3. *List* any new ideas you have that may be connected to your first idea.

For instance, you may decide to work with the list gathered through freewriting:

work clothes	casual clothes
sports clothes	clothes shopping
sizes	price
thrift shops	uniforms
military uniforms	running shoes
sweatshirts	tee shirts
expensive sneakers	ads on tees
sports tees	

Looking at this list, you might decide you want to write something about this topic: tee shirts.

One way to add details is to go back and check your list for other ideas that seem to fit with the topic of tee shirts. You find

sports clothes, ads on tees, sports clothes

Another way to add details is to brainstorm some questions that will lead you to more details. The questions do not have to be connected to each other; they are just questions that could lead you to ideas and details. Here are some possibilities:

Who wears tee shirts?

Athletes, children, teens, movie stars, musicians, parents, old people, restaurant workers.

How much do they cost?

Some are cheap, but some are expensive.

What kinds of tees are there?

Sports tees, concert tees, college names on tees, designer tees.

Why do people wear them?

They're comfortable, fashionable, too.

What ads are on tees?

Beer, sporting goods.

Another way to add details is to list any ideas that may be connected to your first idea, tee shirts. The list might give you more specific details:

Mickey Mouse shirts
surfer tee shirts
souvenir tee shirts
political slogans on tees
tee shirts under suit jackets

If you had tried all three ways of adding details, you would end up with this list of details connected to the topic of tee shirts:

sports clothes	some expensive
sports tees	concert tees
ads on tees	college names on tees
athletes	designer tees
children	beer ads on tees
teens	sporting goods on tees
movie stars	Mickey Mouse shirts
musicians	surfer tees
parents	souvenir tees
old people	political slogans on tees
restaurant workers	tees under suit jackets
some cheap	

Infobox

Beginning the Thought Lines: A Summary

The thought lines stage of writing a paragraph enables you to gather ideas. This process begins with several steps:

1. *Think on paper and write down any ideas you have about a general topic.* You can do this by freewriting, by brainstorming, or by keeping a journal.

2. *Scan your writing for specific ideas that have come from your first efforts.* List these specific ideas.

3. *Pick one specific idea.* Then, by reviewing your early writing, by questioning, and by thinking further, you can add details to the one specific idea.

This process may seem long, but once you have worked through it several times, it will become nearly automatic. When you think about ideas before you try to shape them into a paragraph, you are off to a good start. Confidence comes from having something to say, and once you have a specific idea, you will be ready to begin shaping and developing details that support your idea.

Creating Questions for Brainstorming

Following are several topics. For each one, brainstorm by writing at least six questions related to the topic that could lead you to further details. The first topic is done for you.

1. topic: dogs

Question 1: Why are dogs such popular pets?

Question 2: What kind of dog is a favorite pet in America?

Question 3: Are dogs hard to train?

Question 4: What dog, in your life, do you remember best?

Question 5: What's the most famous dog on television?

Question 6: Are there dogs as cartoon characters?

2. topic: driving

Question 1: What is most enjoyable part of driving?

Question 2: Who are the best drivers?

Question 3: Who are the worst drivers?

Question 4: What makes a good driver?

Question 5: Is it difficult to be a good driver?

Question 6: What's the longest drive you ever took?

3. topic: shopping

Question 1: Where do you like to shop for clothes?

Question 2: Where do you like to shop for food?

Question 3: Where are the best bargains on clothes?

Question 4: Where are the best bargains on food?

Question 5: Do you think you spend too much time shopping?

Question 6: Do you know any compulsive shoppers?

4. topic: sports

Question 1: <u>Who is the greatest football player of all time?</u>

Question 2: <u>Is football dangerous?</u>

Question 3: <u>Are basketball players good role models for children?</u>

Question 4: <u>Do parents interfere at Little League games?</u>

Question 5: <u>Are ticket prices for professional games too high?</u>

Question 6: <u>Is television wrestling real?</u>

Exercise 2
Practice

Finding Specific Details in Freewriting

Below are two samples of freewriting. Each is a written response to a different topic. Read each sample, and then underline any words and phrases that could become the focus of a paragraph.

Freewriting Reaction to the Topic of Getting Up in the Morning

Answers Will Vary. Possible answers shown at right.

I hate to get up. <u>Night owl</u>. Night owls stay up late, get up late. <u>Not a morning person</u>. Alarm clock screams at me. But if I use a clock radio, I fall asleep again. Bed feels so warm. <u>Getting up in the dark</u> is the worst. <u>Morning people</u> just spring up out of bed. They love to get up. They talk. They eat big breakfasts. I swig a diet cola. Ugh! No cereal or toast. <u>Breakfast food</u> is disgusting!

Freewriting Reaction to the Topic of Recycling

Recycling. Save the planet. <u>Throwing away what's still good</u> is wrong. Save old clothes. They can be mended. Shoe repair instead of new shoes. <u>Recycled paper</u> is another way to save. Lots of <u>paper is wasted at work</u>. Memos. Announcements. <u>Styrofoam cups</u> at work. Why not mugs? Greeting cards on recycled paper. I put the newspaper in a recycling bin at home. <u>Recycling glass</u> containers is another way to save and reuse. But washing out glass jars and bottles is a hassle. <u>Where is the recycling center?</u>

Exercise 3
Practice

Finding Specific Details in a List

Below are several lists of words or phrases. In each list, one item is a general term; the others are more specific. Underline the words or phrases that are more specific. The first list is done for you.

1. <u>apple pie</u>
<u>ice cream</u>
desserts
<u>butterscotch pudding</u>
<u>jello</u>
<u>chocolate brownies</u>

2. children and television
<u>Saturday morning cartoons</u>
<u>toy commercials</u>
<u>child actors</u>
<u>frightening fairy tales</u>

4. <u>late registration</u>
<u>closed classes</u>
going to college
<u>finding an advisor</u>
<u>buying the right textbooks</u>
<u>selecting the right courses</u>

5. <u>baseball caps</u>
<u>bandanna</u>
covering for the head
<u>scarf</u>
<u>beret</u>

3. tennis commentators
sports
halftime shows
instant replay
Monday night football
artificial turf

6. uniforms
military stripes
football numbers
school colors
regulation boots
team insignia

Exercise 4
Practice

Finding Specific Words to Match General Terms

Below are some general terms. On the numbered lines, list four specific words or phrases connected to each general term. The first question is done for you.

1. general term: furniture
specific words or phrases:

a. chair   c. table

b. desk   d. stool

Answers Will Vary.
Possible answers
shown at right.

2. general term: relatives
specific words or phrases:

a. aunt   c. sister

b. grandmother   d. cousin

3. general term: greeting cards
specific words or phrases:

a. valentine   c. sympathy card

b. birthday card   d. get well card

4. general term: insects
specific words or phrases:

a. spiders   c. roaches

b. wasps   d. beetles

Exercise 5
Collaborate

Finding Topics Through Freewriting

The following exercise must be completed with a partner or a group. Below are several topics. Pick one and freewrite on it for ten minutes. Then read your freewriting to your partner or group. Ask your listener(s) to jot down any words or phrases from your writing that could lead to a specific topic for a paragraph.

Answers Will Vary.

Your listener(s) should read the jotted-down words or phrases to you. You will be hearing a collection of specific ideas that came from *your* writing. As you listen, underline the words in your freewriting.

Freewriting topics (pick one):
1. telephone calls
2. chores
3. friends

Freewriting on (name of topic chosen): _____

_____

_____

_____

_____

_____

_____

_____

FOCUSING THE THOUGHT LINES

The next step of writing is to *focus your ideas around some point*. Your ideas will begin to take a focus if you reexamine them, looking for *related ideas*. Two techniques that you can use are

- marking a list of related ideas
- mapping related ideas

Listing Related Ideas

To develop a marked list, take another look at the list we developed under the topic of tee shirts. The same list is shown below, but you will notice some of the items have been marked with symbols that show related ideas:

K   marks ideas about the **kinds** of people who wear tee shirts

C   marks ideas about the **cost** of tee shirts,

P   marks ideas about what is **pictured** or written on tee shirts.

Here is the marked list of ideas related to the topic of tee shirts:

	sports clothes	C	some expensive
	sports tees	P	concert tees
P	ads on tees	P	college names on tees
K	athletes		designer tees
K	children	P	beer ads on tees
K	teens	P	sporting goods on tees
K	movie stars	P	Mickey Mouse shirts
K	musicians	P	surfer tees
K	parents	P	souvenir tees
K	old people	P	political slogans on tees
K	restaurant workers		tees under suit jackets
C	some cheap		

You have probably noticed that some items are not marked: sports clothes, sports tees, designer tees, tees under suit jackets. Perhaps you can come back to them later, or you may decide you do not need them in your paragraph.

To make it easier to see what ideas you have and how they are related, you could *group related ideas*, giving each list a title, such as the following:

Kinds of People Who Wear Tee Shirts

athletes	movie stars	old people
children	musicians	restaurant workers
teens	parents	

The Cost of Tee Shirts

cheap   some expensive

What Is Pictured or Written on Tee Shirts

ads on tees	beer ads	surfer tees
concert tees	sporting goods	souvenir tees
college names	Mickey Mouse	political slogans

Mapping

Another way to focus your ideas is to mark your first list of ideas, then cluster the related ideas into separate lists. You can **map** your ideas like this:

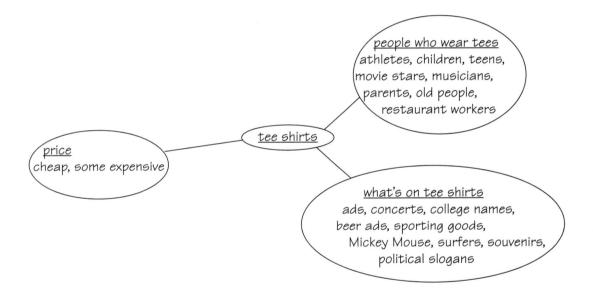

Whatever way you choose to examine and group your detail, you are working toward a *focus*, a *point*. You are asking and beginning to answer the question "Where does the detail lead?" The answer will be the topic sentence of your paragraph. It will be the *main idea* of your paragraph.

Forming a Topic Sentence

To form a topic sentence, you can do the following:

1. Review your details and see if you can form some general idea that can summarize the details.
2. Write that general idea as one sentence.

Your sentence that summarizes the details is the **topic sentence.** It makes a general point, and the more specific details you have gathered will support this point.

To form a topic sentence about tee shirts, you can follow the steps. First, there are many details about tee shirts. It is time to ask questions about the details. You could ask yourself, "What kind of details do I have? Can I summarize them?" You might then write the summary as the topic sentence:

People of various backgrounds and ages wear all kinds of tee shirts.

Check the sentence against your details. Does it cover the people who wear tees? Does it cover what is on the shirts? Yes. The topic sentence says, "*People of various backgrounds and ages* wear *all kinds* of tee shirts."

Writing Good Topic Sentences

Be careful. *Topics are not the same as topic sentences. Topics are the subjects you will write about.* A topic sentence states the *main idea* you have developed on a topic. Consider the differences between the topics and the topic sentences below:

topic: why courtesy is important
topic sentence: Courtesy takes the conflict out of unpleasant encounters.

topic: dogs and their owners
topic sentence: Many dog owners begin to look like their pets.

Topic sentences do not announce; they make a point. Look at the sentences below, and notice the differences between the sentences that announce and the topic sentences:

announcement: I will discuss the process of changing a tire.
topic sentence: Changing a tire is easy if you have the right tools and follow a simple process.

announcement: An analysis of why recycling paper is important will be the subject of this paper.
topic sentence: Recycling paper is important because it saves trees, money, and even certain animals.

Topic sentences can be too big to develop in one paragraph. A topic sentence that is *too broad* may take many paragraphs, even pages of writing, to develop. Look at the very broad sentences below, and then notice how they can be narrowed.

too broad: Athletes get paid too much money. (This sentence is too broad because the term "athletes" could mean anything from professional boxers to college football players to neighborhood softball teams; "too much money" could mean any fee that basketball players receive for endorsing products to bonuses that professional football players get if they make the Super Bowl. The sentence could also refer to all athletes in the world at any time in history.)

a narrower, better topic sentence: Last year, several professional baseball players negotiated high but fair salaries.

too broad: I changed a great deal in my last year of high school. (The phrase "changed a great deal" could refer to physical changes, intellectual changes, or emotional changes or to changes in attitude, changes in goals, or just about any other change you can think of.)

a narrower, better topic sentence: In my last year of high school, I overcame my shyness.

Topic sentences can be too small to develop in one paragraph. A topic sentence that is *too narrow* cannot be supported by details. It may be a fact, which cannot be developed. A topic sentence that is too narrow leaves you with nothing more to say.

too narrow: I hate broccoli.
an expanded topic sentence: I hate broccoli for two reasons.

too narrow: It takes twenty minutes to get out of the airport parking lot.
an expanded topic sentence: Congestion at the airport parking lot is causing problems for travelers.

The thought lines stage begins with free, unstructured thinking and writing. As you work through the thought lines process, your thinking and writing will become more focused.

Infobox

Focusing the Thought Lines: A Summary

The thought lines stage of writing a paragraph enables you to develop an idea into a topic sentence and related details. You can focus your thinking by working in steps:

1. Mark a list of related details, or try mapping to group your ideas.

2. Write a topic sentence that summarizes your details.

3. Check that your topic sentence is a sentence, not a topic. Make sure that it is not too broad or too narrow and that it is not an announcement. Check that it makes a point and focuses the details you have developed.

Exercise 6

Practice

Grouping Related Items in Lists of Details

Below are lists of details. In each list, circle the items that seem to fit into one group; then underline the items that seem to belong to a second group. Some items may not belong in either group. The first list is done for you.

1. topic: rainy weekends
(no sports activities)   (cannot jog in neighborhood)
(picnics canceled)   rains most in autumn
catch up on chores   read a book
not forecast by weather reporters   (park too wet to visit)
go to a mall   watch a movie

2. topic: diets
diet soda   frozen yogurt
crash diet   (junk foods)
(ice cream)   fresh fruit
(pizza with everything)   desired weight
(potato chips)   (rich desserts)

3. topic: living away from home for the first time
an apartment   (doing your own laundry)
no curfew   (cleaning up the mess)
can set your own schedule   unlimited parties
(paying the rent)   (phone bill)
(electric bill)

Writing Topic Sentences for Lists of Details

Below are lists of details that have no topic sentence. Write an appropriate topic sentence for each one.

Answers Will Vary.
Possible answers
shown at right.

1. **topic sentence:** Renting a movie has several advantages over seeing a movie at a theater.

Can watch a movie in the comfort of your own room.
Renting a movie costs little.
No need to dress up.
No crowds to fight.
Do not have to wait in line.
Can watch it when convenient.
Can watch it several times over rental period.

2. **topic sentence:** There are many kinds of cakes.

birthday cakes
wedding cakes
Super Bowl cakes shaped like a football
fruitcakes
pound cakes
angel food cakes
devil's food cakes
heart-shaped cakes for Valentine's Day

3. **topic sentence:** Reese was an asset to his team.

Reese scored the most points on the court.
He never tried to be the center of attention.
He was modest.
He was a team player.
Reese got along well with the coaches.
Reese came to all the practices.

4. **topic sentence:** Tamara made positive contributions to her speech class.

Tamara spoke clearly in speech class.
Her presentations were well organized.
She critiqued classmates' speeches tactfully.
She volunteered to be a speech team leader.
In communicating, Tamara maintained her sense of humor.
She motivated others to complete their speech research.

Turning Topics into Topic Sentences

Below is a list. Some of the items in the list are topic sentences, but some are topics. Put an *X* by the items that are topics. In the lines below the list, rewrite the topics into topic sentences.

1. __X__ Three characteristics of a good friend.
2. _____ Learning to drive takes practice.
3. __X__ The most frightening experience of my life.
4. _____ Many snakes make good pets.
5. __X__ Why I hate giving oral reports.
6. _____ I learned to be punctual on my first job.
7. _____ A younger brother can be a good buddy.
8. __X__ How to meet the person of your dreams.
9. _____ I got the job I wanted through planning and persistence.
10. _____ My twenty-first birthday was the happiest day of my life.

Rewrite the topics. Make each one into a topic sentence.

Answers Will Vary.
Possible answers
shown at right.

1. A good friend is loyal, generous, and sympathetic.

3. A car accident was the most frightening experience of my life.

5. I hate giving oral reports because I am afraid I will forget what I want to say and look foolish.

8. You can meet the person of your dreams by develolping into an interesting person yourself.

Exercise 9

Practice

Revising Topic Sentences That Are Too Broad

Below is a list of topic sentences. Some of them are too broad to support in one paragraph. Put an *X* by the ones that are too broad. Then, in the lines below the list, rewrite those sentences, focusing on a limited idea, a topic sentence that could be supported in one paragraph.

1. __X__ Being a parent is not easy.
2. _____ The toughest part of training my puppy was getting him to walk on a leash.
3. __X__ The economy makes life difficult for many Americans.
4. _____ My habit of gossiping can get me into trouble.
5. _____ Putting my five-year-old to bed at night is a challenge.
6. __X__ Ramon wants to be a success and achieve the American dream.
7. __X__ People have a right to privacy.
8. _____ Amy dreams of owning a restaurant.
9. __X__ Drugs are ruining America.
10. _____ After-school programs keep my children from joining the wrong crowd.

Rewrite the broad sentences. Make each one more limited.

Answers Will Vary.
Possible answers
shown at right.

1. Nursing a toddler through chicken pox is not easy.

3. Holding down two jobs is hard for my mother.

6. Ramon wants to earn enough money to buy a house for his family. _____

7. Parents of teens should not snoop in teenagers' rooms. _____

9. My cousin's drug habit cost him a career in management. _____

_____

Exercise 10
Practice

Making Announcements into Topic Sentences

Below is a list of sentences. Some are topic sentences. Some are announcements. Put an *X* by the announcements. Then, on the lines below the list, rewrite the announcements, making them into topic sentences.

1. _____ Hunting too near a populated area can be dangerous.
2. __X__ The consequences of telling a "white lie" will be the subject of this paper.
3. __X__ The emotional benefits of exercise are going to be explained.
4. _____ Marrying too young often presents financial challenges.
5. _____ Our town needs a better bus system.
6. _____ A network of bike paths through our community would encourage people to leave their cars at home.
7. __X__ Why more day-care centers are needed in this town is the area to be discussed.
8. __X__ This essay concerns the increase in robberies in our community.
9. _____ A neighborhood crime watch can bring greater security to residents.
10. __X__ This paper will be about driving in a snowstorm.

Rewrite the announcements. Make each one a topic sentence.

Answers Will Vary.
Possible answers shown at right.

2. A white lie can hurt others and destroy their trust. _____

3. Exercise can make a person feel calmer and more confident. _____

7. More day care centers in this town would help working parents. _____

8. Cuts in the police budget may have led to more robberies. _____

10. Driving in a snowstorm takes concentration and skill. _____

Exercise 11
Practice

Revising Topic Sentences That Are Too Narrow

Below is a list of topic sentences. Some of them are topics that are too narrow; they cannot be developed with details. Put an *X* by the ones that are too narrow. Then, in the lines below, rewrite those sentences as broader topic sentences that could be developed in one paragraph.

1. __X__ It rained all day yesterday.
2. _____ On rainy days, I have to pay careful attention to the way I drive.
3. __X__ My dog is a mixed breed.
4. _____ A stray cat turned out to be a wonderful pet.
5. __X__ I love bargain hunting.

6. ____ I like working the night shift for several reasons.

7. _X_ My brother failed the written part of his driving test.

8. ____ Inez is a good tennis player because she devotes all her free time to the sport.

9. _X_ Alan plays football.

10. _X_ Dr. Novack leases his car.

Rewrite the narrow sentences. Make each one broader.

Answers Will Vary.
Possible answers
shown at right.

1. Yesterday's rain refreshed our sweltering community.

3. My dog, a mixed breed, is smarter than some purebreds.

5. I love bargain hunting because it gives me a challenge.

7. Carelessness caused my brother to fail the written driving test.

9. Alan plays football with ability and determination.

10. Dr. Novak leases his car because he cannot afford to buy it.

OUTLINES FOR A PARAGRAPH

Checking Your Details

Once you have a topic sentence, you can begin working on an **outline** for your paragraph. The outline is a plan that helps you stay focused in your writing. The outline begins to form when you write your topic sentence and write your list of details beneath the topic sentence. You can now look at your list and ask yourself an important question: "Do I have enough details to support my topic sentence?" Remember, your goal is to write a paragraph of seven to twelve sentences. Consider this topic sentence and list of details:

> **topic sentence:** People can be very rude when they shop in supermarkets.
> **details:** push in line
> express lane
> too many items

Does the list contain enough details for a paragraph of seven to twelve sentences? Probably not.

Adding Details When There Are Not Enough

To add details, try brainstorming. Ask yourself some questions:

> Where else in supermarkets are people rude?
> Are they rude in other lanes besides the express lane?
> Are they rude in the aisles? How?
> Is there crowding anywhere? Where?

By brainstorming, you might come up with these details:

> **topic sentence:** People can be very rude when they shop in supermarkets.
> **details:** push in line
> express lane
> too many items
> hit my cart with theirs in aisles

> block aisles while they decide
> push ahead in deli area
> will not take a number
> argue with cashier over prices
> yell at the bagger

Keep brainstorming until you feel you have enough details for a seven- to twelve-sentence paragraph. Remember that it is better to have too many details than too few, for you can always edit the extra details later.

If you try brainstorming and still do not have many details, you can refer to your original ideas—your freewriting or journal—for other details.

Eliminating Details That Do Not Relate to the Topic Sentence

Sometimes, what you thought were good details do not relate to the topic sentence because they do not fit or support your point. Eliminate details that do not relate to the topic sentence. For example, the following list contains details that really do not relate to the topic sentence. Those details are crossed out.

topic sentence: Waiters have to be very patient in dealing with their customers.
details: customers take a long time ordering
~~waiter's salary is low~~
waiters have to explain specials twice
customers send orders back
customers blame waiters for any delays
customers want food instantly
waiters can't react to sarcasm of customers
waiters can't get angry if customer does
~~waiters work long shifts~~
customers change their mind after ordering

From List to Outline

Take another look at the topic sentence and list of details on tee shirts:

topic sentence: People of various backgrounds and ages wear all kinds of tee shirts.
details:
athletes	children
teens	movie stars
musicians	parents
old people	restaurant workers
ads on tees	concert tees
college names	beer ads
sporting goods	Mickey Mouse shirts
surfer tees	souvenir tees
political slogans	

After you scan that list, you are ready to develop the outline of the paragraph.

An outline is a plan for writing, and it can be a type of draft in list form. It sketches what you want to write and the order in which you want to present it. *An organized, logical list will make your writing unified since each item on the list will relate to your topic sentence.*

When you plan, keep your topic sentence in mind:

> People of <u>various backgrounds</u> and <u>ages</u> wear <u>all kinds</u> of tee shirts.

Notice the underlined key words, which lead to three key phrases:

> people of various backgrounds
> people of various ages
> all kinds of tee shirts

Can you put the details together so that they connect to *one* of these key phrases?

people of various backgrounds

> athletes, movie stars, musicians, restaurant workers

people of various ages

> children, teens, parents, old people

all kinds of tee shirts

> concert tees, college names on tees, beer ads, sporting goods, Mickey Mouse shirts, surfer tees, souvenir tees, political slogans

With this kind of grouping, you have a clearer idea of how to organize a paragraph. You may have noticed that the details grouped under each phrase give *examples* connected to the topic sentence. That is, the details "athletes," "movie stars," "musicians," and "restaurant workers" are all examples of people of various backgrounds who wear tee shirts. When you use examples to support a point, you use a form of writing called **illustration.** In your writing, you often use illustration since you frequently want to explain a general point with a specific example.

Now that you have grouped your ideas with key phrases and examples, you can write an outline.

Note: The outlines for paragraph assignments in this book are simplified, detail-listing formats for easy student reference. In the essay chapter, Chapter 10, students will be introduced to Roman numeral and Arabic letter outlines.

Infobox

An Outline for a Paragraph

topic sentence: People of various backgrounds and ages wear all kinds of tee shirts.

details:

various backgrounds
{
Athletes wear tee shirts.
Movie stars are seen in them.
Musicians perform in tee shirts.
Restaurant workers wear tee shirts.
}

various ages
{
Children and teens wear tee shirts.
Parents and old people wear them.
}

kinds of tees
{
There are tee shirts sold at concerts.
Some shirts have the names of colleges on them.
Others advertise a brand of beer or sporting goods.
Mickey Mouse is a favorite character on them.
Surfers' tee shirts have seascapes on them.
Some shirts are souvenirs.
Others have political slogans.
}

As you can see, the outline combined some of the details from the list. Even with these combinations, the details are very rough in style. As you reread the list of details, you will notice places that need more combination, places where ideas need more explaining, and places that are repetitive. Keep in mind that an outline is merely a very rough organization of your paragraph.

As you work through the steps of designing an outline, you can check for the following points:

✔ Checklist

A Checklist for an Outline

✔ **Unity:** Do all the details relate to the topic sentence? If they do, the paragraph will be unified.

✔ **Support:** Do you have enough suppporting ideas? Can you add to these ideas with even more specific details?

✔ **Coherence:** Are the details listed in the right order? If the order of points is logical, the paragraph will be coherent.

COHERENCE: PUTTING YOUR DETAILS IN PROPER ORDER

Check the sample outline again, and you will notice that the details are grouped in the same order as the topic sentence: first, details about kinds of people; then, details about the ages of people; and next, details about kinds of tee shirts. Putting the details in an order that matches the topic sentence is a logical order for this paragraph.

Putting the details in logical order makes the ideas in your paragraph easy to follow. The most logical order for a pargraph depends on the subject of the paragraph. If you are writing about an event, you might use **time order** (such as telling what happened first, second, and so forth); if you are arguing some point, you might use **emphatic order** (such as saving your most convincing idea for last); if you are describing a room, you might use **space order** (such as from left to right or from top to bottom).

The format of the outline helps to organize your ideas. The topic sentence is written above the list of details. This position helps you to remember that the topic sentence is the *main idea*, and the details that support it are written under it. The topic sentence is the most important sentence of the paragraph. You can easily check the items on your list, one by one, against your main idea. You can also develop the *unity* (relevance) and *coherence* (logical order) of your details.

When you actually write a paragraph, the topic sentence does not necessarily have to be at the beginning of the paragraph. Read the paragraphs below, and notice where each topic sentence is placed.

Note: Students may be uncomfortable learning that topic sentences may not always be at the beginning of a paragraph. They may need assurance that topic sentences in formal, academic essays are usually at the beginning of paragraphs, and your colleagues/department curriculum may prefer such a structure.

Topic Sentence at the Beginning of the Paragraph

Watching a horror movie on the late show can keep me up all night. The movie itself scares me to death, especially if it involves a creepy character sneaking up on someone in the dark. After the movie, I'm afraid to turn out all the lights and be alone in the dark. Then every little noise seems like the sound of a sinister intruder. Strange shapes seem to appear in the shadows. My closet becomes a place where someone could be hiding. There might even be a creature under the bed! And if I go to sleep, these strange invaders might appear from under the bed or in the closet.

Topic Sentence in the Middle of the Paragraph

The kitchen counters gleamed. In the spice rack, every jar was organized neatly. The sink was polished, and not one spot marred its surface. The stove burners were surrounded by dazzling stainless steel rings. <u>The chef kept an immaculate kitchen.</u> There were no finger marks on the refrigerator door. No sticky spots dirtied the floor. No crumbs hid behind the toaster.

Topic Sentence at the End of the Paragraph

On long summer evenings, we would play softball in the street. Sometimes we'd play until it was so dark we could barely see the ball. Then our mothers would come to the front steps of the row houses and call us in, telling us to stop our play. But we'd pretend we couldn't hear them. If they insisted, we'd beg for a few minutes more or for just one more game. It was so good to be outdoors with our friends. It was warm, and we knew we had weeks of summer vacation ahead. There was no school in the morning; there would be more games to play. <u>We loved those street games on summer nights.</u>

Infobox

Since many of your paragraph assignments will require a clear topic sentence, be sure you follow your own instructor's directions about placement of the topic sentence.

Exercise 12   **Adding Details to Support a Topic Sentence**

Practice   The topic sentences below have some—but not enough—details. Write sentences to add details to the list below each topic sentence.

Answers Will Vary.
Possible answers
shown at right.

1. **topic sentence:** My closet is full of items I have saved because of the memories they bring back.
   a. I have an old high school yearbook.
   b. It reminds me of my senior year.
   c. There is an old ragged sweatshirt.

   d. My first girlfriend gave it to me.

   e. A catcher's mitt is stuck in the corner.

   f. I used it in Little League.

   g. I still remember those games.

2. **topic sentence:** Owning a car costs more money than just the cost of the car itself.
   a. Gas is a regular expense.

   b. Changing the oil costs money.

   c. Regular tune-ups are costly.

   d. New tires are needed for safe driving.

   e. Brake linings and brake pads must be replaced.

    f. Batteries wear out. _____

    g. Car insurance can be expensive. _____

  3. topic sentence: When I have a day off, I can find several inexpensive ways to enjoy the time.

    a. I often take a long walk.

    b. Sometimes I walk with a friend. _____

    c. We catch up on each other's news. _____

    d. Other times I listen to music. _____

    e. I play my favorite radio station. _____

    f. On weekends, I play soccer in the park. _____

    g. On rainy days, I go to the bargain movie theater. _____

  4. topic sentence: The first day of college can be confusing and tense.

    a. A student may not know how to find the classroom for his or her first class.

    b. So the student rushes around, terrified of being late to class.

    c. A new student worries about how hard the classes will be.

    d. A new student may feel inferior. _____

    e. Meanwhile, everyone else seems at ease. _____

    f. In the classroom, the instructor may seem frightening. _____

    g. The course outline can look long and complicated. _____

Exercise 13 **Eliminating Details That Do Not Fit**

Practice Below are topic sentences and lists of supporting details. Cross out the details that do not fit the topic sentence.

  1. topic sentence: Toy commercials on television can be deceiving to little children.

  details: Commercials show happy, excited groups of youngsters playing with a toy.
Children viewing may think the toy will make them happy.
They may think the toy will bring them friends.
The commercials show dolls or robots or action figures in motion.
In reality, the figures don't move.
Commercials often show cars or trucks racing around.
~~As a child, I had a collection of model trucks.~~
In small print, the toy car or truck ad says, "Batteries not included."
Small children can't read and don't know about the batteries needed.

2. **topic sentence:** Everywhere I look, I see how sports can influence fashion.

details: Both sexes wear surfer clothes.
Children and adults wear athletic shoes.
~~The NBA playoffs are on prime-time television.~~
Older men wear golf shirts.
People wear sweatpants to the store or to visit friends.
Sweatbands are common headgear.
Baseball caps are seen in many places.
~~Athletes are used to sell soft drinks.~~

3. **topic sentence:** People give many excuses for not voting.

details: Some people say their vote doesn't count.
Others say they don't know where their precinct is.
Some people admit they forgot to vote.
~~There are local elections next week.~~
Some people haven't registered to vote.
Some people say all the candidates are unacceptable.
A few people claim they don't have time to vote.
People who vote get a sticker that says, "I voted."

Exercise 14 **Coherence: Putting Details in the Right Order**

Practice

These outlines have details that are in the wrong order. In the space provided, number the sentences in the right order: *1* would be the number for the first sentence, and so on.

1. **topic sentence:** My first babysitting job was a disaster from start to finish.

___1___ Six-year-old Tyrone cried when his mother said good-bye.

___2___ I tried to distract him from his crying by reading him a story.

___4___ He threw the storybook across the room.

___3___ He pulled the storybook from my hands.

___6___ He wouldn't eat any dinner.

___5___ When it was time for dinner, I made him his favorite food.

___9___ He refused to go to bed.

___7___ I tried to get him to take a bath before bedtime.

___8___ When I got him into the tub, he splashed water all over me.

___10___ His mother came home.

_12 or 11_ I was asleep, exhausted.

_11 or 12_ His mother found Tyrone awake, watching late-night TV.

2. **topic sentence:** I have a hard time wrapping a gift.

___1___ I can never find a box.

___2___ The tissue paper is crumpled.

____7____ I can't get the ribbon to lie flat on the box.

____8____ The bows never turn out nicely.

____4____ The wrapping paper gets wrinkled and lumpy at the ends of the box.

____5____ I use too much tape as I seal the ends of the wrapping paper.

____3____ I always cut too much wrapping paper.

____6____ The tape shines all over the wrapped box.

3. topic sentence: Losing my credit cards was a stressful experience.

____4____ I notified the credit card companies immediately.

____1____ I looked in my wallet and saw that my Visa and Discover cards were missing from their slots.

____3____ I had to look all over the house for the credit card companies' phone numbers.

____2____ I panicked when I saw the cards weren't anywhere in my wallet.

____5____ Even after I called the card companies, I was worried about strangers charging things on my cards.

ROUGH LINES FOR A PARAGRAPH

Drafting a Paragraph

The outline is a draft in list form. You are now ready to write the list in paragraph form, to "rough out" a draft of your assignment. This stage of writing is the time to draft, revise, edit, and draft again. You may write several drafts in this stage, but don't think of this as an unnecessary chore or a punishment. It is a way of taking the pressure off yourself. By revising in steps, you are reminding yourself that the first try does not have to be perfect.

Review the outline on tee shirts on page 20. You can create a first draft of this outline in the form of a paragraph. (Remember that the first line of each paragraph is indented.) In the draft of the paragraph below, the first sentence of the paragraph is the topic sentence.

A First Draft of a Paragraph

```
     People of various backgrounds and ages wear all kinds of
tee shirts. Athletes wear tee shirts. Movie stars are seen in
them. Musicians perform in tee shirts. Restaurant workers wear
tee shirts. Children and teens wear tee shirts. Parents and older
people wear them. There are tee shirts that are sold at concerts.
Some shirts have the names of colleges on them. Others advertise
a brand of beer or sporting goods. Mickey Mouse is a favorite
character on them. Surfer tee shirts have seascapes on them. Some
shirts are souvenirs. Others have political slogans.
```

Revising

Once you have a first draft, you can begin to think about revising and editing it. **Revising** means rewriting the draft, making changes in the structure, in the order of the sentences, and in the content. **Editing** includes making changes in

TEACHING TIP:
Remind students that revising a first draft can take considerable time. Rearranging the sequence of points and adding more details may require going back to the outline first. Students should periodically review the checklist as they revise their draft(s).

the choice of words, in the selection of details, in punctuation, and in the pattern and kinds of sentences. It may also include adding **transitions,** which are words, phrases, or sentences that link ideas.

One way to begin revising and editing is to read your work aloud to yourself. Listen to your words, and consider the questions in the following checklist.

✔ Checklist

A Checklist for Revising the Draft of a Paragraph (with key terms)

✔ Am I staying on my point? (unity)

✔ Should I take out any ideas that do not relate? (unity)

✔ Do I have enough to say about my point? (support)

✔ Should I add any details? (support)

✔ Should I change the order of my sentences? (coherence)

✔ Is my choice of words appropriate? (style)

✔ Is my choice of words repetitive? (style)

✔ Are my sentences too long? Too short? (style)

✔ Should I combine any sentences? (style)

✔ Am I running sentences together? (grammar)

✔ Am I writing conplete sentences? (grammar)

✔ Can I link my ideas more smoothly? (transitions)

If you apply the checklist to the draft of the paragraph on tee shirts, you will probably find these rough spots:

- The sentences are very short and choppy.
- Some sentences could be combined.
- Some words are repeated often.
- Some ideas would be more effective if they were supported by more details.
- The paragraph could use a few transitions.

Consider the following revised draft of the paragraph, and not the underlined changes that have been made in the draft.

A Revised Draft of a Paragraph

---

topic sentence:	People of various backgrounds and ages wear all kinds of tee shirts. <u>Athletes and</u>
sentences combined	<u>movie stars are seen in them. Musicians often</u>
sentences combined	<u>perform in them, and restaurant workers some-</u>
	<u>times work in tee shirts marked with the name</u>

details added	of the restaurant. Children, teens, their par-
sentences combined	ents, and older people all wear tee shirts.
transition sentence added	Almost anything added can be printed or pic-
	tured on a tee shirt. At concerts, fans can
details added	buy tee shirts stamped with the name of the
	group on stage. College students can wear the
	name of their college on a shirt. Some shirts
details added	advertise a brand of beer, like Bud, or a sport-
details added	ing goods company, like Nike. Mickey Mouse is
	a favorite character on tee shirts. Other kinds
transition added	of shirts include shirts with seascapes on
sentences combined	them, and souvenir shirts, like the ones that
details added	say, "My folks visited Philadelphia, and all
transition	I got was this lousy tee shirt." Other shirts
details added	have political slogans like "Save the Whales."

TEACHING TIP:
Group Work. The "Peer Review Form" on p. 35 can help students refine their drafts, and it can reinforce the importance of careful editing. (Peer Review Forms are at the end of each writing chapter.)

When you are revising your own paragraph, you can use the checklist to help you. Read the checklist several times; then reread your draft, looking for answers to the questions on the list. If your instructor agrees, you can work with your classmates. You can read your draft to a partner or a group. Your listener(s) can react to your draft by applying the questions on the checklist and by making notes about your draft as you read. When you are finished reading aloud, your partner(s) can discuss the notes about your work.

Exercise 15

Practice

Note: For more on combining short sentences, see Sentence Variety, Chapter 28.

Revising a Draft by Combining Sentences

The paragraph below has many short, choppy sentences, which are underlined. Wherever you see two or more underlined sentences clustered next to each other, combine them into one clear, smooth sentence. Write your revised version of the paragraph in the spaces above the lines.

Paragraph to Be Revised

My brother is a baseball fanatic. He wakes up in the morning thinking
            He reaches for the newspaper and checks out all the baseball
about the game. <u>He reaches for the newspaper. He checks out all the baseball</u>
<u>scores.</u>
<u>scores.</u> He talks about baseball during breakfast. He can't stop talking and
                    During his break, at lunch, and with
thinking about baseball during work. <u>He talks about his favorite teams during</u>

customers, he has baseball conversations.

his break. He has baseball conversations during lunch. With customers, he

He has seven

argues about the sport. My brother's clothes reflect his obsession. He has seven

baseball caps, three baseball jackets, and at least twelve shirts marked with team

baseball caps. There are three baseball jackets in his closet. He owns at least

insignia.

twelve shirts marked with team insignia. For him, it's always baseball season.

Collaborate

Answers Will Vary.

Exercise 16 Adding Details to a Draft

The paragraph below lacks the kind of details that would make it more interesting. Working with a partner or a group, add details to the blank spaces provided. When you are finished, read the revised paragraph to the class.

Paragraph to Be Revised

Radio stations offer something for almost everyone. For teenagers, there

are stations like _____ that play the top forty hits of the

day. Other stations for teens ignore the current top forty selections and play

different kinds of music. For example, teens can listen to _____

or _____ music instead of the same forty hits played over and

over. Older listeners also have a wide selection of music stations, from those

that play _____ music to those that play _____

tunes. And for those radio listeners who aren't interested in music at all, other

stations offer other kinds of programming. Some stations broadcast

_____, _____, or _____ instead of music.

FINAL LINES FOR A PARAGRAPH

The final version of your paragraph is the result of careful thinking, planning, and revising. After as many drafts as it takes, you read to polish and proofread. You can avoid having too many last-minute corrections if you check your draft carefully for the following:

- spelling errors
- punctuation errors
- mechanical errors
- word choice
- a final statement

Take a look at the last draft of the tee shirt paragraph. Wherever something is crossed out, the draft has been corrected directly above the crossed-out material. At the end of the paragraph, you will notice a concluding sentence that has been added to unify the paragraph.

Correcting the Last Draft of a Paragraph

People of various backgrounds and ages wear all kinds of tee shirts.

~~Atheletes~~ and movie ~~star's~~ are seen in them, musicians often perform in them,
Athletes   *stars*

and ~~restraunt~~ workers sometimes work in tee shirts marked with the name of
restaurant

the restaurant. Children, teens, their parents, and ~~older~~ people all wear tee
elderly

shirts. Almost anything can be painted or pictured on a tee shirt. At concerts,

fans can buy tee shirts stamped with the name of the group ~~of~~ stage.
on

~~Collegestudents~~ can wear the name of ~~there~~ college on a shirt. Some shirts
College students   *their*

advertise a brand of beer, like Bud, or a sporting goods company, like Nike.

Mickey Mouse is a favorite character on tee shirts. Other kinds of tee shirts

include surfer shirts with seascapes on them and souvenir shirts, like the ones

that say, "~~my folk's~~ visited Philadelphia, and all I got was this lousy tee shirt."
"My folks

Other shirts have political slogans, like "Save the Whales." What is written or

pictured on tee shirts is as varied as the people who wear them.

Giving Your Paragraph a Title

Note: Students often underline titles, place quotation marks around them, or capitalize each letter. If you require titles on student submissions, a brief reminder about avoiding these pitfalls may be necessary. For more on punctuating and capitalizing titles, see Chapter 24.

When you prepare the final version of your paragraph, you may be asked to give it a title. The title should be short and should fit the subject of the paragraph. For example, an appropriate title for the paragraph on tee shirts could be "Tee Shirts" or "The Variety of Tee Shirts." Check with your instructor to see whether your paragraph needs a title. In this book, the paragraphs do not have titles.

The Final Version of a Paragraph

Following is the final version of the paragraph on tee shirts. As you read it, you will notice a few more changes. Even though the paragraph went through several drafts and many revisions, the final copy still reflects some additional polishing: some details have been added, some have been made more specific, and a transition has been added. These changes were made as the final version was prepared.

A Final Version of a Paragraph (Changes from the last draft are underlined.)

People of various backgrounds and ages wear all kinds of

tee shirts. Athletes and movie stars are seen in them. Musicians

often perform in <u>ragged tees</u>, and restaurant workers sometimes

work in tee shirts marked with the name of the restaurant. Children, teens, their parents, and elderly people all wear tee shirts. Almost anything can be painted or pictured on a tee shirt. At concerts, <u>for example</u>, fans can buy tee shirts stamped with the name of the group <u>onstage</u>. College students can wear the name of their college on a shirt. Some <u>popular</u> shirts advertise a brand of beer, like Bud, or a sporting goods company, like Nike. Mickey Mouse is a favorite character on tee shirts. Other kinds of tee shirts include surfer shirts with seascapes on them and souvenir shirts, like the <u>surly</u> ones that say, "My folks visited Philadelphia, and all I got was this lousy tee shirt." Other shirts have political slogans, like "Save the Whales." What is written or pictured on tee shirts is as varied as the people who wear them.

Reviewing the Writing Process

This chapter has taken you through four important stages in writing. As you become more comfortable with them, you will be able to work through them more quickly. For now, try to remember the four stages.

Infobox

The Stages of the Writing Process

Thought Lines: gathering and developing ideas, thinking on paper through freewriting, brainstorming, mapping, or keeping a journal.

Outlines: planning the paragraph by combining and dividing details, focusing the details with a topic sentence, listing the supporting details in proper order, and devising an outline.

Rough Lines: writing a rough draft of the paragraph, then revising and editing it.

Final Lines: preparing the final version of the paragraph, with one last proofreading check for errors in preparation, punctuation, and mechanics.

Exercise 17 **Proofreading to Prepare the Final Version**

Practice

Following is an illustration paragraph with the kinds of errors that are easy to overlook when you prepare the final version of an assignment. Correct the errors by writing above the lines. There are ten errors.

Every time I am on the telephone and I need to write something down, I
       terrible   *there*
am caught in a terible dilemma. First of all, their is never any paper nearby.
   though   ,   ,
Even thou I live in an apartment full of schoolbooks notebooks pads, and typ-
        there   *paper*
ing paper, they're is never any papper near the telephone. I wind up desperate-
                                                   |
ly looking for anything I can write on. Sometimes i write on coupons my

mother has saved in the kitchen, but coupons are shiny and don't take writing

well. If I do manage to find some better paper, I can't find a pen or pencil! Our
         pens   *pencils*
home is full of pen's and pencil's, but I can never find even a stubbby old pencil

or a leaky old ballpoint when I need it. In emergencies, I have taken telephone

messages with a crayon and a lipstick.

Lines of Detail: A Walk-Through Assignment

This assignment involves working within a group to write a paragraph.

Step 1: Read the three sentences below. Pick the one sentence you prefer as a possible topic sentence for a paragraph. Fill in the blank for the sentence you choose:

a. The most frightening movie I have ever seen was

_____ (Fill in the title.)

b. If money were no problem, the car I would buy is

_____ (Fill in the name of the car.)

c. The one food I refuse to eat is _____ (Fill in the name of the food.)

Step 2: Join a group composed of other students who picked the same topic sentence you picked. In your class, you'll have "movie" people, "car" people, and "food" people. Brainstorm in a group. Discuss questions that could be used to get ideas for your paragraph.

For the movie topic, sample questions could include "What was the most frightening part of the movie?" or "What kind of movie was it—a ghost story, a horror movie, or another type?" For the car topic, sample questions could include "Have you ever driven this kind of car?" or "Do you know anyone who has one?" For the food topic, sample questions could include, "Did you hate this food when you were a child?" or "Where has this food been served to you?"

As you discuss, write the questions, not the answers, below. Keep the questions flowing. Do not stop to say, "That's silly" or "I can't answer that." Try to devise at least ten questions.

1. _____

2. _____

3. _____

4. _____

5. _____

6. _____

7. _____

8. _____

9. _____

10. _____

Step 3: Split up. Alone, begin to think on paper. Answer as many questions as you can, or add more questions and answers, or freewrite.

Step 4: Draft an outline of the paragraph. You will probably have to change the topic sentence to fit the details you have gathered. For example, your new topic sentence might be something like

_____ was the most frightening movie I have ever seen;

it creates fear by using _____, _____, and

_____.

or

If money were no problem, I would buy a _____ for its

performance, _____, and _____.

or

I refuse to eat _____ because _____.

Remember to look at your details to see where they lead you. The details will help you refine your topic sentence.

Step 5: Prepare the first draft of the paragraph.

Step 6: Read the draft aloud to your writing group, the same people who met to brainstorm. Ask each member of your group to make at least one positive comment and one suggestion for revision.

Step 7: Revise and edit your draft, considering the group's ideas and your own ideas for improvement.

Step 8: Prepare a final version of the paragraph.

Writing Your Own Paragraph

When you write on any of these topics, follow the four basic stages of the writing process in preparing your illustration paragraph.

1. Begin this assignment with a partner. The assignment requires an interview. Your final goal is to write a paragraph that will introduce a class member, your partner, to the rest of the class. In the final paragraph, you may design your own topic sentence or use one of the topic sentences below, filling in the blanks with the material you have discovered.

There are several things you should know about _____ (fill in your partner's name).

or

Three unusual events have happened to _____ (fill in your partner's name).

Before you write the paragraph, follow these steps:

Step 1: Prepare to interview a classmate. Make a list of six questions you might want to ask. They can be questions like "Where are you from?" or "Have you ever done anything unusual?" Write *at least six questions* before you start the interview. List the questions on the following interview form, leaving room to fill in short answers later.

Interview Form

Question 1: _____

Answer: _____

Question 2: _____

Answer: _____

Question 3: _____

Answer: _____

Question 4: _____

Answer: _____

Question 5: _____

Answer: _____

Question 6: _____

Answer: _____

Additional questions and answers: _____

_____

_____

_____

Step 2: Meet and interview your partner. Ask the questions on your list. Jot down brief answers. Ask *any other questions* you think of as you are talking; write down the answers on the additional lines at the end of the interview form.

Step 3: Change places. Let your partner interview you.

Step 4: Split up. Use the list of questions and answers about your partner as the thought lines part of your assignment. Work on the outline and draft steps.

Step 5: Ask your partner to read the draft version of your paragraph, to write any comments or suggestions for improvement below the paragraph, and to mark any spelling or grammar errors in the paragraph itself.

Step 6: When you have completed a final version of the paragraph, read the paragraph to the class.

2. Below are some topic sentences. Select one and use it to write a paragraph.

Many kinds of people wear _____ for a variety of reasons.

My daily life provides several irritations.

High school students should never forget that _____

College is a good place to _____ and _____

3. Select one of the topics listed below. Write a paragraph on some *narrowed* part of the topic. If you choose the topic of exams, for example, you might narrow the topic of your paragraph to your experiences with the SAT test.

List of Topics for a Paragraph

a part-time job	a way to reduce stress	music
single parents	voice mail	toys
exams	boyfriends/girlfriends	cars
old songs	saving money	gossip

Name: _____   **Section:** _____

Peer Review Form for a Paragraph

After you have written a draft of your paragraph, let a writing partner read it. When your partner has completed the form below, discuss the comments. Then repeat the same process for your partner's paragraph.

The topic sentence of this paragraph is _____

_____

_____

The detail that I liked best begins with the words _____

_____

The paragraph has _____ (enough, too many, too few) details to support

the topic sentence.

A particularly good part of the paragraph begins with the words

_____

I have questions about _____

_____

_____

Other comments on the paragraph: _____

_____

_____

_____

_____

_____

_____

_____

_____

_____

_____

_____

_____

Reviewer's Name: _____

WRITING FROM READING: Illustration

Spanglish
Janice Castro, with Dan Cook and Cristina Garcia

The authors of this article discuss the "free-form blend of Spanish and English" that has developed from a mix of cultures. They explain this blend by using many examples.

Words You May Need to Know

bemused (paragraph 1): confused
Quiero un (**1**): I want a . . . .
cerveza (**1**): beer
linguistic currency (2): way of speaking
syntax (3): word order
patter (3): quick talk
Anglo (3): native-born Americans
ir al (**4**): go to the

counterparts (5): duplicates
phenomena (5): remarkable things
implicit (5): contained
languorous (5): lacking energy
almuerzo (**5**): lunch
hybrids (6): blends
wielded (9): used
gaffes (9): social mistakes

1   In Manhattan a first-grader greets her visiting grandparents, happily exclaiming, "Come here, *siéntate!*" Her bemused grandfather, who does not speak Spanish, nevertheless knows she is asking him to sit down. A Miami personnel officer understands what a job applicant means when he says, "Quiero un part time." Nor do drivers miss a beat reading a billboard alongside a Los Angeles street advertising CERVEZA—SIX-PACK!

2   This free-form blend of Spanish and English, known as Spanglish, is common linguistic currency wherever concentrations of Hispanic Americans are found in the U.S. In Los Angeles, where 55% of the city's three million inhabitants speak Spanish, Spanglish is as much a part of daily life as sunglasses. Unlike the broken-English efforts of earlier immigrants from Europe, Asia, and other regions, Spanglish has become a widely accepted conversational mode used casually—even playfully—by Spanish-speaking immigrants and native-born Americans alike.

3   Consisting of one part Hispanicized English, one part Americanized Spanish and more than a little fractured syntax, Spanglish is a bit like a Robin Williams comedy routine: a crackling line of cross-cultural patter straight from the melting pot. Often it enters Anglo homes and families through the children, who pick it up at school or at play with their young Hispanic contemporaries. In other cases, it comes from watching TV; many an Anglo child has learned *uno dos tres* almost as quickly as one two three.

4   Spanglish takes a variety of forms, from the Southern California Anglos who bid farewell with the utterly silly "*hasta la* bye-bye" to the Cuban-American drivers in Miami who *parquean* their *carros* (park their cars). Some Spanglish sentences are mostly Spanish, with a quick detour for an English word or two. A

Latino friend may cut short a conversation by glancing at his watch and excusing himself with the explanation that he must "*ir al* supermarket."

5   Many of the English words transplanted this way are simply handier than their Spanish counterparts. No matter how distasteful the subject, for example, it is still easier to say "income tax" than *impuesto sobre la renta*. At the same time, many Spanish-speaking immigrants have adopted such terms as VCR, microwave and dishwasher for what they view as largely American phenomena. Still other English words convey a cultural context that is not implicit in the Spanish. A friend who invites you to *lonche* most likely has in mind the brisk American custom of "doing lunch" rather than the languorous afternoon break traditionally implied by *almuerzo*.

6   Mainstream Americans exposed to similar hybrids of German, Chinese, or Hindi might be mystified. But even Anglos who speak little or no Spanish are somewhat familiar with Spanglish. Living among them, for one thing, are nineteen million Hispanics. In addition, more American high school and university students sign up for Spanish than for any other foreign language.

7   Only in the past ten years, though, has Spanish begun to turn into a national slang. Its popularity has grown with the explosive increases in U.S. immigration from Latin American countries. English has increasingly collided with Spanish in retail stores, offices and classrooms, in pop music and on street corners. Anglos whose ancestors picked up such Spanish words as *rancho, bronco, tornado*, and *incommunicado*, for instance, now freely use such Spanish words as *gracias, bueno, amigo*, and *por favor*.

8   Among Latinos, Spanglish comnversations often flow easily from Spanish into several sentences of English and back. Spanglish is a sort of code for Latinos: the speakers know Spanish, but their hybrid language reflects the American culture in which they live. Many lean to shorter, clipped phrases in place of the longer, more graceful expressions their parents used. Says Leonel de la Cuesta, an assistant professor of modern languages at Florida International University in Miami: "In the U.S., time is money, and that is showing up in Spanglish as as economy of language." Conversational examples: *taipiar* (type) and *winshiwiper* (windshield wiper) replace *escribir a maquina* and *limpiaparabrisas*.

9   Major advertisers, eager to tap the estimated $134 billion in spending power wielded by Spanish-speaking Americans, have ventured into Spanish to promote their products. In some cases, attempts to sprinkle Spanish through commercials have produced embarrassing gaffes. A Braniff Airlines ad that sought to tell Spanish-speaking audiences they could settle back *en* (in) luxuriant *cuero* (leather) seats, for example, inadvertently said they could fly without clothes (*encuero*). A fractured translation of the Miller Lite slogan told readers the beer was "Filling, and less delicious." Similar blunders are often made by Anglos trying to impress Spanish-speaking pals. But if Latinos are amused by mangled Spanish, they also recognize these goofs as a sort of friendly acceptance. As they might put it, *no problema*.

WRITING FROM READING: "Spanglish"

When you write on any of the following topics, work through the stages of the writing process in preparing your illustration paragraph.

1. "Spanglish" gives several reasons for the growth of this blend of languages. In a paragraph, explain how and why Spanglish has become so widespread.

2. Groups often share their own special language. Computer users, for example, use many terms that a non-user would not understand. Police officers, health-care workers, restaurant workers, musicians, and others all use words or terms that are understood only by their group. In a paragraph, write about four key words or phrases used by a specific group. Use a topic sentence like the following:

   There are four key terms in the language of _____ (name the group.)

   You can write from your own experience or interview a member of a specific group.

3. In a paragraph, discuss the blending of two languages in your life. You can discuss the language of two cultures or countries (like English and Creole, or English and Portuguese) or of two parts of your life (like the formal language you use at work and the informal language you use at home). Give several specific examples of each language.

4. In a paragraph, show how two cultures can blend in a person's choice of clothing, music, or family rituals.

5. The authors of "Spanglish" say that "English has increasingly collided with Spanish in retail stores, offices and classrooms, in pop music and on street corners." Working with a partner or group, brainstorm examples to support that statement. For example, ask and answer such questions as "Where and how does Spanish appear in music popular with both Anglos and Hispanics?" and "How is Spanish appearing in offices?"

   When you have at least five examples, work individually on a paragraph that uses the statement as its topic sentence.

6. If English is not your native language, write a paragraph on the problems you have had in learning English. Give specific examples of each problem.

7. Write a paragraph about the slang you and your friends use. Focus on four key terms.

8. Write a paragraph starting with one of the following topic sentences:

   What we think of as "American" food really includes food from many cultures.

   or

   Americans regularly use words or phrases from other languages. (If you use this topic sentence, avoid using the examples given in "Spanglish.")

CHAPTER **2** # Description

WHAT IS DESCRIPTION?

Description shows a reader what a person, place, thing, or situation is like. When you write description, you try to *show*, *not tell*, about something. You want to make the reader see that person, place, or situation, and then, perhaps, to make the reader think about or act on what you have shown.

Hints for Writing a Descriptive Paragraph

Using Specific Words and Phrases Your description will help the reader see if it uses specific words and phrases. If a word or phrase is *specific*, it is *exact and precise*. The opposite of specific language is language that is vague, general, or fuzzy. Think of the difference between specific and general in this way:

> Imagine that you are browsing through a used car lot. A salesperson approaches you.

> "Can I help you?" the salesperson asks.
> "I'm looking for a good, reliable car," you say.
> "Well, what kind of car did you have in mind?" asks the salesperson.
> "Not too old," you say.
> "A sports car?" asks the salesperson.
> "Maybe," you say.

The conversation could go on and on. You are being very general in saying that you want a "good, reliable" car. The salesperson is looking for specific details: How old a car do you want? What model car?

In writing, if you use words like "good" or "nice" or "bad" or "interesting," you will not have a specific description or a very effective piece of writing. Whenever you can, try to use a more explicit word instead of a general term. To find a more explicit term, ask yourself such questions as "What type?" or "How?" The examples below show how a general term can be replaced by a more specific one:

general word: hat (Ask, "What type?")
more specific words: beret, fedora, baseball cap

general word: lettuce (Ask, "What type?")
more specific words: iceberg lettuce, romaine, arugula

Discussion Questions: To help your class understand the importance of specific details, ask if any of them work with the public. Are their customers or guests often vague or unclear about what they want? What kinds of details do customers need to provide? (Students may be eager to share or vent frustrations about ineffective communication.)

Note: For more on specific language, see Chapter 27 on word choice.

general word: ran (Ask, "How?")
more specific words: raced, sprinted, loped

general word: nice (Ask, "How?")
more specific words: friendly, outgoing, courteous

Exercise 1 **Identifying General and Specific Words**

Practice

Below are lists of words. Put an *X* by the one term in each list that is more general than the others. The first one is done for you.

List 1

_____ waiter

__X__ restaurant employee

_____ cook

_____ cashier

_____ dishwasher

List 2

_____ toaster

_____ electric can opener

_____ coffeemaker

__X__ kitchen appliance

_____ blender

List 3

_____ fiesta

_____ luau

_____ barbecue

__X__ party

_____ clambake

List 4

_____ weather forecaster

_____ news reporter

_____ news anchor

_____ sports reporter

__X__ TV newsperson

List 5

_____ watch

_____ pin

_____ ring

_____ cuff links

__X__ jewelry

List 6

__X__ science

_____ biology

_____ chemistry

_____ astronomy

_____ physics

Exercise 2 **Ranking General and Specific Items**

Practice

Below are lists of items. In each list, rank the items from the most general (*1*) to the most specific (*4*).

List 1

__1__ reading material

__2__ magazine

List 3

__1__ government program

__4__ college loan

_3_ weekly magazine	_3_ money for students
_4_ *Time*	_2_ financial aid

List 2

_2_ dairy product

_4_ low-fat cottage cheese

_3_ cheese

_1_ source of calcium

List 4

_3_ stinging insect

_1_ insect

_2_ dangerous insect

_4_ killer bee

Exercise 3 Collaborate | **Interviewing for Specific Answers**

To practice being specific, interview a partner. Ask your partner to answer the questions below. Write his or her answers in the spaces provided. When you have finished, change places. In both interviews, your goal is to find specific answers, so you should both be as explicit as you can in your answers.

Interview Questions

1. What is your favorite flavor of ice cream? _____

2. What did you eat and drink for breakfast this morning? _____

   _____

3. What is your favorite football team? _____

4. What television personality do you most dislike? _____

5. If you were painting your room, what color would you choose? _____

   _____

6. What fabric do you think is the softest? _____

7. When you think of a fierce dog, what breed comes to mind? _____

8. When you think of a fast car, what car do you picture? _____

9. What specific items of clothing are your most comfortable clothes?

   _____

10. What is the hottest city you have visited? _____

    _____

Exercise 4 Practice | **Finding Specific Words or Phrases**

List four specific words or phrases beneath each general one. You may use brand names where they are appropriate. The first word on List 1 is done for you.

Answers Will Vary.
Possible answers
shown at right.

List 1

general word: blue
specific word or phrase: aquamarine

turquoise

midnight blue

navy blue

List 2

general word: walked
specific word or phrase: strolled

strutted

sashayed

staggered

List 3

general word: athletic shoe
specific word or phrase: sneakers

Nikes

Reeboks

tennis shoes

List 4

general word: hungry
specific word or phrase: starving

famished

voracious

ravenous

List 5

general word: musician
specific word or phrase: drummer

rapper

singer

guitar player

Exercise 5 **Identifying Sentences That Are Too General**

Practice Below are lists of sentences. Put an *X* by one sentence in each group that is general and vague.

1. **a.** _X_ Jose is an easygoing person.

    b. ____ Jose will smile at an insult.

    c. ____ Jose's most typical remark is "No problem."

2. **a.** ____ Her eyes were red and swollen.

    b. ____ Her mouth was turned down at the corners.

    c. _X_ She looked unhappy.

3. **a.** _X_ The dress was pretty.

    b. ____ The dress had peach and yellow flowers on it.

    c. ____ The dress was pale green silk.

4. **a.** ____ Children pushed in line for the swings at the park.

    b. ____ The park was swarming with joggers.

    c. _X_ The park was busy.

5. **a.** _X_ He will always be there for me.

    b. ____ When I was sick, he took care of my daughter.

    c. ____ He gave me a loan when I lost my job.

Using Sense Words in Your Descriptions

One way to make your description specific and vivid is to *use sense words*. As you plan a description, ask yourself these questions:

What does it **look** like?
What does it **sound** like?
What does it **smell** like?
What does it **taste** like?
What does it **feel** like?

The sense details can make the description vivid. Try to include details about the five senses in your descriptions. Often you can brainstorm sense details more easily if you focus your thinking.

Infobox

Devising Sense Details

For the sense of	think about
sight	colors, light and dark, shadows, or brightness
hearing	noise, silence, or the kinds of sounds you hear
smell	fragrance, odors, scents, aromas, or perfume
taste	bitter, sour, sweet, or compare the taste of one thing to another
touch	the feel of things: texture, hardness, softness, roughness, smoothness

Exercise 6

👥 Collaborate

Brainstorming Sense Details for a Description Paragraph

With a partner or a group, brainstorm the following ideas for a paragraph. That is, for each topic, list at least six questions and answers that could help you find sense details. Be prepared to read your completed exercise to another group or to the class.

1. **topic:** The kitchen was the messiest I have ever seen.

Brainstorm questions and answers: Q: What was the first thing you noticed? A: Dirty pots and pans.

Q: What else did you see? A: Food crusted on the pots.

Q: What kind of food? A: Moldy tomato sauce, burnt spaghetti.

Q: Did the food smell? A: It smelled rotten.

Q: Did you touch anything? A: I touched a counter.

Q: What did it feel like? A: It felt slimy.

2. **topic:** The beach provided a soothing environment.

Brainstorm questions and answers: Q: What was so soothing?

A: The sound of the waves rushing to the shore and back to sea.

Q: Any other sounds? A: The wind in the trees.

Q: Were you alone? A: Yes.

Q: So you didn't hear anyone talking? A: No.

Q: No cars going by? A: No, it was late at night.

Q; Could you see anything? A: The stars.

3. **topic:** The Halloween party thrilled the kindergartners.

Brainstorm questions and answers: Q: What did the children like? A: The decorations.

Q: What were the decoration? A: Paper ghosts, yarn spiders.

Q: What else? A: A haunted room.

Q: What was in it? A: Spider webs, dark curtains, scary sounds.

Q: What sounds? A: Groans and wicked laughter.

Q: Wasn't it all too scary for kindergartners? A: No, they giggled and ran

around, shrieking with pleasure.

Exercise 7	**Writing Sense Words**
Practice	

Write sense descriptions for the items below.

1. Write four words or phrases to describe the texture of a blanket:

Answers Will Vary.
Possible answers
shown at right.

soft, rough, itchy, coarse

2. Write four words or phrases to describe what a silver ring looks like:

a shiny circle, a polished gray ring, gleaming, dazzling

3. Write four words or phrases to describe the sounds of a nightclub:

music blasting, the bass beating off the walls, women shrieking,

men shouting

4. Write four words or phrases to describe the taste of burnt toast:

like cinders, gritty, sandy, like charcoal

WRITING THE DESCRIPTION PARAGRAPH IN STEPS

Thought Lines

DESCRIPTION

Writing a description paragraph begins with thinking on paper, looking for specific details and sense descriptions. You can think by brainstorming, freewriting, or writing in a journal. For example, you might decide to write about your first apartment. Brainstorming might lead you to something like the following list of ideas.

Brainstorming a List for a Descriptive Paragraph

- small apartment—one room and a kitchenette
- kitchenette was old but had working refrigerator, stove, and sink
- looked thrown together
- an old bed from a thrift shop
- took off the headboard, covered the bed with a blue tablecloth to look like a couch—covered the wall side of the bed with blue and red pillows
- thrift shop armchair with yellow plastic cushions, camouflaged with lots of blue pillows
- a bookcase I made out of bricks and lumber—5 feet high, looked like a wall unit
- my casette player and speakers on the bookcase
- also had books, framed photos, a candle in a wine bottle dripped with wax
- curtains out of blue and red striped sheets
- proud of them—hung them on brass rods
- movie posters of 2001: A Space Odyssey and Close Encounters of the Third Kind—lots of blue in them
- wheezy old fan, round, with wires around blades
- also a coffee table I got at a garage sale
- one table leg shorter than the others

The Dominant Impression

When you think you have enough details, you can begin to think about focusing them. Look over these details and consider where they are taking you. If you were to look at the list above, you might identify ideas that keep appearing in the details:

— I didn't have much money to furnish my first apartment.
— I was creative.
— I was proud of some of my ideas.
— I had to rely on thrift shops and garage sales.
— I had to be resourceful.

If you decided to use one main idea from the list above, this idea would be the **dominant impression,** or the main point of the description. You could also combine ideas to create a dominant impression. For example, your dominant impression could be

My first apartment showed what I could do with a little cash and plenty of ideas.

Once you have a dominant impression, you are ready to add more ideas to explain and support it. You should try to make the added details specific by using sense description where appropriate.

Exercise 8
Practice

Adding Details to a Dominant Impression

Following are sentences that could be used as a dominant impression in a description paragraph. Add more details. Some details to explain and support the dominant impression are already given.

    1. dominant impression: The teenager looked like he had dressed in a hurry.

    details: **a.** His shirt was hanging over his jeans.

                b. The laces of his sneakers were untied.

                c. His socks didn't match.

                d. Three buttons on his shirt were unbuttoned

                e. The shirt looked like a pajama top

    2. dominant impression: The hallway of the apartment was cluttered.

    details: **a.** A bicycle leaned against one wall.

                b. A skateboard was shoved under the bike.

                c. A pair of rubber boots lay on the welcome mat.

                d. An umbrella was stuck into the top of one boot.

                e. A backpack hung on the doorknob.

    3. dominant impression: The bakery invited me to come in and buy something.

    details: **a.** The display window was filled with sticky cinnamon rolls.

                b. Next to the rolls was a pyramid of dark chocolate brownies.

                c. Cupcakes gleamed with mounds of vanilla icing.

                d. Long French breads with crispy crusts stood upright.

                e. Chocolate chip cookies filled a tray.

Exercise 9
Practice

Creating a Dominant Impression from a List of Details

Following are lists of details. For each list, write one sentence that could be used as the dominant impression created by the details.

    1. dominant impression: The restaurant was busy and crowded.

    details: People were pushed together behind the cash register, waiting for tables.

The waiters raced from the tables to the kitchen, carrying plates of fajitas, burritos, and tacos.
Every table was filled with people.
The hostess zigzagged between tables, trying to give newcomers their menus.
The tables were so close together that strangers elbowed each other.

2. dominant impression: The examination room was tense and silent.

details: Thirty students sat at thirty desks, looking at the tests before them.
Their eyes never strayed to the left or right.
A few students tapped nervously with their pencils.
The only sounds were the pacing of the instructor and the turning of the test pages.
The instructor held a watch in her hand.
One student's knees were shaking.

3. dominant impression: The old car was well cared for.

details: The paint on the old car had been buffed to a deep shine.
The chrome dazzled.
Each spoke of the hubcaps reflected light.
The hood ornament was a bright silver.
The finish on the car's paint was as smooth as porcelain.

Outlines

Description

You can use the sentence you created as the dominant impression as the topic sentence of your outline. Beneath the topic sentence, list the details you have collected. Once you have this rough list, check the details, asking:

Do all the details relate to the topic sentence?
Are the details in logical order?

Following are the topic sentence and list of details for the paragraph describing an apartment. The details that are crossed out do not "fit" the topic sentence.

topic sentence: My first apartment showed what I could do with little cash and plenty of ideas.

- small apartment—one room and a kitchenette

- kitchenette was old but had working refrigerator, stove, and sink

- looked thrown together

```
-  an old bed from a thrift shop

-  took off the headboard, covered the bed with a blue

   tablecloth to look like a couch—covered the wall side of

   the bed with blue and red pillows

-  thrift shop armchair with yellow plastic cushions, camou-

   flaged with lots of blue pillows

-  a bookcase I made out of bricks and lumber—5 feet high,

   looked like a wall unit

-  my casette player and speakers on the bookcase

-  also had books, framed photos, a candle in a wine bottle

   dripped with wax

-  curtains out of blue and red striped sheets

-  proud of them—hung them on brass rods

-  movie posters of 2001: A Space Odyssey and Close

   Encounters of the Third Kind—lots of blue in them.

-  wheezy old fan, round, with wires around blades

-  also a coffee table I got at a garage sale

-  one table leg shorter than the others
```

Notice what is crossed out. The details about the kitchen, the fan, and the coffee table do not really have much to do with the topic sentence. The topic sentence is about decorating with little money and plenty of ideas. Since the kitchen is not really discussed in the rest of the details, and since the fan is not part of the decorating, the sentences about the kitchen and the fan do not fit. And, if you want the paragraph to make a point about your clever decorating skills, you do not want a detail that says the apartment "looked thrown together," so that detail is eliminated, too.

Remember that as you write and revise, you may decide to eliminate other ideas, to reinsert ideas you once rejected, or even to add new ideas. Changing your mind is a natural part of revising.

Once you have decided on your best list of details, check their order. Remember, when you write a description, you are trying to make the reader *see*. It will be easier for the reader to imagine what you see if you put your description in a simple, logical order. You might want to put descriptions in order by **time sequence** (first to last), by **spatial position** (top to bottom or right to left), or by **similar types** (for example, all about the flowers, then all about the trees in a park).

If you are describing a house, for instance, you may want to start with the outside of the house and then describe the inside. You do not want the details to shift back and forth, from outside to inside and back to outside. If you are describing a person, you might want to group all the details about his or her face before you describe the person's body. You might describe a meal from first course to dessert.

Look again at the details of the outline describing the apartment. It is logical to use three categories to create a simple order: furniture in general, furniture against the wall, and windows and walls.

An Outline for a Descriptive Paragraph

```
topic sentence:  My first apartment showed what I could do with a
                 little cash and plenty of ideas.

details:         It was a small apartment.
                 I got an old bed from a thrift shop.
                 I took off the headboard.
                 I covered the bed with a blue tablecloth to make
  furniture       the bed look like a couch.
                 I covered the wall side with red and blue pillows.
                 I got an armchair from a thrift shop.
                 It had plastic cushions.
                 I camouflaged the yellow plastic cushions with lots
                  of blue pillows.

  furniture       I made a bookcase out of bricks and lumber.
  against         It was five feet high, like a wall unit.
  the wall        I put my casette player and speakers on the bookcase.
                 I set out some books, framed photos, and a candle in
                  a wine bottle dripped with wax.

                 I made curtains out of blue and red striped sheets.
                 I hung them on brass rods.
  windows         I was proud of them.
  and             On the wall I had movie posters of 2001: A Space
  walls            Odyssey and Close Encounters of the Third Kind.
                 They had lots of blue in them.
```

Once you have a list of details focused on a topic sentence and arranged in some logical order, you can begin writing a draft of your description paragraph.

Exercise 10
Practice

Finding Details That Do Not Relate

Survey the following lists. Each includes a topic sentence and several details. In each list, cross out the details that do not relate to the topic sentence.

1. **topic sentence:** My brother's garden was neglected.
   details: Weeds cluttered the flower beds.
   Grass peeped through the cracks in the sidewalks.
   Yellow dandelions bloomed in the lawn.
   ~~The apple tree had many apples.~~
   ~~The yard was bordered by a fence.~~
   The long, uncut grass tickled my ankles.
   An overgrown vine strangled a small tree.
   Ants swarmed from anthills, stinging me.
   Some flowers wilted from lack of water.

2. **topic sentence:** My Aunt Maria was a motherly woman.
   details: She always greeted me with a big hug.
   She crushed me against her plump body.
   She smelled like the gingerbread cookies she always made for me.
   ~~She was born in Guatemala.~~
   She always checked to see if I was dressed warmly enough to go outside.
   She carried small treats in her apron.
   She made me wash my hands before meals.
   ~~She had deep brown eyes.~~

3. **topic sentence:** Levar was a very spoiled child.
   details: He would interrupt his mother when she was talking to people.
   He'd pull at her sleeve or the hem of her dress.
   He'd whine, "Mom, Mom, I want to go now," or "Mom, can I have a dollar?"
   He had about a hundred toys.
   Whenever he broke one, he got a new one right away.
   Levar wore designer clothes, even to play in.
   Levar had no set bedtime; he was allowed to stay up as long as he wanted.
   ~~Levar had a little sister, Denise.~~
   ~~Levar had big black eyes with long, soft lashes.~~

| Exercise 11 | **Putting Details in Order** |

Practice

Following are lists that start with a topic sentence. The details under each topic sentence are not in the right order. Put the details in logical order by labeling them, with *1* being the first detail, *2* the second, and so forth.

1. **topic sentence:** The picnic turned out to be a disaster.
   (Arrange the details in time order.)

   details: _2_ We got lost on the way to the picnic.

   _3_ The ice in the ice chest melted.

   _4_ The lemonade was warm.

   _1_ Back home, we forgot to close the lid on the cooler when we were packing.

2. **topic sentence:** The Jackson house looked haunted.
   (Arrange the details from outside to inside.)

   details: _1_ The tall iron fence around the house was rusted and crumbling.

   _4_ The front hall smelled like a dead rat.

   _2_ The house was covered by a dark green vine.

   _3_ The front door creaked and groaned.

   _5_ A long, twisting staircase loomed at the end of the hall.

3. topic sentence: The bodyguard was a frightening person.
(Arrange the details from head to foot.)

   details: _1_ His cold eyes stared straight ahead.

   _2_ His mouth never moved.

   _6_ He stood poised on the balls of his feet, ready to spring.

   _4_ His wide shoulders strained against the fabric of his shirt.

   _3_ His neck was as thick as a tree trunk.

   _5_ His fists were half clenched.

Exercise 12 **Creating Details Using a Logical Order**

Practice

The following lists include a topic sentence and indicate a required order for the details. Write five sentences of details in the required order.

Answers Will Vary.
Possible answers
shown at right.

1. topic sentence: Her new truck dazzled my eyes.
(Describe the truck from inside to outside.)

   a. The upholstery was a soft brown leather.

   b. The dashboard matched the leather with wood panels.

   c. A center console contained wood grain cupholders.

   d. The truck was painted a deep metallic blue.

   e. The hubcaps gleamed.

2. topic sentence: The movie was full of exciting moments.
(Describe the movie from beginning to end.)

   a. It started with a rescue from a mountaintop.

   b. Then three convicts escaped from prison.

   c. They stole a truck full of toxic chemicals.

   d. They were chased by cars and helicopters.

   e. A huge explosion came at the end.

3. topic sentence: The traffic jam showed people at their worst.
(First describe what the scene looked like; then describe the drivers' behavior.)

   a. A huge tractor-trailer had overturned.

   b. Traffic was backed up for five miles.

c. Some drivers tried to drive on the median.

d. Others began blowing their horns.

e. Others tried to pass by driving on people's lawns.

4. **topic sentence:** His clothes showed a lack of style. (Describe him from head to foot.)

a. He wore a hat covered with lint

b. He had on an open-necked, flowered shirt.

c. His trousers were wildly striped bellbottoms.

d. His socks had Mickey Mouse on them.

e. On his feet were patent-leather shoes.

Rough Lines

DESCRIPTION

After you have an outline, the next step is creating a rough draft of the paragraph. At this point, you can begin combining some of the ideas in your outline, making two or more short sentences into one longer one. You can also write your first draft in short sentences and combine the sentences later. Your goal is simply to put your ideas in paragraph form so that you can see how they look. You can check them to see what needs to be improved.

The first draft of a paragraph will not be perfect. If it were perfect, it would not be a first draft. Once you have the first draft, look it over, using the following checklist.

✔ Checklist

A Checklist for Revising a Descriptive Paragraph

✔ Are there enough details?

✔ Are the details specific?

✔ Do the details use sense words?

✔ Are the details in order?

✔ Is there a dominant impression?

✔ Do the details connect to the dominant impression?

✔ Have I made my point?

A common problem in writing description is creating a fuzzy, vague description. Take a look at the following fuzzy description:

```
The football fans were rowdy and excited. They shouted
when their team scored. Some people jumped up. The fans
showed their support by cheering and stomping. They were
enjoying every minute of the game.
```

The description could be revised so that it is more specific and vivid:

```
     The football fans were rowdy and excited. When their team
scored, they yelled, "Way to go!" or "Stomp 'em! Crush 'em!"
until they were hoarse. Three fans, wearing the team colors
of blue and white on their shirts, shorts, and socks, jumped
up, spilling their drinks on the teenagers seated below them.
During time-outs, the fans chanted rhythmically, and through-
out the game they stomped their feet in a steady beat against
the wooden bleachers. As people chanted, whooped, and woofed,
they turned to grin at each other and thrust their clenched
fists into the air.
```

The vivid description meets the requirements of the checklist. It has sufficient specific details, and uses sense words to describe how the fans looked and sounded. The details also support a dominant impression of rowdy, excited fans. The vivid, specific details make the point.

Exercise 13
Practice

Revising a Paragraph: Finding Irrelevant Sentences

Following are two descriptive paragraphs. In each, there are sentences that are irrelevant, meaning they do not have anything to do with the first sentence, the topic sentence. Cross out the irrelevant sentences in the paragraphs below.

1. John looked and sounded like he had a bad cold. His voice was hoarse and raspy, and it sounded like it hurt him to talk. His nostrils were red and chafed around the edges, as if he had wiped his nose with hundreds of Kleenex. His cheeks looked flushed and feverish. His eyes had a watery sheen. ~~Sometimes my eyes get like that when I have an allergy. I am allergic to cats.~~ John sneezed four times in thirty seconds. ~~There's nothing worse than sneezing constantly, unless it's a cold that won't quit.~~

2. The van was in bad shape. One door panel had been deeply dented, and since the dent had never been repaired, rust filled the dented places. The rear tires were so worn out that they shone smoothly where tread should have been. ~~Tires like that are really dangerous, especially on slick roads.~~ One of the van windows was missing, and a piece of cardboard covered the opening. The whole van was covered in dust. ~~It doesn't cost that much to run a van through a car wash, so they could have taken care of it.~~ An odor of burnt oil seeped from under the vehicle.

Exercise 14
Practice

Revising a Paragraph for More Specific Details

In the following paragraphs, the details that are underlined are not specific. Change the underlined sentences to a more specific description. Write the changes in the lines below each paragraph.

1. It was the most beautiful beach I had ever seen. The beach itself was very wide; it was almost a quarter mile from the sand to the water. The sand was a pale beige, almost white in color, and it was as fine as cake flour. Shining up from the sand were small pink and ivory shells. <u>The water was nice, too.</u>

revisions: <u>The turquoise water was so clear that I could see small fish swimming in schools.</u>

2. The house seemed to say, "We don't want you here." There was a heavy iron fence around the yard, and the iron gate had two locks on it. <u>A plant clung to the iron fence, and a dog patrolled the yard.</u> Black bars crossed the windows of the first story of the house, and the second-story windows were tinted black.

revisions: <u>A wilted brown plant clung to the iron fence, and a snarling rottweiler patrolled the yard.</u>

Transitions

As you revise your description paragraph, you may notice places in the paragraph that seem choppy or abrupt. That is, one sentence may end, and another may start, but the two sentences don't seem to be connected. Reading your paragraph aloud, you may sense that it is not very smooth.

You can make the writing smoother and make the content clearer by using **transitions,** which are words or phrases that link one idea to another idea. They tell the reader what he or she has just read and what is coming next. Here are some transitions you may want to use in writing a description:

Infobox

Transitions for a Descriptive Paragraph

To show ideas brought together: and, also, in addition, next

To show a contrast: but, although, on the other hand, however, in contrast, unlike, yet, on the contrary

To show a similarity: both, like, similarly, all, each

To show a time sequence: after, always, before, first, second, third (etc.), often, meanwhile, next, soon, then, when, while

To show a position in space: above, ahead of, alongside, among, around, away, below, beside, between, beneath, beyond, by, close, down, far, here, in front of, inside, near, nearby, next to, on, on top of, outside, over, there, toward, under, up, underneath, where

---

Note: For more sentence combining options that incorporate transitions, see Chapter 13 on coordination, and Chapter 14 on subordination.

There are many other transitions you can use, depending on what you need to link your ideas. Take a look at a draft of a description paragraph on an apartment. Compare it to the outline on page 50. Pay particular attention to the transitions in this draft.

A Draft of a Descriptive Paragraph (Transitions are underlined.)

My first apartment showed what I could do with a little cash and plenty of ideas. To furnish my small apartment, I started with an old bed I got at a thrift shop. I took off the headboard and covered the bed with a blue tablecloth. <u>Then,</u> to make the bed look like a couch, I covered the wall side of the bed with lots of

```
blue and red pillows. I also got an armchair from the thrift
shop. It had yellow plastic cushions, but I camouflaged those
cushions with lots of blue pillows. I made a bookcase out of
bricks and lumber. The bookcase was five feet high, and I used it
as a wall unit. On it, I put my casette player and speakers, some
books, some framed photos, and a candle in a wine bottle dripped
with wax. For the windows, I made curtains out of red and blue
striped sheets and hung them on brass rods. I was proud of those
curtains. On the wall, I had movie posters of 2001: A Space
Odyssey and Close Encounters of the Third Kind. They had lots of
blue in them.
```

Exercise 15 **Recognizing Transitions**

Practice Underline the transitions in the paragraph below.

My sister designed a children's fantasy for her little boy's birthday party. She decorated the walls with streamers in neon yellow and green. From the ceiling she hung clusters of yellow and blue balloons. Then, on the food table, she spread a tablecloth printed with hundreds of Barney dinosaurs. Meanwhile, my brother finished decorating an enormous cake slathered in white and yellow icing. On top of the cake he placed a small purple dinosaur. After he put the cake in the middle of the table, my sister added baskets filled with cookies and candy. Beneath the table she hid a huge box of prizes for all the party games. When she added a bag of treats for each child at the party, my sister finished her work. Now came the enjoyment of seeing her son celebrate his third birthday.

Final Lines

DESCRIPTION

In preparing the final version of a descriptive paragraph, you add the finishing touches to your paragraph, making changes in words, combining sentences, changing or adding transitions, and sharpening details. In the draft of the description of an apartment, the phrase "lots of" is used often, as in

> lots of blue and red pillows
> lots of blue pillows
> lots of blue in them

When you are drafting, it is easy to get into the habit of using "lots of" or "a lot" and of being repetitive or vague. In the final version of the description paragraph, the "lots of" phrases are replaced.

In the draft paragraph, the ending of the paragraph is a little sudden. The paragraph needs a sentence that pulls all the details together and reminds the reader of the topic sentence. The final version has an added sentence that ties the paragraph together.

A Final Version of a Descriptive Paragraph
(Changes from the draft are underlined)

```
    My first apartment showed what I could do with a little cash
and plenty of ideas. To furnish my apartment, I started with an
old bed I got at a thrift shop. I took off the headboard and cov-
ered the bed with a blue tablecloth. Then, to make the bed look
like a couch, I covered the wall side of the bed with piles of
blue and red pillows. I also got an armchair from the thrift
shop. It had yellow plastic cushions, but I camouflaged those
cushions with more blue pillows. I made a bookcase out of bricks
and lumber. The bookcase was five feet high, and I used it as a
wall unit. On it, I put my cassette player and speakers, some
books, some framed photos, and a candle in a wine bottle dripped
with wax. For the windows, I made curtains out of red and blue
striped sheets and hung them on brass rods. I was proud of those
curtains. On the wall I had movie posters of 2001: A Space
Odyssey and Close Encounters of the Third Kind. They were filled
with shades of blue, and I thought they added the perfect final
touch to my stylish but inexpensive apartment.
```

Before you prepare the final copy of your own descriptive paragraph, check your last draft for errors in spelling and punctuation and for any errors made in typing or copying.

Exercise 16

Practice

Proofreading to Prepare the Final Version

Following is a descriptive paragraph with the kinds of errors that are easy to overlook when you write the final version of an assignment. Correct the errors, writing above the lines. There are thirteen errors.

I have a dilapidated old sweatshirt that I'll *always* allways cherish for the *memories* memmories it holds. It is a ratty-looking, gray shirt that belongs in the rag pile, but I wore that shirt on many happy *occasions* occassions. The greasy stain on one sleeve reminds me how I got covered in oil when *I* i was working on my first motorcy-cle*.* The tear at the neck reminds me of a crazy game of football. At the game where I tore the shirt, I also met my current *girlfriend* girlfreind. The pale white blotches *across* acrost the front of the shirt are from *bleach* bleech. But to me they are a memory of the time my girlfriend and I *were* was fooling around at the laundry room and put *too* to much bleach in the washer. Every mark or stain on my shirt has a meaning to me *,* and I'll never *throw* through that old shirt away.

Lines of Detail: A Walk-Through Assignment

Your assignment is to write a paragraph describing a popular place for socializing. Follow these steps:

Step 1: Freewrite about a place where people socialize. For example, you could write about a place where people go to eat, or dance, or swim, or just "hang out."

Step 2: Read your freewriting. Underline all the words, phrases, and sentences of description.

Step 3: List everything you underlined, grouping the ideas in some order. Maybe the details can be listed from inside to outside, or maybe they can be put into categories, like "walls, floor, and furniture" or "scenery and people."

Step 4: After you've surveyed the list, write a sentence about the dominant impression of the details.

Step 5: Using the dominant impression as your topic sentence, write an outline. Add specific details where you need them. Concentrate on details that appeal to the senses.

Step 6: Write a first draft of your paragraph. Be sure to check the order of your details. Combine short sentences and add transitions.

Note: A Peer Review Form for student editing/interaction is on p. 61.

Step 7: Revise your first draft version, paying particular attention to order, specific details, and transitions.

Step 8: After a final check for punctuation, spelling, and word choice, prepare the final version of the paragraph.

TEACHING TIP:
(1) Assignments #1, 2, or 3 can be given as an in-class writing topic to get students used to writing within time constraints.
(2) Assignments #4, 5, or 6 are more appropriate as homework. **(3)** You may decide to assign the topics prompted by the reading "A Present for Popo" on pp. 62–63.

Writing Your Own Descriptive Paragraph

When you write on any of the following topics, work through the stages of the writing process in preparing your descriptive paragraph. Be sure that your paragraph is based on a dominant impression, and put the dominant impression into your topic sentence.

1. Write a paragraph that describes one of the items below:

   a piece of clothing   a hospital waiting room
   a perfect meal   a family member
   a favorite relative   an enemy
   a very young baby   an irritating customer
   what is in your top bureau drawer
   what is in your top kitchen drawer
   the contents of your purse or wallet
   items in the glove compartment of your car
   what you wear on your day off
   your first impression of a school
   a person who was a positive influence in your life

2. Describe a place that creates one of these impressions:

peace	tension	depression
excitement	cheerfulness	hurry
friendliness	danger	safety

3. Describe a person who conveys one of these impressions:

confidence	warmth	pride
hostility	fear	style
shyness	rebellion	intelligence
conformity	strength	beauty

4. Select a photograph of a person or place. You can use a photograph from a magazine or newspaper or one of your own photographs. Write a paragraph describing that photograph. Attach the photograph to the completed paragraph.

5. Interview a partner so that you and your partner can gather details; then write a description paragraph with the title "My Perfect Room."

First, prepare a list of at least six questions to ask your partner. Write down the answers your partner gives, and use those answers to form more questions. For example, if your partner says her dream room would be a game room, ask her what games she'd like to have in it. If your partner says his perfect room would be a workshop, ask him what kind of workshop.

When you've finished the interview, switch roles. Let your partner interview you. Feel free to add more questions or to follow up on previous ones.

Give your partner his or her interview responses. Take your own responses and use them as the basis for gathering as much details as you can on your perfect room. Finally, build the thoughtlines part of your paragraph. Then go to the outline, draft, and final version. Be prepared to read your completed paragraph to your partner.

6. Describe photograph A on page 60. Be sure that your description includes specific details about the man, the lake, and the mountains.

7. Describe the scene in photograph B on page 60. Look carefully at the people's expressions and include them in your description.

Photograph A

Photograph B

Name: _____ **Section:** _____

Peer Review Form for a Descriptive Paragraph

After you have written a draft of your descriptive paragraph, let a writing partner read it. When your partner has completed the form below, discuss the comments. Then repeat the same process for your partner's paragraph.

The dominant impression of the paragraph is this sentence:

_____

_____

The details of the description are in a specific order. That order is (for example, top to bottom, time order, etc.)

_____

_____

The part of the description I liked best begins with the words

_____

_____

The part that could use more or better details begins with the words

_____

_____

I have questions about

_____

_____

I noticed these transitions:

_____

_____

A place where transitions could be added or improved is right before the words

_____

_____

Other comments

_____

Reviewer's Name: _____

WRITING FROM READING: Description

A Present for Popo
Elizabeth Wong

The child of Chinese immigrants, Elizabeth Wong was born in Los Angeles, California. She has a master of fine arts degree and has worked as a writer for newspapers and television. She has also written several plays. In "A Present for Popo," Wong describes a beloved grandmother.

Words You May Need to Know

nimbly (paragraph 1): quickly, gracefully
vain (2): proud of your appearance
co-opted (3): taken over
niggling (4): unimportant
dim sum **(6):** a light meal

terrarium (7): a small container in which plants and small creatures are kept alive under conditions imitating their natural environment

1 When my Popo opened a Christmas gift, she would shake it, smell it, listen to it. She would size it up. She would open it nimbly, with all enthusiasm and delight, and even though the mittens were ugly or the blouse too small or the card obviously homemade, she would coo over it as if it were the baby Jesus.

2 Despite that, buying a gift for my grandmother was always problematic. Being in her late 80s, Popo didn't seem to need any more sweaters or handbags. No books certainly, as she only knew six words of English. Cosmetics might be a good idea, for she was just a wee bit vain.

3 But ultimately, nothing worked. "No place to put anything anyway," she used to tell me in Chinese. For in the last few years of her life, Popo had a bed in a room in a house in San Gabriel owned by one of her sons. All her belongings, her money, her very life was now co-opted and controlled by her sons and their wives. Popo's daughters had little power in this matter. This was a traditional Chinese family.

4 For you see, Popo had begun to forget things. Ask her about something that happened 20 years ago, and she could recount the details in the heartbeat of a New York minute. But it was those niggling little everyday matters that became so troubling. She would forget to take her heart medicine. She would forget where she put her handbag. She would forget she talked to you just moments before. She would count the few dollars in her billfold, over and over again. She would ask me for the millionth time, "So when are you going to get married?" For her own good, the family decided she should give up her beloved one-room Chinatown flat. Popo herself recognized she might be a danger to herself. "I think your grandmother is going crazy," she would say.

5 That little flat was a bothersome place, but Popo loved it. Her window had a view of several import-export shops below, not to mention the grotesque plas-

tic hanging lanterns and that nasty loudspeaker serenading tourists with 18 hours of top-40 popular hits.

6　　My brother Will and I used to stand under her balcony on Mei Ling Way, shouting up, "Grandmother on the Third Floor! Grandmother on the Third Floor!" Simultaneously, the wrinkled faces of a half-dozen grannies would peek cautiously out their windows. Popo would come to the balcony and proudly claim us: "These are my grandchildren coming to take me to *dim sum.*" Her neighbors would cluck and sigh, "You have such good grandchildren. Not like mine."

7　　In that cramped room of Popo's, I could see past Christmas presents. A full-wall collage of family photos that my mother and I made together and presented one year with lots of fanfare. Popo had attached additional snapshots by way of paper clips and Scotch tape. And there, on the window sill, a little terrarium to which Popo had tied a small red ribbon. "For good luck," as she gleefully pointed out the sprouting buds. "See, it's having babies."

8　　Also, there were the utility shelves on the wall, groaning from a wide assortment of junk, stuff and whatnot. Popo was fond of salvaging discarded things. After my brother had installed the shelving, she did a little jig, then took a whisk broom and lightly swept away any naughty spirits that might be lurking on the walls. "Shoo, shoo, shoo, away with you, Mischievous Ones!" That apartment was her independence, and her pioneer spirit was everywhere in it.

9　　Popo was my mother's mother, but she was also a second mother to me. Her death was a great blow. The last time I saw her was Christmas, 1990, when she looked hale and hearty. I thought she would live forever. Last October, at 91, she had her final heart attack. The next time I saw her, it was at her funeral.

10　　An open casket, and there she was, with a shiny new penny poised between her lips, a silenced warrior woman. Her sons and daughters placed colorful pieces of cloth in her casket. They burned incense and paper money. A small marching band led a New Orleans–like procession through the streets of Chinatown. Popo's picture, larger than life, in a flatbed truck to survey the world of her adopted country.

11　　This little 4-foot, 9-inch woman had been the glue of our family. She wasn't perfect, she wasn't always even nice, but she learned from her mistakes, and, ultimately, she forgave herself for being human. It is a lesson of forgiveness that seems to have eluded her own sons and daughters.

12　　And now she is gone. And with her—the tenuous, cohesive ties of blood and duty that bound us to family. My mother predicted that once the distribution of what was left of Popo's estate took place, no further words would be exchanged between Popo's children. She was right.

13　　But this year, six of the 27 grandchildren and two of the 18 great-grandchildren came together for a holiday feast of honey-baked ham and mashed potatoes. Not a gigantic family reunion. But I think, for now, it's the one yuletide present my grandmother might have truly enjoyed.

14　　Merry Christmas, Popo!

WRITING FROM READING: "A Present for Popo"

When you write on any of the following topics, work through the stages of the writing process in preparing your descriptive paragraph.

1. Elizabeth Wong uses many details about her grandmother's apartment to describe the woman. Write a paragraph in which you use many details about a person's environment (for example, her office, his apartment) to describe that person.

2. Wong's essay includes a description of a funeral in a Chinese-American family. Write a description of some custom or ritual in your family. You could write, for instance, about a wedding, a funeral, a celebration of a holiday, or a religious occasion.

3. "A Present for Popo" is a tribute to a beloved person. Write a description of someone who holds a special place in your life.

4. The grandmother in Wong's essay is an immigrant, a Chinese woman who moved to America. Describe an immigrant you know. Focus on how the person is a combination of two countries or cultures.

5. Describe an older person you know well. In your description, you can use details of appearance and behavior. Focus on how these details reveal personality.

6. Describe yourself at age ninety. Use your imagination to give details of appearance, behavior, and family relationships.

3 Narration

WHAT IS NARRATION?

Narration means telling a story. Everybody tells stories; some people are better storytellers than others. When you write a **narrative** paragraph, you can tell a story about something that happened to you or to someone else, or about something that you saw or read.

A narrative, like a description, relies on specific details, but it is also different from a description because it covers events in a time sequence. While a description can be about a person, a place, or an object, a narrative is always about happenings: events, actions, incidents.

Interesting narratives do more than just tell what happened. They help the reader become involved in the story by providing vivid details. These details come from your memory, your observation, or your reading. Using good details, you don't just tell the story; you *show* it.

Give the Narrative a Point

We all know people who tell long stories that seem to lead nowhere. These people talk on and on; they recite an endless list of activities and soon become boring. Their narratives have no point.

The difficult part of writing a narrative is making sure that it has a point. That point will be included in the topic sentence. The point of a narrative is the meaning of the incident or incidents you are writing about. To get to the point of your narrative, ask yourself questions like these:

> What did I learn?
> What is the meaning of this story?
> What is my attitude toward what happened?
> Did it change me?
> What emotion did it make me feel?
> Was the experience a good example of unfairness, kindness, generosity, or some other quality?

The answers to such questions can lead you to a point. An effective topic sentence for a narrative is

TEACHING TIP:

Students often need to be reminded that topic sentences should not be announcements. Some students may have developed the habit in speech classes, in informal presentations, or in high school classes that rewarded content over structure.

not this: I am going to tell you about the time I flunked my driving test. (This is an announcement; it does not make a point.)

but this: When I failed my driving test, I learned not to be overconfident.

not this: Yesterday my car stalled in rush-hour traffic. (This sentence identifies the incident but does not make a point. It is also too narrow to be a good topic sentence.)

but this: When my car stalled in rush-hour traffic, I was annoyed and embarrassed.

The topic sentence, stating the point of your narrative paragraph, can be placed in the beginning or middle or at the end of the paragraph. You may want to start your story with the point, so that the reader knows exactly where your story is headed, or you may want to conclude your story by leaving the point until last. Sometimes the point can even fit smoothly into the middle of your paragraph.

Consider the narrative paragraphs below. The topic sentences are in various places.

Topic Sentence at the Beginning

<u>When I was five, I learned how serious it is to tell a lie.</u> One afternoon, my seven-year-old friend Tina asked me if I wanted to walk down the block to play ball in an empty lot. When I asked my mother, she said I couldn't go because it was too near dinnertime. I don't know why I lied, but when Tina asked me if my mother had said yes, I nodded my head in a lie. I wanted to go play, and I did. Yet as I played in the dusty lot, a dull buzz of guilt or fear distracted me. As soon as I got home, my mother confronted me. She asked me whether I had gone to the sandlot and whether I had lied to Tina about getting permission. This time, I told the truth. Something about my mother's tone of voice made me feel very dirty and ashamed. I had let her down.

Topic Sentence in the Middle

TEACHING TIP:

For students who say they have always been taught that topic sentences of paragraphs must be at the beginning, reassure them that they can follow the pattern in the first example.

When I was little, I was afraid of diving into water. I thought I would go down and never come back up. Then one day, my father took me to a pool where we swam and fooled around, but he never forced me to try a dive. After about an hour of playing, I walked round and round the edge of the pool, trying to get the courage to dive in. Finally, I did it. <u>When I made that first dive, I felt blissful because I did something I had been afraid to do.</u> As I came to the surface, I wiped the water from my eyes and looked around. The sun seemed more dazzling, and the water sparkled. Best of all, I saw my father looking at me with a smile. "You did it," he said. "Good for you! I'm proud of you."

Topic Sentence at the End

It seemed like I'd been in love with Reeza for years. Unfortunately, Reeza was always in love with someone else. Finally, she broke up with her boyfriend Nelson. I saw my chance. I asked Reeza out. After dinner, we talked and talked. Reeza told me all about her hopes and dreams. She told me about her family and her job, and I felt very close

to her. We talked late into the night. When she left, Reeza
kissed me. "Thanks for listening," she said. "You're like a
brother to me." <u>Reeza meant to be kind, but she shattered my
hopes and dreams</u>.

Exercise 1 — Finding the Topic Sentence in a Narrative Paragraph

Practice

Underline the topic sentence in each narrative paragraph below.

Paragraph 1

I was eager to get a place of my own. I figured that having my own apartment meant I was free at last since there would be no rules, no curfew, no living by someone else's schedule. My first day in the apartment started well. I arranged the furniture, put up all my pictures, and called all my friends. Then I called out for pizza. When it came, I tried to start a conversation with the delivery man, but he was in a hurry. I ate my pizza alone while I watched the late movie. It was too late to call any of my friends, and I definitely wasn't going to call my mother and let her know I wanted some company. <u>In truth, my first day in my apartment showed me the lonely side of living on my own.</u>

Paragraph 2

Last Saturday I took a bus downtown to have lunch with a friend. After lunch, my friend and I split the bill, and I reached for my wallet to pay my share. I was horrified to discover I had lost my wallet. My friend drove me home, and the first thing I saw was the blinking message light on my answering machine. The message said someone had found my wallet and wanted to return it. <u>I couldn't believe anyone in the city would be so kind and honest, but losing something changed my mind.</u> When I met the man in a nearby coffee shop, he gave me the wallet with all my money and credit cards still in it. He said he had found it on a seat in the bus and had been calling my apartment for hours. He was such a good person he wouldn't even take a small reward. He even paid the check at the coffee shop because he said I'd had a bad day and deserved a break!

Paragraph 3

<u>Yesterday, one person showed me what it means to be a good parent.</u> I was walking in the mall, and just ahead of me a toddler was holding his father's hand and struggling to keep up. Pretty soon, the child got tired and started to cry. Within minutes, his crying had become a full-fledged tantrum. The little boy squatted on the ground, refusing to go any farther, his face purple. Some parents would have shouted at the child, threatened him, or scooped him up and carried him away. This father, however, just sat down on the ground by his son and talked to him, very calmly and quietly. I couldn't hear his words, but I got the feeling he was sympathizing with the tired little boy. Pretty soon, the child's screams became little sniffles, and father and son walked quietly away.

Exercise 2 — Writing the Missing Topic Sentences in Narrative Paragraphs

Practice

Below are three paragraphs. If the paragraph already has a topic sentence, write it in the lines provided. If it does not have a topic sentence, create one. (Two of the paragraphs have no topic sentence.)

Paragraph 1

When I got up, I realized I must have turned off my alarm clock and gone

Note: Paragraph 2 has a topic sentence. Answers for paragraphs 1 and 3 will vary. Possible answers shown at right.

back to sleep, because I was already an hour behind schedule. I raced into the shower, only to find I had used up the last of the shampoo the day before. I barely had time to make a cup of coffee to take with me in the car. I grabbed the cup of coffee, rushed to the car, and turned the ignition. The car wouldn't start. Two hours later, the emergency service finally came to jump-start the car. I arrived at work three hours late, and the supervisor was not happy with me.

If the paragraph already has a topic sentence, write it here. If it does not

have a topic sentence, create one. <u>Yesterday morning brought me one</u>

<u>problem after another.</u>

_____

Paragraph 2

Since I gave my first speech in my public speaking class, I'm not as shy as I used to be. On the day I was supposed to give my speech, I seriously considered cutting class, taking an F on the speech, or even dropping the course. All I could think of was what could go wrong. I could freeze up and go blank, or I could say something really stupid. In spite of my terror, I managed to walk up to the front of the class. When I started talking, I could hear my voice shaking. I wondered if everyone in the room could see the cold sweat on my forehead. By the middle of the speech, I was concentrating so intensely on what to say that I forgot about my nerves. When I finished, I couldn't believe people were clapping! I never believed I could stand up and speak to the entire class. Once I did that, it seemed so easy to talk in a class discussion. Best of all, the idea of making another speech doesn't seem as frightening any more.

If the paragraph already has a topic sentence, write it here. If it does not

have a topic sentence, create one. <u>Since I gave my first speech in public</u>

<u>speaking class, I'm not as shy as I used to be.</u>

_____

Paragraph 3

Last weekend I was driving home alone, at about 10:00 p.m., when a carload of young men pulled their car beside mine. They began shouting and making strange motions with their hands. At first I ignored them, hoping they'd go away. But then I got scared because they wouldn't pass me. They kept driving right alongside of my car. I rolled up my car windows and locked the doors. I couldn't hear their shouts, but I was still afraid. I was more afraid when I stopped at a red light and they pulled up next to me. Suddenly, one of the men screamed at me, at the top of his lungs. "Hey! You have a broken taillight!"

If the paragraph already has a topic sentence, write it here. If it does not

have a topic sentence, create one. <u>I misinterpreted some people's good</u>

<u>intentions last week.</u>

_____

Hints for Writing a Narrative Paragraph

Everyone tells stories, but some people tell stories better than others. When you write a story, be sure to follow these rules:

- Be clear.
- Be interesting.
- Stay in order.
- Pick a topic that is not too big.

1. Be clear. Put in all the information the reader needs in order to follow your story. Sometimes you need to explain the time or place or the relationships of the people in your story in order to make the story clear. Sometimes you need to explain how much time has elapsed between one action and another. This paragraph is not clear:

> I've never felt so stupid as I did on my first day of work. I was stocking the shelves when Mr. Cimino came up to me and said, "You're doing it wrong." Then he showed me how to do it. An hour later, he told me to call the produce supplier and check on the order for grapefruit. Well, I didn't know how to tell Mr. Cimino that I didn't know what phone to use or how to get an outside line. I also didn't know how to get the phone number of the produce supplier, or what the order for the grapefruit was supposed to be and when it was supposed to arrive. I felt really stupid asking these questions.

What is wrong with the paragraph? It lacks all kinds of information. Who is Mr. Cimino? Is he the boss? Is he a produce supervisor? What was the writer doing wrong? And, more important, what kind of place is the writer's workplace? The reader knows the place has something to do with food, but is it a supermarket, or a fruit market, or a warehouse?

2. Be interesting. A boring narrative can make the greatest adventure sound dull. Here is a dull narrative:

> I had a wonderful time on prom night. First, we went out to dinner. The meal was excellent. Then we went to the dance and saw all our friends. Everyone was dressed up great. We stayed until late. Then we went out to breakfast. After breakfast we watched the sun come up.

Good specific details are the difference between an interesting story and a dull one.

3. Stay in order. Put the details in a clear order, so that the reader can follow your story. Usually, time order is the order you follow in narration. This narrative has a confusing order:

> My impatience cost me twenty dollars last week. There was a pair of shoes I really wanted. I had wanted them for weeks. So, when payday came around, I went to the mall and checked the price on the shoes. I had been checking the price for weeks before. The shoes were expensive, but I really wanted them. On payday, my friend who works at the shoe store told me the shoes were about to go on sale. But I was impatient. I bought them at full price, and three days later, the shoes were marked down twenty dollars.

Discussion Questions: Ask students why the paragraph is dull. What words are vague? What details could be added?

There is something wrong with the order of these sentences. Tell the story in the order it happened: first, I saw the shoes and wanted them; second, the shoes were expensive; third, I checked the price for several weeks; fourth, I got paid; fifth, I checked the price again; sixth, my friend told me the shoes were about to go on sale; seventh, I paid full price right away; eighth, the shoes went on sale. A clear time sequence helps the reader follow your narrative.

4. Pick a topic that is not too big. If you try to write about too many events in a short space, you run the risk of being superficial. You cannot describe anything well if you cover too much. This paragraph covers too much:

> Starting my sophomore year at a new high school was a difficult experience. Because my family had just moved to town, I didn't know anybody at school. On the first day of school, I sat by myself at lunch. Finally, two students at another table started a conversation with me. I thought they were just feeling sorry for me. At the end of the first week, it seemed like the whole school was talking about exciting plans for the weekend. I spent Friday and Saturday night at home, doing all kinds of things to keep my mind off my loneliness. On Monday, people casually asked, "Have a good weekend?" I lied and said, "Of course."

This paragraph would be better if it discussed one shorter time period in greater depth and detail. It could cover the first day at school, or the first lunch at school, or the first Saturday night at home alone, when the writer was doing "all kinds of things" to keep from feeling lonely.

Using a Speaker's Exact Words in Narrative

Some of the examples of narrative that you have already seen have included the exact words someone said. You may want to include part of a conversation in your narrative. To do so, you need to know how to punctuate speech.

A person's exact words get quotation marks around them. If you change the words, you do not use quotation marks:

Note: For more on punctuating dialogue (direct quotes), students can review Chapter 24.

exact words: "You're being silly," he told me.
not exact words: He told me that I was being silly.

exact words: My sister said, "I'd love to go to the party."
not exact words: My sister said she would love to go to the party.

There are a few other points to remember about punctuating a person's exact words. Once you've started quoting a person's exact words, periods and commas generally go inside the quotation marks. Here are two examples:

Richard said, "Nothing can be done."
"Be careful," my mother warned us.

When you introduce a person's exact words with phrases like "She said" or "The teacher told us," put a comma before the quotation marks. Here are two examples:

She said, "You'd better watch out."
The teacher told us, "This will be a challenging class."

If you are using a person's exact words and have other questions about punctuation, check the information about punctuation in the grammar section of this book.

WRITING THE NARRATIVE PARAGRAPH IN STEPS

Thought Lines

Narration

Finding something to write about can be the hardest part of writing a narrative paragraph because it is usually difficult to think of anything interesting or significant that you have experienced. By answering the following questions, you can gather topics for your paragraph.

 **Exercise 3** Collaborate

Questionnaire for Gathering Narrative Topics

Answer the questions below as best you can. Then read your answers to a group. The members of the group should then ask you follow-up questions. Write your answers on the lines provided; the answers will add details to your list.

Finally, ask each member of your group to circle one topic or detail on your questionnaire that could be developed into a narrative paragraph. Discuss the suggestions. Repeat this process for each member of the group.

Narrative Questionnaire

1. Did you ever have a close call? When? _____

Write four things you remember about it:

   a. _____

   b. _____

   c. _____

   d. _____

More details, to be added after working with the group:

_____

_____

2. Have you ever tried out for a team? Write four details about what happened before, during, and after:

   a. _____

   b. _____

   c. _____

   d. _____

More details, to be added after working with the group:

_____

_____

3. Have you ever had a day when everything went wrong? Write four details about that day:

a. _____

b. _____

c. _____

d. _____

More details, to be added after working with the group:

_____

_____

4. Have you ever applied for a job? Write four details about what happened when you applied for a job:

a. _____

b. _____

c. _____

d. _____

More details, to be added after working with the group:

_____

_____

Freewriting for a Narrative Topic

One good way to discover something to write about is to freewrite. For example, if your instructor asks you to write a narrative paragraph about something that changed you, you might begin by freewriting.

Freewriting for a Narrative Paragraph

Topic: Something That Changed Me

Something that changed me. I don't know. What changed me? Lots of things happened to me, but I can't find one that changed me. Graduating from high school? Everybody will write about that, how boring, and anyway, what was the big deal? I haven't gotten married. No big change there. Divorce. My parents' divorce really changed the whole family. A big shock to me. I couldn't believe it was happening. I was really scared. Who would I live with? They were real calm when they told me. I've never been so scared. I was too young to understand. Kept thinking they'd just get back together. They didn't. Then I got a stepmother. The year of the divorce a hard time for me. Kids suffer in divorce.

Narrowing and Selecting a Suitable Narrative Topic

After you freewrite, you can assess your writing, looking for words, phrases, or sentences that you could expand into a paragraph. The sample freewriting has several ideas for a narrative:

— high school graduation
— learning about my parents' divorce
— adjusting to a stepmother
— the year of my parents' divorce

Looking for a topic that is not too big, you could use

high school graduation
learning about my parents' divorce

Since the freewriting has already called graduation a boring topic, the divorce seems to be a more attractive subject. In the freewriting, you already have some details related to the divorce; add to these details by brainstorming. Follow-up questions and answers might include these:

How old were you when your parents got divorced?

I was seven years old when my mom and dad divorced.

Are you an only child?

My sister was ten.

Where did you parents tell you? Did they both tell you at the same time?

They told us at breakfast, in the kitchen. Both of my parents were there. I was eating toast. I remember I couldn't eat anything after they started talking. I remember a piece of toast with one bite out of it.

What reasons did they give?

They said they loved us, but they couldn't get along. They said they would always love us kids.

If you didn't understand, what did you *think* was happening?

At first I just thought they were having another fight.

Did you cry? Did they cry?

I didn't cry. My sister cried. Then I knew it was serious. I kept thinking I would have to choose which parent to live with. Then I knew I would really hurt the one I didn't choose. I felt so much guilt about hurting one of them.

What were you thinking?

I felt ripped apart.

Questions can help you form the point of your narrative After brainstorming, you can go back and survey all the details. Do they lead you to a point? Try asking yourself the questions listed earlier in this chapter: What did I learn? What is the meaning of this story? What is my attitude toward what happened? Did it change me? What emotion did it make me feel? Was the experience a good example of something (such as unfairness, or kindness, or generosity)?

For the topic of the divorce, the details mention a number of emotions: confusion, pain, shock, disbelief, fear, guilt. The *point* of the paragraph cannot list all these emotions, but it could be stated

When my parents announced they were divorcing, I felt confused by all my emotions.

Now that you have a point and several details, you can move on to the outlines stage of writing a narrative paragraph.

| **Exercise 4** | **Distinguishing Good Topic Sentences from Bad Ones in Narration** |

Practice

Below are sentences. Some would make good topic sentences for a narrative paragraph. Others would not: they are too big to develop in a single paragraph, or they are so narrow they cannot be developed, or they make no point about an incident or incidents. Put an *X* by the sentences that would not make good topic sentences.

1. __X__ Sarah went to her first job interview last week.

2. __X__ I learned a lot when I was in the Marines.

3. _____ The motorist who stopped to help me on the highway taught me a valuable lesson about trust.

4. __X__ My two-year battle for child custody was a nightmare.

5. __X__ This is the story of the birth of my son.

6. _____ I saw true compassion when I visited the home for babies with AIDS.

7. _____ Our team's victory over the Rangers demonstrated the power of endurance.

8. __X__ I've seen guns ruin the lives of four of my friends in four years.

9. __X__ The robbery took place at the deli near my house.

10. _____ I never knew what it was like to be afraid until our house was burglarized.

| **Exercise 5** | **Developing a Topic Sentence from a List of Details** |

Practice

Following are two lists of details. Each has an incomplete topic sentence. Read the details carefully; then complete each topic sentence.

Answers Will Vary.
Possible answers
shown at right.

1. **topic sentence:** When he borrowed my new leather jacket,

my brother made me feel angry and cheated.

details: My brother always borrows my clothes.
Sometimes I wish he wouldn't.
Last week he took my new leather jacket.
I went to my closet, and the jacket wasn't there.
I wanted to wear it that night.
Later, he came home wearing it.
I could have punched him.
He gave it back.
He swore he didn't know it had a big slash in the back.
He acted innocent.
I told him he'd have to pay to fix the jacket.
He still hasn't paid me.

2. **topic sentence:** An incident at a traffic light showed me

that violence can break out anywhere.

details: I was stopped at a traffic light one afternoon.

Cars were stopped on all sides of me.

Suddenly, a driver from the car beside me leaped out of his car.

He ran to the car in front of me.

He started screaming at the driver of the car.

The driver inside that car wouldn't open his window.

The man who was screaming began to pound on the window.

Then he started kicking the car, hard.

I watched in terror.

I couldn't drive out of this situation.

I was stuck and afraid of being the next victim.

The crazy, shouting driver stopped.

He got back in his car.

When the light changed, he raced into the intersection.

I felt safer, but still shaken.

Outlines

Narration

The topic of how an experience changed you has led you to a point and a list of details. You can now write a rough outline, with the point as the topic sentence. Once you have the rough outline, check it for these qualities:

Relevance: Do all the details connect to the topic sentence?
Order: Are the details in a clear order?
Development: Does the outline need more details? Are the details specific enough?

Your revised outline might look like this:

An Outline for a Narrative Paragraph

topic sentence: When my parents announced that they were divorcing, I felt confused by all my emotions.

details:

background of the narrative
- I was seven when my mom and dad divorced.
- My sister was ten.
- Both of my parents were there.
- They told us at breakfast, in the kitchen.
- I was eating toast.
- I remember I couldn't eat anything after they started talking.
- I remember a piece of toast with one bite out of it.

story of the divorce announcement
- My parents were very calm when they told us.
- They said they loved us but couldn't get along.
- They said they would always love us kids.

my reactions at each stage
{
It was a big shock to me.
I couldn't believe it was happening.
At first I just thought they were having another fight.
I was too young to understand.
I didn't cry.
My sister cried.
Then I knew it was serious.
I kept thinking I would have to choose which parent to live with.
I knew I would really hurt the one I didn't choose.
I felt so much guilt about hurting one of them.
I felt ripped apart.
}

Once you have a revised outline, you will be ready to write a rough draft of your narrative paragraph.

Exercise 6 **Finding Details That Are Out of Order in a Narrative Outline**

Practice The outlines below have details that are out of order. Put the details in correct order by numbering them, using *1* for the detail that should be first, and so on.

1. **topic sentence:** Renewing my driver's license was a frustrating experience.

   details: _4_ I got in the shortest line.

   _1_ The office was packed with people.

   _2_ When I got through the crowd, I went straight to the information desk.

   _3_ The clerk at the information desk just gave me a form and said, "Get in line."

   _6_ After an hour, I got to the head of the line.

   _7_ I gave my form to the man behind the counter.

   _5_ I waited in line for an hour.

   _8_ The man behind the counter said, "You're in the wrong line."

2. **topic sentence:** Yesterday I saw something that showed me the good side of people.

   details: _2_ My traffic lane was at a standstill, so I had time to look around.

   _1_ I was driving down the highway.

   _3_ As I waited for the traffic to move, I saw a ragged man by the side of the road, holding a sign.

   _4_ The sign said, "Will Work for Food."

   _5_ I saw a car pull off the road, right next to the man.

   _6_ The ragged man shrank back as if he were afraid the car would hit him.

_____8_____ The driver motioned to the homeless man through the open window.

_____7_____ The driver of the car rolled down his window on the passenger side.

_____9_____ The homeless man crept over.

____10____ The driver handed him a big bag of food from Burger King.

Exercise 7 **Recognizing Irrelevant Details in a Narrative Outline**

Practice

Below are two outlines. One of them has details that are not relevant to the topic sentence. Cross out the details that do not fit.

1. **topic sentence:** I saw another side of my sister when her husband was in a car accident. (Outline *1* is correct as is.)

details: My sister Julia is usually helpless.
She lets her husband Leo make all the decisions.
She doesn't like to go anywhere without him.
Then one day she got a call from the hospital.
Leo had been in a car accident.
He was in critical condition.
Julia suddenly became very strong.
She calmly told us she was going to the hospital to wait.
She went right up to the desk at the emergency room and asked to see Leo.
When the nurses tried to make her wait, she demanded to see him.
She stayed by Leo's side for twenty-four hours.
The only time she left was to talk to his doctors.
She was very firm and businesslike with the doctors.
She questioned them about the right treatment for Leo.
She got the name of a famous surgeon.
She called the surgeon and got him to come to the hospital.
Today, Leo says she saved his life.

2. **topic sentence:** The most embarrassing thing I've ever experienced happened to me in the supermarket checkout line.

details: ~~I always shop with a list of what I need to buy.~~
The cashier was running the items through the scanner.
~~Our store uses scanners now instead of cash registers.~~
When he was finished, he said, "That'll be $23.50."
I reached into my wallet for the money.
All I found was a ten-dollar bill.
I searched frantically through all the folds of my wallet.
There was nothing but the ten-dollar bill.
I was *sure* I had put a twenty in my wallet when I left for the store.
Then I remembered—I had spent the twenty at the gas station.
I whispered to the cashier, "Oops! I didn't bring enough money."
He just looked at me.
The groceries were already bagged.
I had to take them out of the bags and get rid of enough of them to add up to $13.50.
Meanwhile, the people in line behind me wanted to kill me.
At that moment, I wished they had.

Rough Lines

Narration

After you have a revised outline for your narration paragraph, you can begin working on a rough draft of the paragraph. As you write your first draft, you can combine some of the short sentences of the outline. Once you have a draft, you can check it for places you would like to improve. The checklist below may help you review your draft.

✔ Checklist

A Checklist for Revising the Draft of a Narrative Paragraph

✔ Is my narrative vivid?

✔ Are the details clear and specific?

✔ Does the topic sentence fit all the details?

✔ Are the details written in a clear order?

✔ Do the transitions make the narrative easy to follow?

✔ Have I made my point?

Revising for Sharper Details

A good idea for a narrative can be made better if you revise for sharper details. In the first-draft paragraph below, the underlined words and phrases could be revised to create better details. See how the second draft has more vivid details than the first draft.

First Draft: Details Are Dull

A woman at the movies showed me just how rude and selfish people can be. It all started when I was in line with <u>a lot</u> of other people. We had been waiting <u>a long time</u> to buy our tickets. We were outside, and it <u>wasn't pleasant.</u> We were impatient because time was running out and the movie was about to start. <u>Some people</u> were <u>making remarks,</u> and <u>others were pushing</u>. Then <u>a woman</u> <u>cut to</u> the front of the line. The cashier at the ticket window <u>told</u> the woman there was a line and she would have to go to the end of it. The woman <u>said she didn't want to wait because her son didn't want to miss the beginning of the movie.</u>

Second Draft: Better Details

A woman at the movies showed me just how rude and selfish people can be. It all started when I was in line with <u>forty or fifty other people.</u> We had been waiting to buy our tickets for <u>twenty minutes.</u> We were outside, <u>where the temperature was about 90 degrees, and it looked like rain.</u> We were all getting impatient because time was running out and the movie was about to start. <u>I heard two people mutter about how ridiculous the wait was, and someone else kept saying, "Let's go!" The man directly behind me kept pushing me, and each new</u>

Discussion Question: Have students jot down the underlined words in the first draft and then match them with the additional details in the second draft (in two columns). Ask them what details they find effective. Why? This activity will help them understand the difference between vague and specific.

<u>person at the end of the line pushed the whole line forward against the ticket window.</u> Then a woman <u>with a loud voice and a large purse thrust her purse and her body in front of the ticket window.</u> The cashier <u>politely</u> told the woman there was a line and she had to go the end of it. But the woman answered <u>indignantly.</u> <u>"Oh no," she said. "I'm with my son Mickey. And Mickey really wants to see Tarzan. And he hates to miss the first part of any movie. So I can't wait. I've got to have those tickets now."</u>

Checking the Topic Sentence

Sometimes you think you have a good idea, a good topic sentence, and specific details, but when you write the draft of the paragraph, you realize the topic sentence does not quite fit all the details. When that happens, you can either revise the detail or rewrite the topic sentence.

In the paragraph below, the topic sentence (underlined) does not quite fit all the details, so the topic sentence should be rewritten.

> <u>I did not know what to do when a crime occurred in front of my house.</u> At 9:00 p.m. I was sitting in my living room, watching television, when I heard what sounded like a crash outside. At first I thought it was a garbage can that had fallen over. Then I heard another crash and a shout. I ran to the window and looked out into the dark. I could not see anything because the street light in front of my house was broken. But I heard at least two voices, and they sounded angry and threatening. I heard another voice, and it sounded like someone moaning. I was afraid. I ran to the telephone. I was going to call 911, but then I froze in fear. What if the police came and people got arrested? Would the suspects find out I was the one who called the police? Would they come after *me*? Would I be a witness at a trial? I didn't want to get involved. So I just stood behind the curtain, peeking out and listening. Pretty soon the shouting stopped, but I still heard sounds like hitting. I could not stand it any more. I called the police. When they came, they found a young teenager, badly beaten, in the street. They said my call may have saved his life.

The paragraph above has good details, but the story has more of a point than "I did not know what to do." The person telling the story did, finally, do something. Following is a better topic sentence that covers the whole story:

> **topic sentence rewritten:** I finally found the courage to do the right thing when a crime occurred in front of my house.

Exercise 8

Practice

Adding Better Details to a Draft of a Narrative

The following paragraph has some details that could be more vivid. Rewrite the paragraph in the lines below, replacing the underlined details with more vivid words, phrases, or sentences.

Roberto showed he is a great athlete when he lost the wrestling match. The match was very close, but someone had to lose, and that someone turned out to be Roberto. After the match, the winner, Tom, was <u>getting all the attention.</u> He was acting very <u>full of himself.</u> Roberto was just <u>keeping to himself.</u> Roberto <u>looked hurt.</u> His eyes <u>were sad.</u> Nevertheless, he went to Tom and shook hands. Tom looked <u>mean</u> and <u>did not say much.</u> Roberto, on the other hand, <u>said the right thing.</u> Then Roberto walked away, his head held high.

Answers Will Vary.
Possible answers
shown at right in
italics.

Rewrite: *Roberto showed he is a great athlete when he lost the wrestling match.*

The match had been very close, but someone had to lose, and that someone

turned out to be Roberto. After the match, the winner, Tom, was surrounded by

TV cameras and fans. He was acting very loud and boastful. Roberto was just

standing alone and silent. Roberto looked humiliated by his defeat. His eyes were

bleak. Nevertheless, he went to Tom and shook hands. Tom looked at him coldly

and snarled, "Hey, man." Roberto, on the other hand, said, "Congratulations. Nice

work." Then Roberto walked away, his head held high.

Exercise 9
Practice

Writing a Better Topic Sentence for a Narrative

The paragraphs below need better topic sentences. (In each paragraph, the current topic sentence is underlined.) Read each paragraph carefully; then write a new topic sentence for it in the lines below.

1. <u>My visit to my old school was interesting.</u> I had not been back to Miller Road Elementary since fifth grade, so I expected it to be changed, but I never thought it would be so drastically different. When I entered the schoolyard, I saw that the playground that had once been full of trees and bright green grass was now a muddy, empty lot. All the trees were gone. The school, once a new, golden brick building, was sooty and decrepit. Several of the windows were broken. I walked into the entrance hall and saw graffiti all over the walls. The school was silent. Wandering the halls, I peeked into the classrooms. I saw rickety desks and blackboards so faded you could hardly see the chalked-on words on them. Then I found room 110, my old first-grade classroom. I went in and sat down at one of the desks, and the room that had once seemed so big and so exciting suddenly seemed small and sad.

Answers Will Vary.
Possible answers
shown at right.

New topic sentence: *When I visited my old school, I saw many depressing*

changes.

2. <u>I had dinner with my family last week.</u> My two younger brothers, Simon and David, started fighting over who was going to sit in the seat next to my father. When we all sat down to eat, my sister provoked my mother by complaining, "Chicken again? All we eat is chicken." Of course, my mother jumped right in and said that if my sister wanted to take the responsibility for planning menus and cooking meals, she could go right ahead. Meanwhile, my father was telling David not to kick Simon under the table, and Simon was spitting mashed potatoes at David. I got irritated and said I wished that once, just once, we could eat dinner like a normal family. So then my father and I had an argument about what I meant by a "normal" family. By that time, Simon had spilled his milk on the floor, and my mother had caught my sister feeding chicken to the dog. We all left the dinner table in a bad mood.

New topic sentence: <u>Last week's dinner with my family was a series of</u>

<u>conflicts.</u>

Using Transitions Effectively in Narration

When you tell a story, you have to be sure that your reader can follow you as you move through the steps of your story. One way to make your story easier to follow is to use transitions. Most of the transitions in narration have to do with time. Below is a list of transitions writers often use in writing narration.

Infobox

Transitions for a Narrative Paragraph

after, again, always, at first, at last, at once, at the same time, before, during, finally, first (second, etc.), frequently, immediately, in the meantime, later, later on, meanwhile, next, now, soon, soon after, still, suddenly, then, until, when, while

---

The Draft

Below is a draft of the paragraph on divorce. As you read it, you will notice that some ideas from the outline on pages 75–76 have been combined, the details have been put in order, and transitions have been added. Exact words of dialogue have been used to add vivid details.

A Draft of a Narrative Paragraph (Transitions are underlined.)

<u>When</u> my parents announced that they were divorcing, I felt confused by all my emotions. <u>At the time</u> of their announcement, I was seven, and my sister was ten. Both of my parents were there to tell us. They told us at breakfast, in the kitchen. I was eating toast, but I remember I could not eat anything after they started talking. I remember a piece of toast with one bite taken out of it. My parents were very calm when they told us. "We love both of you kids very much," my dad said, "but your mother and I aren't getting along." They said they would always love us. The announcement was such a shock to me that I could not believe it was happening. <u>At first</u>, I just thought they were having another fight. Because I was too young to understand, I didn't cry. <u>Suddenly</u>, my sister started to cry, <u>and then</u> I knew it was serious. I kept thinking I would have to choose which parent to live with. I knew I would really hurt the one I didn't choose, <u>so</u> I felt so much guilt about hurting one of them. I felt ripped apart.

Exercise 10
Practice

Recognizing Transitions in a Narrative Paragraph

Underline the transitions in the following paragraph.

The salesman who called last night was a master of manipulation. He <u>first</u> asked for me by name. He did not ask for the head of the house, which is always a sure sign that the call is a sales pitch. <u>After</u> confirming I was Mr. Johnson, he told me he was checking on my newspaper delivery. <u>Then</u> he asked whether I had been getting my paper regularly and on time. <u>When</u> I said yes, he quickly added that I could get a better deal by extending my subscription, right away, at a discounted rate for longtime customers. <u>By that time,</u> I was getting tired of what I now knew was a sales call. <u>Just before</u> I tried to end the conversation, the salesman offered me a chance to win a trip to the Bahamas. <u>Suddenly,</u> he had my interest again. <u>While</u> I listened to him explain the contest, I seriously thought about extending my newspaper subscription. <u>Finally,</u> I even thanked him for the information about the vacation contest. Maybe <u>the next time</u> a salesperson calls, I will <u>first</u> ask about any contests and my real chances of winning.

Exercise 11
Practice

Adding the Right Transitions to a Narrative Paragraph

In the following paragraph, circle the correct transition in each of the pairs.

I wasted an entire Saturday trying to get my refrigerator repaired. (First)/Now I noticed that the ice cream in my freezer was melting. Then I checked some other items in the freezer: the frozen hamburger patties were soft, and the ice cubes had turned into water. (Immediately)/Frequently I called a repair service, and a recorded message said the service was closed during/(until) Monday. I tried six more repair shops when/(before) I found one that would send anyone to do repairs on a Saturday. (Meanwhile)/Suddenly, more food was spoiling. The frozen fish was beginning to smell, and the frozen vegetables were bags of mush. I spent six hours swabbing up dripping water and trying to save my remaining food in a foam ice chest. Soon/(Finally) the repair person arrived at 5:00 p.m. By 7:00 p.m., I had a functioning refrigerator, the only good part of a frustrating day.

Final Lines

Narration

As you prepare the final version of your narrative paragraph, make any minor changes in word choice or transitions that can refine your writing. Below is the final copy of the narrative paragraph on divorce. Notice these changes in the final version:

- The draft used both formal and informal words like "dad" and "father." The final version uses only "father."
- A few details have been added.
- A few details have been changed.
- A transition has been added.

A Final Version of a Narrative Paragraph (Changes from the draft are underlined.)

When my parents announced that they were divorcing, I felt confused by all my emotions. At the time of their announcement, I was seven, and my sister was ten. Both of my parents were there to tell us. They told us at breakfast, in the kitchen. I was eating toast, but I remember I could not eat anything after they started talking. <u>In fact,</u> I remember <u>staring</u> at a piece of toast with one bite taken out of it. My parents were very calm when they told us. "We <u>love you both</u> very much," my <u>father</u> said, "but your mother and I aren't getting along." They said they would always love us. The announcement was such a shock to me that I could not believe it was happening. At first, I just thought they were having another fight. Because I was too young to understand, I didn't cry. Suddenly, my sister started to cry, and then I knew it was serious. I kept thinking I would have to choose which parent to live with. I knew I would really hurt the one I didn't choose, so I felt <u>terrible</u> guilt about hurting one of them. I felt ripped apart.

Before you prepare the final version of your narrative paragraph, check your latest draft for errors in spelling or punctuation and for any errors made in typing and copying.

Proofreading to Prepare the Final Version

Following is a narrative paragraph with the kinds of errors that are easy to overlook when you prepare the final version of an assignment. Correct the errors, writing above the lines. There are eleven errors.

Remind students that basic computer spellcheckers cannot always give them the appropriate spelling (e.g., threw vs. through).

     girlfriend
When my girl friend tossed my ring out the window, I knew she was not

            McDonald's
ready to forgive me one more time. It all started on Saturday, at MacDonald's,

          wasn't
when I ran into my girlfriend Lakisha. I could see she was'nt in a good mood. As

            , a girl
soon as we sat down, she asked me about Yvonne. A girl I've been seeing behind

          (no quotation marks needed)
Lakisha's back. Well, of course I lied and said "Yvonne was nothing to me."

      had
However, Lakisha said she seen me and Yvonne at the mall the night before, and

     were romantically
we looked like we was rommanticly involved. I asked, "How could you tell?"

Well, naturally that was the wrong thing to say since I was admitting Yvonne and

I had been together. After I asked that stupid question, Lakisha took my ring off

        through   McDonald's
her finger and tossed that ring right threw the window at McDonalds.

Lines of Detail: A Walk-Through Assignment

Write a paragraph about an incident in your life that embarrassed, or amused, or frightened, or saddened, or angered you. In writing the paragraph, follow these steps:

Step 1: Begin by freewriting. Then read your freewriting, looking for both the details and focus of your paragraph.

Step 2: Brainstorm for more details. Then write all the freewriting and brainstorming as a list.

Step 3: Survey your list. Write a topic sentence that makes a point about the details.

Step 4: Write an outline. As you write the outline, check that your details fit the topic sentence and are in clear order. As you revise your outline, add details where they are needed.

Step 5: Write and revise a draft of your paragraph. Revise until your details are specific and in a clear order and your transitions are smooth. Combine any sentences that are short and choppy. Add a speaker's exact words if they will make the details more specific.

Step 6: In preparing the final copy, check for punctuation, spelling, and word choice.

Writing Your Own Narrative Paragraph

When you write on any of the following topics, be sure to work through the stages of the writing process in preparing your narrative paragraph.

1. Write about some event you saw that you will never forget. Begin by freewriting. Then read your freewriting, looking for both the details and the focus of your paragraph. If your instructor agrees, ask a writing partner or group to (a) listen to you read your freewriting, (b) help you focus it, and (c) help you add details by asking questions.

2. Write a narrative paragraph about how you met your boyfriend or girlfriend or husband or wife. Start by listing as many details as you can, and, if your instructor agrees, ask a writing partner or a group to (a) survey your list of details and (b) ask questions that can lead you to more details.

3. Write about a time when you got what you wanted. Start by listing as many details as you can, and, if your instructor agrees, ask a writing partner or a group to (a) survey your list of details and (b) ask questions that can lead you to more details.

4. Interview an older family member or friend who will tell you an interesting story about his or her past. Ask questions as the person speaks. Take notes. If you have a tape recorder, you can tape the interview, but take notes as well.

   When you have finished the interview, review the information with the person you interviewed. Ask the person whether he or she would like to add anything. If you wish, ask follow-up questions.

   Next, on your own, find a point to the story. Work through the stages of the writing process to turn the interview into a narrative paragraph.

5. Write a narrative paragraph about the lions and the cars in photograph A on page 85. In your paragraph, explain about events before, during, and after this scene. You may want to include some dialogue in your paragraph.

6. Study photograph B on page 85, and write a narrative paragraph in the present tense about the reactions of the children to the puppy. You can also imagine what the dog is thinking.

Photograph A

Photograph B

Name: _____ Section: _____

Peer Review Form for a Narrative Paragraph

After you have written a draft of your narrative paragraph, let a writing partner read it. When your partner has completed the form below, discuss the responses. Repeat the same process for your partner's paragraph.

I think the topic sentence of this paragraph is _____

_____ (Write the sentence.)

I think the topic sentence (a) states the point well or (b) could be revised. (Choose one.)

The part of the narrative I liked best begins with the words _____

_____

The part that could use more or better details begins with the words _____

_____

An effective transition was _____

_____ (Write the words of a good transition.)

I have questions about _____

I would like to see something added about _____

I would like to take out the part about _____

I think the narrative is (a) easy to follow or (b) a little confusing. (Choose one.)

Other comments: _____

_____

_____

_____

_____

_____

_____

_____

_____

_____

Reviewer's Name: _____

WRITING FROM READING: Narration

Rocky Rowf
Edna Buchanan

Edna Buchanan is famous as a former crime reporter for the Miami Herald *and as the author of nonfiction books and novels about murder and mayhem. In this essay, she writes about a lighter subject: how she met and got to know Rocky Rowf, her dog.*

Words You May Need to Know

dehydrated (paragraph 4): lacking water
clambered (7): climbed
nonchalantly (13): coolly, casually
dotes (14): shows great love for
deferential (14): respectful
obsequious (14): slavelike, submissive

abject (14): humiliating
fawning (14): submissive behavior
disdainfully (14): scornfully, arrogantly
pretext (29): excuse
repertoire (34): collection of tricks

1   I was a pushover.

2   I met Rocky on a sizzling Fourth of July weekend. I never intended to take him home with me. He was sprawled under a park bench on South Beach trying to stay cool. I was there to exercise, to bend and stretch in the shade of the sea grape trees, and to look at the blue-green summer sea. Two elderly men, friendly regulars in the park, were sitting on the bench.

3   "Is that your dog?" I asked.

4   They said no. He was so quiet they had barely noticed him. He was panting in the heat, and I grew alarmed as I patted him. His tongue was purple—eggplant purple. I was certain that it meant the animal was dangerously dehydrated. I filled a paper cup several times from a faucet used by bathers to rinse sand off their feet and he drank politely. But his tongue stayed purple.

5   That is its normal color, something I did not learn until later. It may mean he is part chow chow, though he does not look it. He looks like the kind of mutt that everybody has owned at some time in their life: black with buff-colored paws, medium sized, and affable. His ears are floppy, his grin silly. He wore a battered old leather collar with no tag. After he drank, he watched me exercise, then followed as I walked along the seawall. This little romance will end now, I thought, as I returned to my car.

6   When I opened the door, he pushed right past me, scrambling into the front seat. Obviously accustomed to traveling by car, he was determined to have his way. When ordered out, he slunk into the backseat and settled stubbornly on the

floor, on the far side, out of arm's reach. What the heck, I thought, I'll keep him until I find his owner. As we pulled away from the curb, however, I reconsidered: I can't take this dog home, what about all those cats?

7   I stopped at the main lifeguard station, and the dog clambered out after me, trotting right alongside. The guard said he had seen the dog roaming the beach alone for the past three days. He would call Animal Control, he said, and held the dog, so I could get away. "Bye, puppy," I said, and headed for the car. My mistake was in looking back. The dog was whimpering and struggling to follow, his eyes fixed on me, pleading.

8   "You sure this isn't your dog?" Th lifeguard looked suspicious.

9   I insisted I had never seen that animal before in my life. The lifeguard let go, and the dog bounded to me, wagging his tail.

10   On the way home we stopped at the supermarket for dog food. It was too hot to leave him in the car, so I left him just outside the store and told him to wait. He'll probably be gone, finding a new friend, by the time I get the dog food through the checkout counter, I thought. But as I turned into the next aisle, there he was, trotting past the produce, wriggling with delight when he spotted me. Somebody had opened the door.

11   "Is that your dog?" the store manager wanted to know. I denied it.

12   "Are you sure?" he said, staring pointedly at the dog food and the Milk-Bone box in my cart.

13   He ejected the dog, who was waiting when I came out. I looked around the parking lot vaguely, wondering where I had left my car. He knew. All I had to do was follow as he trotted briskly ahead, found the car, and sat down next to it waiting for me. When we got home, he scampered up the front steps without hesitation and waited as I unlocked the door. It was as though he had lived there all his life. Misty and Flossie were snoozing on the highly polished hardwood floor in the living room when this strange dog walked nonchalantly into their home. Both shot straight up in the air, then fled so fast that for several seconds they ran in place on the slick surface. They skidded into my bedroom and dove out the window. Luckily it was open. The screen landed in the middle of the lawn.

14   After the initial shock, they sized him up at once. He must have lived with other animals, because he dotes on them, especially the smaller ones, and is particularly deferential to cats. He was so obsequious in fact, rolling on his back in abject surrender whenever they entered the room, that they quickly became disgusted at his fawning. Within two days the cats were stealing his food and stepping disdainfully over him as he napped.

15   For two weeks we walked up and down that stretch of South Beach seawall looking for his owner. Lots of people had seen the friendly dog, but always alone. A middle-aged Puerto Rican busboy with no teeth grinned and greeted him as Blackie. I thought we had found the owner, but he said he had fed the dog a hamburger and some water at about one o'clock the same morning I found him performing his hungry-and-thirsty act.

16   After two weeks I gave up, took him to the vet [and] got him a license, and he joined the household.

17   He chose his own name. I ran through dozens of appropriate possibilities. None appealed to him. He would not even open his eyes at most. But when I said Rocky, he looked up, wagged his tail, and grinned. So Rocky it is—Rocky Rowf.

18   His past remains a mystery. Housebroken and well-behaved, he did not seem to understand even the most simple commands. Perhaps, I decided, his owner spoke a language other than English. We went to an obedience school, taught by a cop in charge of the Coral Gables police K-9 unit. The only mutt, Rocky was the smartest in the class. However, he did refuse to be a watchdog. In an attempt to agitate him, they thrust him between a Doberman pinscher and a German shepherd. The big dogs were ferocious, leaping in frenzies, snarling, and barking. Rocky Rowf sat between them, grinning and drooling. A very laid-back dog, he hates trouble, rolling his eyes and whining when the cats quarrel among themselves. If the chips were down and we were attacked by strangers, he would do the sensible thing—run for his life.

19   The day after his first visit to the vet, I got home from the *Herald* after nine o'clock at night. When I opened the back door and called, he did not come bounding in from the yard as usual. I stepped out into the dark and could barely make him out, curled up next to the banana tree. I called to him again and again. He did not move. My heart sank. Frightened, I approached the still form, reached out, and touched the fur ruffled by a summer breeze. It felt cool.

20   He was dead.

21   Poor stray dog, doing fine until I took him home; now he was dead. How did it happen? My mind raced. The vet had said he was in good health thirty-six hours earlier. It had to be poison, or maybe he had been shot. It was too dark to see anything in the yard. I dialed the vet's emergency number. He's dead, I cried accusingly, probably an allergic reaction to the shots you gave him.

22   "What makes you think he's dead?" asked Dr. Hal Nass.

23   "I know a dead dog when I see one!" I screamed.

24   He told me to bring the body to his office. He would get dressed and meet me there; together we would find out what happened.

25   The dog weighed forty-seven pounds. The backyard was dark, and I didn't even own a flashlight. The only neighbor I knew was across the street, in a big house on the bay. When I had moved in months earlier he introduced himself and invited me to call on him if I ever needed help.

26   His wife answered. They had gone to bed early. I said I needed her husband's assistance. I whimpered to him that somebody or something had killed my dog and asked if he had seen any strangers prowling the neighborhood. I told him I had to get the dead dog out of my shadowy and unlit backyard and into my car. Poor Rocky Rowf's last ride would be to the vet for an autopsy.

27   A sympathetic man and a good neighbor, Larry Helfer climbed out of bed,

got dressed and brought a flashlight. "I think it was poison," I said, greeting him in tears. "The doctor said he was fine yesterday."

28   I offered him a blanket to wrap the body in. "Where is it?" he said grimly. Out there, I said, pointing. He pushed open the back door, stared into the darkness, then slowly turned and looked at me, his face strange. I stepped past him to look. Sitting at the back door, gazing up at us was Rocky. He was grinning.

29   Never taking his eyes off me, Larry Helfer began to back slowly toward the front door. He obviously believed that, using the pretext of a dead dog, I had lured him out of his bed and across the street, for some unknown purpose.

30   "I could have sworn he was dead. He didn't answer when I called him," I babbled. "He was just lying there."

31   It was his turn to babble. "My, eh, wife, is worried. I better go tell her everything's all right," he said and made a run for it.

32   I caught the vet, just as he was leaving his home. "Never mind," I said.

33   Larry Helfer and his wife avoided me for several years after that. When we did meet by chance, they always asked politely after the health of my dog.

34   Nowadays, I point an index finger at Rocky Rowf and say, "Bang, you're dead!" He falls on the floor, then rolls over on his back. It's one of the best tricks in his repertoire.

35   It wasn't difficult to teach him at all. He already knew how.

WRITING FROM READING: "Rocky Rowf"

When you write on any of the following topics, be sure to work through the stages of the writing process in preparing your narrative paragraph.

1. Write a narrative paragraph about an animal you know that has a distinct personality. To begin, you may want to freewrite about all your memories of this animal.

2. Write a narrative paragraph about how you got a pet. To begin, you may want to list all the steps included in getting your pet.

3. Write the story of an emergency with a pet. If your instructor agrees, you may want to begin by asking a writing partner to interview you, asking questions like these:

    How did you feel during this emergency?
    What was the worst part of the incident?
    Did your feelings change during the emergency?

    Next, you can interview your partner to collect ideas for his or her paragraph.

4. Write the story of how your pet got its name.

5. Write a narrative paragraph that shows that dogs (or cats) are smarter than people.

6. Edna Buchanan writes about a time she helped an animal, a lost dog. Write a narrative paragraph about a time you helped a person who was in trouble.

CHAPTER 4 Process

WHAT IS PROCESS?

A **process** writing explains how to do something or describes how something happens or is done. When you tell the reader how to do something (a **directional process**), you speak directly to the reader, giving clear, specific instructions about performing some activity. Your purpose is to explain an activity so that a reader can do it. For example, you may have to leave instructions telling a new employee how to close the cash register or use the copy machine.

When you describe how something happens or is done (an **informational process**), your purpose is to explain an activity without telling a reader how to do it. For example, you can explain how a boxer trains for a fight or how the special effects for a movie were created. Instead of speaking directly to the reader, an informational process speaks about "I," "he," "she," "we," or "they" or speaks about a person by his or her name. A directional process uses "you," or, in the way it gives directions, the word "you" is understood.

Discussion Questions: (1) Ask students to list the steps involved in preparing for an important event (i.e., a ceremony, a party, a trip, etc.) This will generate several ideas. **(2)** Have they observed how someone else completes the steps of a process? (e.g., a friend who trains for sports competition, a family member who prepares for a job interview.)

A Process Involves Steps in Time Order

Whether a process is directional or informational, it describes something that is done in steps, and these steps are in a specific order: a **time order.** The process can involve steps that are followed in minutes, hours, days, weeks, months, or even years. For example, the steps in changing a tire may take minutes, whereas the steps taken to lose ten pounds may take months.

You should keep in mind that a process involves steps that *must follow a certain order,* not just a range of activities that can be placed in any order.

This sentence *signals a process:*

Learning to use a word processor is easy if you follow a few simple directions. (Using a word processor involves following steps in order; for example, you cannot set the margins before you turn the machine on.)

This sentence *does not signal a process:*

There are several ways to get a person to like you. (Each way is separate; there is no time sequence here.)

Telling a person, in a conversation, how to do something or how something is done gives you the opportunity to add important points you may have overlooked or to add details you may have skipped at first. Your listener can ask questions if he or she does not understand you. Writing a process, however, is more difficult. Your reader is not there to stop you, to ask you to explain further, or to question you. In writing a process, you must be organized and clear.

Hints for Writing a Process Paragraph

1. In choosing a topic, find an activity you know well. If you write about something familiar to you, you will have a clearer paragraph.

2. Choose a topic that includes steps that must be done in a specific time sequence.

not this: I find lots of things to do on a rainy day.
but this: I have a plan for cleaning out my closet.

3. Choose a topic that is fairly small. A complicated process cannot be covered well in one paragraph. If your topic is too big, the paragraph can become vague, incomplete, or boring.

too big: There are many stages in the process of a bill before Congress becoming a new law.
smaller and manageable: Willpower and support were the most important elements in my struggle to quit smoking.

4. Write a topic sentence that makes a point. Your topic sentence should do more than announce. Like the topic sentence for any paragraph, it should have a point. As you plan the steps of your process and gather details, ask yourself some questions: What point do I want to make about this process? Is the process hard? Is it easy? Does the process require certain tools? Does the process require certain skills, like organization, patience, endurance?

an announcement: This paragraph is about how to change the oil in your car.
a topic sentence: You do not have to be a mechanic to change the oil in your car, but you do have to take a few simple precautions.

5. Include all the steps. If you are explaining a process, you are writing for someone who does not know the process as well as you do. Keep in mind that what seems clear or simple to you may not be clear or simple to the reader, and be sure to tell what is needed before the process starts. For instance, what ingredients are needed to cook the dish? Or what tools are needed to assemble the toy?

6. Put the steps in the right order. Nothing is more irritating to a reader than trying to follow directions that skip back and forth. Careful planning, drafting, and revision can help you get the time sequence right.

7. Be specific in the details and steps. To be sure you have sufficient details and clear steps, keep your reader in mind. Put yourself in the reader's place. Could you follow your own directions or understand your steps?

If you remember that a process explains, you will focus on being clear. Now that you know the purpose and strategies of writing a process, you can begin the thought lines stage of writing one.

| **Exercise 1** | **Recognizing Good Topic Sentences for Process Paragraphs** |

Practice

If a sentence is a good topic sentence for a process paragraph, write *OK* on the line provided. If a sentence has a problem, label that sentence with one of these letters:

A This is an **announcement**; it makes no point.
B This sentence covers a topic that is too **big** for one paragraph.
S This sentence describes a topic that does not require **steps.**

1. _OK_ I've developed a plan for doing my laundry that saves time and keeps my clothes in good shape.
2. _A_ How I learned to wash and wax my car is the subject of this paragraph.
3. _S_ There are several reasons for buying a home computer.
4. _B_ The steps involved in brain surgery are complicated.
5. _OK_ Trying out for the cheerleading squad meant I had to overcome a series of obstacles.
6. _A_ This paper shows the method of refinishing an antique chair.
7. _B_ Civil rights in America evolved in several stages.
8. _S_ There are many things to remember when you enter college.
9. _OK_ If you learn just a few professional secrets, you can give yourself a good manicure at home.
10. _OK_ Fred learned the right way to apply for a car loan.

| **Exercise 2** | **Including Necessary Materials in a Process** |

Collaborate

Below are three possible topics for a process paragraph. For each topic, work with a partner or a group and list the items (materials, ingredients, tools, utensils, supplies) the reader would have to gather before he or she began the process. When you have finished the exercise, check your lists with another group to see if you have missed any items.

1. topic: washing a car

Answers Will Vary.
Possible answers shown at right.

needed items: _a bucket, a hose attached to a faucet, a cloth or a sponge,_

towels, soap, a brush

2. topic: cooking a hamburger on a grill

needed items: _hamburger meat, a grill, charcoal, matches, charcoal starter,_

a hamburger flipper, salt and pepper

3. topic: preparing a package for mailing (the package contains a breakable item) needed items: <u>a box, bubble wrap or shredded newspaper, tissue paper, mailing tape, address label</u>

WRITING THE PROCESS PARAGRAPH IN STEPS
Thought Lines

Process

The easiest way to start writing a process paragraph is to pick a small topic, one that you can cover well in one paragraph. Then you can gather ideas by freewriting or listing or both.

If you decided to write about how you entertained your nephew for an afternoon, you might begin by freewriting.

Then you might check your freewriting, looking for details that have to do with the process of that afternoon. You can underline those details, as in the example that follows.

Freewriting for a Process Paragraph

Topic: Entertaining a nephew

I had to find something to do with Albert for a whole afternoon. I don't know Albert that well. I see him only two or three times a year when my sister visits my mom. I like Albert. What do I know about <u>five-year-olds?</u> Sports? But I can't play sports well. I can't get him on a team of kids his own age. So <u>I decided, the zoo.</u> Everybody likes zoos. I like the zoo. Probably why I decided on the zoo. Albert was awfully quiet in the car <u>on the way there. A little scared of me.</u> Then, <u>at the zoo,</u> wouldn't go near the animals <u>at first.</u> And <u>he raced</u> from exhibit to exhibit. I thought he'd want to spend some time looking at each animal. But he was always <u>racing ahead</u> to see what was next. He warmed up to me a lot <u>later.</u> Even <u>at the zoo, when he got excited,</u> he really talked up a storm. I had to drag him out of the souvenir shop at the zoo exit, or I'd have been broke! One souvenir is enough! What a racket. But I let him go at his own pace <u>through the zoo.</u> Let him eat what he wanted later, too.

Next, you can put what you've underlined into a list, in correct time sequence:

before the trip

> decided on the zoo
> Albert was quiet on the way there
> a little scared of me

at the zoo

> at first, wouldn't go near the animals
> raced from exhibit to exhibit to see what was ahead
> then, after he got excited, talked up a storm

after the zoo

> he warmed up to me

Check the list. Are some details missing? Yes. A reader might ask, "Did you tell Albert how to behave before he got to the zoo? How did you keep control of a five-year-old? What else happened at the zoo? What animals did you see? In what order? How did the afternoon end? Was it a success?" Answers to questions like these can give you the details needed to write a clear and interesting informational process paragraphs.

Writing a Topic Sentence for a Process Paragraph

Freewriting and a list can now help you focus your paragraph by identifying the point of your process. You already know what the subject of your paragraph is: entertaining a five-year-old for a whole afternoon. But what's the point? Is it easy to entertain a five-year-old? Is it difficult? What does it take to have a successful afternoon with a five-year-old?

Maybe a topic sentence could be

I have learned that the way to have an enjoyable afternoon with a five-year-old is to plan for both our interests but to let him set the pace and make some choices.

Once you have a topic sentence, you can think about adding details that explain your topic sentence, and you can begin the outlines stage of writing.

Exercise 3
Practice

Finding the Steps of a Process in Freewriting

Read the following freewriting. Then reread it, looking for all the words, phrases, or sentences that have to do with steps. Underline all those items. Then once you have underlined the freewriting, put what you have underlined into a list in a correct time sequence.

How I Found My First Apartment: Freewriting

Answers Will Vary. Possible answers shown at right.

My first apartment. Could I afford the rent was my first question. So I <u>designed a budget and came up with a figure for the highest rent</u> I could pay. Rents are high in this area. I didn't know what places went for until I looked around. <u>Looked in the classified ads in the paper to see what typical one-bedroom apartments cost</u> in different neighborhoods. Had <u>decided I needed a one-bedroom,</u> not an efficiency. <u>Found the names of two or three places that matched my budget.</u> Didn't call right away. Why call if the place is a dump? So <u>took a ride in my car first. Checked out those two or three places.</u> Then <u>called the phone numbers of the two nicest-looking places. Set up a time to visit. Asked to see a copy of the leases at the visits. Brought my older brother with me</u> on the visits. He's experienced. Took leases home. <u>Drove back to apartments at several times of day</u> to see how noisy the neighborhoods were, how safe, <u>to check out things I forgot to look for.</u> Read leases carefully. <u>Considered which apartment was cheaper.</u> Which was <u>newer</u> and <u>cleaner</u> and nicer. The cheaper one was not so new but was <u>larger. Called apartment manager and set up a time to sign lease.</u>

Your List of Steps in Time Sequence

1. Designed a budget and came up with a figure for rent

2. Decided I needed a one-bedroom

3. Looked in the classified ads to see costs

4. Found the names of two or three places within my budget

5. Took a ride, checked out two or three places

6. Called the two nicest-looking places and set up a visit

7. Brought my brother to the visits, got lease copies

8. Drove back to neighborhoods several times

9. Read the leases carefully (or reverse 9 and 10.)

10. Considered which apartment was cheaper, newer, etc.

11. Picked the cheaper, larger one

12. Set up a time to sign the lease

Outlines

Process

Using the freewriting and topic sentence on entertaining a nephew, you could make an outline. Then you could revise it, checking the topic sentence and improving the list of details, improving them where you think they could be better. A revised outline of an afternoon with Albert is shown below.

An Outline for a Process Paragraph

topic sentence: I've learned that the way to have an enjoyable afternoon with a five-year-old is to plan for both our interests but to let him set the pace and make some choices.

details:

before the zoo
Albert, my five-year-old nephew, was visiting.
I had to find a way to entertain him one Saturday afternoon.
Before Saturday, I decided on the zoo.
When I picked Albert up, he was quiet in the car.
He was a little scared of me.
I left him alone.
I just told him what to expect at the zoo.
I told him to stay close to me.

at the zoo
At the zoo, the first animals we saw were gorillas.
Albert was scared.
He would not go near the gorilla compound.
I didn't push him.
Then he raced from exhibit to exhibit to see what was ahead.
The second group of animals was lions.
Albert loved them.
But he raced on to the next animals.
I let him set his own pace.
The last animals were in the snake house.
Albert started talking up a storm.

| after the zoo | At the end of the afternoon, he wanted to do it again— the next day! |

The following checklist may help you revise an outline for your own process paragraph.

✔ Checklist

A Checklist for Revising a Process Outline

✔ Is my topic sentence focused on some point about the process?

✔ Does it cover the whole process?

✔ Do I have all the steps?

✔ Are they in the right order?

✔ Have I explained clearly?

✔ Do I need better details?

Exercise 4
Practice

Revising the Topic Sentence in a Process Outline

The topic sentence below does not cover all the steps of the process. Read the outline details several times; then write a topic sentence that covers all the steps of the process and has a point.

topic sentence: If you want to save money at the supermarket, write a list at home.

details: First, leave a pencil and a piece of paper near your refrigerator. Each time you use the last of some item, like milk, write that item on the paper. Before you go to the store, read what's written on the paper and add to the list. Then rewrite the list, organizing it according to the layout of your store. Put all the dairy products together on the list, for instance. Put all the fresh fruits and vegetables together. At the store, begin with the first items on your list. Move purposefully through the aisles. Keep your eyes on your list so you don't see all kinds of goodies you don't need. Pass by the gourmet items. Keep going through each aisle, buying only what is on your list. At the end of the last aisle, check what's in your cart against your list. Get any item you forgot. When you stand in the checkout line, avoid looking at the over-priced and tempting snacks that fill the area.

Answers Will Vary. Possible answer shown at right.

Revised topic sentence: <u>If you want to save money at the supermarket,</u>

<u>write a list at home and stick to it at the store.</u>

Exercise 5

Practice

Revising the Order of Steps in a Process Outline

The steps in each of these outlines are out of order. Put numbers in the spaces provided, indicating what step should be first, second, and so on.

1. **topic sentence:** Danielle knows all the steps in spreading a rumor.

   details: ___3___ Danielle thinks it is fine to tell *one* person, her best friend Vicky.

   ___4___ Vicky believes it is all right to tell *one* person, her dear friend Jack.

   ___1___ Danielle always swears she can keep a secret.

   ___2___ Somebody tells Danielle some great gossip, making her promise to keep it a secret.

   ___5___ Jack believes that his whole group of friends, except him, has already heard the gossip, so he thinks he can tell anybody.

   ___6___ Jack tells several people.

   ___7___ The whole town is talking about the big secret.

2. **topic sentence:** My neighbor has a Saturday routine that never changes.

   details: ___1___ Every Saturday at 8 a.m. he starts cutting his lawn.

   ___2___ The roar of his lawn mower wakes me up.

   ___6___ He barbecues steaks on Saturday nights.

   ___4___ In the afternoon, he sits on a lawn chair in his yard.

   ___5___ After he's been in the lawn chair for a while, he falls asleep.

   ___7___ He reads the paper as he grills the steaks.

   ___3___ I see him in the deli at noon, buying pumpernickel bagels for lunch.

3. **topic sentence:** Getting my cat to take a pill is a frustrating chore.

   details: ___4___ I have to hide the pill inside a lump of mashed tuna.

   ___1___ My cat Princess hates pills.

   ___2___ She runs when she hears the rattle of the pill container.

   ___3___ I have to take out one pill, very quietly.

   ___5___ I coax Princess by allowing her to sniff at the tuna.

   ___6___ I lure her farther, until I have her out in the open.

   ___7___ I pop the tuna into her mouth.

   ___8___ Princess swallows the tuna and the hidden pill.

Exercise 6

Practice

Listing All the Steps in an Outline

Following are three topic sentences for process paragraphs. Write all the steps needed to complete an outline for each sentence. After you have listed all the steps, number them in the correct time order.

1. topic sentence: There are a few simple steps for giving a dog a bath.

Steps: 1. Get soap, a sponge or cloth, and towels.

2. Fill a bathtub or large metal tub with warm water.

3. Carry or coax the dog to the tub.

4. Gently put the dog in the water.

5. Hold the dog firmly while you wet the dog.

6. Lather the dog with soap, avoiding the eyes.

7. Wash the dog thoroughly.

8. Rinse the dog.

9. Lift the dog from the tub and towel the dog dry.

2. topic sentence: Anyone can make a delicious salad.

Steps: 1. Gather lettuce, tomatoes, cucumbers, a large bowl, a paring knife,

a slicing knife, a salad fork and spoon, and some bottled salad dressing.

2. Rinse and dry, and shred the lettuce.

3. Rinse and slice the tomatoes.

4. Peel and slice the cucumbers

5. Place the lettuce, tomatoes, and cucumbers in the bowl.

6. Mix in the dressing, using the salad fork and spoon.

3. topic sentence: You can devise a plan for getting to work on time.

Steps: 1. The night before, lay out your clothes.

2. Lay out your coffee mug, cereal bowl, etc.

3. Lay out any money, notebooks, or bags you will need.

4. Set your alarm for fifteen minutes earlier than usual.

5. The next morning, get up as soon as the alarm goes off.

6. Shower and dress quickly.

7. Eat breakfast without watching TV or reading the paper.

8. Grab your money, notebooks, etc. and go out the door.

Rough Lines

Process

You can take the outline and write it in paragraph form, and you'll have a first draft of the process paragraph. As you write the first draft, you can combine some of the short sentences from the outline. Then you can review your draft and revise it for organization, details, clarity, grammar, style, and word choice.

Using the Same Grammatical Person

Remember that the *directional* process speaks directly to the reader, calling him or her "you." Sentences in a directional process use the word "you," or they imply "you."

> **directional:** *You* need a good paintbrush to get started.
> Begin by making a list. ("You" is implied.)

Remember that the *informational* process involves somebody doing the process. Sentences in an informational process use words like "I," "we," "he," "she," or "they" or a person's name.

> **informational:** *Chip* needed a good paintbrush to get started.
> First, *I* can make a list.

One problem in writing a process is shifting from describing how somebody did something to telling the reader how to do an activity. When that shift happens, the two kinds of processes get mixed. That shift is called a **shift in person.** In grammar, the words "I" and "we" are considered to be in the first person; "you" is in the second person; and "he," "she," "it," and "they" are in the third person.

If these words refer to one, they are *singular;* if they refer to more than one, they are *plural.* The following list may help.

Discussion Question: Ask students to give reasons why shifting to "you" is so common a practice. See if anyone starts shifting to "you" in his or her answer. A humorous discussion of this shift in persons can help students understand how common and easy it is to shift to an illogical use of "you" in a paper.

Infobox

A List of Persons

1st person singular: I
2nd person singular: you
3rd person singular: he, she, it, or a person's name

1st person plural: we
2nd person plural: you
3rd person plural: they, or the names of more than one person

---

In writing your process paragraph, decide whether your process will be directional or informational, and stay with one kind.

Below are two examples of a shift in person. Look at them carefully and study how the shift is corrected.

> **shift in person:** After *I* preheat the oven to 350 degrees, *I* mix the egg whites and sugar with an electric mixer set at high speed. *Mix* until stiff peaks form. Then *I* put the mixture in small mounds on an ungreased cookie sheet. ("Mix until stiff peaks form" is a shift to the "you" person.)

shift corrected: After *I* preheat the oven to 350 degrees, *I* mix the egg whites and sugar with an electric mixer set at high speed. *I* mix until stiff peaks form. Then *I* put the mixture in small mounds on an ungreased cookie sheet.

shift in person: A *salesperson* has to be very tactful when customers try on clothes. *The clerk* can't hint that a suit may be a size too small. *You* can insult a customer with a hint like that. (The sentences shifted from "salesperson" and "clerk" to "you.")

Note: For more on shifts in persons, see Chapter 23.

shift corrected: A *salesperson* has to be very careful when customers try on clothes. *The clerk* can't hint that a suit may be a size too small. *He or she* can insult a customer with a hint like that.

Using Transitions Effectively

As you revise your draft, you can add transitions. Transitions are particularly important in a process paragraph because you are trying to show the steps in a *specific sequence*, and you are trying to show the *connections* between steps. Good transitions will also keep your paragraph from sounding like a choppy, boring list.

Following is a list of some of the transitions you can use in writing a process paragraph. Be sure that you use transitional words and phrases only when it is logical to do so, and try not to overuse the same transitions in a paragraph.

Infobox

Transitions for a Process Paragraph

after, afterward, as, as he is . . ., as soon as . . ., as you are . . ., at last, at the same time, before, begin by, during, eventually, finally, first (second, third, etc.), first of all, gradually, in the beginning, immediately, initially, last, later, meanwhile, next, now, quickly, sometimes, soon, suddenly, the first step (the second step, etc.), then, to begin, to start, until, when, whenever, while, while I am . . .

When you write a process paragraph, you must pay particular attention to clarity. As you revise, keep thinking about your audience to be sure your steps are easy to follow. The following checklist can help you revise your draft.

✔ Checklist

A Checklist for Revising a Process Paragraph

✔ Does the topic sentence cover the whole paragraph?

✔ Does the topic sentence make a point about the process?

✔ Is any important step left out?

✔ Should any step be explained further?

✔ Are the steps in the right order?

✔ Should any sentences be combined?

✔ Have I used the same person throughout the paragraph to describe the process?

✔ Have I used transitions effectively?

Exercise 7
Practice

Correcting Shifts in Person in a Process Paragraph

Below is a paragraph that shifts from being an informational to a directional process in several places. Those places are underlined. Rewrite the underlined parts, directly above the underlining, so that the whole paragraph is an informational process.

Jesse has perfected a whole routine for getting out of chores. He starts as soon as his mother says, "Jesse?" with that certain tone in her voice. Before she can go any further, he says, "What?" in a hurt, tired, exasperated way. He also looks very tired as he says this. <u>You have to look tired,</u> [He has to look tired] or the trick won't work. When she asks him to do something like take out the garbage, he goes into phase two of the routine. He tells her he always takes out the garbage and now it's Lynette's turn. Of course, Lynette instantly chimes in and says she's sick of doing all the chores for a lazy bum like Jesse. The fight between Lynette and Jesse usually distracts their mother. Sometimes she forgets what she originally <u>wanted you to do.</u> [wanted Jesse to do] If she can remember, Jesse has one last tactic. <u>You can always agree to do the chore</u> [He can always agree to do the chore] and then procrastinate until somebody else does it. <u>Live by the rule</u> [He lives by the rule] "Always put off till tomorrow what you could do today."

Exercise 8
Practice

Revising Transitions in a Process Paragraph

The transitions in the following directional paragraph could be better. Rewrite the underlined transitions, directly above each one, so that the transitions are smoother.

Answers Will Vary.
Possible answers
shown at right.

You can set an attractive dinner table by following just a few steps with a little creativity. <u>First,</u> clear the table and make sure the surface is clean. [Then] <u>Second,</u> put some placemats on the table. You can use your imagination with placemats. You can use different colored ones, or different shaped ones, from different sets; you can also use brightly colored dish towels. [After you have laid the place mats,] <u>Third,</u> set out your prettiest dinner plates on the mats. [Next] <u>Fourth,</u> put a knife and fork on either side of each plate. [Now] <u>Fifth,</u> find pretty, bright-colored napkins and find an interesting way to place them. You can twist each napkin into a roll or fold it so it stands in the middle of the plate. [When you have placed the napkins,] <u>Sixth,</u> choose a matching glass for each place setting. [The last step is to] <u>Seventh,</u> find a centerpiece for the table. The centerpiece can be anything from a bowl of fruit or fresh vegetables to a single flower in a vase. [As soon as the centerpiece is in place,] <u>Eighth,</u> sit back and enjoy your creativity.

The Draft

Below is a draft of the process paragraph on entertaining a five-year-old. This draft has more details than the outline on page 96, and one detail from the outline, about Albert racing around, has been moved. Some short sentences have been combined, and transitions have been added.

A Draft of a Process Paragraph

I have learned that the way to have an enjoyable afternoon with a five-year-old is to plan for both our interests but to let him set the pace and make some choices. I learned all this when Albert, my five-year-old nephew, was visiting and I had to find a way to entertain him one Saturday afternoon. Before Saturday rolled around, I wanted to pick something we both liked, so I decided on the zoo. When I picked Albert up on Saturday, he was quiet, as if he was scared of me. But I didn't pump him with questions. I left him alone, just telling him what to expect at the zoo and warning him to stay close to me once we got there. At the zoo, Albert was scared by the gorillas, the first animals we saw. He would not go near the gorilla compound. I didn't push him. The second group of animals was the lions, and Albert loved them. Still, he raced on to the next group of animals. Throughout our visit, Albert raced from exhibit to exhibit to see what was ahead. I thought he would spend some time looking at each exhibit, but I let him set his own pace and just stayed close to him. The last animals were in the snake house, and Albert was so fascinated he started talking up a storm. By the end of our afternoon, Albert had warmed up to me so much that he said he wanted to do it all over again, the next day!

Final Lines

Process

Before you prepare the final copy of your process paragraph, you can check your latest draft for any problems in grammar, word choice, and style.

Following is the final version of the process paragraph on entertaining a five-year-old. You'll notice that it contains several changes from the previous draft.

- The topic sentence has been rewritten; the meaning has not been changed, but it is more clearly stated.
- The point of the topic sentence is reinforced in a new sentence, placed just before the last sentence.
- A transition, "again," has been added to stress the point of the topic sentence.
- The word "raced" has been changed to "ran" to avoid repetition.

A Final Version of a Process Paragraph (Changes from the draft are underlined.)

I have learned that the way to have an enjoyable afternoon with a five-year-old is to plan something that interests us both but to let him set the pace and make some choices. I learned all this when Albert, my five-year-old nephew, was visiting and I

```
had to find a way to entertain him one Saturday afternoon.
Before Saturday rolled around, I wanted to pick something we
both liked to do, so I decided on the zoo. When I picked Albert
up on Saturday, he was quiet, as if he was scared of me. But I
didn't pump him with questions. I left him alone, just telling
him what to expect at the zoo and warning him to stay close to me
once we got there. At the zoo, Albert was scared by the gorillas,
the first animals we saw. He would not go near the gorilla com-
pound. Again, I didn't push him. The second group of animals was
lions, and Albert loved them. Still, he ran on to the next group
of animals. Throughout our visit, Albert raced from exhibit to
exhibit to see what was ahead. I thought he would spend some time
looking at each exhibit, but I let him set his own pace and just
stayed close to him. The last animals were in the snake house,
and Albert was so fascinated he started talking up a storm. By
letting Albert move and talk according to his own timetable, I
had given him a good time. By the end of our afternoon, Albert
had warmed up to me so much that he said he wanted to do it all
again, the next day!
```

Before you prepare the final copy of your process paragraph, check your latest draft for errors in spelling and punctuation and for any errors made in typing or copying.

Exercise 9 **Proofreading to Prepare the Final Paragraph**

Practice

Following is a process paragraph with the kinds of errors that are easy to overlook when you prepare the final version of an assignment. Correct the errors, writing above the lines. There are eight errors.

I have a foolproof system for making my bed neatly. First, I dump all the pillow's [pillows] on the flore [floor]. I then pull the bedspread back to the bottom of the bed. Once you've [I've] pulled the bedspread back, I can pull back the blanket and the top sheet. Next, i [I] smooth the bottom sheet and pull it tight, tucking the extra material under the corners of the mattress. When the bottom sheet is tucked in tightly, I pull up the top sheet and the blanket, smoothing them as I go and making sure they are tucked under the bottom and lower corners of the mattress. At the top end of the bed, fold [I (fold)] the edge of the top sheet over the blanket, and I smooth the folded sheet and blanket across the bed. Finly, [Finally,] I arrange the bedspread over the bed, making sure the bedspread dosen't [doesn't] drag on one side. In a few move [moves], I have a well-made bed.

Lines of Detail: A Walk-Through Assignment

Your assignment is to write a paragraph on how you planned a special day. Follow these steps:

Step 1: Focus on one special day. If you cannot think of a day you planned, ask yourself such questions as these: "Have I ever planned a birthday party? A baby or wedding shower? A surprise party? A picnic? A reunion? A celebration of a religious holiday?"

Step 2: Once you have picked the day, freewrite. Write anything you can remember about the day and how you planned it.

Step 3: When you have completed the freewriting, read it. Underline all the details that refer to steps in planning that event. List the underlined details in time order.

Step 4: Add to the list by brainstorming. Ask yourself questions that can lead to more details. For example, if an item on your list is "I decorated the room," ask questions like "What did I use for decorations? What colors did I use?"

Step 5: Survey your expanded list. Write a topic sentence that makes some point about your planning for this special day. To reach a point, think of more questions like these: "Was the planning successful?" "What did I learn from the planning?"

Step 6: Use the topic sentence to prepare an outline. Be sure that the steps in the outline are in the correct time order.

Step 7: Write a draft of the paragraph. In this first draft, add more detail and combine short sentences.

Step 8: Revise your draft. Be careful to use smooth transitions, and check that you have included all the necessary steps.

Step 9: Prepare and proofread the final copy of your paragraph.

Writing Your Own Process Paragraph

When you write on one of these topics, be sure to work through the stages of the writing process in preparing your process paragraph.

1. Write a *directional* or *informational* process about one of these topics:

Note: Remind students that a directional process sounds as though one is giving orders; an informational process requires that one observe or analyze steps objectively.

packing a suitcase	fixing a clogged drain
preparing for a garage sale	changing the oil in a car
painting a room	washing and waxing a car
taking a test	breaking a specific habit
losing weight	gaining weight
training a roommate	giving a pet a bath
finding the right mate	falling out of love
doing holiday shopping early	getting up in the morning

breaking up with a boyfriend or girlfriend
getting good tips while working as a waiter or waitress
getting ready to go out for a special occasion
sizing up a new acquaintance

2. Write about the wrong way to do something or the wrong way you (or someone else) did it. You can use any of the topics in the list above, or you can choose your own topic.

3. Imagine that a relative who has never been to your state is coming to visit. This relative will arrive at the nearest airport, rent a car, and drive to your house. Write a paragraph giving your relative clear directions for getting from the airport to your house. Be sure to have an appropriate topic sentence.

4. Interview one of the counselors at your college. Ask the counselor to tell you the steps for applying for financial aid. Take notes or tape the interview. Get copies of any forms that are included in the application process, and ask questions about these forms. After the interview, write a paragraph explaining the process of applying for financial aid. Your explanation is directed at a high school senior who has never applied for aid.

5. Interview someone whose cooking you admire. Ask that person to tell you the steps involved in making a certain dish. Take notes or tape the interview. After the interview, write a paragraph, *not* a recipe, explaining how to prepare the dish. Your paragraph will explain the process to someone who is a beginner at cooking.

Name: _____ **Section:** _____

Peer Review Form for a Process Paragraph

After you have written a draft version of your process paragraph, let a writing partner read it. When your partner has completed the form below, discuss your draft. Then repeat the same process for your partner's paragraph.

The steps that are most clearly described are _____

_____

_____

I would like more explanation about this step: _____

_____

Some details could be added to the part that begins with the words _____

_____

A transition could be added to the part that begins with the words _____

_____

I have questions about _____

_____

The best thing about this paragraph is _____

Other comments: _____

_____

_____

_____

_____

_____

_____

_____

_____

_____

Reviewer's Name: _____

WRITING FROM READING: Process

How to Land the Job You Want
Davidyne Mayleas

Davidyne Mayleas studied banking and finance before becoming a writer. She has published books and articles about the job market. In this essay, she gives a step-by-step explanation of how you can become your own job counselor and teach yourself to get the job you want. Her explanation is made clear and interesting through her use of examples.

Words You May Need to Know

résumé (paragraph 1): a brief account of personal, educational, and professional qualifications and experience, used in applying for a job

asset (2): useful thing or quality

classified ads (4): small advertisements in the newspaper, often called the want ads

actuarial department (9): a department that calculates insurance rates, risks, and so on according to probabilities based on statistical records

prospective (15): potential

route (15): send, direct

geriatric (16): having to do with elderly people

perseverance (18): persistence

traits (18): personal characteristics

leads (21): guides to other jobs, suggestions to follow

1   Louis Albert, 39, lost his job as an electrical engineer when his firm made extensive cutbacks. He spent two months answering classified ads and visiting employment agencies—with zero results. Albert might still be hunting if a friend, a specialist in the employment field, had not shown him how to be his own job counselor. Albert learned how to research unlisted openings, write a forceful résumé, perform smoothly in an interview, even transform a turndown into a job.

2   Although there seemed to be a shortage of engineering jobs, Albert realized that he still persuaded potential employers to see him. This taught him something—that his naturally outgoing personality might be as great an asset as his engineering degree. When the production head of a small electronics company told him that they did not have an immediate opening, Albert told his interviewer, "You people make a fine product. I think you could use additional sales representation—someone like me who understands and talks electrical engineer's language, and who enjoys selling." The interviewer decided to send Albert to a senior vice president. Albert got a job in sales.

3   You too can be your own counselor if you put the same vigorous effort into *getting* a job as you would into *keeping one*. Follow these three basic rules, developed by placement experts:

4   1. *Find the hidden job market.* Classified ads and agency listings reveal only a small percentage of available jobs. Some of the openings that occur through promotions, retirements and reorganization never reach the personnel department. There are three ways to get in touch with this hidden market:

5   *Write a strong résumé with a well-directed cover letter and mail it to the appropriate department manager in the company where you'd like to work.* Don't worry whether there's a current opening. Many managers fill vacancies by reviewing the résumés already in their files. Dennis Mollura, press-relations manager in the public-relations department of American Telephone and Telegraph, says, "In my own case, the company called me months after I sent in my résumé."

6   *Get in touch with people who work in or know the companies that interest you.* Jobs are so often filled through personal referral that Charles R. Lops, executive employment manager of the J. C. Penney Co., says, "Probably our best source for outside people comes from recommendations made by Penney associates themselves."

7   *"Drop in" on the company.* Lillian Reveille, employment manager of Equitable Life Assurance Society of the United States, reports: "A large percentage of the applicants we see are 'walk-ins'—and we do employ many of these people."

8   2. *Locate hidden openings.* This step requires energy and determination to make telephone calls, see people, do research, and keep moving despite turndowns.

9   *Contact anyone who may know of openings*, including relatives, friends, teachers, bank officers, insurance agents—anyone you know in your own or an adjacent field. When the teachers' union and employment agencies produced no teaching openings, Eric Olson, an unemployed high-school math instructor, reviewed his talent and decided that where an analytical math mind was useful, there he'd find a job. He called his insurance agent, who set up an interview with the actuarial department of one of the companies he represented. They hired Olson.

10   It's a good idea to contact not only professional or trade associations in your field, but also your local chamber of commerce and people involved in community activities. After Laura Bailey lost her job as retirement counselor in a bank's personnel department, she found a position in customer relations in another bank. Her contact: a member of the senior-citizens club that Mrs. Bailey ran on a volunteer basis.

11   *Use local or business-school libraries.* Almost every field has its own directory of companies, which provides names, addresses, products and/or services, and lists officers and other executives. Write to the company president or to the executive to whom you'd report. The vice president of personnel at Warner-Lambert Co. says, "When a résumé of someone we could use—now or in the near future—shows up 'cold' in my in-basket, that's luck for both of us."

12   3. *After you find the job opening, get the job.* The applicants who actually get hired are those who polish these six job-getting skills to perfection:

13   *Compose a better résumé.* A résumé is a self-advertisement, designed to get you an interview. Start by putting yourself in an employer's place. Take stock of your job history and personal achievements. Make an inventory of your skills and accomplishments that might be useful from the employer's standpoint. Choose the most important and describe them in words that stress accomplishments. Avoid such phrases as "my duties included . . ." Use action words like planned, sold, trained, managed.

14   Ask a knowledgeable business friend to review your résumé. Does it stress accomplishment rather than duties? Does it tell an employer what you can do for him? Can it be shortened? (One or two pages should suffice.) Generally, it's not wise to mention salary requirements.

15   *Write a convincing cover letter.* While the résumé may be a copy, the cover letter must be personal. Sy Mann, director of research for Aceto Chemical Co., says: "When I see a photocopied letter that states. 'Dear Sir, I'm sincerely interested in working for your company,' I wonder, 'How many other companies got this valentine?'" Use the name and title of the person who can give you the interview, and be absolutely certain of accuracy here. Using a wrong title or misspelling a prospective employer's name may route your correspondence directly to an automatic turndown.

16   *Prepare specifically for each interview.* Research the company thoroughly; know its history and competition. Try to grasp the problems of the job you're applying for. For example, a line in an industry journal that a food company was "developing a new geriatric food" convinced one man that he should emphasize his marketing experience with vitamins rather than with frozen foods.

17   You'll increase your edge by anticipating questions the interviewer might raise. Why do you want to work for us? What can you offer us that someone else cannot? Why did you leave your last position? What are your salary requirements?

18   An employer holds an interview to get a clearer picture of your work history and accomplishments, and to look for characteristics he or she considers valuable. These vary with jobs. Does the position require emphasis on attention to detail or on creativity? Perseverance or aggressiveness? Prior to the interview decide what traits are most in demand. And always send a thank-you note immediately after the interview.

19   *Follow-up.* They said you would hear in a week; now it's two. Call them. Don't wait and hope. Hope and act.

20   *Supply additional information.* That's the way Karen Halloway got her job as fashion director with a department store. "After my interview I sensed that the merchandise manager felt I was short on retail experience. So I wrote to him describing twenty-five fashion shows I'd staged yearly for the pattern company I'd worked for."

21   *Don't take no for an answer.* Hank Newell called to find out why he had been turned down. The credit manager felt he had insufficient collection experience. Hank thanked him for his time and frankness. The next day, Hank called back saying, "My collection experience is limited, but I don't think I fully emphasized my training in credit checking." They explored this area and found Hank still not qualified. But the credit manger was so impressed with how well Hank took criticism that when Hank asked him if he could suggest other employers, he did, even going so far as to call one. Probing for leads when an interview or follow-up turns negative is a prime technique for getting personal referrals.

22   The challenge of finding a job, approached in an active, organized, realistic way, can be a valuable personal adventure. You can meet new people, develop new ideas about yourself and your career goals, and improve your skills in dealing with individuals. These in turn can contribute to your long-term job security.

WRITING FROM READING: "How to Land the Job You Want"

When you write on any of these topics, be sure to work through the stages of the writing process in preparing your process paragraph.

1. Interview someone who has a job you would like to have. Ask him or her how you can prepare yourself, with the proper education and job experience, to be ready for a similar job. Use the information from the interview to write a process paragraph.

2. Write a paragraph on how to fire an employee as painlessly as possible. To begin, you might want to freewrite on how it feels to be fired or to fire someone. Then you can consider how to minimize those bad feelings.

3. Write a process paragraph on how you—or someone else—recovered from losing a job.

4. Interview a business instructor or a job placement counselor at your college. Ask him or her to explain how to put together a good résumé. Take notes.

   After the interview, do further research on writing a résumé. Ask the person you interviewed and/or your college librarian for books on the subject. Use the information from the interview and from books to write a paragraph on how to prepare an effective résumé.

5. Since this article was written a few years ago, the Internet has become a valuable tool for job searches. Interview your college's job placement counselor or your college's reference librarian about the best ways to research job listings/qualifications through the Internet.

6. Write a summary of "How to Land the Job You Want." Include Mayleas's three basic rules, and give some details about each rule.

5

Comparison and Contrast

WHAT IS COMPARISON? WHAT IS CONTRAST?

To **compare** means to point out *similarities.* To **contrast** means to point out *differences.* When you compare or contrast, you need to come to some *conclusion.* It's not enough to say, "These two things are similar" or "They are different." Your reader will be asking, "So what? What's your point?" You may be showing the differences between two restaurants to explain which is the better buy:

> If you like Mexican food, you can go to either Café Mexicana or Juanita's, but Juanita's has lower prices.

Or you may be describing the similarities between two family members to explain how people with similar personalities can clash:

> My cousin Bill and my brother Karram are both so stubborn they can't get along.

Hints for Writing a Comparison or Contrast Paragraph

1. Limit your topic. When you write a comparison or contrast paragraph, you might think that the easiest topics to write about are broad ones with many similarities or differences. However, if you make your topic too large, you will not be able to cover it well, and your paragraph will be full of boring statements.

Here are some topics that are too large for a comparison or contrast paragraph: two countries, two periods in history, two kinds of addiction, two wars, two economic or political systems, two presidents.

2. Avoid the obvious topic. Some people think it is easier to write about two items if the similarities or differences between them are obvious, but with an obvious topic, you will have nothing new to say, and you will risk writing a boring paragraph.

Here are some obvious topics: the differences between high school and college, the similarities between *Lethal Weapon 2* and *Lethal Weapon 3.* If you are drawn to an obvious topic, *try a new angle* on the topic. Write about the unexpected, using the same topic. Write about the similarities between high school and college or about the differences between *Lethal Weapon 2* and *Lethal*

TEACHING TIPS:
Point out to students that on most days, we all do some type of comparing or contrasting automatically. Examples: **(1)** When we decide what presents to buy for family members, we think about their different personalities and their preferences. **(2)** When we choose one fast-food restaurant over another, we may be making a choice based on similarities in service but differences in advertised specials or promotional campaigns (toys, dolls, etc)

Hint

112

Weapon 3. You may have to do more thinking before you come up with ideas, but your ideas may be more interesting to write about and to read.

3. Make your point in the topic sentence of your comparison or contrast paragraph. Indicate whether the paragraph is about similarities or differences in a topic sentence like this:

> Because he is so reliable and loyal, Michael is a much better friend to me than Stefan. (The phrase "much better" indicates differences.)
> My two botany teachers share a love of the environment and a passion for protecting it. (The word "share" indicates similarities.)

4. Do not announce in the topic sentence. The sentences below are announcements, not topic sentences:

> This paper will explain the similarities between my two botany teachers.
> Let me tell you about why Michael is a different kind of friend than Stefan.

5. Make sure your topic sentence has a focus. It should indicate similarities or differences; it should focus on the specific kind of comparison or contrast you will make.

> **not focused:** My old house and my new one are different.
> **focused:** My new home is bigger, brighter, and more comfortable than my old one.

6. In the topic sentence, cover both subjects to be compared or contrasted.

> **covers only one subject:** The beach at Santa Lucia was dirty and crowded.
> **covers both subjects:** The beach at Santa Lucia was dirty and crowded, but the beach at Fisher Bay was clean and private.

Be careful. It is easy to get so carried away by the details of your paragraph that you forget to put both subjects into one sentence.

Note: Before analyzing the exercises and reviewing sample paragraphs, you may want students to preview the various topics they could write about. Sample topics for a comparison or contrast paragraph are on pp. 135–136 and p. 139.

| **Exercise 1** |
| Practice |

Identifying Suitable Topic Sentences for a Comparison or Contrast Paragraph

Following is a list of possible topic sentences for a comparison or contrast paragraph. Some would make good topic sentences. The ones that would not make good topic sentences have one or more of these problems: they are announcements, they do not indicate whether the paragraph will be about similarities or differences, they do not focus on the specific kind of comparison or contrast to be made, they cover subjects that are too big to write about in one paragraph, or they do not cover both subjects.

Mark the problem sentences with an *X*. If a sentence would make a good topic sentence for a comparison or contrast paragraph, mark it *OK*.

1. __X__ I have two friends, Rick and Luke.

2. __X__ My two close friends, Rick and Luke, are very similar.

3. __OK__ My two close friends, Rick and Luke, are alike in their athletic ability and obsession with sports.

4. __X__ The United States and Canada are similar in their economic systems, history, and culture.

5. __X__ The Palm Club has better music and a friendlier atmosphere.

6. __X__ I'd like to discuss the similarities between my cat and my beagle.

7. __X__ Men and women are different in their physical, intellectual, and emotional make-up.

8. __X__ On the one hand, there is Jack's Pizza Parlor, and then there is the Italian Palace.

9. __OK__ Mr. Sheridan is a more energetic and enthusiastic teacher than Mr. Smith.

10. __OK__ My second date with Carla was a big improvement over my first one.

Organizing Your Comparison or Contrast Paragraph

Whether you decide to write about similarities (to compare) or differences (to contrast), you will have to decide how to organize your paragraph. You can choose between two patterns of organization: subject by subject or point by point.

Subject-by-Subject Organization In the subject-by-subject pattern, you support and explain your topic sentence by first writing all your details on one subject and then writing all your details on the other subject. If you choose a subject-by-subject pattern, be sure to discuss the points for your second subject *in the same order* as you did for the first subject. For example, if your first subject is an amusement park and you cover (1) the price of admission, (2) the long lines at rides, and (3) the quality of the rides, when you discuss the second subject, another amusement park, you should write about its prices, lines, and quality of rides *in the same order.* Look carefully at the outline and comparison paragraph below for a subject-by-subject pattern.

A Comparison Outline: Subject-by-Subject Pattern

topic sentence:	Once I realized that my brother and my mother are very much alike in temperament, I realized why they do not get along.
details:	
subject 1, James—temper	My brother James is a hot-tempered person. It is easy for him to lose control of his temper.
unkind words	When he does, he often says things he later regrets.
stubbornness	James is also very stubborn. In an argument, he will never admit he is wrong. Once we were arguing about baseball scores. Even when I showed him the right score printed in the paper, he would not admit he was wrong. He said the newspaper had made a mistake. James's stubbornness overtakes his common sense.
subject 2, mother—temper	James inherited many of his character traits from our mother. She has a quick temper, and anything can provoke it. She gets angry if she has to wait too long at a traffic light.
unkind words	She also has a tendency to use unkind words when she is mad.
stubbornness	She never backs down from a disagreement or concedes she was wrong. My mother even quit a job because she refused to admit she had made a mistake in taking inventory.

Her pride can lead her into foolish acts.
After I realized how similar my brother and mother are, I understood how such inflexible people are likely to clash.

A Comparison Paragraph: Subject-by-Subject Pattern

subject 1,
James—temper
unkind words,
stubbornness

subject 2,
mother—temper

unkind words

stubbornness

Once I realized that my brother and my mother are very much alike in temperament, I realized why they do not get along. My brother James is a hot-tempered person. It is easy for him to lose control of his temper, and when he does, he often says things he regrets. James is also very stubborn. In an argument, he will never admit he is wrong. I remember one time when we were arguing about baseball scores. Even when I showed him the right score printed in the newspaper, he would not admit he was wrong. James insisted that that the newspaper must have made a mistake in printing the score. As this example shows, sometimes James' stubbornness overtakes his common sense. It took me a while to realize that my stubborn brother James has inherited many of his traits from our mother. Like James, she has a quick temper, and almost anything can provoke it. She gets angry if she has to wait too long at a traffic light. She also shares James' habit of saying unkind things when she is angry. And just as James refuses to back down when he is wrong, my mother will never back down from a disagreement or concede she is wrong. In fact, my mother once quit a job because she refused to admit she had made a mistake in taking inventory. Her pride is as powerful as James' pride, and it can be just as foolish. After I realized how similar my mother and brother are, I understood why such inflexible people are likely to clash.

Look carefully at the paragraph in the subject-by-subject pattern, and you'll note that it

- begins with a topic sentence about both subjects—James and his mother
- gives all the details about one subject—James
- then gives all the details about the second subject—his mother—in the same order

Point-by-Point Organization In the point-by-point pattern, you support and explain your topic sentence by discussing each point of comparison or contrast, switching back and forth between your subjects. You explain one point for each subject, then explain another point for each subject, and so on.

Look carefully at the outline and the comparison paragraph below for the point-by-point pattern.

A Comparison Paragraph: Point-by-Point Outline

topic sentence: Once I realized that my brother and my mother are very much alike in temperament, I realized why they do not get along.

details:

point 1, temper	My brother James is a hot-tempered person.
James and mother	It is easy for him to lose control of his temper.
	My mother has a quick temper, and anything can provoke it.
	She gets angry if she has to wait too long at a traffic light.
point 2, unkind words	When my brother gets mad, he often says things he regrets.
James and mother	My mother has a tendency to use unkind words when she is mad.
point 3, stubbornness	James is very stubborn.
	In an argument, he will never admit he is wrong.
James and mother	Once we were arguing about baseball scores.
	Even when I showed him the right score printed in the paper, he would not admit he was wrong.
	He said the newspaper had made a mistake.
	James' stubbornness overtakes his common sense.
	My mother will never back down from a disagreement or admit she is wrong.
	She even quit a job because she refused to admit she had made a mistake in taking inventory.
	She was foolish in her stubbornness.
	After I realized how similar my mother and brother are, I understood why such inflexible people are likely to clash.

A Comparison Paragraph: Point-by-Point Pattern

	Once I realized that my brother and my mother are very much alike in temperament, I realized why they do not get along. My brother is a hot-tempered
point 1 James and mother	person, and it is easy for him to lose control of his temper. My mother shares James's quick temper, and anything can provoke her anger. She gets angry if she has to wait too long at a traffic light. When my
point 2 James and mother	brother gets mad, he often says things he regrets. Similarly, my mother is known for the unkind things she has said in anger. James is a very stubborn per-
point 3 James and mother	son. In an argument, he will never admit he is wrong. I remember one argument we were having over baseball scores. Even when I showed him the right score printed in the newspaper, he would not admit he had been wrong. He simply insisted the paper had made a mistake. At times like that, James' stubbornness overtakes his common sense. Like her son, my mother will never back down from an argument or admit she was wrong. She even quit a job because she refused to admit she had made a mistake in taking inventory. In that case, her stubbornness was as foolish as James'. It took me a while to see the similarities between my brother and mother. Yet after I realized how similar these two people are, I understood why two inflexible people are likely to clash.

Look carefully at the paragraph in the point-by-point pattern, and you'll note that it

- begins with a topic sentence about both subjects—James and his mother
- discusses how both James and his mother are alike in these points: their quick tempers, the unkind things they say in a temper, their often foolish stubbornness
- switches back and forth between the two subjects

Hints for Using Patterns of Organization

The subject-by-subject and point-by-point patterns can be used for either a comparison or contrast paragraph. But whatever pattern you choose, remember these hints:

1. Be sure to use the same points to compare or contrast both subjects. If you are contrasting two cars, you can't discuss the price and safety features of one, then the styling and speed of the other. You must discuss the price of both or the safety features, styling, or speed of both.

You don't have to list the points in your topic sentence, but you can include them, like this: "My old Celica turned out to be a cheaper, safer, and more reliable car than my boyfriend's new Taurus."

2. Be sure to give roughly equal space to both subjects. This rule doesn't mean you must write the same number of words—or even sentences—on both subjects. It does mean you should give fairly equal attention to the details of both subjects.

Since you will be writing about two subjects, this type of paragraph can involve more details than other paragraph formats. Thus, a comparison or contrast paragraph may be longer than twelve sentences.

Using Transitions Effectively for Comparison or Contrast

The transitions you use in a comparison or contrast paragraph, as well as how and when you use them, depend on the answers to two questions:

1. Are you writing a comparison paragraph or a contrast paragraph?
   - When you choose to write a *comparison* paragraph, you use transition words, phrases, or sentences that point out *similarities*.
   - When you choose to write a *contrast* paragraph, you use transition words, phrases, or sentences that point out *differences*.

2. Are you organizing your paragraph in the point-by-point or subject-by-subject pattern?
   - When you choose to organize your paragraph in the *point-by-point* pattern, you need transitions *within each point and between points*.
   - When you choose to organize in the *subject-by-subject pattern,* you need most of your transitions *in the second half* of the paragraph to remind the reader of the points you made in the first half.

Here are some transitions you can use in writing comparison or contrast. There are many others you may think of that will be appropriate for your ideas.

Note: Students may need to review the use of commas and semicolons in transitions. For a review of punctuating sentences with coordinating conjunctions, conjunctive adverbs, and subordinate adverbs, see the chart in Chapter 14.

> **Infobox**
>
> ### Transitions for a Comparison or Contrast Paragraph
>
> **To show similarities:** additionally, again, also, and, as well as, both, each of, equally, furthermore, in addition, in the same way, just like, like, likewise, similarly, similar to, so, too
>
> **To show differences:** although, but, conversely, different from, despite, even though, except, however, in contrast to, instead of, in spite of, nevertheless, on the other hand, otherwise, still, though, unlike, whereas, while, yet.

Writing a comparison or contrast paragraph challenges you to make decisions like these: Will I compare or contrast? Will I use a point-by-point or a subject-by-subject pattern? Those decisions will determine what kind of transitions you will use, as well as where you will use them.

Exercise 2
Practice

Writing Appropriate Transitions for a Comparison or Contrast Paragraph

Below are pairs of sentences. First, decide whether each pair shows a comparison or a contrast. Then combine the two sentences into one, using an appropriate transition (either a word or a phrase). You may have to rewrite parts of the original sentences to create one smooth sentence. The first pair is done for you.

1. Dr. Cheung is a professor of art.
   Dr. Mbala is a professor of history.

   Combined: <u>Dr. Cheung is a professor of art while Dr. Mbala is a professor of</u>

   <u>history.</u>

Answers Will Vary.
Possible answers shown at right.

Note: Remind students not to rely on the word "and."

2. *The Brady Bunch* was a show about a happy, well-adjusted family that was too good to be true.
   The Fresh Prince of Bel Air was a show about a family that lived a fantasy lifestyle.

   Combined: <u>The Brady Bunch was a show about a happy, well-adjusted family that was too good to be true; similarly, The Fresh Prince of Bel Air was about a family that lived a fantasy lifestyle.</u>

3. Small children are often afraid to leave their parents.
   Teenagers are often anxious to get away from their parents.

   Combined: <u>Although small children are often afraid to leave their parents, teenagers can't wait to get away from their parents.</u>

4. Phillippe was an intelligent dog who learned all sorts of tricks.
   Elvis, our basset hound, refused to do the simplest tricks.

   Combined: <u>Phillippe was an intelligent dog who learned all sorts of new tricks, unlike Elvis, our basset hound, who refused to do the simplest tricks.</u>

5. Exercise can help you lower cholesterol levels, fight heart disease, and relieve stress.
    A doctor can give you medicine for heart disease, high cholesterol, or stress.

Combined: <u>Both exercise and medication can help you lower cholesterol</u>

<u>levels, fight heart disease, and relieve stress.</u>

6. Edward is dedicated to helping the homeless at the food bank where he works.
    His sister Irene has devoted her life to protecting the rights of Central American refugees.

Combined: <u>Edward is dedicated to helping the homeless at the food bank</u>

<u>where he works; on the other hand, his sister Irene has devoted her life to</u>

<u>protecting the rights of Central American refugees.</u>

7. My father spends many hours volunteering at a local food bank.
    Every Saturday, my boyfriend donates his time to the food bank, where he collects free food from donors.

Combined: <u>My father spends many hours volunteering at a local food bank,</u>

<u>and my boyfriend also donates his time to the food bank, where he collects</u>

<u>free food from donors every Saturday.</u>

8. Camping out takes work and can be uncomfortable.
    Staying in a motel is easy and pleasant.

Combined: <u>Camping out takes work and can be uncomfortable, but staying</u>

<u>in a motel is easy and pleasant.</u>

9. Staying in a motel costs money.
    Camping out takes expensive supplies.

Combined: <u>Staying in a motel costs money; so does camping out, which</u>

<u>takes expensive supplies.</u>

10. My co-workers at the Sports Store were friendly and supportive.
    The people I worked with at Bruno's Subs created a warm and helpful working environment.

Combined: <u>My co-workers at the Sports Store were friendly and supportive,</u>

<u>just like the people I worked with at Bruno's Subs.</u>

WRITING THE COMPARISON OR CONTRAST PARAGRAPH IN STEPS

Thought Lines

Comparison or Contrast

One way to get started on a comparison or contrast paragraph is to list as many differences or similarities as you can on one topic. Then you can see whether you have more similarities (comparisons) or differences (contrasts), and decide which approach to use. For example, if you are asked to compare or contrast two restaurants, you could begin with a list like this.

List for Two Restaurants: Victor's or The Garden

similarities

both offer lunch and dinner
very popular
nearby

differences

Victor's	*The Garden*
formal dress	informal dress
tablecloths	placemats
food is bland	spicy food
expensive	moderate
statues, fountains, fresh flowers	dark wood, hanging plants

Getting Points of Comparison or Contrast

Whether you compare or contrast, you are looking for points of comparison or contrast, items you can discuss about both subjects. If you surveyed the list on the two restaurants and decided you wanted to contrast the two restaurants, you'd see that you already have these points of contrast:

dress	food
decor	prices

To write your paragraph, start with several points of comparison or contrast. As you work through the stages of writing, you may decide you don't need all the points you have jotted down, but it is better to start with too many points than with too few.

Exercise 3
👥 Collaborate

Developing Points of Comparison or Contrast

Do this exercise with a partner or a group. Below are some topics that could be used for a comparison or contrast paragraph. Underneath each topic, write three points of comparison or contrast. Be ready to share your answers with another group or with the class. The first topic is done for you.

1. **topic:** Compare or contrast two television talk shows.
   points of comparison or contrast:

   a. the host

   b. the kinds of topics discussed on the show

c. what the studio audience is like

2. **topic:** Compare or contrast a movie and its sequel.
   points of comparison or contrast:

   a. the acting

   b. the plot

   c. the special effects

3. **topic:** Compare or contrast two friends.
   points of comparison or contrast:

   a. the way they walk

   b. the way they talk

   c. the way they dress

4. **topic:** Compare or contrast two college courses.
   points of comparison or contrast:

   a. the textbooks

   b. the assignments

   c. the instructor

5. **topic:** Compare or contrast two professional basketball players.
   points of comparison or contrast:

   a. their skill

   b. their attitude toward their teammates

   c. their fame

Exercise 4 **Finding Differences in Subjects That Look Similar**

Practice

Following are pairs of subjects that seem very similar but that do have differences. List three differences for each pair.

1. **subjects:** Burger King and McDonald's
   differences:

   a. method of cooking burgers

   b. slogans

   c. exterior of restaurants

2. **subjects:** Pepsi and Coke
   differences:

a. advertising

b. shape of bottles

c. taste

3. **subjects:** swimming in the ocean and swimming in a pool
   differences:

a. water contents - salt vs. chlorine

b. calmness of the water

c. space for swimming

4. **subjects:** preschool and kindergarten
   differences:

a. ages of children

b. curriculum

c. length of the school day

5. **subjects:** cell phones and traditional home and office phones
   differences:

a. portability

b. costs

c. likelihood of being stolen

Exercise 5 **Finding Similarities in Subjects That Look Different**

Practice

Following are pairs of subjects that are different but have some similarities. List three similarities for each pair.

Answers Will Vary.
Possible answers
shown at right.

1. **subjects:** attending college while living with your family and attending college while living with a roommate
   similarities:

a. respecting others' rights

b. doing household chores

c. finding time to study

2. **subjects:** watching television and going to a movie
   similarities:

a. sitting for a length of time

b. snacking while watching

c. watching to relax

3. subjects: working the night shift and working daytime hours
similarities:

a. must keep to a schedule

b. look forward to breaks

c. must fulfill specific responsibilities

4. subjects: learning to dance and learning to drive
similarities:

a. take concentration

b. take practice

c. bring a sense of achievement

5. subjects: traveling by car and traveling by plane
similarities:

a. can be hectic

b. can involve crowds

c. can be affected by the weather

Adding Details to Your Points

Once you have some points, you can begin adding details to them. The details may lead you to more points. If they do not, they will still help you develop the ideas of your paragraph. If you were to write about the differences in restaurants, for example, your new list with added details might look like this:

List for a Contrast of Restaurants

Victor's	The Garden
dress—formal	informal dress
men in jackets, women in dresses	all in jeans
decor—pretty, elegant	place mats, on table is
statues, fountains,	a card listing specials,
fresh flowers on tables,	lots of dark wood, brass,
tablecloths	green hanging plants
food—bland tasting	spicy and adventurous
traditional, broiled fish or	pasta in tomato sauces,
chicken, traditional steaks,	garlic in everything,
appetizers like shrimp	curry, appetizers like
cocktail, onion soup	tiny tortillas, ribs in
	honey-mustard sauce
price—expensive	moderate
everything costs extra,	price of dinner includes
like appetizer, salad	appetizer and salad

Once you have a list of points and some details, you can review your list and ask yourself, "What's my main idea? Where is the list taking me?"

Reading the list about restaurants, you might conclude that some people may prefer The Garden to Victor's. Why? There are several hints in your list: The Garden has cheaper food, better food, and a more casual atmosphere. Now that you have a point, you can put it into a topic sentence. A topic sentence contrasting the restaurants could be

Some people would rather eat at The Garden than at Victor's because The Garden offers better, cheaper food in a more casual environment.

Once you have a possible topic sentence, you can begin working on the outlines stage of your paragraph.

Exercise 6
Practice

Writing Topic Sentences for Comparison or Contrast

Below are lists of details. Some lists are for comparison paragraphs; some are for contrast paragraphs. Read each list carefully; then write a topic sentence for each list.

Answers Will Vary.
Possible answers
shown at right.

1. **topic sentence:** Frozen yogurt and ice cream differ in taste, nutritional value, and appeal.

List of Details

frozen yogurt	ice cream
taste—light, milky, a little sour	sweet, heavy, creamy
nutritional value—low fat or fat free, low calorie, a healthy dessert or snack	more fat, higher calories, acceptable as an occasional treat
popularity—younger generation, parents with small children who want a healthy snack, dieters	lovers of gourmet food, people who want to splurge on calories

2. **topic sentence:** Both frozen yogurt and ice cream are widely available in a variety of forms and flavors.

List of Details

frozen yogurt	ice cream
availability—frozen yogurt stores, supermarkets, fast food places, college cafeterias	ice cream stores, supermarkets, college cafeterias, snack bars
ways to buy it—in cones, cups, quarts, pints, in cakes, soft serve	cones, cups, pints, quarts, half gallons, gallons, cakes, a little soft serve
flavors—mostly fruit, some chocolate, some with mixed-in ingredients like Heath bars	chocolate, fruit, mixed-in ingredients like cherries or cookies

3. **topic sentence:** A pick-up truck has different seating, carrying capacity, and uses than a sport utility vehicle.

List of Details

pickup truck	sport-utility vehicle (like Bronco, Explorer)
seating—for two	seats four or five
room to carry things—large truck bed, can be open space, covered by a canvas cover, or permanently closed	large covered space behind seats, but not as big as pickup's space
uses—good for rough terrain, hunting and fishing, hauling and moving, construction work	good for country driving but also for suburban families, with space for toys, baby strollers, car seats

4. topic sentence: <u>Pick-up trucks and sport utility vehicles appeal to</u>

<u>similar buyers, convey a similar image, and offer similar accessories.</u>

List of Details

pick-up truck	sport-utility vehicle
buyers—popular with young people, hunters, farmers	people in their twenties, people who camp or fish
image—a rugged, solid, practical vehicle	fashionable, rugged, useful
accessories available—CD fancy speakers, air conditioning	luxurious interiors, CD players and speakers, air conditioning

Outlines

Comparison or Contrast

With a topic sentence, you can begin to draft an outline. Before you can write an outline, however, you have to make a decision: what pattern do you want to use in organizing your paragraph? Do you want to use the subject-by-subject or the point-by-point pattern?

The following is an outline of a contrast paragraph in point-by-point form.

An Outline of a Contrast Paragraph: Point-by-Point

topic sentence: Some people would rather eat at The Garden than at Victor's because The Garden offers better, cheaper food in a more casual environment.

details:
point 1:
food

Food at Victor's is bland-tasting and traditional.
The menu has broiled fish, chicken, traditional steaks.
The spices used are mostly parsley and salt.
The food is the usual American food, with a little French food on the list.
Appetizers are the usual things like shrimp cocktail and onion soup.

point 2:
prices

{
Food at The Garden is more spicy and adventurous.
There are many pasta dishes in tomato sauce.
There is garlic in just about everything.
The Garden serves five different curry dishes.
It has all kinds of ethnic food.
Appetizers include items like tiny tortillas and
hot honey-mustard ribs.

The prices of the two restaurants differ.
Victor's is expensive.
Everything you order costs extra.
An appetizer or a salad costs extra.
Food at The Garden is more moderately priced.
The price of a dinner includes an appetizer and a
salad.

point 3:
environment

{
Certain diners may feel uncomfortable in Victor's,
which has a formal atmosphere.
Everyone is dressed up, the men in jackets and ties
and the women in dresses.
Less formal diners would rather eat in a more
casual place.
People don't dress up to go to The Garden; they
wear jeans.

conclusion

{
Many people prefer a place where they can relax,
with reasonable prices and unusual food, to a place
that's a little stuffy, with a traditional and
expensive menu.

Once you have drafted an outline, check it. Use the following checklist to help you review and revise your outline.

✔ **Checklist**

A Checklist for an Outline of a Comparison or Contrast Paragraph

✔ Do I have enough details?

✔ Are all my details relevant?

✔ Have I covered all the points on both sides?

✔ If I'm using a subject-by-subject pattern, have I covered the points in the same order on both sides?

✔ Have I tried to cover too many points?

✔ Have I made my main idea clear?

Using this checklist as your guide, compare the outline with the thought lines list on page 120. You may notice several changes:

- Some details on decor in the list have been omitted because there were too many points.
- A concluding sentence has been added to reinforce the main idea.

Exercise 7	**Adding a Point and Details to a Comparison or Contrast Outline**

Practice   The following outline is too short. Develop it by adding a point of contrast and details to both subjects to develop the contrast.

topic sentence: Carson College is a friendlier place than Wellington College.

details: When a person enters Carson College, he or she sees groups of students who seem happy.
They are sprawled on the steps and on the lawns, looking like they are having a good time.
They are laughing and talking to each other.
At Wellington College, everyone seems to be a stranger.
Students are isolated.
They lean against the wall or sit alone, reading intently or staring into space.
The buildings at Carson seem open and inviting.
There are many large glass windows in each classroom.
There are wide corridors.
Many signs help newcomers find their way around.
Wellington College seems closed and forbidding.
It has dark, windowless classrooms.
The halls are narrow and dirty.
There are no signs or directions posted on the buildings.

Answers Will Vary.
Possible answers
shown at right.

**Discussion
Question:** If students
have difficulty adding
details about fictitious
schools, ask students
what other points
about the schools
could be contrasted
based on what they
might need to know
about the appearance
and/or atmosphere of
the schools.

Add a new point of contrast and details about each college: _____

The staff at Carson College are helpful.

Counselors smile at new students.

They offer to sit and answer students' questions.

The security officers ask, "Need directions?"

At Wellington College, the staff is intimidating.

The counselors tell newcomers to make an appointment.

The security guards glare at strangers.

Exercise 8	**Finding Irrelevant Details in a Comparison or Contrast Outline**

Practice   The following outline contains some irrelevant details. Cross out the details that do not fit.

topic sentence: Bill, a student in my chemistry class, behaves like my two-year-old son Toby.

details: Toby has a hard time sitting still for very long.
When we go to a restaurant, Toby gets impatient waiting for his food.
He will sit still only until he is finished eating.
Then he begins to fidget.
Sometimes he starts dropping things, like French fries or spoons, on the floor.
Bill finds it hard to sit through class.

Sometimes he gets impatient when the instructor is explaining something complicated.

~~Bill does not have good grades in this class.~~

If Bill is taking a quiz, he will sit quietly only until he has finished.

~~Dr. Berthoff's quizzes are hard.~~

Then Bill begins to squirm at his desk.

He shifts his seat around.

Sometimes he drops pencils on the floor.

Toby likes a great deal of attention.

~~I am divorced, and Toby does not see his father often.~~

To get my attention, Toby misbehaves.

He interrupts when I have company.

He teases our dog.

He throws things.

Bill likes attention, too.

He misbehaves in class to get attention from the instructor.

Sometimes he makes smart-aleck remarks while the instructor is lecturing.

Sometimes he teases the girl who sits next to him.

Once he threw a crumpled ball of paper across the room into the wastebasket.

Bill and Tony both behave like children, but in Bill's case, it's time to grow up.

Exercise 9   **Revising the Order in a Comparison or Contrast Outline**

Practice

Below is an outline written in the subject-by-subject pattern. Rewrite the part of the outline that is in italics so that the points in the second half follow the order of the first half. You do not have to change any sentences; just rearrange them.

topic sentence: Young people and old people are both victims of society's prejudices.

details: Some people think young people are not capable of mature thinking.

They think the young are on drugs.

They think the young are alcoholics.

The young are considered parasites because they do not earn a great deal of money.

Many young people are in college and not working full time.

Many young people rely on help from their parents.

The young are outcasts because their appearance is different.

They young wear trendy fashions.

They have strange haircuts.

People may think the young are punks.

The way young people look makes other people afraid.

Old people are also judged by their appearance.

They are wrinkled or scarred or frail-looking.

People are afraid of growing old and looking like that.

So they are afraid of the old.

Some people think elderly people are not capable of mature thinking.

They think the old are on too much medication to think straight.

They think the old are senile.
Some people consider the old to be parasites because elderly
people do not earn a great deal of money.
Some of the elderly have small pensions.
Some have only Social Security benefits.
The young and the old are often stereotyped.

Rewritten order: 1. Some people think elderly people are not capable of

mature thinking.

2. They think the old are on too much medication to think straight

3. They think the old are senile.

4. Some people consider the old to be parasites because elderly people do

    not earn a great deal of money.

5. Some of the elderly have small pensions.

6. Some have only Social Security benefits.

7. Old people are also judged by their appearance.

8. They are wrinkled or scarred or frail-looking.

9. People are afraid of growing old and looking like that.

10. So they are afraid of the old.

11. The young and the old are often stereotyped.

Rough Lines

Comparison or Contrast

When you have revised your outline, you can write the first draft of the restaurant paragraph. After making a first draft, you may want to combine more sentences, rearrange your points, fix your topic sentence, or add vivid details. You may also need to add transitions.

The Draft

Here is a draft version of the paragraph on contrasting two restaurants. As you read it, notice the changes from the outline on pages 126–27: the order of some details in the outline has been changed, sentences have been combined, and transitions have been added.

A Draft of a Contrast Paragraph: Point by Point (Transitions are underlined.)

Some people would rather eat at The Garden than at Victor's because The Garden offers better and cheaper food in a more casual environment. The food at Victor's is bland-tasting and traditional. The menu has broiled fish, chicken, and traditional steaks. The food is the usual American food with a little French food on the list. Appetizers are the usual things like shrimp cocktail and onion soup. The spices used are mainly parsley and salt. Food at The Garden, <u>however,</u> is more spicy and adventurous. The restaurant has all kinds of ethnic food. There are many pasta dishes with tomato sauce. The menu has five kinds of curry on it. The appetizers include items like tiny tortillas and hot honey-mustard ribs. <u>And if parsley is the spice of choice at Victor's,</u> garlic is the favorite spice at The Garden. The prices at the restaurants differ, <u>too.</u> Victor's is expensive because everything you order costs extra. An appetizer or a salad costs extra. Food at The Garden, <u>in contrast,</u> is more moderately priced because the price of a dinner includes an appetizer and a salad. <u>Price and menu are important, but the most important difference between the restaurants has to do with environment.</u> Certain diners may feel uncomfortable at Victor's, which has a formal atmosphere. Everyone is dressed up, the men in jackets and ties and the women in dresses. Less formal diners would rather eat in a more casual place like The Garden, where everyone wears jeans. Many people prefer a place where they can relax, with reasonable prices and unusual food, to a place that is a little stuffy, with a traditional and expensive menu.

The following checklist may help you revise your own draft.

✔ Checklist

A Checklist for Revising the Draft of a Comparison or Contrast Paragraph

✔ Did I include a topic sentence that covers both subjects?

✔ Is the paragraph in a clear order?

✔ Does it stick to one pattern, either subject by subject or point by point?

✔ Are both subjects given roughly the same amount of space?

✔ Do all the details fit?

✔ Are the details specific and vivid?

✔ Do I need to combine any sentences?

✔ Are transitions used effectively?

✔ Have I made my point?

Exercise 10
Practice

Revising the Draft of a Comparison or Contrast Paragraph by Adding Vivid Details

You can do this exercise alone, with a writing partner, or with a group. The following contrast paragraph lacks the vivid details that could make it interesting. Read it; then rewrite the underlined parts in the space above the underlining. Replace the original words with more vivid details.

Answers Will Vary.
Possible answers
shown at right.

Nelson and Byron are so different in appearance that most people would not

believe the men are brothers. Nelson is tall and lanky. At six feet, he seems even taller *a crew cut*   *black*

because he has a bony, long-limbed body. His hair is <u>cut short,</u> and it is a <u>dark color.</u>

Nelson's face is notable for its bone structure. He has prominent cheekbones, a sharp nose, and a long chin. His face has a lean, sculptured look. Byron looks nothing like his

5′ 5″

brother. First of all, he is short and stocky. He is <u>short in height</u> and seems even short-

pudgy

er because his body is <u>kind of fat.</u> His hair, unlike Nelson's, is long and straight and is

pale brown

usually pulled into a ponytail. Byron's hair is <u>lighter than Nelson's.</u> His face is rounded, with a snub nose, round cheeks like apples, and a round chin. Byron's face has a soft, chubby look. Byron looks like an overweight wrestler while Nelson looks like a basket-ball player.

Final Lines

Comparison or Contrast

Contrast Paragraph: Point-by-Point Pattern

Following is the final version of the paragraph contrasting restaurants, using a point-by-point pattern. When you read it, you will notice several changes from the draft on page 129:

- "Usual" or "usually" was used too often, so synonyms were substituted.
- "Onion soup" became "*French* onion soup" to polish the detail.
- "Everything *you* order" was changed to "everything *a person* orders" to avoid sounding as if the reader is ordering food at Victor's.
- "A formal *atmosphere*" became "a formal environment."

A Final Version of a Contrast Paragraph: Point by Point
(Changes from the draft are underlined.)

Some people would rather eat at The Garden than at Victor's because The Garden offers better and cheaper food in a more casual environment. The food at Victor's is bland-tasting and traditional. The menu has broiled fish, chicken, and traditional steaks. The food is <u>typical</u> American food with a little French food on the list. Appetizers are <u>standard items</u> like shrimp cocktail and <u>French</u> onion soup. The spices are mostly parsley and salt. Food at The Garden, however, is more spicy and adventurous. The restaurant has all kinds of ethnic food. There are many pasta dishes with tomato sauce. The menu has five kinds of curry on it. The appetizers include items like tiny tortillas and hot honey-mustard ribs. And if parsley is the spice of choice at Victor's, garlic is the favorite spice at The Garden. The prices at the restaurants differ, too. Victor's is expensive because everything <u>a person orders</u> costs extra. An appetizer or a salad costs extra. Food at The Garden, in contrast, is more moderately priced because the price of a dinner includes an appetizer and a salad.

Price and menu are important, but the most important difference between the two restaurants has to do with environment. Certain diners may feel uncomfortable at Victor's, which has a formal <u>environment</u>. Everyone is dressed up, the men in jackets and ties and the women in dresses. Less formal diners would rather eat in a more casual place like The Garden, where everyone wears jeans. Many people prefer a place where they can relax, with reasonable prices and unusual food, to a place that is a little stuffy, with a traditional and expensive menu.

Before you prepare the final copy of your comparison or contrast paragraph, check your latest draft for errors in spelling and punctuation and for any errors made in typing or copying.

The Same Contrast Paragraph: Subject by Subject

To show you what the same paragraph contrasting restaurants would look like in a subject-by-subject pattern, the outline, draft, and final version are shown below.

An Outline: Subject by Subject

topic sentence:	Some people would rather eat at The Garden than at Victor's because The Garden offers better, cheaper food in a more casual environment.
details:	Food at Victor's is bland-tasting and traditional. The menu has broiled fish, chicken, and traditional steaks.
subject 1: Victor's	The spices used are mostly parsley and salt. The food is the usual American food, with a little French food on the list. Appetizers are the usual things like shrimp cocktail and onion soup. Victor's is expensive. Everything you order costs extra. An appetizer or a salad costs extra. Certain diners may feel uncomfortable at Victor's, which has a formal atmosphere. Everyone is dressed up, the men in jackets and ties and the women in dresses.
subject 2: The Garden	Food at The Garden is more spicy and adventurous. There are many pasta dishes in tomato sauce. There is garlic in just about everything. The Garden serves five different curry dishes. It has all kinds of ethnic food. Appetizers include items like tiny tortillas and hot honey-mustard ribs. Food at The Garden is moderately priced. The price of a dinner includes an appetizer and a salad. The Garden is casual.

People don't dress up to go there; they wear jeans. Many people prefer a place where they can relax, with reasonable prices and unusual food, to a place that's a little stuffy, with a traditional and expensive menu.

A Draft Version of a Contrast Paragraph: Subject by Subject
(Transitions are underlined.)

Some people would rather eat at The Garden than at Victor's because The Garden offers better, cheaper food in a more casual environment. The food at Victor's is bland-tasting and traditional. The menu has broiled fish, chicken, and traditional steaks on it. The food is the usual American food, with a little French food on the list. Appetizers are the usual things like shrimp cocktail and onion soup. At Victor's, the spices are mostly parsley and salt. Eating traditional food at Victor's is expensive since everything you order costs extra. An appetizer or a salad, for instance, costs extra. Victor's prices make some people nervous, and the restaurant's formal atmosphere makes them uncomfortable. At Victor's, everyone is dressed up, the men in jackets and ties and the women in dresses. <u>The formal atmosphere, the food, and the prices attract some diners, but others would rather go to The Garden for a meal.</u> The food at The Garden is more spicy and adventurous <u>than the offerings at Victor's.</u> The place has all kinds of ethnic food. There are many pasta dishes in tomato sauce, and The Garden serves five different curry dishes. Appetizers include items like tiny tortillas and hot honey-mustard ribs. <u>If Victor's relies on parsely and salt to flavor its food,</u> The Garden sticks to garlic, which is in just about everything. Prices are lower at The Garden <u>than they are at Victor's.</u> The Garden's meals are more moderately priced because, <u>unlike Victor's,</u> The Garden includes an appetizer and a salad in the price of a dinner. <u>And in contrast to Victor's,</u> The Garden is a casual restaurant. People don't dress up to go to The Garden; everyone wears jeans. Many people prefer a place where they can relax, with unusual food at reasonable prices, to a place that's a little stuffy, with a traditional and expensive menu.

A Final Version of a Contrast Paragraph: Subject by Subject
(Changes from the draft are underlined.)

Some people would rather eat at The Garden than at Victor's because The Garden offers better, cheaper food in a more casual environment. The food at Victor's is bland-tasting and traditional. The menu has broiled fish, chicken, and traditional steaks on it. The food is typical American food, with a little French food on the list. Appetizers are the <u>standard</u> things like shrimp cocktail and <u>French</u> onion soup. At Victor's, the spices are mostly parsley and salt. Eating traditional food at Victor's is expensive since everything <u>a person orders</u> costs extra. An appetizer or a salad, for instance, costs extra. Victor's prices make some people nervous, and the restaurant's formal <u>environment</u> makes them uncomfortable. At Victor's, everyone is dressed up, the men in jackets and ties and the women in dresses. The formal <u>environment</u> and the prices attract some diners, but others would rather go to The Garden for a meal. The food at The Garden is more spicy and adventurous than the offerings at Victor's. The place has all kinds of ethnic food. There are many pasta dishes in tomato sauce, and The Garden serves five different curry dishes. Appetizers include items like tiny tortillas and hot honey-mustard ribs. If Victor's relies on parsley and salt to flavor its food, The Garden sticks to garlic, which is in just about everything. Prices are lower at The Garden than they are at Victor's. The Garden's meals are more moderately priced because, unlike Victor's, The Garden includes an appetizer and a salad in the price of a dinner. And in contrast to Victor's, The Garden is a casual restaurant. People don't dress up to go to The Garden; everyone wears jeans. Many people prefer place where they can relax, with unusual food at reasonable prices, to a place that's a little stuffy, with a traditional and expensive menu.

Exercise 11

Practice

Proofreading to Prepare the Final Version

Following is a comparison paragraph with the kinds of errors that are easy to overlook in a final copy of an assignment. Correct the errors, writing your corrections above the lines. There are eleven errors.

My nephew's stuffed dog and my portable tape player meet the same needs in both

of us. Brendan, who is four, will not go anywhere without the ragged stufed dog he loves. [*stuffed*]

To him, that dog represents security I have seen him cry so long and so hard that his

parents had to turn the car around and drive fifty miles to pick up the dog they forgot.

My tape player is my security, and I take it everywere. I even take it to the library when

I study; I just plug in the earphones. When Brendan feels tense, he runs to grab his dog.

One day Brendans mother was yelling at him, an his face got puckered up and red. [*Brendan's* / *and*]

Brendan ran out of the room and hid in the corner of the hallway. He was clutching his

dog. While I dont clutch my tape player, I do turn to my mussic to relax whenever I felt [*don't* / *music*]

anxious. Brendan uses his toy to excape the world. I seen him sit silent for half an [*feel* / *escape* / *have seen*]

hour, holding his dog and starring into space. He is involved in some fantasy with his [*staring*]

puppy. Whenever I feel tense, I turn on my music. It soothes me and puts me in a world

of my own. I guess adults and children have there own ways of coping with conflict, [*their*]

and they have their own toys, too!

Lines of Detail: A Walk-Through Assignment

Write a paragraph that compares or contrasts any experience you have heard about with the same experience as you have lived it. For example, you could compare or contrast what you heard about starting college with your actual experience of starting college. You could compare or contrast what you heard about falling in love with your experience of falling in love, or what you heard about playing a sport with your own experience playing that sport. To write your paragraph, follow these steps:

Step 1: Choose the experience you will write about; then list all the similarities and differences between the experience as you heard about it and the experience as you lived it.

Step 2: To decide whether to write a comparison paragraph or a contrast paragraph, survey your list to see which has more details, the similarities or the differences.

Step 3: Add details to your comparison or contrast list. Survey your list again, and group the details into points of comparison or contrast.

Step 4: Write a topic sentence that includes both subjects, focuses on comparison or contrast, and makes a point.

Step 5: Decide whether your paragraph will be in the subject-by-subject or point-by-point pattern. Write your outline in the pattern you choose.

Step 6: Write a draft of your paragraph. Revise your draft, checking the transitions, the order of the points, the space given to each point for each subject, and the relevance and vividness of details. Combine any short, choppy sentences.

Step 7: Before you prepare the final copy of your paragraph, edit for word choice, spelling, punctuation, and transitions.

Writing Your Own Comparison or Contrast Paragraph

When you write on one of these topics, be sure to follow the stages of the writing process in preparing your comparison or contrast paragraph.

1. Contrast what your appearance (or your behavior) makes others think of you and what you are like below the surface of your appearance (or behavior). If your instructor agrees, you can ask a writing partner or group to give you ideas on what your appearance or behavior says about you.

2. Contrast something you did in the past with the way you do the same thing today. For example, you could contrast the two ways (past and present) of studying, shopping, treating your friends, spending your free time, driving a car, or getting along with a parent or child.

3. Compare or contrast any of the following:

two pets	two performers	two movies
two cars	two bosses	two TV shows
two stores	two family members	two jobs
two athletic teams	two birthdays	two classes

If your instructor agrees, you may want to brainstorm points of comparison or contrast with a writing partner or a group.

4. Imagine that you are a reporter who specializes in helping consumers get the best for their money. Imagine that you are asked to rate two brands of the same supermarket item. Write a paragraph advising your readers which is the better buy. You can rate two brands of cola, or yogurt, or potato chips, or toothpaste, or ice cream, or chocolate chip cookies, or paper towels—any item you can get in a supermarket.

   Be sure to come up with *enough* points to contrast. You can't, for example, do a well-developed paragraph on just the taste of two cookies. But you can also discuss texture, color, smell, price, fat content, calories, number of chocolate chips, and so on. If your instructor agrees, you may want to brainstorm topics or points of contrast with a group, as a way of beginning the writing process. Then work on your own on the outline, draft, and final version.

5. Contrast your taste in music, or dress, or ways of spending leisure time, with the same taste of another generation.

6. Interview a person of your age group who comes from a different part of the country. (There may be quite a few people from different parts of the country in your class.) Ask this person about similarities or differences between his or her former home and this part of the country. You could ask about similarities or differences in dress, music, dating, nightlife, ways to spend leisure time, favorite entertainers, or anything else you like.

   After the interview, write a paragraph that shows how people of the same age group, but from different parts of the country, either have *different* tastes in something like music or dress or share the *same* tastes in that area. Whichever approach you use, be sure to include details you collected in the interview.

Name: _____   **Section:** _____

Peer Review Form for a Comparison or Contrast Paragraph

After you have written a draft of your paragraph, let a writing partner read it. When your partner has completed the form below, discuss the comments. Then repeat the same process for your partner's paragraph.

I think the topic sentence of this paragraph is _____

_____

_____

The pattern of this paragraph is (a) subject by subject or (b) point by point. (Choose one.)

The points used to compare or contrast are _____

_____

_____

The part of the paragraph I like best is about _____

_____

The comparison or contrast is (a) easy to follow or (b) a little confusing. (Choose one.)

I have questions about _____

I would like to see something added about _____

I would like to take out the part about _____

I would like to add or change a transition in front of the words _____

_____

Other comments: _____

_____

_____

_____

_____

_____

_____

_____

Reviewer's Name: _____

WRITING FROM READING: Comparison or Contrast

Against All Odds, I'm Just Fine
Brad Wackerlin

When Brad Wackerlin wrote this essay in 1990, he had just graduated from high school. He writes about the differences between society's view of teenagers and the real teens who "do fine" in the real world.

Words You May Need to Know

baby boomers (paragraph 1): People born between 1946 and 1964, when the record number of births was called a "baby boom."

generation gap (1): the distance (in attitudes, values, goals, etc.) between two generations

warping (2): twisting out of shape

preconceived (3): formed in advance

1   What troubled times the American teenager lives in! Ads for Nike shoes urge us to "Just do it!" while the White House tells us to "Just say no." The baby boomers have watched their babies grow into teens and history has repeated itself: the punk teens of the '80s have taken the place of the hippie teens of the '60s. Once again, the generation gap has widened and the adults have finally remembered to remember that teenagers are just no good. They have even coined a name for their persecution of adolescents: "teen-bashing."

2   If what is being printed in the newspapers, viewed on television and repeated by adults is correct, it is against all odds that I am able to write this article. Adults say the average teenager can't write complete sentences and has trouble spelling big words. Their surveys report that I can't find Canada on a map. According to their statistics, my favorite hobbies are sexual intercourse and recreational drug use. It's amazing that I've found time to write this; from what they say, my time is spent committing violent crimes or just hanging out with a gang. In fact, it is even more amazing that I'm here at all, when you consider that the music I listen to supposedly "warping" my mind and influencing me to commit suicide.

3   Nonetheless, here I am. I write this article to show that a teenager can survive in today's society. Actually, I'm doing quite well. I haven't fathered any children, I'm not addicted to any drugs, I've never worshiped Satan and I don't have a police record. I can even find Canada on a map along with its capital, Ottawa. I guess my family and friends have been supportive of me, for I've never been tempted to become one of those teenage runaways I'm always reading about. Call me a rebel, but I've stayed in school and (can it be true?!) I enjoy it. This month, I graduate from high school and join other graduates as the newest generation of adults. I'm looking forward to four years of college and becoming a

productive member of society. I may not be America's stereotypical teen, but that only proves there is something wrong with our society's preconceived image of today's teenager.

4   My only goal in writing this article is to point out the "bum rap" today's teenager faces. I feel the stereotypical teen is, in fact, a minority. The true majority are the teenagers who, day in and day out, prepare themselves for the future and work at becoming responsible adults. Our time is coming. Soon we will be the adults passing judgment on the teenagers of tomorrow. Hopefully, by then, we will have realized that support and encouragement have a far more positive effect on teenagers than does "bashing" them.

WRITING FROM READING: "Against All Odds, I'm Just Fine"

When you write on any of the topics below, be sure to work through the stages of the writing process in preparing your comparison or contrast paragraph.

1. Write a paragraph that contrasts society's image of any age group (teens, twenties, thirties, etc.) with the reality. As part of the thought lines stage of writing, interview one or more members of that age group. Before the interview, prepare a list of questions such as these:

   How does television depict your age group?
   What do others think is wrong with people in your age group?
   Are there stereotypes about how people in your age group dress, talk, and so on?

   Prepare at least eight questions before you begin the interview. At the interview, jot down answers, ask follow-up questions, and ask the person(s) being interviewed to review and add to your notes.

2. Contrast your first impression of someone with the way you feel about the person after knowing him or her longer.

3. Show the similarities between teens of today and teens of thirty years ago. If your instructor agrees, brainstorm for similarities with a partner or group.

4. Compare or contrast yourself with the kind of person you think is typical of your age group.

6

Classification

WHAT IS CLASSIFICATION?

When you **classify,** you divide something into different categories, and you do it according to some basis. For example, you may classify the people in your neighborhood into three types: those you know well, those you know slightly, and those you don't know at all. Although you may not be aware of it, you have chosen a basis for this classification. You are classifying the people in your neighborhood according to *how well you know them.*

Hints for Writing a Classification Paragraph

Hint

1. Divide your subject into three or more categories or types. If you are thinking about classifying VCRs, for instance, you might think about dividing them into cheap VCRs and expensive VCRs. Your basis for classification would be the price of VCRs. But you would need at least one more type—moderately priced VCRs. Using at least three types helps you to be reasonably complete in your classification.

2. Pick one basis for classification and use it. If you are classifying VCRs by price, you cannot divide them into cheap, expensive, and Japanese. Two of the categories relate to price, but "Japanese" does not. In the following examples, notice how one item does not fit its classification and has been crossed out:

fishermen

fishermen who fish every day
weekend fishermen
~~fishermen who own their own boats~~
(If you are classifying fishermen on the basis of how often they fish, "fishermen who own their own boats" does not fit.)

tests

essay tests
objective tests
~~math tests~~
combination essay and objective tests

Emphasize the difference between a category (or type) and an example (or details) within a category. Students may initially confuse the two until they see that a category is a larger concept than an example within a category.

TEACHING TIP:
Emphasize the difference between a category (or type) and an example (or details) within a category. Students may initially confuse the two until they see that a category is a larger concept than an example within a category.

140

(If you are classifying tests on the basis of the type of questions they ask, "math tests" does not fit, because it describes the subject being tested.)

3. Be creative in your classification. While it is easy to classify drivers according to their age, your paragraph will be more interesting if you choose another basis for comparison, such as how drivers react to a very slow driver in front of them.

4. Have a reason for your classification. You may be classifying to help a reader understand a topic or to help a reader choose something, or you may be trying to prove a point, to criticize, or to attack.

A classification paragraph must have a unifying reason behind it, and the details for each type should be as descriptive and specific as possible. Determining your audience and deciding why you are classifying can help you stay focused and make your paragraph more interesting.

Discussion Questions: Ask students how they would classify types of neighbors in their neighborhood on the basis of how *friendly* they are. (Possibilities: outgoing, cordial, and reserved.)

Exercise 1	**Finding a Basis for Classifying**

Practice

Write three bases for classifying each of the following topics. The first topic is done for you.

TEACHING TIP:
Before students begin the exercises, review the following key terms: classifying, category/type, basis for classifying, and examples/details within a category. Understanding these concepts' distinctions helps students organize more logically and specifically.

TEACHING TIP:
Remind students that each basis for classifying is a subject by itself; in this exercises there are no categories. This is an exercise in devising a possible focus for a paragraph. When you review basis possibilities, ask students which bases could be extended into categories.

Answers Will Vary.
Possible answers shown at right.

1. topic to classify: dogs
You can classify dogs on the basis of

a. How easy they are to train

b. Their size

c. How frisky they are

2. topic to classify: cars
You can classify cars on the basis of

a. Their price

b. Their size

c. How fast they can go

3. topic to classify: football players
You can classify football players on the basis of

a. How they treat fans

b. The position they play

c. How famous they are

4. topic to classify: music videos
You can classify music videos on the basis of

a. How violent they are

b. Who they appeal to

c. How old they are

Exercise 2 **Identifying What Does Not Fit the Classification**

Practice   In each list below, one item does not fit because it is not classified on the same basis as the others on the list. First, determine the basis for the classification. Then cross out the one item on each list that does not fit.

1. **topic:** parties

   basis for classification: *the occasion they celebrate*

   list: anniversary parties
   birthday parties
   ~~small parties~~
   retirement parties

2. **topic:** hair

   basis for classification: *color*

   list: black
   gray
   brown
   ~~straight~~

3. **topic:** jewelry

   basis for classification: *on what part of the body it is worn*

   list: earring
   ~~diamond~~
   necklace
   bracelet

4. **topic:** sleepers

   basis for classification: *what sleepers do in their sleep*

   list: ~~late sleepers~~
   people who snore
   people who toss and turn
   sleepers who talk in their sleep

5. **topic:** police

   basis for classification: *rank*

   list: captain
   detective
   ~~officer of the year~~
   sergeant

Exercise 3 **Finding Categories That Fit One Basis for Classification**

Practice   In the lines under each topic, write three categories that fit the basis of classification that is given. The first one is done for you.

1. **topic:** cartoons on television
   basis for classification: when they are shown
   categories:

   a. Saturday morning cartoons

   b. weekly cartoon series shown in the evening

   c. cartoons that are holiday specials

2. **topic:** desserts
   basis for classification: how fattening they are
   categories:

Answers Will Vary.
Possible answers
shown at right.

   a. low-fat desserts

   b. moderately fattening desserts

   c. very fattening desserts

3. **topic:** teenagers
   basis for classification: popularity with peers
   categories:

   a. popular with a few peers

   b. popular with many peers

   c. popular with all his/her peers

4. **topic:** toys
   basis for classification: price
   categories:

   a. cheap toys

   b. moderately priced toys

   c. expensive toys

5. **topic:** chicken
   basis for classification: how it is cooked
   categories:

   a. fried chicken

   b. baked chicken

   c. barbecued chicken

WRITING THE CLASSIFICATION PARAGRAPH IN STEPS
Thought Lines

Classification

Note: For classification activities, refer to the following: "Lines of Detail: A Walk-Through Assignment," p. 154; "Writing Your Own Classification Paragraph," pp. 154–55; and "Writing From Reading," pp. 157–59.

First, pick a topic for your classification. Next, choose some basis for your classification.

Brainstorming a Basis for Classification

Sometimes the easiest way to choose one basis is to brainstorm about different things related to your topic and see where your brainstorming leads you. For example, if you were to write a paragraph classifying phone calls, you could begin by listing anything about phone calls that occurs to you:

Phone Calls

sales calls at dinnertime	people who talk too long
short calls	calls I hate getting
calls in the middle of the night	wrong numbers
long distance calls	waiting for a call

The next step is to survey your list. See where it is leading you. The list on phone calls seems to have a few items about unpleasant phone calls:

sales calls at dinnertime
calls in the middle of the night
wrong numbers

Maybe you can label these "Calls I Do Not Want," and that will lead you toward a basis for classification. You might think about calls you do *not* want, and calls you *do* want. You think further and realize that you want or do not want certain calls because of their effect on you. You decide to use the effect of the calls on you as the basis for classification. Remember, however, that you need at least three categories. If you stick with this basis for classification, you can come up with three categories:

calls that please me
calls that irritate me
calls that frighten me

By brainstorming, you can then gather details about your three categories.

Added Details for Three Categories

calls that please me

from boyfriend

good friends

catch-up calls—someone I haven't talked to for a while

make me feel close

calls that irritate me

sales calls at dinnertime

wrong numbers

calls that interrupt

invade privacy

calls that frighten me

emergency call in the middle of the night

"let's break up" call from boyfriend

change my life, indicate some bad change

Matching the Points Within the Categories

As you begin thinking about details for each of your categories, try to write about the same points in each type. For instance, in the list on phone calls, each category includes some details about who made the call:

calls that please me—from good friends, my boyfriend

calls that irritate me—from salespeople, unknown callers

calls that frighten me—from the emergency room, my boyfriend

Each category also includes some details about why you react to them in a specific way:

calls that please me—make me feel close

calls that irritate me—invade my privacy

calls that frighten me—indicate some bad change

You achieve unity by covering the same points for each category.

Writing a Topic Sentence for a Classification Paragraph

The topic sentence for a classification paragraph should do two things:

1. It should mention what you are classifying.
2. It should indicate the basis for your classification by stating the basis or listing your categories, or both.

Consider the details on phone calls. To write a topic sentence about the details, you

1. Mention what you are classifying: phone calls.
2. Indicate the basis for classifying by (a) stating the basis ("their effect on me") or (b) listing the categories ("calls that please me," "calls that irritate me," and "calls that frighten me"). You may also state both the basis and the categories in the topic sentence.

Following these guidelines, you can write a topic sentence like this:

I can classify phone calls according to their effect on me.

or

Phone calls can be grouped into the ones that please me, the ones that irritate me, and the ones that frighten me.

Both of these topic sentences state what you're classifying and give some indication of the basis for the classification. Once you have a topic sentence, you are ready to begin the outlines stage of writing the classification paragraph.

Exercise 4   Creating Questions to Get Details for a Classification Paragraph

Do this exercise with a partner or group. Each list below includes a topic, the basis for classifying that topic, and three categories. For each list, think of three questions that you could ask to find more details about the types. The first list is done for you.

1. **topic:** moviegoers
   basis for classification: what they eat and drink during the movie
   categories: the traditional munchers, the healthy munchers, the really hungry munchers
   questions you can ask:

   a. What does each type eat and drink?

   b. What does each type look like?

   c. Does each group stock up on more supplies during the movie?

Answers Will Vary. Possible answers shown at right.

2. **topic:** sports fans at a game
   basis for classification: how much they like the sport
   categories: fanatics, ordinary fans, and bored observers
   questions you can ask:

   a. What does each type wear to the game?

   b. How long does each type stay at the game?

   c. What does each type say during the game?

3. **topic:** people at the dentist's office
   basis for classification: how nervous they are
   categories: the mildly anxious, the anxious, and the terrified
   questions you can ask:

   a. How does each type behave in the waiting room?

   b. How does each type sit in the dentist's chair?

   c. How does each type react to the sight of the dentist's drill?

4. **topic:** children at a preschool
   basis for classification: how they interact with others
   categories: shy, friendly, aggressive
   questions you can ask:

   a. How does each type handle toys?

   b. What tone of voice does each type use?

   c. Which type gets the most attention from the teacher?

5. **topic:** older female relatives
   basis for classification: how they greet you
   categories: those who shake hands, those who peck you on the cheek, those who hug you to death
   questions you can ask:

a. How is each type dressed? _____

b. What does each type say? _____

c. Which type do children like best? _____

Exercise 5	**Writing Topic Sentences for a Classification Paragraph**
Practice	

Review the topics, bases for classification, and categories in Exercise 4. Then, using that material, write a good topic sentence for each topic.

TEACHING TIP:

Group Work: This exercise can be done in groups to practice collaborative brainstorming and peer revision for precise wording of these topic sentences.

Answers Will Vary. Possible answers shown at right.

topic sentences

for topic 1: Moviegoers can be classified on the basis of what they eat and drink during the movie.

_____

for topic 2: Sports fans at a game can be grouped into fanatics, ordinary fans, and bored observers.

_____

for topic 3: People at a dentist's office can be categorized according to how nervous they are.

_____

for topic 4: At a pre-school, children can be grouped into shy, friendly, or aggressive categories.

_____

for topic 5: Older female relatives can be classified according to how they greet you.

_____

Outlines

Classification

Effective Order in Classifying

After you have a topic sentence and a list of details, you can create an outline. Think about which category you want to write about first, second, and so on. The order of your categories will depend on what you're writing about. If you're classifying ways to meet people, you can save the best one for last. If you're classifying three habits that are bad for your health, you can save the worst one for last.

If you list your categories in the topic sentence, list them in the same order you will use to explain them in the paragraph.

Following is an outline for a paragraph classifying phone calls. The details have been put into categories. The underlined sentences have been added to define each category clearly before the details are given.

An Outline for a Classification Paragraph

---

topic sentence: Phone calls can be grouped into the ones that please me, the ones that irritate me, and the ones that frighten me.

category 1 details
<u>There are some calls that please me.</u>
They make me feel close to someone.
I like calls from my boyfriend, especially when he calls just to say he is thinking of me.
I like to hear from good friends.
I like catch-up calls.
These are calls from people I haven't talked to in a while.

category 2 details
<u>There are some calls that irritate me.</u>
These calls invade my privacy.
Sales calls always come at dinnertime.
They offer me newspaper subscriptions or "free" vacations.
I get at least four wrong number calls each week.
All these calls irritate me, and I have to interrupt what I'm doing to answer them.

category 3 details
<u>There are some calls that frighten me.</u>
They are the calls that tell me about some bad change in my life.
I once got a call in the middle of the night.
It was from a hospital emergency room.
The nurse said my brother had been in an accident.
I once got a call from a boyfriend who said he wanted to break up.

You can use the following checklist to help you revise your own classification outline.

> **✔ Checklist**
>
> **A Checklist for Revising the Classification Outline**
>
> ✔ Do I have a consistent basis for classifying?
>
> ✔ Does my topic sentence mention what I am classifying and indicate the basis for classification?
>
> ✔ Do I have enough to say about each category in my classification?
>
> ✔ Are the categories presented in the most effective order?
>
> ✔ Am I using clear and specific details?

With a revised outline, you can begin writing your draft.

Exercise 6
Practice

Recognizing the Basis for Classification Within the Topic Sentence

The topic sentences below do not state a basis for classification, but you can recognize the basis nevertheless. After you have read each topic sentence, write the basis for classification on the lines provided. The first one is done for you.

1. **topic sentence:** Neighbors can be classified into complete strangers, acquaintances, and buddies.

   basis for classification: <u>how well you know them</u>

2. **topic sentence:** In the dog world, there are yipper-yappers, authoritative barkers, and boom-box barkers.

   basis for classification: <u>how they bark</u>

3. **topic sentence:** At the Thai restaurant, you can order three kinds of hot sauce: hot sauce for beginners, hot sauce for the adventurous, and hot sauce for fire eaters.

   basis for classification: <u>how hot the sauce is</u>

4. **topic sentence:** When it comes to photographs of yourself, there are three types: the ones that make you look good, the ones that make you look fat, and the ones that make you look ridiculous.

   basis for classification: <u>how they make you look</u>

5. **topic sentence:** Beer commercials on television can be grouped into the ones with pretty women, the ones with celebrities, and the ones with good buddies having good times.

   basis for classification: <u>the people they use to advertise</u>

Exercise 7
Practice

Adding Details to a Classification Outline

Do this exercise with a partner or group. In this outline, add details where the blank lines indicate. Match the points covered in the other categories.

topic sentence: My friends can be categorized as best friends, good friends, and casual friends.

Answers Will Vary. However, they must cover the following: **(1)** what good friends talk about, **(2)** what casual friends talk about, and **(3)** how long you have known casual friends. Possible answers shown at right.

details: I know my best friends so well they are like family.
I have two best friends.
We talk about everything, from our problems to our secret ambitions.
I have known my best friends for years.
I can spend time with my best friends any time, good or bad.
I am close to my good friends, but not that close.
I have about six good friends.

<u>We talk about school, work, family, weekend plans.</u>

I have known all my good friends for at least a year.
I like to be around good friends when I'm in a good mood and want to share it.

Casual friends are people I like but am not close to. I have about a dozen casual friends.

We talk about sports, the weather, or the news.

I have known my casual friends for weeks or months.

I like to be around casual friends when I am in a large crowd, so I feel less alone.

Rough Lines

Classification

You can transform your outline into a first draft of a paragraph by writing the topic sentence and the details in paragraph form. As you write, you can begin combining some of the short sentences, adding details, and inserting transitions.

Transitions in Classification

Various transitions can be used in a classification paragraph. The transitions you select will depend on what you are classifying and the basis you choose for classifying. For example, if you are classifying roses according to how pretty they are, you can use transitions like "one lovely kind of rose," "another, more beautiful kind," and "the most beautiful kind." In other classifications, you can use transitions like "the first type," "another type," or "the final type." In revising your classification paragraph, use the transitions that most clearly connect your ideas.

As you write your own paragraph, you may want to refer to a "kind" or a "type." For variety, try other words like "class," "group," "species," "form," or "version" if it is logical to do so.

After you have a draft of your paragraph, you can revise and review it. The following checklist may help you with your revisions.

✔ Checklist

A Checklist for Revising the Draft of a Classification Paragraph

✔ Does my topic sentence state what I am classifying?

✔ Does it indicate the basis of my classification?

✔ Should any of my sentences be combined?

✔ Do my transitions clearly connect my ideas?

✔ Should I add more details to any of the categories?

✔ Are the categories presented in the most effective order?

Below is a draft of the classification paragraph on phone calls with these changes from the outline on page 148:

- An introduction has been added, in front of the topic sentence, to make the paragraph smoother.
- Some sentences have been combined.
- Some details have been added.
- Transitions have been added.
- A final sentence has been added so that the paragraph makes a stronger point.

A Draft of a Classification Paragraph

```
     I get many phone calls, but they fit into three types. Phone
calls can be grouped into the ones that please me, the ones that
irritate me, and the ones that frighten me. There are some calls
that please me because they make me feel close to someone. I like
calls from my boyfriend, especially when he calls just to say he
is thinking of me. I like to hear from my good friends. I like
catch-up calls, the calls from people I have not talked to in a
while that fill me in on what friends have been doing. There are
also calls that irritate me because they invade my privacy. Sales
calls, offering me newspaper subscriptions and "free" vacations,
always come at dinnertime. In addition, I get at least four wrong
number calls each week. All these calls irritate me, and I have
to interrupt what I am doing to answer them. The more serious
calls are the ones that frighten me. They are the calls that tell
me about some bad change in my life. Once, in the middle of the
night, a call from a hospital emergency room told me my brother
had been in an accident. Another time, a boyfriend called to tell
me he wanted to break up. When I get bad news by phone, I real-
ize that the telephone can bring frightening calls as well as
friendly or irritating ones.
```

Exercise 8

Practice

Combining Sentences for a Better Classification Paragraph

Note: For more on combining short sentences, see Chapter 28 on sentence variety.

The paragraph below has some short sentences that would be more effective if they were combined. Combine each pair of underlined sentences into one sentence. Write the new sentence in the space above the old ones.

The first kind of junk mail

I categorize my junk mail according to how sneaky it is. <u>The first kind of junk mail</u>

isn't very sneaky at all because it looks like junk mail.

<u>is not very sneaky at all. It looks like junk mail.</u> This kind of mail is obviously out to

sell me something. It is a catalog or an envelope that has the name of the product right

This

there, so I can see what is for sale. A second type of junk mail is more deceptive. <u>This</u>

type comes in an envelope that tells me I am a big winner in a sweepstakes.

<u>type comes in an envelope. The envelope tells me I am a big winner in a sweepstakes.</u> I

am not sure what this letter is selling until I open the envelope. Last, and most sneaky,

Some junk mail now

is the mail disguised to look like something important. <u>Some junk mail now comes in</u>

comes in an envelope that says, "Important Tax Information."

<u>an envelope. The envelope says, "Important Tax Information."</u> It looks like an envelope

Other junk

from the Internal Revenue Service, but it is just another piece of junk mail. <u>Other junk</u>

mail is made to look like it contains a telegram or a check.

<u>mail is made to look like it contains a telegram. And some other sneaky junk mail is</u>

<u>made to look like it contains a check.</u> All these tricks have made me more suspicious

than ever about what comes in the mail.

Exercise 9
Practice

Identifying Transitions in a Classification Paragraph

Underline all the transitions in the paragraph below. The transitions may be words or groups of words.

I classify my jeans according to when and where I wear them. <u>At the bottom of the list</u> are the ragged, worn-out old jeans I wear around the house—and *only* around the house. I wouldn't want to be seen in public in such disgraceful clothes. These jeans have holes in them, and they are faded, ripped, and out of style. However, they are also comfortable and perfect for relaxing and for doing chores. <u>My mid-level jeans</u> are the ones I wear to school. These jeans are presentable, and they are a classic style. I have worn and washed them enough to soften them up, and they are perfect for long days of sitting at a desk or studying in the library. <u>Finally, the highest class of jeans</u> I have is my good jeans. I wear my good jeans to parties and clubs. They are stylish and new and carry the label of a trendy company. Yet I must admit they are a little stiff and tight. <u>When it comes to jeans,</u> I guess I have to give up comfort to have style.

Final Lines

Classification

Below is the final version of the classification paragraph on phone calls. Compare the draft of the paragraph on page 151 to the final version, and you will notice these changes:

- The first sentence has been rewritten so that it is less choppy, and a word of transition, "My," links the second sentence to the first.
- Some words have been eliminated and sentences rewritten so that they are not too wordy.
- The word choice has been refined: "bad change" has been replaced by "crisis," "someone" has been changed to "a person I care about" to make the detail more precise, and "irritate" has been changed to "annoy" to avoid repetition.

A Final Version of a Classification Paragraph
(Changes from the draft are underlined.)

TEACHING TIP:
Have several students read aloud different portions of this paragraph. If their assigned portion includes an underlined section, have them identify the type of editing change (i.e., transitional link, less wordy, more precise details, less repetition). They will need to cross reference this final version with the rough draft on p. 151.

```
    I get many phone calls, but most of them fall into one of
three types. My phone calls can be grouped into the ones that
please me, the ones that irritate me, and the ones that fright-
en me. There are some calls I want to receive because they make
me feel close to a person I care about. I like calls from my
boyfriend, especially when he calls just to say he is thinking
of me. I like to hear from my good friends. I like catch-up calls
from friends I have not talked to in a while. There are also
```

calls <u>I do not want</u> because they invade my privacy. Sales calls, offering me newspaper subscriptions and "free" vacations, always come at dinnertime. In addition, I get at least four wrong number calls each week. All these calls <u>annoy</u> me, and I have to interrupt what I am doing to answer them. The more serious calls are the ones that frighten me. They are the calls that tell me about some <u>crisis</u> in my life. <u>I once got a midnight call from a hospital emergency room, informing me my brother had been in an accident.</u> Another time, a boyfriend called to tell me he wanted to break up. When I get bad news by phone, I realize that the telephone can bring frightening calls as well as friendly or irritating ones.

Before you prepare the final version of your own classification paragraph, check your latest draft for errors in spelling and punctuation and for any errors made in typing or copying.

Exercise 10
Practice

Proofreading to Prepare the Final Version

Following is a classification paragraph with the kinds of errors that are easy to overlook when you prepare the final version of an assignment. Correct the errors, writing above the lines. There are twelve errors.

      experience   *there*
My experince in school has shown me their are three kinds of pencils, and they are
                                                           don't
the pencils that work great, the pencils that barely work, and the pencils that dont
                 pencils
work at all. The pencil's that work are the ones that are perfectly sharpened to a razor-

fine point and have huge, clean erasers at the end. These pencils produce a dark, clear
                                       . Unfortunately
line when I write with them unfortunatly, I never do write with them. Great pencils are
                       across   *I'm*
the ones I always come accross, all over the house, when i'm looking for something
                  write
else. The pencils I usually rite with are the damaged pencils. They work, but not well.

They need sharpening, or their erasers are worn so far down that using them leaves

rips across the page. Sometimes these pencils leave a faded, weak line on the paper.
                              looks
Sometimes the line is so thick it look like a crayon. The third kind of pencil is the

worst of all. Pencils in this group just don't work. They have no point. Or if they have a
                breaks
point, it brakes off as soon as I write. They have no eraser. The pencils are so chewed

and mutilated they might have been previously owned by woodpeckers. Nonworking
                                      don't
pencils are the ones I bring to class on test days. I just do'nt seem to have much luck

with pencils.

Lines of Detail: A Walk-Through Assignment

Write a paragraph that classifies bosses on the basis of how they treat their employees. To write the paragraph, follow these steps.

Step 1: List all the details you can remember about bosses you have worked for or known.

Step 2: Survey your list. Then list three categories of bosses, based on how they treat their employees.

Step 3: Now that you have three categories, study your list again, looking for matching points for all three categories. For example, all three categories could be described by this matching point: where the boss works.

Step 4: Write a topic sentence that (a) names what you are classifying and (b) states the basis for classification or names all three categories.

Step 5: Write an outline. Check that your outline defines each category, uses matching points for each category, and puts the categories in an effective order.

Step 6: Write a draft of the classification paragraph. Check the draft, revising it until it has specific details, smooth transitions, and effective word choice.

Step 7: Before you prepare the final copy of your paragraph, check your latest draft for any errors in punctuation, spelling, and word choice.

Writing Your Own Classification Paragraph

When you write on any of these topics, be sure to work through the stages of the writing process in preparing your classification paragraph.

1. Write a classification paragraph on any of the topics below. If your instructor agrees, brainstorm with a partner or a group to come up with (a) a basis for your classification, (b) categories related to the basis, and (c) points you can make to give details about each of the categories.

horror movies	cars	salespeople
romantic movies	football players	cats
children	fans at a concert	dogs
parents	fans at a sports event	fears
students	neighbors	weddings
teachers	restaurants	insects
drivers	dates	excuses
birthdays		

2. Adapt one of the the topics in question 1 by making your topic smaller. For example, you can classify Chinese restaurants instead of restaurants or classify sports cars instead of cars. Then write a classification paragraph that helps your reader make a choice about your topic.

3. Below are some topics. Each one already has a basis for classification. Write a classification paragraph on one of these choices. If your instructor agrees, work with a partner or group to brainstorm categories, matching points and details for the categories.

Classify

a. Exams on the basis of how difficult they are.
b. Weekends on the basis of how busy they are.
c. Valentines on the basis of how romantic they are.
d. Breakfasts on the basis of how healthy they are.
e. Skin divers (or some other recreational athletes) on the basis of how experienced they are.
f. Singers on the basis of the kind of audience they appeal to.
g. Parties on the basis of how much fun they are.
h. Television commercials on the basis of what time of day or night they are broadcast.
i. Radio stations on the basis of what kind of music they play.

Name: _____ Section: _____

Peer Review Form for Classification Paragraph

After you have written a draft of your classification paragraph, let a writing partner read it. When your partner has completed the form below, discuss his or her comments. Then repeat the same process for your partner's paragraph.

This paragraph classifies _____ (Write the topic.)

The basis for classification is according to _____

_____

The matching points are _____

_____

The part that could use more or better details is _____

_____

_____

I have questions about _____

I would like to see something added about _____

_____

I would like to take out the part about _____

_____

The part of this paragraph I like best is _____

_____

Additional comments: _____

_____

_____

_____

_____

_____

_____

Reviewer's Name: _____

WRITING FROM READING: Classification

Three Disciplines for Children
John Holt

John Holt is an educator and activist who believes our system of education needs a major overhaul. In this essay, he classifies the ways children learn from discipline, and he warns against overusing one kind of discipline.

Words You May Need to Know

disciplines (paragraph 1): the training effect of experience
impersonal (1): without personal or human connection
impartial (1): fair
indifferent (1): not biased, not prejudiced

wheedled (1): persuaded by flattery or coaxing
ritual (2): an established procedure, a ceremony
yield (3): give in to, submit
impotent (3): powerless

1   A child, in growing up, may meet and learn from three different kinds of disciplines. The first and most important is what we might call the Discipline of Nature or of Reality. When he is trying to do something real, if he does the wrong thing or doesn't do the right one, he doesn't get the result he wants. If he doesn't pile one block right on top of another, or tries to build on a slanting surface, his tower falls down. If he hits the wrong key, he hears the wrong note. If he doesn't hit the nail squarely on the head, it bends, and he has to pull it out and start with another. If he doesn't measure properly what he is trying to build, it won't open, close, fit, stand up, fly, float, whistle, or do whatever he wants it to do. If he closes his eyes when he swings, he doesn't hit the ball. A child meets this kind of discipline every time he tries to *do* something, which is why it is so important in school to give children more chances to do things, instead of just reading or listening to someone talk (or pretending to). This discipline is a great teacher. The learner never has to wait long for his answer; it usually comes quickly, often instantly. Also it is clear, and very often points toward the needed correction; from what happened he cannot only see what he did was wrong, but also why, and what he needs to do instead. Finally, and most important, the giver of the answer, call it Nature, is impersonal, impartial, and indifferent. She does not give opinions, or make judgments; she cannot be wheedled, bullied, or fooled; she does not get angry or disappointed; she does not praise or blame; she does not remember past failures or hold grudges; with her one always gets a fresh start, this time is the one that counts.

2   The next discipline we might call the Discipline of Culture, of Society, of What People Really Do. Man is a social, a cultural animal. Children sense around them this culture, this network of agreements, customs, habits, and rules binding the adults together. They want to understand it and be a part of it. They

watch very carefully what people around them are doing and want to do the same. They want to do right, unless they become convinced they can't do right. Thus children rarely misbehave seriously in church, but sit as quietly as they can. The example of all those grownups is contagious. Some mysterious ritual is going on, and children, who like rituals, want to be part of it. In the same way, the little children that I see at concerts or operas, though they may fidget a little, or perhaps take a nap now and then, rarely make any disturbance. With all those grownups sitting there, neither moving or talking, it is the most natural thing in the world to imitate them. Children who live among adults who are habitually courteous to each other, and to them, will soon learn to be courteous. Children who live surrounded by people who speak a certain way will speak that way, however much we may try to tell them that speaking that way is bad or wrong.

3   The third discipline is the one most people mean when they speak of discipline—the Discipline of Superior Force, of sergeant to private, of "you do what I tell you or I'll make you wish you had." There is bound to be some of this in a child's life. Living as we do surrounded by things that can hurt children, or that children can hurt, we cannot avoid it. We can't afford to let a small child find out from experience the danger of playing in a busy street, or of fooling with the pots on top of a stove, or of eating up the pills in the medicine cabinet. So, along with other precautions, we say to him, "Don't play in the street, or touch things on the stove, or go into the medicine cabinet, or I'll punish you." Between him and the danger too great for him to imagine we put a lesser danger, but one he can imagine and maybe therefore want to avoid. He can have no idea of what it would be like to be hit by a car, but he can imagine being shouted at, or spanked, or sent to his room. He avoids these substitutes for the greater danger until he can understand it and avoid it for its own sake. But we ought to use this discipline only when it is necessary to protect the life, health, safety, or well-being of people or other living creatures, or to prevent destruction of things that people care about. We ought not to assume too long, as we usually do, that a child cannot understand the real nature of the danger from which we want to protect him. The sooner he avoids the danger, not to escape our punishment, but as a matter of good sense, the better. He can learn that faster than we think. In Mexico, for example, where people drive their cars with a good deal of spirit, I saw many children no older than five or four walking unattended on the streets. They understood about cars, they knew what to do. A child whose life is full of the threat and fear of punishment is locked into babyhood. There is no way for him to grow up, to learn to take responsibility for his life and acts. Most important of all, we should not assume that having to yield to the threat of our superior force is good for the child's character. It is never good for anyone's character. To bow to superior force makes us feel impotent and cowardly for not having had the strength or courage to resist. Worse, it makes us resentful and vengeful. We can hardly wait to make someone pay for our humiliation, yield to us as we were once made to yield. No, if we cannot always avoid using the Discipline of Superior Force, we should at least use it as seldom as we can.

WRITING FROM READING: "Three Disciplines for Children"

When you write on any of the topics below, be sure to work through the stages of the writing process in preparing your classification paragraph.

1. John Holt writes a very clear classification with a clear purpose: he is trying to explain how children should learn. Write a one-paragraph summary of the article. In your summary, include his definitions of all three types of discipline, and state when they should be used.

2. Holt says that it is very important "in school to give children more chances to do things, instead of just reading or listening to someone talk." Write a paragraph classifying your elementary or high school classes according to how much they allowed you to do. In your paragraph include your opinion of each category.

   If your instructor agrees, begin this assignment with an interview. Ask a writing partner to interview you about your learning experiences, as a way of gathering ideas for this topic. Then interview your partner. Before any interviewing begins, write at least seven questions to ask your partner.

3. Holt says that children want to understand society and to be a part of it: "They watch very carefully what people around them are doing and want to do the same." Write a paragraph classifying children according to the behavior they have learned from their parents. If your instructor agrees, freewrite on this topic, and then share your freewriting with a writing partner or group, asking for reactions and further ideas.

4. Instead of classifying disciplines for children, write a paragraph classifying parents according to their attitudes toward their children.

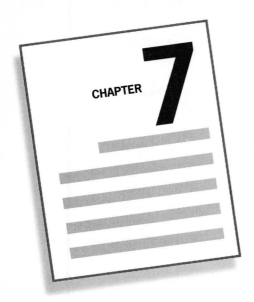

Definition

CHAPTER **7**

WHAT IS DEFINITION?

A **definition** paragraph is one that *explains what a term means to you.* You can begin thinking about what a term means by consulting the dictionary, but your paragraph will include much more than a dictionary definition. It will include a *personal* definition.

You can select several ways to explain the meaning of a term. You can give examples, you can tell a story, or you can contrast your term with another term. If you were writing a definition of perseverance, for example, you could do one or more of the following: you could give examples of people you know who have persevered, you could tell a story about someone who persevered, or you could contrast perseverence with another quality, like impatience. You could also write about times when perseverance is most needed or about the rewards of perseverance.

Hints for Writing a Definition Paragraph

1. Pick a word or phrase that has a personal meaning for you and that allows you room to develop your idea. Remember that you will be writing a full paragraph on this term. Therefore, a term that can be defined quickly, in only one way, is not a good choice. For example, you would not have much to say about terms like "cauliflower" or "dental floss" unless you had strong personal feelings about cauliflower or dental floss. If you didn't have such feelings, your paragraph would be very short.

When you think about a term to define, you might think about some personal quality you admire or dislike. If some quality provokes a strong reaction in you, you will probably have something to write about that term.

2. The topic sentence should have three parts. Include these items:

- the *term* you are defining
- the broad *class* or *category* into which your term fits
- the specific *distinguishing characteristics* that make the term different from all the others in the class or category

160

Each of the following topic sentences could be a topic sentence for a definition paragraph because it has the three parts.

    term   **category**   **distinguishing characteristics**
Resentment is the *feeling* that *life has been unfair.*

    term   **category**   **distinguishing characteristics**
A *clock-watcher* is a *worker* who *is just putting in time, not effort.*

3. Select an appropriate class or category when you write your topic sentence.

    not this: Resentment is a thing that makes you feel life has been unfair. (Resentment is a feeling or an attitude. Say so.)
    not this: Resentment is when you feel life has been unfair. ("When" is a word that refers to a time, like noon or 7:00 p.m. Resentment is a feeling, not a time.)
    not this: Resentment is where a person feels life has been unfair. ("Where" is a word that refers to a place, like a kitchen or a beach. Resentment is not a place; it is a feeling.)
    but this: Resentment is the feeling that life has been unfair.

4. Express your attitude toward the term you are defining in the "distinguishing characteristics" part of the topic sentence. Make that attitude clear and specific.

    not this: Resentment is the feeling that can be bad for a person. (Many feelings can be bad for a person. Hate, envy, anger, and impatience, for instance, can all be bad. What is special about resentment?)
    not this: Resentment is an attitude of resenting another person or a circumstance. (Do not define a word with another form of the word.)
    but this: Resentment is the feeling that life has been unfair.

5. Use specific and concrete examples to explain your definition. *Concrete* terms refer to things you can see, touch, taste, smell, or hear. Using concrete terms and specific examples will make your definition interesting and clear.

You may be asked to define an *abstract* idea like happiness. Even though an abstract idea cannot be seen, touched, tasted, smelled, or heard directly, you can give a personal definition of it by using concrete terms and specific examples:

    not this: Happiness takes place when you feel the joy of reaching a special goal. ("Joy" and "special goal" are abstract terms. Avoid defining one abstract term by using other abstract terms.)
    but this: I felt happiness when I saw my name at the top of the list of athletes picked for the team. Three months of daily six-hour practices had paid off, and I had achieved more than I had set out to do. (The abstract idea of happiness is linked to a specific, concrete idea of feeling happiness.)

If you remember to show, not tell, your reader what your term means, you'll have a better definition. Be especially careful not to define a term with another form of that term.

Exercise 1 **Recognizing Abstract and Concrete Words**

Practice

In the following list, put an *A* by the abstract words and a *C* by the concrete words.

1.	_A_ stubbornness	11.	_A_ mercy
2.	_C_ stowaway	12.	_C_ infant
3.	_A_ faith	13.	_A_ equality
4.	_A_ cruelty	14.	_C_ coin
5.	_C_ pencil	15.	_C_ crimson
6.	_A_ independence	16.	_A_ affection
7.	_C_ supermarket	17.	_C_ skyscraper
8.	_A_ apathy	18.	_C_ newspaper
9.	_A_ creativity	19.	_A_ thoughtfulness
10.	_A_ duty	20.	_A_ respect

Exercise 2
Practice

Completing a Topic Sentence for a Definition

Following are unfinished topic sentences for definition pargraphs. Finish each sentence so that it expresses a personal definition of the term and satisfies the three requirements for the topic sentence of a definition paragraph.

TEACHING TIP:
Remind students to refer to the three-part topic sentence format on p. 161 to reinforce the importance of precise wording in their writing. They should be particularly careful not to define a word or term with another form of the word or term.

Answers Will Vary.
Possible answers shown at right.

1. A blabbermouth is a friend who talks about his or her friends' secrets.

2. A road hog is a driver who takes up more than his or her share of the road.

3. A con artist is a salesperson who tricks and manipulates people into buying a product.

4. A best buddy is a friend who offers loyalty, support, and understanding in good and bad times.

5. The life of the party is the guest who openly enjoys the party and encourages other guests to enjoy it, too.

6. A role model is a person who serves as an example for others who share the same situation or goals.

7. A disciplinarian is an authority figure who establishes strict rules and enforces them.

8. A bargain hunter is a shopper who sees shopping as a challenge to find the best deal.

9. The black sheep in the family is the relative who <u>who has not met the</u>

   <u>family's standards of behavior.</u>

10. A brat is a child who <u>insists on having his or her own way.</u>

Exercise 3
Practice

Recognizing Problems in Topic Sentences for Definition Paragraphs

Review the three components that should be included in the topic sentence for a definition paragraph. Then read the topic sentences below, put an *X* next to each sentence that has a problem, and underline the part of the sentence that is faulty.

1. _____ Poise is an attitude of cool, calm control.

2. __X__ Generosity is the quality <u>of being generous</u> to others.

3. __X__ Spite is <u>when</u> people feel a mean desire to hurt others.

4. _____ Empathy is the ability to feel what someone else is feeling.

5. _____ Terror is a feeling of extreme fear.

6. __X__ An unreliable friend is a friend who cannot <u>be relied on.</u>

7. __X__ Obsession is <u>where</u> a person cannot stop thinking about some person or problem.

8. _____ Environmentalism is a movement to preserve the natural world.

9. __X__ Consideration is <u>when</u> you are concerned about the impact of your actions on the lives of others.

10. __X__ Cooperation is the ability to <u>cooperate</u> with other people.

Exercise 4
👥 *Collaborate*

Writing Examples for Definition Paragraphs

Below are incomplete statements from a definition paragraph. Complete them in the spaces below by writing specific examples. When you have completed the statements, share your work with a group. After each group member has read his or her examples aloud, discuss the examples. Which examples did you like best? Which are the clearest and most specific? Do some examples lead to a different definition of a term than other examples do? The first part of the exercise has been started for you.

Answers Will Vary.
Possible answers
shown at right.

1. I first saw greed in action when <u>I saw a four-year-old boy at the pre-</u>

   <u>school where I work. He scooped up all the toys around him. He snatched</u>

   <u>all the toy turtles a little three-year-old was playing with. The five-year-old</u>

   <u>didn't play with any of the toys. He just guarded them, grinning.</u>

Another example of greed was my experience with <u>a singing group. My</u> <u>friend and I sang backup for a popular recording artist. Whenever we did a</u> <u>live concert, we were allowed only one curtain call; then we had to go off-</u> <u>stage. The lead singer wanted all the applause to himself.</u>

2. The most hypocritical comment I ever heard was <u>my cousin's state-</u> <u>ment that people should always tell the truth. He was scolding my little</u> <u>nephew for telling a fib.</u>

It was hypocritical because <u>my cousin had just told a whopping lie to his</u> <u>girlfriend about where he had been last night. He had also been laughing</u> <u>about how trusting his girl was.</u>

A person in the news that I think is hypocritical is <u>the mayor of our city</u>

because he/she <u>said he was for law and order but is now on trial for</u> <u>taking bribes.</u>

3. The person who represents inner strength to me is <u>my sister</u>

because this person <u>lost her vision when she was sixteen years old but</u> <u>has never felt sorry for herself. Instead, she has even gone to college to</u> <u>study music.</u>

I was called on to show inner strength when <u>my friends urged me to try</u> <u>some bourbon they had stolen from their parents' house. I was only eleven</u> <u>at the time and wanted to fit in by drinking the stuff. But I stayed strong</u> <u>and refused the drink.</u>

4. A situation when a person must be tactful is <u>the breakup of a couple,</u> <u>when both partners are a person's good friends. A person should not take</u> <u>sides by letting one partner criticize the other.</u>

A time I saw tact in action was when <u>my aunt asked my uncle how he</u>

<u>liked her new haircut. He said it was a whole new look for her, which was a</u>

<u>very tactful remark since she looked hideous.</u>

_____

WRITING THE DEFINITION PARAGRAPH IN STEPS
Thought Lines

Definition

To pick a topic for your definition paragraph, begin with some personality trait or type of person. For instance, you might define "the insecure person." If you listed your first thoughts, you list might look like this:

> the insecure person
> someone who is not emotionally secure
> wants (needs?) other people to make him or her feel good
> no self-respect

Using Questions to Get Details

Often, when you look for ideas to define a term, you get stuck with big, general statements or abstract words, or you simply cannot come up with enough to say. If you are having trouble getting ideas, think of questions about your term. Jot these questions down, without stopping to answer them. One question can lead you to another question. Once you have five or more questions, you can answer them, and the answers will provide details for your definition paragraph.

If you were writing about "the insecure person," for example, you could begin with questions like these:

> What are insecure people like?
> What behavior shows a person is insecure?
> How do insecure people dress or talk?
> What makes a person insecure?
> Why is insecurity a bad trait?
> How do insecure people relate to others?
> Does insecurity hurt the insecure person? If so, how?
> Does the insecure person hurt others? If so, how?

By scanning the questions and answering as many as you can, you can add details to your list. Once you have a longer list, you can review it and begin to group the items on the list. Following is a list of grouped details on the insecure person.

Grouped Details on the Insecure Person

wants (needs?) other people to make him or her feel important

> no self-respect

insecure people have to brag about everything

> a friend who brags about his car

> they tell you the price of everything

they put others down

saying bad things about other people makes insecure people feel better

insecure people can never relax inside

can never enjoy being with other people

other people are always their competitors

must always worry about what others think of them

The Topic Sentence

Grouping the details can help you arrive at several main ideas. Can they be combined and revised to create a topic sentence? Following is a topic sentence on the insecure person that meets the requirements of naming the term, placing it in a category, and distinguishing the term from others in the category:

term   **category**   **distinguishing**

The *insecure person* is a *person* who *needs other people to*

characteristic
make him or her feel respected and important.

Once you have a topic sentence, you can begin working on the outlines stage of the paragraph.

Exercise 5
Practice

Designing Questions to Gather Details

Following are terms that could be defined in a paragraph. For each term, write five questions that could lead you to details for the definition. The first one has been done for you.

TEACHING TIP:
Group Work. This exercise works well as a small group activity.

1. **term:** arrogance
   questions:

   a. Do I know anyone who displays arrogance?

   b. Is there any celebrity I think is arrogant?

   c. What is an arrogant action?

   d. What kind of remark is an example of arrogance?

   e. Why are people arrogant?

Answers Will Vary.
Possible answers shown at right.

2. **term:** enthusiasm
   questions:

   a. Have I ever been enthusiastic?

   b. What made me feel enthusiastic?

   c. Who's the most enthusiastic person I know?

   d. Can a person have too much enthusiasm?

   e. Is enthusiasm contagious?

3. **term:** the conformist
   questions:

   a. Is it good to be a conformist? _____

   b. When is it better not to conform? _____

   c. Are there conformists in every age group? _____

   d. Is there one age group that is most conformist? _____

   e. Why does someone become a conformist? _____

4. **term:** common sense
   questions:

   a. Do I know anyone with no common sense? _____

   b. What's an example of common sense in action? _____

   c. How do you get common sense? _____

   d. Why is common sense so important? _____

   e. Do heroes always use common sense? _____

5. **term:** a leader
   questions:

   a. What traits do leaders share? _____

   b. Who is a leader in the news today? _____

   c. Are all leaders good people? _____

   d. Are all leaders born to lead? _____

   e. How do leaders get others to follow them? _____

Exercise 6   **Grouping Related Ideas for a Definition Paragraph**

Practice   Following is a list of ideas for a definition paragraph. Read the list several times; then group all the ideas on the list into one of the three categories below. Put the letter of the category next to each idea.

Categories

B how ambition can be **bad**
E an **example** of ambition in action
P the **positive** qualities of ambition and ambitious people

List

1. __B__ Too much ambition leads to obsession.

2. __P__ Ambitious people have established their goals.

3. __B__ Ambitious people can destroy whatever gets in their way.

4. __E__ I was determined to win a scholarship by scoring high on a national test.

5. __E__ I devised a plan to get my scholarship.

6. __E__ I studied many hours to prepare for the test.

7. __P__ Ambition can motivate people and help them organize their time.

8. __E__ Everyone thought my ambition was unrealistic, but I earned a scholarship.

9. __P__ Achieving an ambition takes discipline.

10. __B__ Ambitious people risk losing their enjoyment of daily life.

Outlines

Definition

To make an outline for a definition paragraph, start with the topic sentence and list the grouped details. Often a first outline does not have many examples or concrete, specific details. A good way to be sure you put specific details and concrete examples into your paragraph is to put some shortened version of them into your revised outline. If you compare the following outline to the grouped list of details on pages 165–66, you will see how specific details and concrete examples have been added.

An Outline for a Definition Paragraph

topic sentence:	The insecure person is a person who needs other people to make him or her feel respected and important.
details:	Insecure people have to brag about everything.
	An insecure friend may brag about his car.
added detail	Insecure people wear expensive jewelry and tell you what it costs.
added detail	They brag about their expensive clothes.
added detail	They make sure they wear clothes with trendy labels, another kind of bragging.
	Insecure people put others down.
	Saying bad things about others make insecure people feel better.
added example	When some friends were talking about Susan's great new job, Jill had to make mean remarks about Susan.
	Jill hated having Susan look like a winner.
	Insecure people can never relax inside.
	They can never enjoy being with other people.
	Other people are always their competitors.
added example	Luke can't enjoy any game of basketball unless he is the star.
	Insecure people must always worry about what others think of them.

When you prepare your own definition outline, use the following checklist to help you revise.

✔ Checklist

A Checklist for Revising a Definition Outline

✔ Does my topic sentence include a category and the characteristics that show how my term is different from others in the category?

✔ Have I defined my term so that it is different from any other term?

✔ Am I being concrete and specific in the details?

✔ Do I have enough examples?

✔ Do my examples relate to the topic sentence?

✔ Are my details in the most effective order?

With a revised outline, you are ready to begin writing a rough draft of your definition paragraph.

Exercise 7

Practice

Rewriting a Topic Sentence for a Definition Paragraph

Below is an outline in which the topic sentence does not make the same point as the rest of the outline. Rewrite the topic sentence so that it relates to the details.

Answers Will Vary.
Possible answer
shown at right.

topic sentence: Regret is a feeling of extreme pain.

details: When I was seventeen, I had a chance to go on a major class trip.
The same weekend was my brother's graduation from the police academy.
I chose to go on the class trip.
My brother never said anything, but he was hurt.
To this day, I regret my choice.
I regret many things.
I regret being the class clown instead of earning good grades.
My decision to break up with my girlfriend instead of working things out fills me with regret.
I am sorry I was always too busy to spend time with my grandmother when she asked me to come over.

Rewrite the topic sentence: _Regret is the feeling that a person has made_

the wrong choices.

Exercise 8

Practice

Revising an Example to Make It More Concrete and Specific

The following outline contains one example that is too abstract. In the lines provided, rewrite the example that is too abstract, using more specific, concrete details.

topic sentence: A true friend is a friend who puts the other person first.

details:

example 1	Rafael is such a good friend that he will lend me money he really needs himself.
	I once took his last twenty dollars because I needed to pay a parking ticket.
	Rafael, meanwhile, lived on peanut butter sandwiches for two days.
example 2	Carla is another friend who is always there for me whenever I need her.
	She is always ready to give her time generously.
	She does not think of what she could be doing instead of helping me.
example 3	Theo was the truest friend of all.
	He let me borrow his brand-new motorcyle when I desperately needed to get to school for a test.
	I know he was worried I would smash up his bike.
	Nevertheless, he handed me the keys without a whimper.
	I could see him looking worried as I rode off on the cycle he had worked so long to buy.

Answers Will Vary.
Possible answers shown at right.

Revised example: Once I had to move out of my apartment within forty-eight hours.

Carla came to my rescue; she packed boxes and moved furniture.

She even cleaned the apartment after it was empty.

She worked all night when she should have been sleeping.

Rough Lines

Definition

To write the first draft of your definition paragraph, you can rewrite the outline in paragraph form, combining some of the short sentences and adding more details. Remember that your purpose in this definition paragraph is to explain your *personal* understanding of a term. Therefore, you want to be sure that your topic sentence is clear and that your explanation connects your details to the topic sentence. A careful use of transitions will link your details to your topic sentence.

Transitions

Since you can define a term in many ways, you can also use many transitions. If you are listing several examples in your paragraph, you can use transitions like "first," "second," and "finally." If you are contrasting your term with another, you can use transitions like "on the other hand" or "in contrast." You may want to alert or remind the reader that you are writing a definition paragraph by using phrases like "can be defined as," "can be considered," "means that," or "implies that."

Because many definitions rely on examples, the transitions below are ones you may want to use.

Infobox

Transitions for a Definition Paragraph

A classic case of _____ is _____, another case, for example, for instance, in fact, in one case, in one instance, one time, another time, sometimes, specifically

---

The Draft

Following is a draft of the definition paragraph on the insecure person. When you read it, you'll notice several changes from the outline on page 168:

- Transitions have been added in several places. Some transitions let the reader know an example is coming, some transitions link one point about the topic to another point, and other transitions connect an example to the topic sentence.
- Examples have been made concrete and specific.
- The word choice has been improved.

TEACHING TIPS:
(1) Remind students not to include transitional words/phrases just to have them. Students too often think that the more transitions they use, the better. Stress that such links should be *logical* rather than forced. **(2)** Have students label each underlined change according to the type of change it represents (Refer to above list of changes.)

A Draft of a Definition Paragraph (Transitions are underlined.)

The insecure person is a person who needs other people to make him or her feel respected and important. The insecure person loves to brag about everything. <u>For instance,</u> a friend may brag about his car. He tells everyone he meets that he drives a Corvette. An insecure person tells you the price of everything. He wears expensive jewelry and tells you what it costs, <u>like</u> the person who always flashes a Rolex watch. <u>Another</u> insecure person will brag about her expensive clothes or make sure she always wears clothes with trendy labels, <u>another kind</u> of bragging. <u>Bragging is not the only way an insecure person tries to look good;</u> he or she may put other people down. Saying bad things about other people can put the insecure person on top. <u>For instance,</u> some friends were recently talking about another friend, Susan, who had just started a great new job. Jill had to add some mean remarks about how lucky Susan had been to get the job since Susan really was not qualified for it. Jill hated having Susan look like a winner. The insecure person can hurt others <u>but also</u> suffers inside. <u>Such a person</u> can never relax because he or she always sees other people as competitors. <u>An example of this attitude</u> is seen in Luke, a college acquaintance who always plays pickup basketball games. Even though the games are just for fun, Luke does not enjoy any game unless he is the star. Luke is a typically insecure person, for he must always worry about what others think of him.

The following checklist may help you revise the draft of your own definition paragraph.

> **✔ Checklist**
>
> ### A Checklist for Revising the Draft of a Definition Paragraph
>
> ✔ Is my topic sentence clear?
>
> ✔ Have I written enough to define my term clearly?
>
> ✔ Is my definition interesting?
>
> ✔ Could it use another example?
>
> ✔ Could it use more details?
>
> ✔ Do I need to combine any sentences?
>
> ✔ Do I need any words, phrase, or sentences to link the examples or details to the topic sentence?
>
> ✔ Do I need any words, phrase, or sentences to reinforce the topic sentence?

Exercise 9
Practice

Adding Examples to a Draft of a Definition Paragraph

Two of the following paragraphs need examples with concrete, specific details to explain their points. Fill in the blank lines with examples of concrete, specific details. Each example should be at least two sentences long. The first paragraph is done for you.

1. Listlessness is the feeling that nothing is worth starting. After a hectic week, I often wake up on Saturday morning feeling listless. I just do not have the energy to do the things I intended to do. I may have planned to wash my car, for example, but I cannot bring myself to get going. I cannot put together the bucket, detergent, brushes, and window cleaner I need to start the process. I tell myself, "Why wash the car? It will probably rain anyway." Another time I feel listless is when I am faced with a big assignment. For instance, I hate to start a term paper because there is so much to do. I have to think of a topic, do research, read, take notes, plan, write, and revise. When I am faced with so many things to do, I don't do anything. I tell myself it is not worth starting because I will probably get a bad grade on the paper anyway. I put off getting started. I let listlessness get the better of me.

2. Nosy people are people who think they have a right to invade the private lives of others. Nosy people do not hesitate to ask personal questions. Recently I bought a new car. I was very proud of my car and wanted to show it to my friends, so I drove it to campus. Several of my friends were in the parking lot, and they all admired

TEACHING TIP:
After students work on developing specific details, call on them to read their entries. Discuss whether they think they have been as specific as possible. Classmates can suggest other possible details. Stress the difference between concrete and abstract words.

Answers Will Vary.
Possible answers shown at right.

the car's engine and style. However, one person was nosy enough to ask how much I had paid for the car. People who are nosy also spy on their friends or neighbors. One of my neighbors watches me from behind his window curtains every time I go outside. I have even caught him flipping through the letters in my mailbox. He said he was returning a letter that had been put in the wrong box, but I think he was spying. At work, nosy people also invade their co-workers' privacy. One of the women at the store where I work listens to all my private calls. If I have to leave early, she wants to know why. Nosy people must not like their own lives. Instead, they are fascinated by the lives of other people.

3. "Senioritis" is a disease that afflicts high school students in the last year of high school; its symptoms are restlessness, laziness, and craziness. Students with senioritis have had enough of high school. They are thinking about life after graduation, and so they cannot think about high school any more. Consequently, they are restless in school. They fidget at their desks and daydream about the freedom of leaving high school forever. They look out the window or stare at the clock. Some of them sing songs under their breath or tap the fingers on their desks, repeating the beat of a song. Seniors suffering from senioritis just do not want to do any more schoolwork. They are lazy. Many seniors skip school, and some skip so often that they wind up in summer school. Others just give up on turning in assignments or studying for tests. If they are asked a question about the homework, they just stare. Senioritis makes people crazy as well as lazy. Senior year is the time when students try all kinds of pranks and stunts. Some put toilet paper all over a friend's car, and others come to school dressed as their favorite cartoon characters. Some even spread rumors of an "official" Senior Skip Day when all seniors are expected to stay away from school. Years after high school, people say, "I can't believe I did such silly things! I must have had senioritis."

Exercise 10
Practice

Identifying the Words That Need Revision in a Definition Paragraph

The following paragraph has too many vague, abstract words. Underline the words that you think should be replaced with more specific or concrete words or examples.

Answers Will Vary.
Possible answers shown at right.

Resourcefulness is the ability to come up with <u>whatever is needed</u>. My mother is the most resourceful person I know. <u>Under all circumstances,</u> she has <u>things at hand</u> to <u>do the job</u>. Resourcefulness is needed <u>at unexpected moments</u>. Therefore, to be resourceful a person must be organized. A person must also be able to plan so that he or she can keep <u>things under control in all situations</u>. The person we admire most is the one who is carrying an umbrella when it suddenly begins to rain, or the one who remembered to bring spare flashlight batteries on the camping trip. Such people think ahead because they are blessed with resourcefulness.

Exercise 11
Practice

Combining Sentences in a Definition Paragraph

The following definition paragraph has some short, choppy sentences that could be combined. These pairs or clusters of sentences are underlined. Combine each pair or cluster into one smooth sentence, and write the new sentence in the lines above the old ones.

Note: For more sentence combining practice, see Chapter 25 on sentence variety.

Answers Will Vary.
Possible answers shown at right.

A green thumb is a gift for making plants thrive. *My father, who owns a plant* <u>My father owns a plant nursery.</u>
nursery has a green thumb.
<u>He has a green thumb.</u> I have seen my father take the most dried-out, rocky, bare soil
Once he received a shipment of ragged, spindly
and grow amazing flowers in it. <u>Once he received a shipment of chrysanthemums. The</u>
chrysanthemums.
<u>chrysanthemums all looked ragged. They looked spindly.</u> With loving care, my father

nursed those chrysanthemums back to health. His love for plants is a big part of his
If a plant
gift, but another part of his green thumb is my father's knowledge of botany. <u>A plant</u>
is diseased, my father knows what to use to treat it.
<u>may have a disease. My father knows what to use to treat the disease.</u> He can identify
He is constantly reading books and magazines
almost any kind of shrub or tree. <u>He is constantly reading books. They are books about</u>
about plants and gardening.
<u>plants and gardening. He is constantly reading magazines. They are magazines about</u>

<u>gardening and plants.</u> My father knows and loves the plants he works with, and he

brings life to everything he touches with his green thumb.

Final Lines

Definition

Before you prepare the final version of your definition paragraph, check your latest draft to see if it needs a few changes. You may want to check for good transitions, appropriate word choice, and effective details. If you compare the draft on page 171 to the following final version of the paragraph on the insecure person, you will see a few more revisions:

- The wording has been improved so that it is more precise.
- Transitions have been added to reinforce the topic sentence.
- The word "you" has been taken out so that the paragraph is consistent in person.

A Final Version of a Definition Paragraph
(Changes from the draft are underlined.)

    The insecure person is a person who needs other people to make him or her feel respected and important. <u>To get respect</u>, the insecure person loves to brag about everything. For instance, a friend may brag about his car. He tells everyone he meets that he drives a Corvette. An insecure person tells <u>people</u> the price of everything. He wears expensive jewelry and tells <u>people</u> what it costs, like the person who always flashes a Rolex watch. Another insecure person will brag about her expensive clothes or make sure she wears clothes with trendy labels, another kind of bragging. Bragging is not the only way an insecure person tries to look good; he or she may also <u>criticize</u> other people. <u>Criticizing</u> others can put the insecure person on top. For instance, some friends were recently talking about another friend, Susan, who had just started a great new job. Jill had to add some mean remarks about how lucky Susan had been to get the job since Susan really was not qualified for it. Jill hated having Susan look like a winner. The insecure person <u>like Jill</u> can hurt others but also suffers inside. Such a person can never relax because he or she always sees other people as competitors. An example of this attitude can be seen in Luke, a college acquaintance who always plays pickup basketball games. Even though the games are just for fun, Luke does not enjoy any game unless he is the star. Luke is a typically insecure person, for he must always worry about what others think of him.

As you prepare the final version of your definition paragraph, check your latest draft for any errors in spelling and any errors made in typing or copying.

Exercise 12
Practice

Correcting Errors in the Final Version of a Definition Paragraph

Below is a definition paragraph with the kinds of errors that are easy to overlook in a final version. Correct the errors by writing above the lines. There are fourteen errors.

    Nerve is a talent for pushing forward when most people would stay back. We've all
exclaimed,
exclamed "That really takes nerve!" when somebody has cut us off on the road or cut
        Nervy   have
ahead of us in line. Nervey people has an ability to do what most people would not
      . T   victims
think of doing they can be selfish, rude, or inconsiderate right in front of their victim's.

For example, a nervy person can walk right by an older lady and takes^(take) the last seat on the buss^(bus.) A nervy person can reach right out and grab the last sale-priced sweater in the store, right out of another custumers^(customer's) hands. nervy^(Nervy) people seem to be blind to the rights of others. And why shouldn't they be? After all, the only person they think about is the one they see in the mirror every morning.

Lines of Detail: A Walk-Through Assignment

Write a paragraph that gives a personal definition of a secure person. To write the paragraph, follow these steps:

Step 1: List all your ideas about a secure person.

Step 2: Write at least five questions that can add details about a secure person. Answer the questions as a way of adding details to your list.

Step 3: Group your details; then survey your groups.

Step 4: Write a topic sentence that includes the term you are defining, puts the term into a category, and distinguishes the term from others in the category.

Step 5: Write an outline. Begin by writing the topic sentence and the groups of details. Then add more details and specific examples.

Step 6: Write a draft of your paragraph. To revise, check that you have enough examples, that your examples fit your definition, and that the examples are in an effective order. Combine any choppy sentences, and add transitions.

Step 7: Before you prepare the final version of your definition paragraph, check the punctuation, word choice, transitions, and grammar of your latest draft.

Writing Your Own Definition Paragraph

When you write on any of these topics, be sure to work through the stages of the writing process in preparing your definition paragraph.

1. Define an abstract term using concrete, specific details. Choose from the following list. You can begin by looking up the term in a dictionary to be sure you understand the meaning. Then write a personal definition.

   You can begin by freewriting. If your instructor agrees, you can read your freewriting to a group for reactions and suggestions. If you prefer, you can begin by brainstorming a list of questions to help you define the term. Again, if your instructor agrees, you can work with a group to develop brainstorming questions. Here is the list of abstract terms:

loyalty	generosity	fun
charm	style	patience
boredom	charisma	persistence
rudeness	consideration	impulsiveness

ambition	selfishness	jealousy
suspicion	fear	loneliness
failure	shame	irritation
anger	self-deception	self-discipline
initiative	bliss	prejudice

2. Write a definition of a type of person. Develop your personal definition with specific, concrete details. You can choose one of the following types or choose your own type.

   Freewriting on the topic is one way to begin. If your instructor agrees, you can read your freewriting to a group for reactions and suggestions. You can also begin by brainstorming a list of questions to help you define your term. If your instructor agrees, you can work with a group to develop brainstorming questions. Here is the list of types of people:

the procrastinator	the bully	the daredevil
the braggart	the bodybuilder	the jock
the chocaholic	the neatness fanatic	the apologizer
the organizer	the fitness fanatic	the joker
the inventor	the manipulator	the dreamer
the worrywart	the whiner	the buddy
the workaholic	the reliable friend	the fan
the compulsive liar	the Mr./Ms. Fixit	the achiever

3. Think of one word that best defines you. In a paragraph, define that word, using yourself as a source of examples and details. To begin, you may want to freewrite about several words that define you; then you can select the most appropriate one.

Name: _____ **Section:** _____

Peer Review Form for a Definition Paragraph

After you have written a draft of your definition paragraph, let a writing partner read it. When your partner has completed the form below, discuss the comments. Then repeat the same process for your partner's paragraph.

In the topic sentence, the term being defined is placed in this category or class: _____

_____

In the topic sentence, the characteristic(s) that make(s) the term different from others in its

class or category is/are _____

_____

_____

The most enjoyable or interesting part of this definition starts with the words _____

_____

The part that could use a clear example more details starts with the words _____

_____

I have questions about _____

I would like to take out the part about _____

_____

_____

_____

Other comments: _____

_____

_____

_____

_____

_____

_____

_____

Reviewer's Name: _____

WRITING FROM READING: Definition

Breaking the Bonds of Hate
Virak Khiev

Khiev, who immigrated to the United States at age ten, wrote this essay when he was a nineteen-year-old senior at the Blake School in Minneapolis, Minnesota. As you read his essay, you will notice how he defines the American Dream and two kinds of war.

Words You May Need to Know

carrion (paragraph 4): dead flesh
stereotype (5): an established image of someone or something, believed in by many people
unscrupulous (5): without a conscience
mentality (6): attitude, way of thinking

adversaries (7): enemies
immortalized (9): given the ability to live forever
"the melting pot" (10): an image of America in which all the races and ethnic groups blend in harmony
mind-set (10): attitude

1   Ever since I can remember, I wanted the ideal life: a big house, lots of money, cars. I wanted to find the perfect happiness that so many people have longed for. I wanted more than life in the jungle of Cambodia. America was the place, the land of tall skyscrapers, televisions, cars and airplanes.

2   In the jungles of Cambodia, I lived in a refugee camp. We didn't have good sanitation or modern conveniences. For example, there were no inside bathrooms—only ones made from palm-tree leaves, surrounded by millions of flies. When walking down the street, I could smell the aroma of the outhouse; in the afternoon, the five- and six-year-olds played with the dirt in front of it. It was the only thing thay had to play with, and the "fragrance" never seemed to bother them. And it never bothered me. Because I smelled it every day, I was used to it.

3   The only thing that bothered me was the war. I have spent half of my life in war. The killing is still implanted in my mind. I hate Cambodia. When I came to America nine years ago at the age of ten, I thought I was being born into a new life. No more being hungry, no more fighting, no more killing. I thought I had escaped the war.

4   In America, there are more kinds of material things than Cambodians could ever want. And here we don't have to live in the jungle like monkeys, we don't have to hide from mortar bombing and we don't have to smell the rotten human carrion. But for the immigrant, America presents a different type of jungle, a different type of war and a smell as bad as the waste of Cambodia.

5   Most Americans believe the stereotype that immigrants work hard, get a good education and have a very good life. Maybe it used to be like that, but not anymore. You have to be deceptive and unscrupulous in order to make it. If you

are not, then you will end up like most immigrants I've known: living in the ghetto in a cockroach-infested house, working on the assembly line or in the chicken factory to support your family, getting up at three o'clock in the morning to take the bus to work and not getting home until 5:00 p.m.

6   If you're a kid my age, you drop out of school to work because your parents don't have enough money to buy you clothes for school. You may end up selling drugs because you want cars, money and parties, as all teenagers do. You have to depend on your peers for emotional support because your parents are too busy working in the factory trying to make money to pay the bills. You don't get along with your parents because they have a different mentality: you are an American, and they are Cambodian. You hate them because they are never there for you, so you join a gang as I did.

7   You spend your time drinking, doing drugs and fighting. You beat up people for pleasure. You don't care about anything except your drugs, your beers and your revenge against adversaries. You shoot at people because they've insulted your pride. You shoot at the police because they are always bothering you. They shoot back, and then you're dead like my best friend Sinerth.

8   Sinerth robbed a gas station. He was shot in the head by the police. I'd known him since the sixth grade from my first school in Minneapolis. I can still remember his voice calling me from California. "Virak, come down here, man," he said. "We need you. There are lots of pretty girls down here." I promised him that I would be there to see him. The following year he was dead. I felt sorry for him. But as I thought it over, maybe it is better for him to be dead than to continue with the cycle of violence, to live with hate. I thought, "It is better to die than live like an angry young fool, thinking that everybody is out to get you."

9   When I was like Sinerth, I didn't care about dying. I thought that I was on top of the world, being immortalized by drugs. I could see that my future would be spent working on the assembly line like most of my friends, spending all my paycheck on the weekend and being broke again on Monday morning. I hated going to school because I couldn't see a way to get out of the endless cycle. My philosophy was "Live hard and die young."

10   I hated America because, to me, it was not the place of opportunities or the land of "the melting pot," as I had been told. All I had seen were broken beer bottles on the street and homeless people and drunks using the sky as their roof. I couldn't walk down the street without someone yelling out, "You gook" from his car. Once again I was caught in the web of hatred. I'd become a mad dog with the mind-set of the past: "When trapped in the corner, just bite." The war mentality of Cambodia came back: get what you can and leave. I thought I came to America to escape war, poverty, fighting, to escape the violence, but I wasn't escaping; I was being introduced to a newer version of war—the war of hatred.

11   I was lucky. In Minneapolis, I dropped out of school in the ninth grade to join a gang. Then I moved to Louisiana, where I continued my life of "immortality" as a member of another gang. It came to an abrupt halt when I crashed a car.

I wasn't badly injured but I was underage, and the fine took all my money. I called a good friend of the Cambodian community in Minneapolis for advice (she'd tried to help me earlier). I didn't know where to go or whom to turn to. I saw friends landing in jail, and I didn't want that. She promised to help me get back in school. And she did.

12   Since then I've been given a lot of encouragement and caring by American friends and teachers who've helped me turn my life around. They opened my eyes to a kind of education that frees us all from ignorance and slavery. I could have failed so many times except for those people who believed in me and gave me another chance. Individuals who were willing to help me have taught me that I can help myself. I'm now a twelfth grader and have been at my school for three years; I plan to attend college in the fall. I am struggling to believe I can reach the other side of the mountain.

WRITING FROM READING: "Breaking the Bonds of Hate"

When you write on any of these topics, be sure to work through the stages of the writing process in preparing your paragraph.

1. In a paragraph, trace the turning points in Virak Khiev's life. Consider all the changes in his life and whether they made his life better or worse.

2. Khiev defines "the bonds of hate," a hate that kept him from achieving a good life. He says that he was a prisoner of his hatred for the country that denied him what he hoped for and of his hatred for his parents. He hated the endless cycle of poverty and struggle he found in the ghetto.
   Write your own paragraph defining the bonds of hate. That is, write a personal definition of the kind of hatred that can keep a person in chains.

3. By explaining what a gang does and why he joined one, Khiev defines the term "gang." Write your own definition of a gang.

4. Write a paragraph that gives your personal definition of the American Dream. Use examples from your life or the lives of people you know.

5. Khiev says, "For the immigrant, America presents a different type of jungle, a different type of war and a smell as bad as the waste of Cambodia."
   Write a paragraph defining "the immigrant's experience of America." Define the term using the experiences of one or more immigrants as examples. Your definition does not have to be similar to Khiev's. If you are an immigrant to America, you can use your own experiences as examples. If you are not an immigrant, interview one or more immigrants, taking notes and/or taping the interviews to gather details. Your classmates or teachers may include people to interview. Before you interview, write at least six questions to ask.

6. Khiev defines the luck in his life as the help of other people, particularly one woman who was a friend to the Cambodian community. In a paragraph, define the luck in your life.

8

Cause and Effect

WHAT IS CAUSE AND EFFECT?

Almost every day, you consider the causes or effects of events so that you can make choices and take action. In writing a paragraph, when you explain the **reasons** for something, you are writing about **causes.** When you write about the **results** of something, you are writing about **effects.** Often in writing, you consider both the causes and effects of a decision, an event, a change in your life, or change in society, but in this chapter, you will be asked to *concentrate on either causes (reasons) or effects (results).*

Hints for Writing a Cause or Effect Paragraph

1. Pick a topic you can handle in one paragraph. A topic you can handle in one paragraph is one that (a) is not too big and (b) doesn't require research.

Some topics are so large that you probably can't cover them in one-paragraph. Topics that are too big include ones like

Why People Get Angry
Effects of Unemployment on My Family

Other topics require you to research the facts and to include the opinions of experts. They would be good topics for a research paper but not for a one-paragraph assignment. Topics that require research include ones like

The Causes of Divorce
The Effects of Television Viewing on Children

When you write a cause or effect topic, choose a topic you can write about by using what you already know. That is, make your topic smaller and more personal. Topics that use what you already know are ones like

Why Children Love Video Games
The Causes of My Divorce
What Enlistment in the Navy Did for My Brother
How Alcoholics Anonymous Changed My Life

2. Try to have at least three causes or effects in your paragraph. Be sure you consider immediate and remote causes or immediate and remote effects. Think about your topic and gather as many causes or effects as you can *before* you start drafting your paragraph.

An event usually has more than one cause. Think beyond the obvious, the **immediate cause,** to more **remote causes.** For example, the immediate cause of your car accident might be the other driver who hit the rear end of your car. But more remote causes might include the weather conditions or the condition of the road.

Situations can have more than one result, too. If you take Algebra I for the second time and you pass the course with a C, an **immediate result** is that you fulfill the requirements for graduation. But there may be other, more **remote results.** Your success in Algebra I may help change your attitude toward math courses, build your confidence in your ability to handle college work, or lead you to sign up for another course taught by the same teacher.

3. Make your causes and effects clear and specific. If you are writing about why short haircuts are popular, don't write "Short haircuts are popular because everybody is getting one" or "Short haircuts are popular because they are a trend." If you write either of those statements, you have really said, "Short haircuts are popular because they are popular."

Think further. Have any celebrities been seen with this haircut? Write the names of actors, athletes, or musicians who have the haircut, or find out the name of the movie and the actor who started the trend. By giving specific details that explain, illustrate, or describe a cause or effect, you help the reader understand your point.

4. Write a topic sentence that indicates whether your paragraph is about causes or effects. You should not announce, but you can *indicate*.

> **not this:** The effects of my winning the scholarship are going to be discussed. (an announcement)
> **but this:** Winning the scholarship changed my plans for college. (indicates effects will be discussed)

You can *list* a short version of all your causes or effects in your topic sentence, like this:

> Frozen yogurt's popularity has forced ice cream makers to change their products, driven ice cream parlors out of business, and created a whole new line of products.

You can just *hint* at your points by summarizing them, like this:

> Frozen yogurt's popularity has challenged and even threatened its competition but has also created new business opportunities.

Or you can use words that *signal* causes or effects:

> **words that signal causes:** reasons, why, because, motives, intentions
> **words that signal effects:** results, impact, consequences, changed, threatened, improved

---

TEACHING TIP:

If students have trouble grasping the concept of "remote," ask them to list the immediate benefits of taking a CPR class (or similar safety class) and then list the long-range benefits. Some of your students, especially if they are training to be health professionals, paramedics, or firefighters, will be well aware of the positive effects of taking such a class.

Exercise 1 Selecting a Suitable Topic for a Cause or Effect Paragraph

Practice

Following is a list of topics. Some are suitable for a cause or effect paragraph. Some are too large to handle in one paragraph, some would require research, and some are both too large and would require research. Put an *X* next to any topic that is not suitable.

1. ____ Why My Son Needed a Mentor

2. __X__ Effects of Smoking Cigarettes

3. ____ Reasons I Attend College Part Time

4. __X__ The Impact of Computers on Education

5. __X__ The Causes of Drug Abuse

6. __X__ The Effects of AIDS on Our Society

7. ____ How Magic Johnson Changed My Perception of AIDS

8. __X__ Why Marriages Fail

9. __X__ The Causes of Anorexia

10. __X__ The Impact of Television on American Family Life

Exercise 2 **Recognizing Cause and Effect in Topic Sentences**

Practice

In the list below, if the topic sentence is for a cause paragraph, put a *C* next to it. If the sentence is for an effect paragraph, put an *E* next to it.

1. __E__ Adopting a stray dog had startling consequences for my family.

2. __C__ I decided to pierce my ears out of a desire to look different, to do something exciting, and to shock my parents.

3. __C__ Jack has several motives for proposing marriage.

4. __E__ Until I actually owned one, I never knew how a computer could change a person's work habits.

5. __E__ The television's remote control device has created conflicts in my marriage.

6. __C__ Children enjoy horror movies because the movies allow them to deal with their fears in a nonthreatening way.

7. __C__ People buy clothes with designer labels to impress others, to feel successful, and to feel accepted into a higher social class.

8. __E__ The birth of my little sister had an unexpected impact on my life.

9. __C__ I am beginning to understand why my mother was a strict disciplinarian.

10. __E__ Videocasette recorders have changed the movie industry.

WRITING THE CAUSE OR EFFECT PARAGRAPH IN STEPS

Thought Lines

Cause or Effect

Once you've picked a topic, the next—and very important—step is getting ideas. Because this paragraph will contain only causes *or* effects and details about them, you must be sure you have enough causes or effects to write a developed paragraph.

Freewriting on a Topic

One way to get ideas is to freewrite on your topic. Since causes and effects are so clearly connected, you can begin by freewriting about both and then choose one—causes or effects—later.

If you were thinking about writing a cause or effect paragraph on owning a car, you could begin by freewriting something like this:

Freewriting on Owning a Car

A car of my own. Why? I needed it. Couldn't get a part-time job without one. Because I couldn't get to work. Needed it to get to school. Of course I could have taken the bus to school. But I didn't want to. Feel like a grown-up when you have a car of your own. Freedom to come and go. I was the last of my friends to have a car. Couldn't wait. An old Camaro. But I fixed it up nicely. Costs a lot to maintain. Car payments, car loan. Car insurance.

Now you can review the freewriting and make separate lists of causes and effects you wrote down:

causes (reasons)

needed to get a part-time job
needed to get to school
my friends had cars

effects (results)

feel like a grown-up
freedom to come and go
costs a lot to maintain
car payments
car loan
car insurance

Because you have more details on the effects of owning a car, you decide to write an effects paragraph.

Your list of effects can be used several ways. You can add to it if you think of ideas as you are reviewing your list. You can begin to group ideas in your list and then add to it. Following is a grouping of the list of effects. Grouping helps you see how many effects and details you have.

effects of getting my own car

effect 1: I had to pay for the car and related expenses.
    details: costs a lot to maintain

car payments
car loan
car insurance

effect 2: I had the freedom to come and go.
 details: none

effect 3: I felt like a grown-up.
 details: none

Will these effects work in a paragraph? One way to decide is to try to add details to the effects that have no details. Ask questions to get those details.

effect 2: I had the freedom to come and go.

What do you mean?

Well, I didn't have to beg my father for his truck any more. I didn't have to get rides from friends. I could go to the city when I wanted. I could ride around just for fun.

effect 3: I felt like a grown-up.

What do you mean, "like a grown-up"?

Adults can go where they want, when they want. They drive themselves.

If you look carefully at the answers to the questions above, you'll find that the two effects are really *the same.* By adding details to both effects, you'll find that both are saying that owning a car gives you the adult freedom to come and go.

So the list needs another effect of owning a car. What else happened? How else did things change when you got your car? You might answer

I worried about someone hitting my car.
I worried about bad drivers.
I wanted to avoid the scratches you get in parking lots.

With answers like these, your third effect could be

I became a more careful driver.

Now that you have three effects and some details, you can rewrite your list. You can add details as you rewrite.

Effects of Getting My Own Car

effect 1: I had to pay for the car and related expenses.
 details: costs a lot to maintain
 car payments
 car loans
 car insurance

effect 2: I had the adult freedom to come and go.
 details: didn't have to beg my father for his truck
 didn't have to get rides from friends
 could go to the city when I wanted
 could ride around for fun

effect 3: I became a more careful driver.
 details: worried about someone hitting the car
 worried about bad drivers
 wanted to avoid the scratches cars get in parking lots

Designing a Topic Sentence

With at least three effects and some details for each effect, you can create a topic sentence. The topic sentence for this paragraph should indicate that the subject is the *effects* of getting a car. You can summarize all three effects in your topic sentence, or you can just hint at them. A possible topic sentence for the paragraph can be

> Owning my own car cost me money, gave me freedom, and made me more careful about how I drive.

> or

> Once I got a car of my own, I realized the good and bad sides of ownership.

With a topic sentence and a fairly extensive list of details, you are ready to begin the outlines step in preparing your paragraph.

Exercise 3

👥 Collaborate

Designing Questions for a Cause or Effect Paragraph

Below are four topics for cause or effect paragraphs. For each topic, write five questions that could lead you to ideas on the topic. (The first one is completed for you.) After you have written five questions for each topic, give your list to a member of your writing group. Ask him or her to add one question to each topic and then pass the exercise on to the next member of the group. Repeat the process so that each group member adds to the lists of all the other members.

Later, if your instructor agrees, you can answer the questions (and add more questions and answers) as a way to begin writing a cause or effect paragraph.

1. **topic:** the effects of email on the workplace
   questions that can lead to ideas and details:

   a. Does everyone know how to use email?

   b. What is email used for at work?

   c. Does email save money at work?

   d. Do some workers misuse email?

   e. Can a boss spy on employees through their email?

   additional questions: With email, can some people work at home?

   Will offices be eliminated because of email?

   Does email save paper?

2. **topic:** why teenagers watch soap operas
   questions that can lead to ideas and details:

   a. Are soap operas exciting?

   b. Do they have beautiful actresses?

   c. Do they have handsome actors?

Answers Will Vary.
Possible answers
shown at right.

d. Are the plots interesting? _____

e. Are the stories so stupid that they're funny? _____

additional questions: Is watching soap operas relaxing? _____

Do teens talk about the soaps with friends? _____

Do the shows have teenage characters? _____

3. **topic:** the effects of high ticket prices at concerts
questions that can lead to ideas and details:

a. How high are ticket prices? _____

b. Who wants to attend concerts? _____

c. Can concert fans afford the prices? _____

d. Will some fans be excluded because of prices? _____

e. Will audiences get smaller? _____

additional questions: Will there be fewer concerts? _____

Will concert tickets get more expensive? _____

Will concert tickets become less expensive? _____

4. **topic:** why Americans are eating more meals away from home
questions that could lead to ideas and details:

a. Are there more places to eat outside the home? _____

b. Are there more fast-food restaurants? _____

c. Are there more inexpensive eating places? _____

d. Are teens spending more time outside of the home? _____

e. If so, why are they away from home? _____

additional questions: Are fathers often away from home at dinner? _____

Are college students often away from home? _____

Do working parents take their children out to eat? _____

Exercise 4 **Creating Causes or Effects for Topic Sentences**

Practice

For each of the following topic sentences, create three causes or effects, depending on what the topic sentence requires. The first one is completed for you.

1. **topic sentence:** The telephone answering machine has both improved and complicated my life.

a. I don't miss important calls any more.

b. Now I have to deal with all the messages left on my answering machine.

c. I also have to decide whether to answer my phone or "screen" calls when I am at home and the phone rings.

2. **topic sentence:** Small children may fear the dark for a number of reasons.

Answers Will Vary.
Possible answers
shown at right.

a. They have seen scary movies about dark places.

b. They have active imaginations.

c. They have family members who are afraid of the dark.

3. **topic sentence:** There are many reasons why teens join gangs.

a. Teens may feel peer pressure to join.

b. Some people see the gang as a substitute family.

c. Others join to gain a sense of power.

4. **topic sentence:** Credit cards can have negative effects on those who use them.

a. Credit cards encourage unnecessary spending since they make it easy to buy whatever you see, immediately.

b. They promote financial irresponsibility because they let you owe a large debt and pay what seems a small interest.

c. If you misuse the cards, you can become bankrupt.

5. **topic sentence:** Taking too many college courses at one time can have serious consequences.

   a. <u>Students can fail a course.</u>

     _____

   b. <u>Students may have to drop a course.</u>

     _____

   c. <u>Students may become ill from the pressure of dealing with too many</u>

     <u>classes.</u> _____

Outlines

Cause or Effect

With a topic sentence and a list of causes (or effects) and details, you can draft an outline of your paragraph. Once you have an outline, you can work on revising it. You may want to add to it, take out certain ideas, rewrite the topic sentence, or change the order of the ideas. The following checklist may help you revise your outline.

✔ Checklist

A Checklist for Revising the Outline of a Cause or Effect Paragraph

✔ Does my topic sentence make my point?

✔ Does it indicate whether my paragraph is about causes or effects?

✔ Does the topic sentence fit the rest of the outline?

✔ Have I included enough causes or effects to make my point?

✔ Have I included enough details?

✔ Should I eliminate any ideas?

✔ Is the order of my causes or effects clear and logical?

The Order of Causes or Effects

Looking at a draft outline can help you decide on the best order for your reasons or results. There is no single rule for organizing reasons or results. Instead, you should think about the ideas you are presenting and decide on the most logical and effective order.

For example, if you are writing about some immediate and some long-range effects, you might want to discuss the effects in a **time order.** You might begin with the immediate effect, then discuss what happens later, and end with what happens last. If you are discussing three or four effects that are not in any particular time order, you might save the most important effect for last, for an **emphatic order.** If one cause leads to another, then use the **logical order** of discussing the causes.

Compare the following outline on owning a car to the list of effects on page 185. Notice that in the outline, the carefree side of owning a car comes first, and the cares of owning a car, the expense and the worry, come later. The topic sentence follows the same order.

An Outline for an Effects Paragraph

```
revised      topic sentence: Owning my own car gave me freedom,
topic        cost me money, and made me careful about how
sentence:    I drive.

effect 1     I had the adult freedom to come and go.
           ⎧ I didn't have to beg my father for his truck.
details    ⎨ I didn't have to get rides from my friends.
           ⎪ I could go to the city when I wanted.
           ⎩ I could ride around for fun.

effect 2     I had to pay for the car and related expenses.
           ⎧ A car costs a lot to maintain.
details    ⎨ I had car payments.
           ⎪ I had a car loan to pay.
           ⎩ I had car insurance.

effect 3     I became a more careful driver.
           ⎧ I worried about someone hitting the car.
details    ⎨ I worried about bad drivers.
           ⎪ I wanted to avoid the scratches cars can get in a
           ⎩ parking lot.
```

Once you have a revised outline of your cause or effect paragraph, you are ready to begin writing your draft.

| **Exercise 5** | **Writing Topic Sentences for Cause or Effect Outlines** |

Practice

There are two outlines below. They have no topic sentences. Read the outlines carefully, several times. Then write a topic sentence for each.

Answers Will Vary.
Possible answers shown at right.

1. **topic sentence:** <u>Lack of sleep has several bad effects on me.</u>

_____

_____

   details: When I don't get enough sleep, I get irritable.
   Little things, like my friend's wise remarks, make me angry.
   At work, I am not as patient as usual when a customer complains.
   Lack of sleep also slows me down.
   When I'm tired, I can't think as fast.
   For instance, it takes me ten minutes to find a number in the phone book when I can usually find one in a minute.
   When I'm tired, I am slower in restocking the shelves at the store where I work.
   Worst of all, I make more mistakes when I'm tired.
   Last Monday, I was so tired I locked myself out of my car.
   Also, a sleepless night can cause me to ring up a sale the wrong way.
   Then I have to spend hours trying to fix my mistake before my boss catches it.

2. topic sentence: <u>Because Denise didn't share my interests, wasn't fun to</u>

<u>be with, and didn't trust me, I broke up with her.</u>

_____

     details: Denise wasn't really interested in what I like to do.
              She hated sports.
              She always complained when we went to football games
              together.
              Denise was not much fun to be with.
              Whenever we were together, we wound up fighting over some
              trivial thing.
              For example, we once spent a whole evening fighting about
              what movie we should see.
              My main reason for breaking up was Denise's lack of trust
              in me.
              Denise couldn't believe I cared about her unless I showed her,
              every minute.
              She made me call her at least three times a day.
              She needed to know where I was at all times.
              She was jealous of the time I spent away from her.

Exercise 6   **Revising the Order of Causes or Effects**

Practice

Below are topic sentences and lists of causes or effects. Reorder each list according the directions given at the end of the list. Put a _1_ by the item that would come first, a _2_ by the next one, and so forth.

1. topic sentence: My brother went on a diet for several reasons.

    <u>2</u> He couldn't exercise for as long as he used to.

    <u>1</u> His clothes were too tight.

    <u>3</u> A doctor told him his weight was raising his cholesterol to a dangerous level.

Use this order: from least important to most important.

2. topic sentence: Rappers started something when they began wearing baseball caps backwards.

    <u>2</u> Fans imitated the look.

    <u>1</u> When rap became popular, fans noticed the caps.

    <u>3</u> The caps started showing up on people who never listen to rap.

Use this order: time order.

3. topic sentence: Losing my job had negative and positive effects on me.

_____1_____ I was in a state of shock since I had no idea I'd be laid off.

_____3_____ I eventually realized the job had been a dead-end job and I could do better.

_____2_____ I went from shock to a feeling of failure.

Use this order: the order indicated by the topic sentence, from bad to good.

Exercise 7	**Developing an Outline**

Practice

The outlines below need one more cause or effect and details for that cause or effect. Fill in the missing parts.

Answers Will Vary.
Possible answers
shown at right.

1. **topic sentence:** Stress at work can lead to many emotional and physical problems.
   effect 1:   Stressed-out people get caught in a cycle of worry.
   details   When I am under stress at the office, for instance, I worry about getting everything done on time.
                   The pressure to meet deadlines creates more stress and more worry for me.
   effect 2:   Stress can cause high blood pressure.
   details   I know an executive who pushed herself to work twelve-hour days.
                   She never stopped working and never felt she was good enough.
                   She ended up in the hospital, where she was treated for dangerously high blood pressure.

   effect 3:   Stress and heart attacks are connected.

   details (at least two sentences)   My uncle is recovering from a major heart attack.

   His physician told my uncle to retire from the stressful job of a police officer.

2. **topic sentence:** People look for mates in the personals columns for many reasons.
   cause 1:   It's hard to meet the right person in a bar or club.
   details   Everyone in a bar or club is trying hard to look trendy or rich.
                  Conversation is often insincere or superficial.
   cause 2:   The personals columns allow people to screen their dates.
   details   Those who write the ads can describe who they are and what they want in a mate.
                  For instance, the person who places the ad can say he or she is looking for someone who likes sports or someone who doesn't smoke.
                  Those who answer the personals have to send a letter describing themselves and often send a photo.

cause 3:   People who arrange a meeting in the personals can meet in a safe, non-threatening situation.

details (at least two sentences)   They can arrange to meet for coffee or lunch.

Each person can stay as long as he or she wants and no one has to take the other person home.

Rough Lines

Cause or Effect

Once you have an outline in good order, with a sufficient number of causes or effects and details, you can write a first draft of the paragraph. When the first draft is complete, you can read and reread it, deciding how you'd like to improve it. The following checklist may help you revise.

✔ **Checklist**

A Checklist for Revising the Draft of a Cause or Effect Paragraph

✔ Does my topic sentence indicate cause or effect?

✔ Does it fit the rest of the paragraph?

✔ Do I have enough causes or effects to make my point?

✔ Do I have enough details for each cause or effect?

✔ Are my causes or effects explained clearly?

✔ Is there a clear connection between my ideas?

✔ Have I shown the links between my ideas?

✔ Do I need to combine sentences?

✔ Do I need an opening or closing sentence?

Linking Ideas in Cause or Effect

When you write about how one event or situation causes another, or about how one result leads to another, you have to be very clear in showing the connections between events, situations, or effects.

One way to be clear is to rely on transitions. Some transitions are particularly helpful in writing cause and effect paragraphs.

Infobox

Transitions for a Cause or Effect Paragraph

For cause paragraphs: because, due to, for, for this reason, since

For effect paragraphs: as a result, consequently, hence, in consequence, then, therefore, thus, so

---

Making the Links Clear

Using the right transition word is not always enough to make your point. Sometimes you have to write the missing link in your line of thinking so that the reader can understand your point. To write the missing link means writing phrases, clauses, or sentences that help the reader follow your point.

> **not this:** Many mothers are working outside the home. Consequently, microwave ovens are popular.
> **but this:** Many mothers are working outside the home and have little time to cook. Consequently, microwave ovens, which can cook food in minutes, are popular.

The hard part of making clear links between ideas is that you have to put yourself in your reader's place. Remember that your reader cannot read your mind, only your paper. Connections between ideas may be very clear in your mind, but you must spell them out on paper.

Revising the Draft

Below is a draft of the paragraph on owning a car. When you read it, you'll notice many changes from the outlines stage on page 191.

- The details on "car payments" and "a car loan" said the same thing, so the repetition has been cut.
- Some details about the costs of maintaining a car and about parking have been added.
- The order of the details about the costs of a car has been changed. Now, paying for a car comes first, and maintaining it comes after.
- Sentences have been combined.
- Transitions have been added.

A Draft of an Effects Paragraph (Transitions are underlined.)

Owning my own car gave me freedom, cost me money, and made me more careful about how I drive. <u>First of all</u>, my car gave me the adult freedom to come and go. I didn't have to beg my father for his truck or get rides from my friends anymore. I could go to the city or even ride around for fun when I wanted. <u>On the negative side,</u> I had to pay for the car and related expenses. I had to pay for the car loan. I also paid for car insurance. <u>A car costs a lot to maintain, too</u>. I paid for oil changes, tune-ups, tires, belts, and filters. <u>With so much of my money put into my car,</u> I became a more careful driver. I worried about someone hitting the car and watched out for bad drivers. <u>In addition,</u> I wanted to avoid the scratches a car can get in a parking lot, so I always parked far away from other cars.

Exercise 8

Practice

Making the Connections Clear

Following are ideas that are connected, but the connection is not clearly explained. Rewrite each pair of ideas, making the connection clear.

1. I had a bad attitude toward homework in high school. Therefore I did poorly in my first-year college courses.

TEACHING TIP:

Group Work. This exercise can be challenging for students. They may benefit from collaborating with classmates to see if their revised sentences establish a logical and precisely worded connection between the ideas.

Answers Will Vary. Possible answers shown at right.

Rewritten: I had a bad attitude towards homework in high school.

Because I brought that attitude with me to college, I did poorly in my fresh-man college courses.

(**Hint:** Did the bad attitude follow you to college?)

2. People want stylish clothes. They don't have much money to spend. So they go to discount stores.

Rewritten: People want stylish clothes, but they don't have much money to spend. They go to discount stores, which offer style at a reasonable price.

(**Hint:** Do discount stores offer style? Or cheaper clothes? or both?)

3. I drank three cups of coffee last night. Consequently I couldn't sleep.

Rewritten: I drank three cups of coffee last night. Since I'm not used to drinking coffee at night, the caffeine in the coffee kept me awake.

(**Hint:** Do you usually or rarely drink coffee at night? What substance in the coffee kept you awake?)

4. Pine Tree College was nearer home than Lake College. As a result, I went to Pine Tree College.

Rewritten: Pine Tree College was nearer home than Lake College. I wanted to save money by attending college and living at home, so I went to the closer school, Pine Tree College.

(**Hint:** Did you want to go to a college close to home? Did you want to save money by living at home while attending college? Did you want a shorter trip to school?)

5. Some people believe the government interferes in the private life of the individual. Thus these people refuse to follow a seat belt law.

Rewritten: Some people believe the government interferes in the private life of the individual. They believe the seat belt law is an example of government interference in their private life. Thus these people refuse to follow a seat

belt law.

(**Hint:** Do these people think a seat belt law is an interference in their private life?)

Exercise 9
Practice

Revising a Paragraph by Adding Details

Each of the paragraphs below is missing details. Add details, at least two sentences, to each paragraph.

Answers Will Vary.
Possible answers
shown at right.

1. I had very good reasons for getting a German shepherd. First of all, I have always had a dog, and I needed a dog when my collie, Buff, died. After I lost Buff, I just couldn't stand walking into an empty house. There was no excited buddy, wagging his tail, thrilled to see me. I missed the companionship of walking my dog, talking to my dog, playing with my dog. Second, German shepherds are a breed I've always admired. They are fiercely loyal dogs, and they are very intelligent. My grandmother had a German shepherd who was smarter than some people I know. My third reason for getting my shepherd was for security. German shepherds are known to be good watchdogs. Their intelligence makes them easy to train, and their great loyalty makes them extremely protective of their human family. My dog provides my home with more security than any alarm system.

All in all, a shepherd was the breed that gave me the companionship, loyalty, intelligence, and security I wanted.

2. My first day of college had three significant effects on me. One effect was to reassure me. I had expected my teachers to be very cold, formal, and distant. I was sure they would never stoop to being friendly to a new student like me. But my teachers turned out to be friendly and warm, and they stressed their desire to meet with students during office hours. My reassurance was mixed with a second reaction, excitement. It was exciting to start a new part of my life and to see all the people and places I would be getting to know. Maybe the guy sitting next to me in English class would become a friend. Or maybe the girl in my art class would go out with me. My third reaction was less positive; it was fear. _I couldn't believe the size of the_

course outlines I received in my classes. One teacher gave me an outline that

was five pages long. How would I ever get all these assignments completed? The

thought made me nervous.

So I was afraid on the first day, and I was also reasssured and excited. Only time would

tell how correct my first reactions had been.

Note: For more on combining sentences, see Chapter 13 on coordination and Chapter 14 on subordination.

Exercise 10	**Revising a Draft by Combining Sentences**

Practice

Combine the underlined sentences in the following paragraph. Write your combinations in the space above the original sentences.

Answers Will Vary.
Possible answers shown at right.

The latest television commercial is designed to make viewers think that freedom,

First of all, the ad starts with a tired
excitement, and nature come with the car. First of all, the ad starts with a tired execu-
executive ripping off his tie and leaping into his convertible.
tive. The executive rips off his tie and leaps into his convertible. As he speeds out of

the city, the viewers get a sense of freedom. The freedom is connected to a sense of

The car zips past slower cars as loud rock 'n roll plays on the soundtrack.
excitement. The car zips past slower cars. Loud rock and roll plays on the soundtrack.

The car races around curves and conquers dangerous corners. Soon, viewers see the

The car brings the executive to the middle
ultimate effect of owning a Nighthawk. The car brings the executive to the middle of a
of an unspoiled, green area with a gorgeous lake.
green area. There is a gorgeous lake. Everything is unspoiled. The rock and roll music

fades away, and the only sounds heard are birdcalls and gentle breezes. Truly, this com-

mercial says, a new car can change viewers' lives. This ad is not really for a car;

instead it sells a dream of excitement and escape.

Final Lines

Cause or Effect

Following is the final version of the paragraph on owning a car. When you contrast the final version with the draft on page 195, you'll notice several changes:

- An introductory sentence has been added.
- Some sentences have been combined.
- Transitions have been revised.
- Some words have been changed so that the language is more precise.

Changes in style, word choice, sentence variety, and transitions can all be made before you decide on the final version of your paragraph. You may also want to add an opening or closing sentence to your paragraph.

A Final Version of an Effects Paragraph (Changes from the draft are underlined.)

When I bought my first car, I wasn't prepared for all the changes it made in my life. Owning my own car gave me freedom, cost me money, and made me careful about how I drive. First of all, my car gave me the adult freedom to come and go. I didn't have to beg my father for his truck or get rides from my friends anymore. I could go to the city or even ride around for fun when I wanted. On the negative side, I had to pay for the car and related expenses. I had to pay for both the car loan and car insurance. A car costs money to maintain, too. I paid for oil changes, tune-ups, tires, belts, and filters. With so much of my money put into my car, I became a more careful driver. I worried about someone hitting the car and watched out for bad drivers. To avoid dangers in the parking lot as well as on the road, I always parked my car far away from other cars, keeping my car safe from scratches.

Before you prepare the final copy of your paragraph, check your latest draft for errors in spelling and punctuation and for any errors made in typing or copying.

Exercise 11
Practice

Correcting a Final Copy of a Cause or Effect Paragraph

Following is a cause paragraph with the kinds of errors that are easy to overlook when you prepare the final version of an assignment. Correct the errors, writing above the lines. There are thirteen errors.

                                                     semester

I signed up for an Introduction to Computers class this semster so that I could get

course   *buying*

some useful skills. One reason I took the Course is that I am thinking of bying a home

                 assignments

computer to use for my college assinments. But if I don't know how to use a computer,

             ?

what good would it do to own one. If I can learn to use a computer, I can learn word

processing on it and do my college papers. Second, my ability to use a computer will

         friend

help me at home. I have a freind who does her household accounts and stores financial

          . A

information on her home computer another friend has a program that helps her plan

           studying

her investments. The most important reason I am studing computers is that I think I

will get

get a better job if I know the basics of computers. Even though I am majoring in social

          business

work, not math, science, or buisness, a computer will be essential in my field. I'll use it

to look up clients' records and to store data. I'll use it in research and writing. I think

          knowledge   computers

that in the future, every job will require a knowlege of computer.

Lines of Detail: A Walk-Through Assignment

Write a paragraph on the topic, "Why Americans Are Eating More Meals Away from Home." To write your paragraph, follow these steps:

Step 1: Go back to Exercise 1 on pages 187–88. Topic 4 is on the same topic as this assignment. If you have already done that exercise, you have five or more questions that can lead you to ideas and details. If you have not done the exercise, do topic 4 now.

Step 2: Use the answers to your questions to prepare a list of ideas and details. Put the items on your list into groups of reasons and related details. Add to the groups until you have at least three reasons (and related details) why Americans are eating more meals away from home.

Step 3: Write a topic sentence that fits your reasons.

Step 4: Write an outline. Check that your outline has sufficient details and that you have put the reasons in the best order.

Step 5: Write a rough draft of your paragraph. Revise it until you have enough specific details to explain each reason, and make sure that the links between your ideas are smooth and clear. Check whether any sentences should be combined, and decide whether your paragraph could use an opening sentence or a concluding one.

Step 6: Before you prepare the final copy of your paragraph, check your latest draft for word choice, punctuation, transitions, and spelling.

Writing Your Own Cause or Effect Paragraph

When you write on any of the following topics, be sure to work through the stages of the writing process in preparing your cause or effect paragraph.

1. Write a cause paragraph on one of the following topics. You create the topic by filling in the blanks.

   Why I Chose _____

   Why I Stopped _____

   Why I Enjoy _____

   Why I Started _____

   Why I Hate _____

   Why I Bought _____

   Why I Decided _____

2. Write a one-paragraph letter of complaint to the manufacturer of a product you bought or the company that owns a hotel, restaurant, airline, or some other service you used. In your letter, write at least three reasons why you (1) want your money refunded or (2) want the product replaced. Be clear and specific about your reasons. Be sure your letter has a topic sentence.

If your instructor agrees, read a draft of your letter to a writing partner, and ask your partner to pretend to be the manufacturer or the head of the company. Ask your partner to point out where your ideas are not clear or convincing and where you make your point effectively.

3. Think of a current fad or trend. The fad can be a popular style of clothing, a movie, a kind of music, a sport, a pastime, an actor, an athlete, a gadget, an invention, an appliance, and so on. Write a paragraph on the causes of this fad or trend or the effects of it.

   If your instructor agrees, begin by brainstorming with a group. Create a list of three or four fads or trends. Then create a list of questions to ask (and answer) about each fad or trend. If you are going to write about causes, for example, you might ask questions like

   What changes in society have encouraged this trend?
   Have changes in the economy helped to make it popular?
   Does it appeal to a specific age group? Why?
   Does it meet any hidden emotional needs? For instance, is it a way to gain status or to feel safe or powerful?

   If you are going to write about effects, you might ask questions like

   Will this trend last?
   Has it affected competitors?
   Is it spreading?
   Is the fad changing business, education, or the family?
   Has it improved daily life?

4. If you have ever had one of the following experiences, write a paragraph about its effects on you.

moving to a new place	losing a friend
losing a job	starting a job
being a victim of a crime	breaking a bad habit
winning a contest	entering a relationship
undergoing surgery	ending a relationship

Name: _____ **Section:** _____

Peer Review Form for a Cause or Effect Paragraph

After you have written a draft of your cause or effect paragraph, let a writing partner read it. When your partner has completed the form below, discuss the comments. Then repeat the same process for your partner's paragraph.

This is a cause paragraph/an effect paragraph. (Circle one.)

In this paragraph, the causes or effects are _____

_____

_____

_____

(Briefly list all of them.)

The topic sentence uses these words to indicate cause or effect: _____

_____

_____ (Write the exact words.)

The cause or effect that is most clearly explained is _____

_____

I would like to see more details added to _____

_____

I have questions about _____

I would like to take out the part about _____

Other comments: _____

_____

_____

_____

_____

_____

_____

_____

Reviewer's Name: _____

WRITING FROM READING: Cause and Effect

Students in Shock
John Kellmayer

John Kellmayer, an educator, explores the reasons why college students are stressed beyond their limits. He also discusses how colleges are reacting to student problems.

Words You May Need to Know

warrant (paragraph 6): demand, call for, require
magnitude (9): great importance

biofeedback (10): A method of monitoring your blood pressure, heart rate, and so on as a way of monitoring and controlling stress

1   If you feel overwhelmed by your college experiences, you are not alone—many of today's college students are suffering from a form of shock. Going to college has always had its ups and downs, but today the "downs" of the college experience are more numerous and difficult, a fact that the schools are responding to with increased support services.

2   Lisa is a good example of a student in shock. She is an attractive, intelligent twenty-year-old college junior at a state university. Having been a straight-A student in high school and a member of the basketball and softball teams there, she remembers her high school days with fondness. Lisa was popular then and had a steady boyfriend for the last two years of school.

3   Now, only three years later, Lisa is miserable. She has changed her major four times already and is forced to hold down two part-time jobs in order to pay her tuition. She suffers from sleeping and eating disorders and believes she has no close friends. Sometimes she bursts out crying for no apparent reason. On more than one occasion, she has considered taking her own life.

4   Dan, too, suffers from student shock. He is nineteen and a freshman at a local community college. He began college as an accounting major but hated that field. So he switched to computer programming because he heard the job prospects were excellent in that area. Unfortunately, he discovered that he had little aptitude for programming and changed majors again, this time to psychology. He likes psychology but has heard horror stories about the difficulty of finding a job in that field without a graduate degree. Now he's considering switching majors again. To help pay for school, Dan works nights and weekends as a sales clerk at K-Mart. He doesn't get along with his boss, but since he needs the money, Dan feels he has no choice except to stay on the job. A few months ago, his girlfriend of a year and a half broke up with him.

5   Not surprisingly, Dan has started to suffer from depression and migraine headaches. He believes that in spite of all his hard work, he just isn't getting anywhere. He can't remember ever being this unhappy. A few times he considered

talking to somebody in the college psychological counseling center. He rejected that idea, though, because he doesn't want people to think there's something wrong with him.

6   What is happening to Lisa and Dan happens to millions of college students each year. As a result, one-quarter of the student population at any time will suffer from symptoms of depression. Of that group, almost half will experience depression intense enough to warrant professional help. At schools across the country, psychological counselors are booked up months in advance. Stress-related problems such as anxiety, migraine headaches, insomnia, anorexia, and bulimia are epidemic on college campuses. Suicide rates and self-inflicted injuries among college students are higher now than at any other time in history. The suicide rate among college youth is fifty percent higher than among nonstudents of the same age. It is estimated that each year more than five hundred college students take their own lives. College health officials believe that these reported problems represent only the tip of the iceberg. They fear that most students, like Lisa and Dan, suffer in silence.

7   There are three reasons today's college students are suffering more than in earlier generations. First is a weakening family support structure. The transition from high school to college has always been difficult, but in the past there was more family support to help get through it. Today, with divorce rates at a historical high and many parents experiencing their own psychological difficulties, the traditional family is not always available for guidance and support. And when students who do not find stability at home are bombarded with numerous new and stressful experiences, the results can be devastating.

8   Another problem college students face is financial pressure. In the last decade tuition costs have skyrocketed—up about sixty-six percent at public college and ninety percent at private schools. And at the same time that tuition costs have been rising dramatically, there has been a cutback in federal aid to students. College loans are now much harder to obtain and are available only at near-market interest rates. Consequently, most college students must work at least part-time. And for some students, the pressure to do well in school while holding down a job is too much to handle.

9   A final cause of student shock is the large selection of majors available. Because of the magnitude and difficulty of choosing a major, college can prove a time of great indecision. Many students switch majors, some a number of times. As a result, it is becoming commonplace to take five or six years to get a degree. It can be depressing to students not only to have taken courses that don't count towards a degree but also to be faced with the added tuition costs. In some cases these costs become so high that they force students to drop out of college.

10   While there is no magic cure-all for student shock, colleges have begun to recognize the problem and are trying in a number of ways to help students cope with the pressures they face. First of all, many colleges are upgrading their psychological counseling centers to handle the greater demand for services. Additional staff is being hired, and experts are doing research to learn more about the

psychological problems of college students. Some schools even advertise these services in student newspapers and on campus radio stations. Also, third- and fourth-year students are being trained as peer counselors. These peer counselors may be able to act as a first line of defense in the battle for students' well-being by spotting and helping to solve problems before they become too big for students to handle. In addition, stress-management workshops have become common on college campuses. At these workshops, instructors teach students various techniques for dealing with stress, including biofeedback, meditation, and exercise.

11   Finally, many schools are improving their vocational counseling services. By giving students more relevant information about possible majors and career choices, colleges can lessen the anxiety and indecision often associated with choosing a major.

12   If you ever feel that you're "in shock," remember that your experience is not unique. Try to put things in perspective. Certainly, the end of a romance or failing an exam is not an event to look forward to. But realize that rejection and failure happen to everyone sooner or later. And don't be reluctant to talk to somebody about your problems. The useful services available on campus won't help you if you don't take advantage of them.

WRITING FROM READING: "Students in Shock"

When you write on any of the topics below, be sure to work through the stages of the writing process in preparing your cause or effects paragraph.

1. Write a one-paragraph summary of "Students in Shock." Include the three significant reasons college students are in distress, and discuss how colleges are reacting to student stress. Remember to use logical and effective transitions throughout your summary.

2. Write a paragraph about the main causes of stress in your life. To begin, list everything that caused you stress in the past twenty-four hours. Do not think about whether the cause was minor or major; just list all the causes you can remember. If you felt stress waiting for a traffic light to change, for example, write it down.

    When you have completed your list, read it to a writing partner or group. Ask your listener(s) to help you identify three or more causes of stress in your life. Then work alone to prepare your paragraph.

3. Write a paragraph on the positive effects of your attending college. Be sure you have at least three effects.

4. Write a paragraph on the negative effects of your attending college. Be sure you have at least three effects.

5. Write a letter to your college instructors. Your letter will be a paragraph giving at least three reasons why students seem tired in class.

6. Stress has different effects on different people. Freewrite about the effects of college stress on you and people you know. Use your freewriting to plan and write a paragraph on the effects of college stress. Use your and your friends' experiences as examples of the different effects of college stress.

CHAPTER 9

Argument

WHAT IS ARGUMENT?

A written **argument** is an attempt to *persuade* a reader to think or act in a certain way. When you write an argument paragraph, your goal is to get people to see your point so that they are persuaded to accept it and perhaps to act on it.

In an argument paragraph, you take a stand. Then you support your stand with reasons. In addition, you give details for each reason. Your goal is to persuade your reader by making a point that has convincing reasons and details.

Hints for Writing an Argument Paragraph

1. Pick a topic you can handle. Your topic should be small enough to be covered in one paragraph. For instance, you can't argue effectively for world peace in just one paragraph.

2. Pick a topic you understand from your own experience and observation. Topics like legalizing drugs, or gun control, or capital punishment, or air pollution require research into facts, figures, and expert opinions to make a complete argument. They are topics you can write about convincingly in a longer research paper, but for a one-paragraph argument, pick a topic based on what you've experienced yourself:

not this topic: Organized Crime
but this topic: Starting a Crime Watch Program in My Neighborhood

3. Do two things in your topic sentence: name the subject of your argument, and take a stand. The following topic sentences do both:

       subject   takes a stand
The college cafeteria should serve more healthy snacks.

             subject   takes a stand
High school athletes who fail a course should not be allowed to play on a school team.

You should take a stand, but *don't* announce it.

TEACHING TIP:

Tell students not to associate the word "argument" with yelling or fighting with someone. Stress that in composition, to argue means to write persuasively or logically in favor of a particular stand. Most likely, some of your students will find taking a stand in class a new experience, especially if they are asked to defend it logically and with convincing details.

> **not this:** This paragraph will explain why Springfield needs a teen center.
>
> **but this:** Springfield should open a teen center. (a topic sentence with a subject and a stand.)

Note: For a list of argument topics that ask students to consider their audience of readers, see p. 223 in this chapter.

4. Consider your audience. Think about why these people should support your points. How will they be likely to object? How will you get around these objections? For instance, you might want to argue, to the residents of your community, that the intersection of Hawthorne Road and Sheridan Street needs a traffic light. Would anyone object?

At first, you might think, "No. Why would anyone object? The intersection is dangerous. There's too much traffic there. People risk major accidents getting across the intersection." But if you think further about your audience, the people in your community, you might identify these objections: Some town residents may not want to pay for a traffic signal. Some drivers may not want to spend extra time waiting for a light to change.

There are several ways to handle objections:

> You can *refute* an objection. To refute it means to prove it isn't valid; it isn't true. For instance, if someone says that a light wouldn't do any good, you might say that a new light has already worked in a nearby neighborhood.
>
> Sometimes it's best to admit the other side has a point. You have to *concede* that point. For instance, traffic lights do cost money, and waiting for a light to change does take time.
>
> Sometimes you can *turn an objection into an advantage.* When you acknowledge the objection and yet use it to make your own point, you show that you've considered both sides of the argument. For instance, you might say that the price of a traffic signal at the intersection is well worth it because that light will buy safety for all the drivers who try to cross Hawthorne Road and Sheridan Street. Or you might say that waiting a few moments for the light to change is better than waiting many minutes for an opening in the heavy traffic of the intersection.

Discussion Question: Students who have taken a speech course may have studied ways to refute a point or ways to "consider the opposition." See if any of your students can discuss stands on topics they have debated or researched for other classes.

5. Be specific, clear, and logical in your reasons. As always, think before you write. Think about your point and your audience. Try to come up with at least three reasons for your position.

Be careful that your reasons do not overlap. For instance, you might write the following:

topic sentence:	College students should get discounts on movie tickets.
audience:	Owners of movie theaters.
reasons:	1. Many college students can't afford current ticket prices.
	2. The cost of tickets is high for most students.
	3. More people in the theater means more popcorn and candy sold at the concession stand.

But reasons 1 and 2 overlap; they are really part of the same reason.

Be careful not to argue in a circle. For instance, if you say, "One reason for having an after-school program at Riverside Elementary School is that we need one there," you've just said, "We need an after-school program because we need an afterschool program."

Finally, be specific in stating your reasons:

not this: One reason to start a bus service to and from the college is to help people.

but this: A bus service to and from the college would encourage students to leave their cars at home and use travel time to study.

Exercise 1 **Recognizing Good Topic Sentences in an Argument Paragraph**

Practice

Some of the topic sentences below are appropriate for an argument paragraph. Some are for topics that are too large for one paragraph, and some are for topics that would require research. Some are announcements. Some do not take a stand. Write *OK* next to the sentences that would work well in an argument paragraph.

1. _____ People should try to cure their own addictions.

2. _____ The empty lot by the post office is a serious problem.

3. _____ We must ban offshore oil drilling in American waters.

4. _OK_ Bicycle safety should be taught at Deerfield Elementary School.

5. _____ We need stricter penalties for criminals.

6. _____ Something should be done about victims' rights.

7. _OK_ The city parks and recreation department should put more picnic tables at Veterans' Park.

8. _____ The savings and loan scandal shows the need for stricter banking laws.

9. _OK_ National Federal Savings Bank should be open on Saturday so that working people can do their banking.

10. _____ The reasons to ban skateboarding at Miller Mall will be the subject of this essay.

Exercise 2 **Recognizing and Handling Objections**

Collaborate

Below are the topic sentences of arguments. Working with a group, list two possible objections to each argument that might come from the specific audience identified. Then think of ways to handle each objection, either by refuting it, conceding it, or trying to turn it to your advantage. On the lines provided, write the actual sentence(s) you would use in a paragraph.

Answers Will Vary. Possible answers shown at right.

1. **topic sentence:** The college library, which is currently open until 10:00 p.m., should be open until midnight every night.
audience: the deans, vice president and president of the college possible objections from this audience:

   a. It would be too expensive to pay staff to work later hours.

   b. Few students would use the library late at night.

answering objections:

a. The cost of scheduling extra hours would be worth it, to give students greater access to campus resources.

b. Many students use the library until 10 p.m., so they would most likely stay even later.

2. **topic sentence:** The local mall [you pick a specific mall] needs more security officers to patrol inside and outside the mall.
audience: the owners of the mall
possible objections from this audience:

a. We have enough security officers.

b. Extra security costs too much.

answering objections:

a. Many shoppers do not feel safe at the mall because they do not see security officers out and about.

b. The cost of extra security would be offset by the increased number of shoppers and merchants wanting to rent mall space.

3. **topic sentence:** Atlantic Township should ban parking at the beach parking lot after midnight.
audience: teen residents of Atlantic Township
possible objections from this audience:

a. The beach is the only place teens can "hang out."

b. Teens are being discriminated against.

answering objections:

a. An isolated parking lot after midnight is not safe.

b. The rule would protect the safety of all age groups, not just teens.

4. **topic sentence:** The Crispy Donut Shop should offer fat-free and sugar-free muffins.
audience: the owners of the Crispy Donut Shop
possible objections from this audience:

a. No one would buy them.

b. No other doughnut store in town sells them.

answering objections:

a. Current customers who want to lose weight might try them and become repeat buyers, if the muffins were tasty.

b. The Crispy Donut Shop might attract new customers by offering something competitors don't have.

5. **topic sentence:** Local day-care centers should be required to provide one adult supervisor for every two children under the age of one year.
   audience: The owners of the Happy Child Day Care Center, which currently has one adult supervisor for every three children under the age of one year.
   possible objections from this audience:

   a. We don't need another law to tell us how to do our business.

   b. The cost of extra supervisors would put us out of business.

   answering objections:

   a. Day car providers, parents, and legislators all want to keep babies safe, and this law protects very young children.

   b. Parents will pay the additional cost of extra staff if they know the money protects their children.

WRITING THE ARGUMENT PARAGRAPH IN STEPS

Thought Lines

Argument

Imagine that your instructor has given you this assignment:

Write a one-paragraph letter to the editor of your local newspaper. Argue for something in your town that needs to be changed.

One way to begin is to brainstorm for some specific thing that you can write about:

Is there a part of town that needs to be cleaned up?
Should something be changed at a school?
What do I notice on my way to work or school that needs improvement?
What could be improved in my neighborhood?

By answering these questions, you may come up with one topic, and then you can list ideas on it:

topic
Cleaning Up Roberts Park

ideas

dirty and overgrown
benches are all cracked and broken
full of trash
could be fixed up
people work nearby
they would use it

You can consider your audience and possible objections:

audience

Local people of all ages who read the local paper.

possible objections from this audience

would cost money
more important things to spend money on

answering objections

Money would be well spent to beautify the downtown.
City children could play there in the fresh air and in nature; workers could eat lunch there.

Grouping Your Ideas

Once you have a list, you can start grouping the ideas. Some of the objections you wrote down may actually lead you to reasons that support your argument. That is, by answering objections, you may come up with reasons that support your point. Following is a list with a point to argue, three supporting reasons, and some details about cleaning up Roberts Park.

A List for an Argument Paragraph

point:	We should fix up Roberts Park.
reason:	Improving the park would make the downtown area more attractive to shoppers.
details:	Shoppers could stroll in the park or rest from their shopping.
	Friends could meet in the park for a day of shopping and lunch.
reason:	City children could play in the park.
details:	They could get fresh air.
	They could play in a natural setting.
reason:	Workers could get lunch outdoors.
details:	Several office complexes are nearby.
	Workers would take a break outdoors.

With three reasons and some details for each, you can draft a topic sentence. Remember that your topic sentence for an argument should (1) name your subject and (2) take a stand. Below is a topic sentence about Roberts Park that does both.

       subject   **takes a stand**
Roberts Park should be cleaned up and improved.

With a topic sentence, you are ready to move on to the outlines stage of preparing an argument paragraph.

Exercise 3 **Distinguishing Between Reasons and Details**

Practice Each list below has three reasons and details for each reason. Write *reason 1*, *reason 2*, or *reason 3* next to the reasons on each list. Then write *detail for 1*, *detail for 2*, or *detail for 3* by the items that give details about each reason. There may be more than one sentence of details connected to one reason.

1. **topic sentence:** The city needs to pick up garbage at my apartment complex three times a week, not twice.

   _____detail 1_____ Garbage spills out past the dumpster.

   _____detail 1_____ People throw their garbage on top of already loaded dumpsters; the bags fall and split open.

   _____reason 3_____ Uncovered garbage that piles up is a health hazard.

   _____reason 1_____ Too much garbage accumulates when the schedule allows for only two pickups.

   _____detail 3_____ Flies buzz over the garbage, a sign of dangerous contamination that can spread.

   _____detail 3_____ The roaches from the garbage area spread into the apartments, carrying disease.

   _____reason 2_____ Trash piles make people lose pride in their neighborhood.

   _____detail 2_____ Apartment residents are starting to litter the parking lot because they've lost respect for their homes.

   _____detail 2_____ One longtime resident is thinking of moving to a better neighborhood.

2. **topic sentence:** Children under ten years of age should not be permitted in the Mountain Mall unless they are accompanied by an adult.

   _____reason 3_____ It is not safe for children to be alone in the mall.

   _____reason 2_____ Unsupervised children cause trouble for mall merchants.

   _____reason 1_____ Children left alone in the mall are not always happy with their freedom.

   _____detail 1_____ I've seen one nine-year-old boy roam the mall for hours, looking forlorn.

   _____detail 1_____ Sometimes pairs of sad young girls wait by the food court for an hour, until Mom, who is "late," remembers to pick them up.

   _____detail 1_____ Once I saw two seven-year-old boys walk back and forth in front of my store for half an hour with nothing to do.

<u>   detail 3   </u>   Children have been kidnapped in malls.

<u>   detail 3   </u>   If a child gets sick at the mall, will he or she know what to do?

<u>   detail 2   </u>   Bored children run through stores, chasing each other.

<u>   detail 2   </u>   I saw one child shoplifting.

Exercise 4   **Finding Reasons to Support an Argument**

Practice

Give three reasons that support each point. In each case, the readers of your local newspaper will be the audience for an argument paragraph.

Answers Will Vary.
Possible answers
shown at right.

1. **point:** The state should ban all telephone sales calls between the hours of 5:00 p.m. and 8:00 p.m.
   reasons:

   a. This time is the dinner hour.

   b. Working parents and children need it to communicate.

   c. Sales calls should be made during business hours.

2. **point:** Our state must ban the sale of all fireworks.
   reasons:

   a. Fireworks can start fires, especially wildfires.

   b. They can hurt or kill animals.

   c. They can hurt or kill humans.

3. **point:** Parenting should be a required course for all high school students.
   reasons:

   a. Better parenting skills can make parents confident.

   b. Better skills can lead to healthier children.

   c. Better skills can lead to happier children.

4. **point:** Dogs should not be permitted on the public beach.
   reasons:

   a. Dogs can soil the beach.

   b. Dogs can be a safety hazard to other dogs.

   c. Dogs can be a safety hazard to people.

Outlines

Argument

With a topic sentence and a list of reasons and detail, you can draft an outline. Then you can review it, making whatever changes you think it needs. The following checklist may help you review and revise your outline.

✔ Checklist

A Checklist for Revising an Argument Outline

✔ Does my topic sentence make my point? Does it state a subject and take a stand?

✔ Have I considered the objections to my argument so that I am arguing intelligently?

✔ Do I have all the reasons I need to make my point?

✔ Do any reasons overlap?

✔ Are my reasons specific?

✔ Do I have enough details for each reason?

✔ Are my reasons in the best order?

The Order of Reasons in an Argument

When you are giving several reasons, it is a good idea to keep the most convincing or most important reason for last. Saving the best for last is called using **emphatic order.** For example, you might have these three reasons to tear down an abandoned building in your neighborhood: (1) The building is ugly. (2) Drug dealers are using the building. (3) The building is infested with rats. The most important reason, the drug dealing, should be used last for an emphatic order.

Following is an outline on improving Roberts Park. When you look at the outline, you'll notice several changes from the list on page 211:

- Since the safety of children at play is important, it is put as the last detail.
- Some details have been added.
- A sentence has been added to the end of the outline. It explains why improving the park is good even for people who will never use the park themselves. It is a way of answering these people's objections.

An Outline for an Argument Paragraph

```
topic sentence: Roberts Park should be cleaned up and improved.
reason          Improving the park would make the downtown area more
                attractive to shoppers.
              ⎧ Shoppers could stroll through the park or rest there
              ⎪ after shopping.
details       ⎨
              ⎪ Friends could meet at the park for a day of shop-
              ⎩ ping and lunch.
reason          Workers from nearby offices and stores could eat
                lunch outdoors.
              ⎧ Several office complexes are nearby.
details       ⎨
              ⎩ An hour outdoors is a pleasant break from work.
```

```
reason        City children could play there.
              ⎡ They would get fresh air.
details       ⎢ They would play on grass, not on asphalt.
              ⎣ They would not have to play near traffic.
final idea    An attractive park improves the city, and all res-
              idents benefit when the community is beautified.
```

Exercise 5

Practice

Working with the Order of Reasons in an Argument Outline

Below are topic sentences and lists of reasons. For each list, put an *X* by the reason that is the most significant, the reason you would save for last in an argument paragraph.

1. **topic sentence:** Manufacturers of pain relievers should stop the double packaging of their products.

   reason 1: _____ Putting a small jar into a big box is deceptive, making the buyer think he or she is getting more for the money.

   reason 2: _____ Buyers get irritated trying to open both a box and a jar.

   reason 3: __X__ Double packaging wastes valuable natural resources.

2. **topic sentence:** Our city should permit a snack bar to open at Greenwood Lake.

   reason 1: _____ Visitors to the lake would appreciate the chance to buy hot dogs, potato chips, and soda.

   reason 2: _____ There are no restaurants or stores near the lake.

   reason 3: __X__ The profits from the snack bar could be used to maintain the natural beauty of the lake area, which is currently looking seedy.

3. **topic sentence:** Parents should not let their children play in the sun for hours.

   reason 1: __X__ Too much sun in childhood can lead to skin cancer later in life.

   reason 2: _____ Too much sun, even in childhood, can cause premature wrinkling in adults.

   reason 3: _____ The sun can cause headaches and irritability in all age groups.

4. **topic sentence:** Seven-year-olds should be given a small allowance to spend as they wish.

   reason 1: _____ Seven-year-olds see other children their age with spending money.

   reason 2: __X__ Children need to learn to handle money responsibly.

   reason 3: _____ Learning about making change is good practice in math skills.

Exercise 6 **Recognizing Reasons That Overlap**

Practice

Below are topic sentences and lists of reasons. In each list, two reasons overlap. Put an X by the two reasons that overlap.

1. **topic sentence:** The college cafeteria should lower its prices.

   a. __X__ Prices are too high for most students.

   b. _____ Lower prices would actually mean a profit for the cafeteria because more students would eat there.

   c. __X__ Many students cannot afford to eat in the cafeteria.

   d. _____ The cafeteria has to compete with cheaper restaurants nearby.

2. **topic sentence:** Advertising should be banned from children's Saturday morning television programs.

   a. __X__ Young children are too innocent to know the way ads work.

   b. _____ Much of the advertising is for unhealthy food like sugary cereals and junk food.

   c. __X__ The ads manipulate unsuspecting children.

   d. _____ Ads push expensive toys that many parents cannot afford.

3. **topic sentence:** Our college needs a larger, lighted sign at the entrance.

   a. __X__ Some residents of our town have never heard of our college, so a large sign would be good publicity.

   b. _____ Visitors to the college have a hard time finding it.

   c. _____ Students who are preoccupied sometimes drive right past the entrance to the college at night.

   d. __X__ A better sign would make people more aware of the college.

Exercise 7 **Identifying a Reason That Is Not Specific**

Practice

For each of the following lists, put an X by the reason that is not specific.

1. **topic sentence:** The high school should hold a senior citizens' day to bring elderly people to school for a day of fun and entertainment.

   a. _____ Teenagers would enjoy talking to older people, especially since many teens do not have much contact with their own grandparents.

   b. _____ Planning a day's entertainment would teach teens how to organize a major event.

   c. __X__ The older people would benefit from the day.

   d. _____ Each generation would learn not to stereotype the other.

2. **topic sentence:** American college students should learn a foreign language.

    a. _____ Countries that compete with us economically, such as Japan and Germany, have a competitive edge because their children routinely learn English.

    b. _____ It is often easier for a person to get a good job if he or she speaks two languages.

    c. __X__ Learning a new language broadens a person's horizons.

    d. _____ Most Americans, at home or at work, have to interact with immigrants or visitors who do not speak English.

3. **topic sentence:** Our college should open a fitness center in the gym.

    a. _____ Health clubs are too expensive for many students.

    b. __X__ A fitness center would be good for students.

    c. _____ Students who have an hour or two between classes could work out in the gym.

    d. _____ Students who are new to the college could make friends by using the fitness center.

Exercise 8
Practice

Adding Details to an Outline

Following is part of an outline. It includes a topic sentence and three reasons. Add at least two sentences of details to each reason. Your details may be examples or description.

topic sentence: The staff at Bargain Supermarket should enforce the "9 Items or Less" rule at the express checkout lane.

reason: Customers who follow the rule must suffer because of people who don't obey the rule.

details: I once waited while the customer ahead of me unloaded about thirty items.

details: She said she was in a hurry, so she needed to use the express lane.

reason: Not enforcing the rule can create unpleasant confrontations among customers.

details: One lady started shouting at a man with too many items in his cart.

details: When he laughed at her, she hit him over the head with a bunch of broccoli.

reason: If it fails to enforce the rule, Bargain Supermarket may lose customers.

details: <u>If I am in a hurry and need to buy only one or two items, I avoid Bargain Supermarket.</u>

details: <u>I go to Family Foods, where the rule at the express lane is enforced, and I do my shopping more quickly.</u>

Rough Lines

Argument

Once you are satisfied with your outline, you can write the first draft of your paragraph. When you have completed it, you can begin revising the draft so that your argument is as clear, smooth, and convincing as it can be. The checklist below may help you with your revisions.

✔ Checklist

A Checklist for Revising the Draft of an Argument Paragraph

✔ Do any of my sentences need combining?

✔ Have I left out a serious or obvious reason?

✔ Should I change the order of my reasons?

✔ Do I have enough details?

✔ Are my details specific?

✔ Do I need to explain the problem or issue I am writing about?

✔ Do I need to link my ideas more clearly?

✔ Do I need a final sentence to stress my point?

Checking Your Reasons

Be sure that your argument has covered all the serious or obvious reasons. Sometimes writers get so caught up in drafting their ideas that they forget to mention something very basic to the argument. For instance, if you were arguing for a leash law for your community, you might state that dogs that run free can hurt people and damage property. But don't forget to mention another serious reason to keep dogs on leashes: dogs that are not restrained can get hurt or killed by cars.

One way to see whether you have left out a serious or obvious reason is to ask a friend or classmate to read your draft and react to your argument. Another technique is to put your draft aside for an hour or two and then read it as if you were a reader, not the writer.

Explaining the Problem or the Issue

Sometimes your argument discusses a problem so obvious to your audience that you do not need to explain it. On the other hand, sometimes you need to explain a problem or issue so that your audience can understand your point. If you tell readers of your local paper about teenage vandalism at Central High School, you probably need to explain what kind of vandalism has occurred and how often. Sometimes it's smart to convince readers of the seriousness of a situation by explaining it a little so that they will be more interested in your argument.

Transitions That Emphasize

In writing an argument paragraph, you can use different transitions, depending on how you present your point. But no matter how you present your reasons, you will probably want to *emphasize* one of them. Below are some transitions that can be used for emphasis.

Infobox

Transitions to use for emphasis: above all, especially, finally, mainly, most important, most of all, most significant, primarily

---

For example, by saying, *"Most important,* broken windows at Central High School are a safety problem," you put the emphasis for your audience on this one idea.

A Draft

Following is a draft of the argument paragraph on Roberts Park. When you read it, you'll notice these changes from the outline on pages 214–15:

- A description of the problem has been added.
- Details have been added.
- Short sentences have been combined.
- Transitions, including two sentences, have been added. "Most important" and "best of all"—transitions that show emphasis—have been included.

A Draft of an Argument Paragraph (Transitions are underlined.)

Roberts Park was once a pretty little park, but today it is overgrown with weeds, cluttered with trash and rusty benches. Roberts Park should be cleaned up and improved. Improving the park would make the downtown area more attractive to shoppers. Shoppers could stroll through a renovated park or rest there after shopping. Friends could <u>also</u> meet there for a day of shopping and lunch. <u>Shoppers are not the only ones who could enjoy the park.</u> Workers from nearby offices and stores could eat lunch outdoors. Several office complexes are near the park, and workers from these offices could bring their lunch to work and eat outside in good weather. I think many people would agree that an hour spent outdoors is a pleasant break from work. <u>Most important,</u> city children could play in an improved Roberts Park. They would get fresh air while they played on grass, not asphalt. <u>Best of all,</u> they would not have to play near traffic. <u>Children, shoppers, and workers would benefit from a clean-up of Roberts Park, but so would others.</u> An attractive park improves the city, and all residents benefit when a community is beautified.

Exercise 9	**Adding an Explanation of the Problem to an Argument Paragraph**
Practice	

This paragraph could use an explanation of the problem. Write a short explanation of the problem in the lines provided.

> Crystal Springs Apartments should get rid of its speed bumps. The majority of the residents at Crystal Springs did not want the bumps. They were installed without a vote of the residents. If the management at the apartments had asked the residents to vote, most residents would have voted against the bumps. Residents dislike the bumps because the structures can damage cars. Even when a driver drives at the speed limit, hitting a bump can wreck the alignment of a car because the bumps are very high. More serious damage can occur if a driver drives just five miles over the speed limit. Worst of all, the bumps, which were installed for safety reasons, are creating safety hazards. Drivers are avoiding the bumps by swerving onto the grass. Residents who walk through the apartment complex are in danger of being hit by drivers who swerve onto the lawn. Clearly, the bumps have not improved life at Crystal Springs Apartments; they have made it worse.

Answers Will Vary. Possible answers shown at right.

Crystal Springs is a large and pleasant apartment complex, but recently it has become a less pleasant place to live. Residents at the complex now face large speed bumps installed on all the roads.

Exercise 10	**Recognizing Transitions in an Argument Paragraph**
Practice	

Underline all the transitions—words, phrases, or sentences—in the paragraph below. Put a double line under any transitions that emphasize.

> Every time I go into my favorite restaurant, I am greeted by a server who hands me a menu and then puts a glass of ice water on the table. I need one of those items, the menu, but I may not need the water. Restaurants should not give customers a glass of water unless the customers request it. <u>For one thing</u>, giving everyone a glass of water wastes water. Most people order some kind of drink, like iced tea or Pepsi, and they don't touch the water. At the end of the meal, the water is thrown down the drain. Our whole country is trying to conserve our natural resources, and yet we waste all this water. <u>Water is not the only thing we would save if restaurants stopped giving it routinely.</u> We would save energy. The glasses holding all that water need to be washed. Running the dishwasher takes electricity. More glasses mean more use of the dishwasher. <u>More important</u> than conserving water or energy is the message the new policy would send. If customers had to ask for their water, they would think about the restaurant's reason for not providing it: conservation. People who think about saving water or energy may think about how they can save water or electricity at home. And so a simple restaurant policy can do a little toward saving our earth.

Exercise 11	**Adding a Final Sentence to an Argument Paragraph**
Practice	

The following paragraph can use a final sentence to sum up the reasons or to reinforce the topic sentence. Add that final sentence.

> My boyfriend is away at basic training for the Marines. He calls me often, and I love his calls. But I wish he would write me letters. People who are away from their

loved ones should write letters if they want to show they care. It is easy to pick up the phone, but writing a letter takes more effort. A letter shows me the writer spent some time thinking about me and about what to tell me. Taking that time is a way of telling me I am special. A letter can also say things a speaker can't. Sometimes it's hard to say "I'm sorry" or "I miss you" on the phone. But words of intimacy can be easier to write than to say. Most important, a letter can be read over and over. The words last. I can carry a letter with me or hide it in a special place, and every time I read it, I can feel close to the writer.

Answers Will Vary.
Possible answers shown at right.

A letter has great power; it can bring two people close and reconnect them with each reading.

Final Lines

Argument

Following is the final version of the argument paragraph on Roberts Park. When you read it, you'll notice several changes from the draft on page 219:

Note: For more on parallelism, see Chapter 16.

- Some words have been changed to improve the details.
- The first sentence has been changed so that it is more descriptive and uses a parallel pattern for emphasis.

A Final Version of an Argument Paragraph
(Changes from the draft are underlined.)

Roberts Park was once a pretty little park, but today it is overgrown with weeds, <u>littered with trash, and cluttered with rusty benches.</u> Roberts Park should be cleaned up and improved. Improving the park would make the downtown area more attractive to shoppers. Shoppers could stroll through a <u>restored</u> park or rest there after shopping. Friends could also meet at the park for a day of shopping and lunch. Shoppers are not the only ones who could enjoy the park. Workers from nearby offices and stores could eat lunch outdoors. Several office complexes are near the park, and workers from these offices could bring <u>a bag</u> lunch to work and eat outside in good weather. I think many people would agree that an hour spent outdoors is a pleasant break from work. Most important, city children could play in an improved Roberts Park. They would get fresh air while they played on grass, not asphalt. Best of all, they would not have to play near traffic. Children, shoppers, and workers would benefit from a clean-up of Roberts Park, but so would others. An attractive park improves the city, and all residents benefit when a community is beautified.

Before you prepare the final copy of your argument paragraph, check your latest draft for errors in spelling and punctuation and for any errors made in typing or copying.

Exercise 12 **Proofreading to Prepare the Final Version**

Practice Following is a paragraph with the kinds of errors that are easy to overlook when you prepare the final version of an assignment. Correct the errors, writing above the lines. There are twelve errors.

Our college should put a pencil sharpener in every classroom. First of all‚ putting
                                                                          students
a sharpener in each class would help many students. Most student take notes and

tests in pencil. Often, a pencil point breaks or gets worn down while a student is

writing. A pencil sharpener in the room takes care of the problem. Second, a pencil
sharpener
sharpner would eliminate distractions in class. For instance, I was in my math class
                                              didn't
yesterday when my pencil point broke. I dind't have another pencil, and there was no
                                                          borrow   *Last*
sharpener in the room. I had to interrupt the lesson to ask to borow a pencil. last of all,
        sharpener
a pencil sharpner in each room would solve the problem of wandering students. At

least once a day, a student comes into one of my classes, politely asking, "Does this
                              "It's   *it's*
room have a pencil sharpener? Its embarrassing to have to do this. And its worse
                      through
to wander desperately threw the halls, trying to find one of the few rooms with a

sharpener. Pencil sharpeners wouldn't cost the college much, but they would sure
              difference
make a diference.

Lines of Detail: A Walk-Through Assignment

Write a one-paragraph letter to the editor of your local newspaper. Argue for some change you want for your community. You could argue for a traffic light, turn signal, or stop sign at a specific intersection. Or you could argue for bike paths in certain places, a recycling program, more bus service, or any other specific change you feel is needed. To write your paragraph, follow these steps:

Step 1: Begin by listing all the reasons and details you can about your topic. Survey your list and consider any possible objections. Answer the objections as well as you can, and see if the objections can lead you to more reasons.

Step 2: Group your reasons, listing the details that fit under each reason. Add details where they are needed, and check to see if any reasons overlap.

Step 3: Survey your reasons and details, and draft a topic sentence. Be sure that your topic sentence states the subject and takes a stand.

Step 4: Write an outline. Then revise it, checking that you have enough reasons to make your point. Also check that your reasons are specific and in an effective order. Be sure that you have sufficient details for each reason. Check that your outline includes answers to any significant objections.

Step 5: Write a draft of your argument. Revise the draft until it includes any necessary explanations of the problem being argued, all serious or obvious reasons, and sufficient specific details. Also check that the most important reason is stated last. Add all the transitions that are needed to link your reasons and details.

Step 6: Before you prepare the final copy of your paragraph, decide whether you need a final sentence to stress your point, and check whether your transitions are smooth and logical. Refine your word choice. Then check for errors in spelling, punctuation, and grammar.

Writing Your Own Argument Paragraph

When you write on any of the topics below, be sure to work through the stages of the writing process in preparing your argument paragraph.

1. Write a paragraph for readers of your local newspaper, arguing for one of the following:
   a. a ban on all advertising of alcohol
   b. mandatory jail terms for those convicted of drunk driving
   c. a ban on smoking in all enclosed public places

2. In a paragraph, argue one of the following topics to the audience specified. If your instructor agrees, brainstorm your topic with a group before you start writing. Ask the group to "play audience," reacting to your reasons, raising objections, and asking questions.

   topic a: Early morning classes should be abolished at your college.
   audience: the dean of academic affairs

   topic b: Attendance in college classes should be optional.
   audience: the instructors at your college

   topic c: College students should get discounts at movie theaters.
   audience: the owner of your local movie theater

   topic d: Your college should provide a day-care facility for students with children.
   audience: the president of your college

   topic e: Businesses should hire more student interns.
   audience: the president of a company (name it) you would like to work for

   topic f: You deserve a raise.
   audience: your boss

3. Write a paragraph for or against any of the following topics. Your audience for the argument is your classmates and your instructor.

   For or Against
   a. seat belt laws
   b. ratings for music CDs and tapes
   c. dress codes in high school
   d. uniforms in elementary schools
   e. mandatory student activities fees for commuter students
   f. a law requiring a month waiting period between buying a marriage license and getting married

Name: _____ **Section:** _____

Peer Review Form for an Argument Paragraph

After you have written a draft of your argument paragraph, let a writing partner read it. When your partner has completed the form below, discuss the comments. Then repeat the same process for your partner's paragraph.

The topic sentence has this subject: _____

It takes this stand: _____

The most convincing part of the paragraph starts with the words _____

_____ and ends with the words _____

After reading this paragraph, I can think of an objection to this argument. The objection is

_____

The paragraph has/has not handled this objection. (Choose one.)

The part of the argument with the best details is the part about _____

_____

The part that could use more or better details is the part about _____

_____

The order of the reasons (a) is effective or (b) could be better. (Choose one.)

I have questions about _____

Other comments: _____

_____

_____

_____

_____

_____

_____

_____

_____

_____

_____

Reviewer's Name: _____

WRITING FROM READING: Argument

Athletic Heroes
James Beekman

James Beekman was a junior in high school when he wrote this essay. It was one of thirty-three selected from more than twelve thousand entries in a Newsweek *magazine contest. In his essay, Beekman argues that we overemphasize sports at all levels and should return to the idea of playing sports for fun, not for money and winning.*

Words You May Need to Know

accolades (paragraph 4): awards, honors

generate (6): create

salary caps (7): upper limit of a salary range

1   Almost every child grows up with a professional athlete as his or her hero. Why do some kids choose a hero they don't even know? Maybe it's because society dictates what is popular. I think that sports in general receive too much recognition, not only nationally, but locally, and this preoccupation with athletics distracts society from other equally important activities.

2   This trend toward sports starts when children are very young. At an early age, every child usually picks a sport he or she likes and at which he or she can excel. It is only natural, then, that the child will choose a professional athlete in that sport as a hero. There is nothing wrong with this except that some children, and even their parents, become too interested in that sport and less focused on school. An example of this is the large number of children who play on traveling soccer, hockey, and baseball teams. They spend hours on the road away from home and families. Sports are exciting and can be great for building talent, but I think sports should be reserved for recreation and should not be a substitute for education.

3   Sports receive too much recognition in high school. I am a junior in high school. I have participated in sports all my life. My involvement in sports began when I was three years old and took swimming lessons. Then I moved on to soccer when I was four and to baseball when I was six. I even played basketball in elementary school. I continued to play soccer, baseball, and basketball through the eighth grade and managed to run track a couple of years as well. I have great memories of how much fun these sports were, but I also remember that the coaches' focus on winning became more pronounced the older I became. I thought sports were intended to be fun, but now I question this. I noticed a drastic change in attitude about sports when I entered high school. It seems that the coaches of high school sports make sports more than just an extracurricular activity.

4   Sports seem to receive more attention than other activities in high school. One of these activities is the debate team. I am not part of this team, but I know the members work very hard and practice as many hours as any of the athletes. An activity in which I am involved is the high school show choir. We practice after school from six to fifteen hours a week, and then travel out of town for competitions on weekends. The show choir has consistently won top awards and championships and even has a better record than most of the high school sports teams. And yet who receives all the accolades? One has only to turn to the second section of the *Courier*, our local newspaper, to answer this question. The high school athletes are given front-page coverage. Both the football and the basketball teams had school pep rallies before their big games. There was even a special rally for the boys' soccer team when it went to the state tournament. There have never been any special rallies given for the show choir and its sixty members, however, yet they have repeatedly won contests.

5   The most important thing that is being denied in the overemphasis on high school sports is academic achievement. Many students who excel academically receive far less attention than the stars of the athletic teams. The goal of schools should be to educate the students and not to sensationalize sports. Colleges award many sports scholarships as well as scholarships for academic achievements, and supposedly their main purpose is education. It is possible that some students who do not excel academically but who are eager to learn might be denied an opportunity to attend college, while a star athlete who is not motivated academically might be given a full scholarship.

6   On the professional level, money and winning seem to be the most important goal. Whatever happened to the old idea of playing a sport for fun? Professional athletes seem to be motivated by making the most money for the least amount of work. Most sports last only one season of a few months. The rest of the year the athletes are free to travel and make television commercials and public appearances. Many of these athletes also endorse products to generate additional income. In general, most professional athletes today in basketball, football, baseball, and hockey make more than a million dollars per year. Deion Sanders just signed a $35 million contract with the Dallas Cowboys. In baseball, Ken Griffey, Jr. just signed a multiyear contract with the Seattle Mariners for which he will receive more than $7 million a year. These are the most highly paid players in their sport, but other team members are not far behind. Professional golfer Greg Norman made about $1.6 million in tournament wins last year but raked in an estimated $40 million from his endorsements.

7   Not only do these sports heroes make enormous sums of money, but they also seem to want even more. Last year the major-league baseball teams went on strike for more money before the World Series was even played. The National Hockey League went on strike over salary caps. Hardworking Americans don't make nearly as much as the professional athletes and receive no attention at all.

8   Sports should be for recreation and fun. More recently, sports figures have become more focused on securing large salaries and less focused on entertainment. Almost every child has a star athlete as his or her hero. Maybe if children were better informed about these heroes, they would look elsewhere for a hero. And who would that hero be? Just maybe that hero could be someone as extraordinary as their parents.

WRITING FROM READING: "Athletic Heroes"

When you write on any of the following topics, work through the stages of the writing process in preparing your argument paragraph.

1. Beekman says, "The most important thing that is being denied in the overemphasis on high school sports is academic achievement." Write a paragraph in which you (a) argue for more emphasis on academic achievement in high school or (b) argue that the emphasis on high school sports is healthy for all high school students.

2. Write a paragraph arguing one of the following:

   _____ (name a professional athlete) is too highly paid.

   _____ (name a professional athlete) deserves his/her pay.

   Coaches in children's sports place too much emphasis on winning.

   Sports receive more attention than any other activity in high school.

3. In some high schools, successful athletes may be part of an exclusive group. Write a paragraph arguing that the focus on winning athletes can make other students feel inferior and rejected.

4. Write a paragraph arguing that, instead of sports heroes, children should have other heroes. Be specific in naming who the "other heroes" may be.

5. Write a paragraph arguing that playing a sport for fun is worthwhile, no matter how athletic one is.

Afrocentric Education Pointless if Girls Are Excluded
Julianne Malveaux

Julianne Malveaux is a professor of African-American studies at the University of California at Berkeley. In this editorial, she explores a recent move to create schools exclusively for black males. She identifies several problems with such schools, particularly their impact on black females.

Words You May Need to Know

ACLU (paragraph 1): the American Civil Liberties Union, a national organization that fights to maintain constitutional rights

NOW (1): the National Organization for Women, a group that supports women's rights

role models (2): people others may try to imitate, heroes

gnaws (3): eats away, wears away, wastes

Afrocentric (3): centered on African-American history, culture, and concerns

curriculum (3): a course of study, a plan of study in school

denigrate (4): put down, speak damagingly of

implicitly (5): in a hidden manner, without saying so openly

proponents (6): supporters

stigmatizing (8): branding, giving a mark of disgrace

parochial school (10): an elementary, middle, or high school operated by a religious organization

addressed (11): dealt with, paid attention to

1   They have been proposed in New York and Milwaukee, and public schools just for black boys were supposed to open in Detroit this fall but were stopped by a successful lawsuit filed by the ACLU and the NOW Legal Defense Fund. A federal judge ruled that the Detroit plan for three all-male academies was unconstitutional.

2   Why should black boys have their own schools? Those who support them say black men are "endangered" and cite statistics on dropout status and arrest rates to back themselves up. They say that too many black boys, raised by their mothers, lack positive male role models and are all too vulnerable to negative influences, like gangs.

3   They say that the public school curriculum ignores black achievement and gnaws away at self-esteem, and that an Afrocentric curriculum taught by black men is necessary to rebuild this esteem for black boys. And they say these schools address some of these problems.

4   But every problem that black boys face is also faced by black girls. Girls rarely are arrested, but they, too, drop out and get caught up in all of the urban negatives—teen pregnancy, dead-end careers and sometimes worse. Like black boys, many black girls would benefit from male attention and positive male role models. Like boys, they are vulnerable to gangs and others in the absence of those models. And girls, like boys, read books that denigrate African Americans,

those histories that mention only Booker T. Washington, Dr. Martin Luther King, or blacks in the context of slavery.

5   Black girls, like black boys, would greatly benefit from an improvement in the quality of urban education. These girls are sent a stunning negative message when they observe a shift in resources from all students to male students. They are being told, implicitly, that their educations are less important than black male educations.

6   Proponents of all-black boy schools, like Chicago author Juwanza Kunjufu, would not only segregate students. Kunjufu, alleging that "black women cannot teach black men," would also make teaching environments almost entirely male. Yet if Kunjufu is right, if black women can't teach black men, then the illiteracy rate among African Americans would be even higher than it is now, as black women have historically been the backbone of urban school systems.

7   Those who say black boys need their own schools are crying "crisis." Their argument does not stand up unless we believe that the black man is "endangered." To protect against "endangered species" status, these boys bond under the leadership of African-American male teachers.

8   But these separate schools seem simply to reinforce the notion of "endangerment," stigmatizing black male youngsters and separating them from the general school population. And it sends these boys the message that something is so wrong with girls and women that they are incapable or learning in their presence!

9   The existence of all-black boy schools suggests that black boys are special, but black girls are not. And this is a message girls may carry through womanhood. If black boys/men are so special, must black women support them financially when they cannot find work? Should they put up with violent or abusive behavior because the black man is so special? Should she cling to traditional roles to please this "special" man? Should she make her needs secondary to his?

10   Because of students' different capabilities, there is no one model of education that serves every child. Some learn best in a highly disciplined parochial or military school, others in loosely structured programs for the gifted and talented.

11   Under the umbrella of education, there may well be room for Afrocentric academies targeted toward black male youth. But these academies may cause more problems than they solve unless the educational needs of black girls are also addressed.

WRITING FROM READING: "Afrocentric Education Pointless if Girls Are Excluded"

When you write on any of these topics, work through the stages of the writing process in preparing your paragraph.

   1. Write a summary of Malveaux's article. Focus on the point of her argument and the details she uses to support her point.

2. Write an argument for or against any of the following. Your audience is your classmates and instructor.

all-male schools	all-female schools
all-male colleges	all-female colleges
all-male military colleges	all-male clubs
all-female clubs	

3. Write an argument that agrees or disagrees with any of the statements below. Your audience is your classmates and instructor.

The public school curriculum ignores black achievement.
Black women cannot teach black males effectively.
Black boys need their own schools.

4. Write a letter to your local school board. In it, argue for one of the following:

hiring more male teachers to serve as role models
requiring a class in self-esteem at the (elementary, middle school, or high school) level

10 Writing an Essay

WHAT IS AN ESSAY?

You write an essay when you have more to say than can be covered in one paragraph. An **essay** can consist of one paragraph, but in this book, we take it to mean a writing of more than one paragraph. An essay has a main point, called a *thesis*, supported by subpoints. The subpoints are the *topic sentences*. Each paragraph in the *body*, or main part, of the essay has a topic sentence. In fact, each paragraph in the body of the essay is like the paragraphs you've already written because each one makes a point and then supports it.

COMPARING THE SINGLE PARAGRAPH AND THE ESSAY

Read the paragraph and the essay that follow, both about Bob, the writer's brother. You will notice many similarities.

A Single Paragraph

I think I am lucky to have a brother who is two years older than I am. For one thing, my brother Bob fought all the typical child-parent battles, and I was the real winner. Bob was the one who made my parents understand that seventeen-year-olds shouldn't have an 11:00 p.m. curfew on weekends. He fought for his rights. By the time I turned seventeen, my parents had accepted the later curfew, and I didn't have to fight for it. Bob also paved the way for me at school. He was such a great athlete that I benefited from his reputation. When I tried out for the basketball team, I had an advantage before I hit the court. I was Bob Cruz's younger brother, so the coach thought I had to be a pretty good athlete, too. At home and at school, my big brother was a big help to me.

An Essay

Some people complain about being the youngest child or the middle child in the family. These people believe older children get all the attention and grab all the power. I am the younger brother in my family, and I disagree with the complainers. I think I am lucky to have a brother who is two years older than I am.

For one thing, my brother Bob fought all the typical child-parent battles, and I was the real winner. Bob was the one who made my parents understand that seventeen-year-olds shouldn't have an 11:00 p.m. curfew on weekends. He fought for his rights, and the fighting was not easy. I remember months of arguments between Bob and my parents as Bob tried to explain that not all teens on the street at 11:30 are punks or criminals. Bob was the one who suffered from being grounded or who lost the use of my father's car. By the time I turned seventeen, my parents had accepted the later curfew, and I did not have to fight for it.

Bob also paved the way for me at school. Because he was so popular with the other students and the teachers, he created a positive image of what the boys in our family were like. When I started school, I walked into a place where people were ready to like me, just as they liked Bob. I remember the first day of class when the teachers read the new class rolls. When they got to my name, they asked, "Are you Bob Cruz's brother?" When I said yes, they smiled. Bob's success opened doors for me in school sports, too. He was such a great athlete that I benefited from his reputation. When I tried out for the basketball team, I had an advantage before I hit the court. I was Bob Cruz's younger brother, so the coach thought I had to be a pretty good athlete, too.

I had many battles to fight as I grew up. Like all children, I had to struggle to gain independence and respect. In my struggles at home and at school, my big brother was a big help to me.

If you read the two selections carefully, you noticed that they make the same main point, and they support that point with two subpoints:

> **main point:** I think I am lucky to have a brother who is two years older than I am.
> **subpoints:** 1. My brother Bob fought all the typical child-parent battles, and I was the real winner.
> 2. Bob also paved the way for me at school.

You noticed that the essay is longer because it has more details and examples to support the points.

ORGANIZING AN ESSAY

When you write an essay of more than one paragraph, the **thesis** is the focus of your entire essay; it is the major point of your essay. The other important points that are part of the thesis are in topic sentences.

TEACHING TIP:
Tell students that the thesis statement is the controlling idea for the essay much like a topic sentence is the controlling idea for a paragraph.

> **thesis:** Working as a salesperson has changed my character.
> **topic sentence:** I have had to learn patience.
> **topic sentence:** I have developed the ability to listen.
> **topic sentence:** I have become more tactful.

Notice that the thesis expresses a bigger idea than the topic sentences below it, and it is supported by the topic sentences. The essay has an introduction, a body, and a conclusion.

Note: Throughout this chapter, the terms "thesis" and "thesis statement" are used interchangeably.

1. **Introduction:** The first paragraph is usually the introduction. The thesis goes here.
2. **Body:** This central part of the essay is the part where you support your main point (the thesis). Each paragraph in the body of the essay has its own topic sentence.

3. **Conclusion:** Usually one paragraph long, the conclusion reminds the reader of the thesis.

WRITING THE THESIS

There are several characteristics of a thesis:

1. It is expressed in a sentence. A thesis is *not* the same as the topic or the title of the essay.

   topic: quitting smoking
   title: Why I Quit Smoking
   thesis: I quit smoking because I was concerned for my health, and I wanted to prove to myself that I could break the habit.

2. A thesis *does not announce;* it makes a point about the subject.

   announcement: This essay will explain the reasons why young adults should watch what they eat.
   thesis: Young adults should watch what they eat so they can live healthy lives and prevent future health problems.

   Note: Some students will have difficulty breaking the habit of "announcing" what the essay will be about.

3. A thesis *is not too broad.* Some ideas are just too big to cover well in an essay. A thesis that tries to cover too much can lead to a superficial or boring essay.

   too broad: People all over the world should work on solving their interpersonal communications problems.
   acceptable thesis: As a Southerner, I had a hard time understanding that some New Yorkers think slow speech is ignorant speech.

4. A thesis *is not too narrow.* Sometimes, writers start with a thesis that looks good because it seems specific and precise. Later, when they try to support such a thesis, they can't find anything to say.

   too narrow: My sister pays forty dollars a week for a special formula for her baby.
   acceptable thesis: My sister had no idea what it would cost to care for a baby.

Hints for Writing a Thesis

1. You can mention the specific subpoints of your essay in your thesis. For example, your thesis might be

> I hated *The Silence of the Lambs* because the film was ultraviolent and it glorified criminals.

With this thesis, you have indicated the two subpoints of your essay: *The Silence of the Lambs* was ultraviolent; *The Silence of the Lambs* glorified criminals.

2. You can make a point without listing your subpoints in your thesis. For example, you can write a thesis like this:

> I hated *The Silence of the Lambs* because of the way it made the unspeakable into entertainment.

With this thesis, you can still use the subpoints stating that the movie was ultraviolent and glorified criminals. You just don't have to mention all your subpoints in the thesis. Be sure to check with your instructor about the type of thesis you should devise.

| Exercise 1 | **Recognizing Good Thesis Sentences** |

Practice

Following is a list of thesis statements. Some are acceptable, but others are too broad or too narrow. Some are announcements; others are topics, not sentences. Put a *G* next to the good thesis sentences.

TEACHING TIP:
Ask students to see if they can spot which "statements" are actually fragments and thus not suitable thesis statements.

1. _____ Why oat bran is an important part of a healthy diet will be discussed in the following essay.

2. _____ My family was a small family unit.

3. _____ The environment is a major concern of people in today's society.

4. _____ How to install speakers in a car.

5. _____ Computers are changing the world.

6. _*G*_ Being an only child has its advantages.

7. _*G*_ The government should stop making pennies since they have out-lived their usefulness.

8. _____ St. Augustine, Florida, is the oldest city in the United States.

9. _____ The advantages of buying an American car.

10. _*G*_ Learning to play a musical instrument can bring a person much pleasure.

| Exercise 2 | **Writing a Thesis That Relates to the Subpoints** |

Practice

Following are lists of subpoints that could be discussed in an essay. Write a thesis for each list. Remember that there are two ways to write a thesis: you can write a thesis that includes the specific subpoints, or you can write one that makes a point without listing the subpoints. The first one is done for you, using both kinds of topic sentences.

1. one kind of thesis: *If you want a pet, a cat is easier to care for than a dog.*

another kind of thesis: *Cats make better pets than dogs because cats don't need to be walked, don't mind being alone, and don't make any noise.*

subpoints:
   a. Cats don't have to be walked and exercised like dogs do.
   b. Cats are independent and don't mind being home alone, but a dog gets lonely.
   c. Cats are quieter than dogs.

Answers Will Vary.
Possible answers shown at right.

2. thesis: *Good neighbors can make your life easier.*

subpoints:
    a. Neighbors will often collect your mail when you are out of town.
    b. In an emergency, neighbors can lend you the tools you need.

3. thesis: *Sometimes, neighbors can be helpful; at other times, they can be difficult.*

subpoints:
    a. Neighbors will often collect your mail when you are out of town.
    b. In an emergency, neighbors can lend you the tools you need.
    c. Neighbors can be nosy and critical.
    d. Neighbors can invade your living space.

4. thesis: *Employers look for workers who are hard-working, appropriately trained, and positive.*

subpoints:
    a. Employers look for people who are prepared to work hard.
    b. Employers will hire people with the right training.
    c. Employers want workers who have a positive attitude toward the job.

5. thesis: *Except for a few pleasant surprises, the mail is usually unpleasant or irritating.*

subpoints:
    a. Sometimes the mail includes an unexpected pleasure, such as a card or letter.
    b. Other times, the mail consists of bills.
    c. Mostly, the mail is junk mail.

WRITING THE ESSAY IN STEPS

In an essay, you follow the same steps you learned in writing a paragraph—thought lines, outlines, rough drafts, and final version—but you adapt them to the longer essay form.

Thought Lines

Essay

Often you begin by *narrowing a topic.* Your instructor may give you a large topic so that you can find something smaller within the broad topic that you would like to write about.

Some students think that because they have several paragraphs to write, they should pick a big topic, one that will give them enough to say. But big topics can lead to boring, superficial, general essays. A smaller topic can challenge you to find the specific, concrete examples and details that make an essay effective.

If your instructor asked you to write about college, for instance, you might *freewrite* some ideas as you narrow the topic:

narrowing the topic of college

what college means to me—too big, and it could be boring

college vs. high school—everyone might choose this topic

college students—too big

college students who have jobs—better!

problems of working and going to college—OK!

In your freewriting, you can consider your purpose—to write an essay about some aspect of college—and audience—your instructor and classmates. Your narrowed topic will appeal to this audience because many students hold jobs and instructors are familiar with the problems of working students.

Listing Ideas

Once you have a narrow topic, you can use whatever process works for you. You can brainstorm by writing a series of questions and answers about your topic, you can freewrite on the topic, you can list ideas on the topic, or you can combine these processes. Following is a sample listing of ideas on the topic of the problems of working and going to college:

problems of working and going to college

early classes	weekends only time to study
too tired to pay attention	no social life
tried to study at work	apartment a mess
got caught	missed work for makeup test
got reprimanded	get behind in school
slept in class	need salary for tuition
constantly racing around	rude to customers
no sleep	girlfriend ready to kill me
little time to do homework	

Clustering the Ideas

By clustering related items on the list, you'll find it easier to see the connections between ideas. The following items have been clustered (grouped), and they have been listed under subtitles.

Problems of Working and Going to College: Ideas in Clusters

problems at school	**problems at work**
early classes	tried to study at work
too tired to pay attention	got caught
slept in class	got reprimanded
little time to do homework	missed work for make-up test
get behind in school	rude to customers

problems outside of work and school

weekends only time to study

no social life

apartment a mess

girlfriend ready to kill me

When you surveyed the clusters, you probably noticed that some of the ideas from the original list were left out. These ideas, on racing around, not getting enough sleep, and needing tuition money, could fit into more than one place or might not fit anywhere. You might come back to them later.

When you name each cluster by giving it a subtitle, you move toward a focus for each body paragraph of your essay. And by beginning to focus the body paragraphs, you start thinking about the main point, the thesis of the essay. Concentrating on the thesis and on focused paragraphs helps you *unify* your essay.

Reread the clustered ideas. When you do so, you'll notice that each cluster is about problems at a different place. You can incorporate that concept into a thesis with a sentence like this:

> Students who work while they attend college face problems at school, at work, and at home.

Once you have a thesis and a list of details, you can begin working on the outlines part of the writing process.

TEACHING TIP:
This is a good place to remind students that not all thesis statements are segmented. However, they should be aware that some writing instructors prefer a segmented thesis statement because it provides students with the direction and organization of the essay's body paragraphs.

| **Exercise 3** | **Narrowing Topics** |

👥 Collaborate

Working with a partner or a group, narrow these topics so that the new topics are related but smaller, and suitable for short essays that are between four and six paragraphs long. The first topic is narrowed for you.

1. **topic:** summer vacation
   smaller, related topics:

   a. a car trip with children

   b. Disney World: not a vacation paradise

   c. my vacation job

2. **topic:** cars
   smaller, related topics:

Answers Will Vary.
Possible answers shown at right.

   a. driver's education class

   b. the pleasure of owning a sports car

   c. car alarms

3. **topic:** sports
   smaller, related topics:

   a. my high school football injuries

   b. the worst sports announcers

   c. the best basketball courts in town

4. **topic:** pets
   smaller, related topics:

   a. taking care of parakeets

   b. why ferrets make good pets

   c. my dog, the hero

5. topic: money
smaller, related topics:

a. <u>learning to fill out income tax forms</u>

b. <u>how to use credit cards wisely</u>

c. <u>the best clothes bargains I've found</u>

Exercise 4 **Clustering Related Ideas**

Practice

Below are two topics, each with a list of ideas. Mark all the related items on the list with the same number (*1*, *2*, or *3*). Some items might not get any number. When you have finished marking the list, write a title for each number that explains the cluster of ideas.

1. topic: why teenage marriages fail

_3_ teens are not ready to be responsible to a mate

_3_ one partner is insecure

_1_ jobs do not pay much without college degree

_1_ rent is expensive

_2_ in-laws interfere

_3_ one mate is too critical of the other

_2_ old friends create temptations

_2_ friends gossip to one partner about the other

_3_ novelty of being married wears off

_1_ no cash for entertainment

____ influence of media

Answers Will Vary.
Possible answers
shown at right.

The ideas marked *1* can be titled <u>money problems</u>

The ideas marked *2* can be titled <u>outsiders create problems</u>

The ideas marked *3* can be titled <u>partners' personal problems</u>

2. topic: giving a good party

_3_ circulate among all the guests

_1_ invite people who'd like each other

_1_ plan a menu you can cook ahead of time

_3_ make sure all the guests have someone to talk to

_1_ keep the guest list small

<u> 2 </u> the day of the party, clean up the party area

<u> 2 </u> an hour before the party, set up the buffet table

<u> 2 </u> put out glasses and ice

<u> 2 </u> arrange a selection of things to drink

<u> 2 </u> have music playing before the first guest arrives

<u> 3 </u> look like you're having a good time

<u>   </u> neighbors might complain

<u> 1 </u> invite people at least a week ahead

The items marked *1* can be titled <u>*long before the party*   </u>

The items marked *2* can be titled <u>*the day of the party*   </u>

The items marked *3* can be titled <u>*at the party*   </u>

Outlines

Essay

In the next stage of writing your essay, draft an outline. Use the thesis to focus your ideas. There are many kinds of outlines, but all are used to help a writer organize ideas. When you use a **formal outline,** you show the difference between a main idea and its supporting details by *indenting* the supporting details. In a formal outline, Roman numerals (I, II, III, and so on) and capital letters are used. Each Roman numeral represents a paragraph, and the letters represent supporting details.

The Structure of a Formal Outline

paragraph 1   I. Thesis

paragraph 2   II. Topic sentence

                   A.

                   B.

details   C.

                   D.

                   E.

paragraph 3   III. Topic sentence

                   A.

                   B.

details   C.

                   D.

                   E.

paragraph 4   IV. Topic sentence

                   A.

                   B.

details   C.

                   D.

                   E.

paragraph 5   V. Conclusion

TEACHING TIP:

Tell students that the thesis will be only one sentence (statement), and that they should expect to develop some general statements to lead into the thesis statement. (see "Hints for Writing the Introduction" on pp. 244–46.)

Hints for Outlining

Developing a good, clear outline now can save you hours of confused, disorganized writing later. The extra time you spend to make sure your outline has sufficient details and that *each paragraph stays on one point* will pay off in the long run.

1. Check the topic sentences. Keep in mind that the topic sentence in each body paragraph should support the thesis sentence. If a topic sentence is not carefully connected to the thesis, the structure of the essay will be confusing. In the following list, the topic sentence that does not fit is crossed out:

thesis

topic sentences

   I. A home-cooked dinner can be a rewarding experience for the cook and the guests.

  II. Preparing a meal is a satisfying activity.

 III. It is a pleasure for the cook to see guests enjoy the meal.

 IV. ~~Many recipes are handed down through generations.~~

  V. Dinner guests are flattered that someone cooked for them.

 VI. Dining at home is a treat for everyone at the table or in the kitchen.

Since the thesis of this outline is about the pleasure of dining at home, for the cook and the guests, topic sentence IV doesn't fit: it isn't about the joy of cooking *or* of being a dinner guest. It takes the essay off track. A careful check of the links between the thesis and topic sentences will help keep your essay focused.

2. Include enough details. Some writers believe that they don't need many details in the outline. They think they can fill in the details later, when they actually write the essay. Even though some writers do manage to add details later, others who are in a hurry or who run out of ideas will run into problems. For example, imagine that a writer has included very few details in an outline, like this outline for a paragraph:

  II. A burglary makes the victim feel unsafe.
    A. The person has lost property.
    B. The person's home territory has been invaded.

The paragraph created from that outline might be too short and might lack specific details, like this:

A burglary makes the victim feel unsafe. First of all, the victim has lost property. Second, a person's home territory has been invaded.

If you have difficulty thinking of ideas when you write, try to tackle the problem in the outline. The more details you put into your outline, the more detailed and effective your draft essay will be. For example, suppose the same outline on the burglary topic had more details, like this:

  II. A burglary makes the victim feel unsafe.

more details about burglary

    A. The person has lost property.
    B. The property could be worth hundreds of dollars.
    C. The victim can lose a television or a camera or VCR.
    D. The burglars may take cash.
    E. Worse, items with personal value, like family jewelry or heirlooms, can be stolen.

more details
about
safety
concerns
{
F. Even worse, a person's territory has been invaded.
G. People who thought they were safe know they are not safe.
H. The fear is that the invasion can happen again.

You will probably agree that the paragraph will be more detailed, too.

3. Stay on one point. It is a good idea to check the outline of each body paragraph to see whether each paragraph stays on one point. Compare each topic sentence, which is at the top of the list for the paragraph, against the details indented under it. Staying on one point gives each paragraph unity.

Below is the outline for a body paragraph that has problems staying on one point. See if you can spot the problem areas.

III. Sonya gives warmly of her money and of herself.
   A. I remember how freely she gave her time when our club had a car wash.
   B. She is always willing to share her lecture notes with me.
   C. Sonya gives ten percent of her salary to her church.
   D. She is a member of Big Sisters and spends every Saturday with a disadvantaged child.
   E. She can read people's minds when they are in trouble.
   F. She knows what they are feeling.

The topic sentence of the paragraph is about generosity. But sentences E and F talk about Sonya's insight, not her generosity. When you have a problem staying on one point, you can solve the problem in two ways:

1. Eliminate details that do not fit your main point.
2. Change the topic sentence to cover all the ideas in the paragraph.

For example, you could cut out sentences E and F about Sonya's generosity, getting rid of the details that do not fit. As an alternative, you could change the topic sentence in the paragraph so that it relates to all the ideas in the paragraph. A better topic sentence is "Sonya is a generous and insightful person."

Revisiting the Thought Lines Stage

Writing an outline can help you identify skimpy places in your plan, places where your paragraphs will need to have more details added. You can get these details in two ways:

1. Go back to the writing you did in the thought lines stage. Check whether items on a list or ideas from freewriting can lead you to more details for your outline.
2. Brainstorm for more details by using a question-and-answer approach. For example, if the outline includes "My apartment is a mess," you might ask, "Why? How messy?" Or if the outline includes "I have no social life," you might ask, "What do you mean? No friends? Or no activities? Or what about school organizations?"

The time you spend writing and revising your outline will make it easier for you to write an essay that is well developed, unified, and coherently structured. The following checklist may help you to revise.

> ✔ **Checklist**
>
> ### A Checklist for Revising the Outline of an Essay
>
> ✔ **Unity:** Do the thesis and topic sentences all lead to the same point? Does each paragraph make one, and only one, point? Do the details in each paragraph support the topic sentence? Does the conclusion unify the essay?
>
> ✔ **Support:** Do the body paragraphs have enough supporting details?
>
> ✔ **Coherence:** Are the paragraphs in the most effective order? Are the details in each paragraph arranged in the most effective order?

A sentence outline on the problems of working and going to college follows. It includes the thesis in the first paragraph. The topic sentences have been created from the titles of the ideas clustered earlier. The details have been drawn from ideas in the clusters and from further brainstorming. The conclusion has just one sentence that unifies the essay.

An Outline for an Essay

paragraph 1	I. Thesis: Students who work while going to college face problems at school, at work, and at home.
paragraph 2 topic sentence details	II. Trying to juggle job and school responsibilities creates problems at school. A. Early classes are difficult. B. I am too tired to pay attention. C. Once I slept in class. D. I have little time to do homework. E. I get behind in school assignments.
paragraph 3 topic sentence details	III. Work can suffer when workers attend college. A. I tried to study at work. B. I got caught by my boss. C. I was reprimanded. D. Sometimes I come to work very tired. E. When I don't get enough sleep, I can be rude to customers. F. Rudeness gets me in trouble. G. Another time, I had to cut work to take a makeup test.
paragraph 4 topic sentence details	IV. Working students suffer outside of classes and the workplace. A. I work nights during the week. B. The weekends are the only time I can study. C. My apartment is a mess since I have no time to clean it. D. Worse, my girlfriend is ready to kill me because I have no social life. E. We never even go to the movies any more. F. When she comes over, I am busy studying.
paragraph 5 conclusion	V. I have learned that working students have to be very organized to cope with their responsibilities at college, work, and home.

Exercise 5 **Completing an Outline for an Essay**

Practice

Following is part of an outline that has a thesis and topic sentences but no details. Add the details in complete sentences. Write one sentence for each capital letter. Be sure that the details are connected to the topic sentence.

I. Thesis: Video cameras have several beneficial uses in American society.

II. Americans use their video cameras to record memorable family events.

Answers Will Vary.
Possible answers
shown at right.

A. Parents film their child's first steps.

B. They film their child's first words.

C. Some even film the birth of a child.

D. Video cameras record graduations.

E. Many weddings are captured on videotape.

III. Video cameras are being used to prevent or detect crimes.

A. Many convenience stores have video cameras.

B. Banks use video cameras to discourage robberies.

C. Other stores use cameras to prevent shoplifting.

D. If a crime occurs, the suspect is captured on film.

E. The suspect can be more easily identified.

IV. Video cameras have given ordinary people an entry into many television programs.

A. There are shows that present the funniest home videos.

B. Others present the most embarrassing home videos.

C. Occasionally, a person sees a crime or a disaster.

D. The person may be the only one to film it.

E. That person can sell the film to television news.

V. The video camera has changed the way Americans celebrate family rituals, has contributed to the prevention and detection of crime, and has made ordinary people into television directors, reporters, and performers.

Exercise 6 **Focusing an Outline for an Essay**

Practice

The outline below has a thesis and details, but it has no topic sentences for the body paragraphs. Write the topic sentences.

I. Thesis: After my last meal at Don's Diner, I swore I would never eat there again.

II. The service was terrible.

   A. My friend and I were kept waiting for a table for half an hour.
   B. During that time, several tables were empty, but no one bothered to clear the dirty dishes.
   C. We just stood in the entrance, waiting.
   D. Then, when we were seated, the waitress was surly.
   E. It took fifteen minutes to get a menu.
   F. The plates of food were slammed down on the table.
   G. The orders were mixed up.

Answers Will Vary.
Possible answers
shown at right.

III. The food was awful.

   A. The hamburger was full of gristle.
   B. The French fries were as hard as cardboard.
   C. Our iced tea was instant.
   D. The iced tea powder was floating on top of the water.
   E. The lettuce had brown edges.
   F. Ketchup was caked all over the outside of the ketchup bottle.

IV. I never want to repeat the experience I had at Don's Diner.

Rough Lines

Essay

When you are satisfied with your outline, you can begin drafting and revising the essay. Start by writing a first draft of the essay, which includes these parts: introduction, body paragraphs, and conclusion.

WRITING THE INTRODUCTION

Where Does the Thesis Go?

The thesis should appear in the introduction of the essay, in the first paragraph. But most of the time it should not be the first sentence. In front of the thesis, write a few (three or more) sentences of introduction. Generally, the thesis is the *last sentence* in the introductory paragraph.

Why put the thesis at the end of the first paragraph? First of all, writing several sentences in front of your main idea gives you a chance to lead into it gradually and smoothly. This will help you build interest and gain the reader's attention. Also, by placing the thesis after a few sentences of introduction, you will not startle the reader with your main point.

Finally, if your thesis is at the end of the introduction, it states the main point of the essay just before that point is supported in the body paragraphs. Putting the thesis at the end of the introduction is like using an arrow to point to the supporting ideas in the essay.

Hints for Writing the Introduction

Hint   There are a number of ways to write an introduction.

1. You can begin with general statements that gradually lead to your thesis.

general statements	Students face all kinds of problems when they start college. Some students struggle with a lack of basic math skills; others have never learned to write a term paper. Students who were stars in high school have to cope with being just another social security number at a large institution. Students with small children have to find a way to be good parents and good students, too. Although all these problems are common,
thesis at end	I found an even more typical conflict. <u>My biggest problem in college was learning to organize my time.</u>

2. You can begin with a quotation that smoothly leads into your thesis. The quotation can be from someone famous, or it can be an old saying. It can be something your mother always told you, or it can be a slogan from an advertisement or the words of a song.

quotation	Everybody has heard the old saying, "Time flies," but I never really thought about that statement until I started college. I expected college to challenge me with demanding course work. I expected it to excite me with the range of people I would meet. I even thought it might amuse me with the fun and intrigue of dating and romance. But I never expected
thesis at end	college to exhaust me. <u>I was surprised to discover that my biggest problem in college was learning to organize my time.</u>

Note: You can add transition words or phrases to your thesis, as in the sample above.

3. You can tell a story as a way of leading into your thesis. You can open with the story of something that happened to you or to someone you know or with a story you read about or heard on the news.

story	My friend Phyllis is two years older than I am, and so she started college before I did. When Phyllis came home from college for Thanksgiving weekend, I called her with a long list of activities she and I could enjoy. I was surprised when Phyllis told me she planned to spend most of the weekend sleeping. I did not understand her when she told me she was worn out. However, when I started college myself, I understood her perfectly. Phyllis was a victim of that old college ailment: not knowing how to handle time. I developed the same disease.
thesis at end	<u>My biggest problem in college was learning to organize my time.</u>

4. You can explain why this topic is worth writing about. Explaining could mean giving some background on the topic, or it could mean discussing why the topic is an important one.

explain	I do not remember a word of what was said during my freshman orientation, and I wish I did. I am sure somebody somewhere warned me about the problems I would face in college. I am sure somebody talked about getting organized. Unfortunately, I did not listen, and I had to learn the hard way. I hope other students will listen and learn and be spared my
thesis at end	hard lesson and my big problem. <u>My biggest problem in college was learning to organize my time.</u>

5. You can use one or more questions to lead into your thesis. You can open with a question or questions that will be answered by your thesis. Or you can open with a question or questions that catch the reader's attention and move toward your thesis.

question	Have you ever stayed up all night to study for an exam, then fallen asleep at dawn and slept right through the time of the exam? If you have, then you were probably the same kind of college student I was. I was the student who always ran into class three minutes late, the one who begged for an extension on the term paper, the one who pleaded with the teacher to postpone the test. I just could not get things done on schedule.
thesis at end	<u>My biggest problem in college was learning to organize my time.</u>

6. You can open with a contradiction of your main point as a way of attracting the reader's interest and leading to your thesis. You can begin with an idea that is the opposite of what you will say in your thesis. The opposition of your opening and your thesis creates interest.

contradiction	People who knew me in my first year of college probably felt really sorry for me. They saw a girl with dark circles under her bloodshot eyes, a girl who was always racing from one place to another. Those people probably thought I was exhausted from overwork. But they were wrong. My problem in college was definitely not too much work; it was the way I
thesis at end	handled my work. <u>My biggest problem in college was learning to organize my time.</u>

Exercise 7

Practice

Writing an Introduction

Following are five thesis sentences. Pick one, and then write an introductory paragraph on the lines provided. Your last sentence should be the thesis sentence. If your instructor agrees, read your introduction to others in the class who wrote an introduction to the same thesis, or read your introduction to the entire class.

Thesis sentences:
1. Americans are becoming much too fashion-conscious.
2. A car phone can be a hazard to the user and to other drivers.
3. Credit cards got me into trouble.
4. A diet is only as good as the dieter.
5. People should be more careful in protecting their homes from thieves.

Write an introduction: _____

_____

_____

_____

_____

_____

_____

WRITING THE BODY OF THE ESSAY

In the body of the essay, the paragraphs *explain, support, and develop your thesis*. In this part of the essay, each paragraph has its own topic sentence. The topic sentence in each paragraph does two things:

1. It focuses the sentences in the paragraph.
2. It makes a point connected to the thesis.

The thesis and the topic sentences are ideas that need to be supported by details, explanations, and examples. You can visualize the connections among the parts of an essay like this:

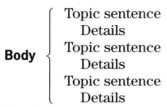

Introduction with Thesis

Body
- Topic sentence
  - Details
- Topic sentence
  - Details
- Topic sentence
  - Details

Conclusion

When you write topic sentences, you can organize your essay by referring to the following checklist.

✔ **Checklist**

A Checklist for the Topic Sentences of an Essay

✔ Does the topic sentence give the point of the paragraph?

✔ Does the topic sentence connect to the thesis of the essay?

How Long Are the Body Paragraphs?

Remember that the body paragraphs of an essay are the place where you explain and develop your thesis. Those paragraphs should be long enough to explain your points, not just list them. To do this well, try to make your body paragraphs *at least seven sentences long*. As you develop your writing skills, you may find that you can support your ideas in fewer than seven sentences.

Developing the Body Paragraphs

You can write well-developed body paragraphs by following the same steps you used in writing single paragraphs for the earlier assignments in this course. By working through the stages of gathering ideas, outlining, drafting, revising, editing, and proofreading, you can create clear, effective paragraphs.

To focus and develop the body paragraphs, ask the following questions as you revise.

✔ **Checklist**

A Checklist for Developing Body Paragraphs for an Essay

✔ Does the topic sentence cover everything in the paragraph?

✔ Do I have enough details to explain the topic sentence?

✔ Do all the details in the paragraph support, develop, or illustrate the topic sentence?

Exercise 8 **Creating Topic Sentences**

Practice Following are thesis sentences. For each thesis, write topic sentences (as many as indicated by the numbered blanks). The first one is done for you.

1. thesis: Cats make good pets.

topic sentence 1: Cats are independent and don't mind being home alone.

topic sentence 2: Cats are easy to litter-train.

topic sentence 3: Cats are fun to play with.

2. thesis: Mr. Thompson is willing to help his students both inside the classroom and during his office hours.

Answers Will Vary.
Possible answers
shown at right.

topic sentence 1: In class, Mr. Thompson will answer all students' questions.

topic sentence 2: Mr. Thompson uses many of his office hours for student conferences.

3. thesis: It is easy to recognize the student who is in college to have a good time.

topic sentence 1: This student is usually late for class.

topic sentence 2: He or she rarely participates or pays attention.

topic sentence 3: He or she often makes excuses to the instructor.

4. thesis: When you want to meet an attractive person at a party, you should follow several steps.

topic sentence 1: Observe the person's behavior and acquaintances.

topic sentence 2: Ask friends about the person.

topic sentence 3: Arrange a friendly, casual introduction.

5. thesis: Moving to a new town has its good and bad points.

topic sentence 1: A new town offers opportunities to make new friends.

topic sentence 2: _A new town is a place to explore._ _____

_____

topic sentence 3: _Leaving old friends behind is difficult._ _____

_____

topic sentence 4: _Giving up familiar places is tough._ _____

_____

WRITING THE CONCLUSION

The last paragraph in the essay is the **conclusion.** It does not have to be as long as a body paragraph, but it should be long enough to tie the essay together and remind the reader of the thesis. You can use any of these strategies in writing the conclusion:

1. You can restate the thesis in new words. Go back to the first paragraph of your essay and reread it. For example, this could be the first paragraph of an essay:

introduction

Because I rarely watch MTV, I had little idea of what today's music videos are like. Last week, however, I happened to be running through the television channels with my remote control, and I stopped at MTV. I was surprised and horrified by what I saw. I saw video after video that looked like a horror flick or a pornographic movie. I wondered how this cable channel could get away with showing such obviously controversial material. Then I realized that parents, the people who might object to the videos,

thesis at end

rarely watch MTV. <u>If parents started watching MTV, they would be shocked by the sex and violence.</u>

The thesis, underlined above, is the sentence that you can restate in your conclusion. Your task is to _keep the point but put it in different words._ Then work that restatement into a short paragraph, like this:

MTV provides a daily program of entertainment for children and teens. That entertainment can include scenes of violence, particularly violence against women, and cruelty. Many parents are crusading against the words on music casettes and disks, but they do not seem to care about the moving pictures that illustrate those words.

restating
the thesis

<u>Parents who turned on MTV would be turned off by what they saw.</u>

2. You can make a judgment, valuation, or recommendation. Instead of simply restating your point, you can end by making some comment on the issue you've described or the problem you've illustrated. If you were looking for another way to end the essay on MTV, for example, you could end with a recommendation:

I am no prude, but I think some of the videos on MTV are too much for my children to handle. Although I do not believe I have the right to take certain videos off the air,

<table>
<tr><td>ending with a
recommendation</td><td><u>I would like MTV to restrict the showing of these videos to</u> <u>adult viewing time, the late evening hours.</u> If the Music Television Network made such a change to help worried parents like me, the network would have many new fans.</td></tr>
</table>

3. You can conclude by framing your essay. You can tie your essay together neatly by *using something from your introduction* as a way of concluding. When you take an example, or a question, or even a quotation from your first paragraph and refer to it in your last paragraph, you are "framing" the essay. Take another look at the introduction to the essay on MTV: the writer talks about flipping through the television channels, seeing images of sex and violence, and being shocked. Now consider how the ideas of the introduction are used in this conclusion:

<table>
<tr><td>frame

frame

frame</td><td><u>The next time I happen to hit the MTV channel with</u> <u>my remote control,</u> I will know what to expect. I will not be surprised by the <u>cruelty, sadism, and rage</u> I see on the screen. But I wonder how many parents will get the <u>same big surprise that I got</u> last week by accidentally switching to MTV. And I wonder how long it will take those shocked parents to start complaining to their cable companies.</td></tr>
</table>

Exercise 9 **Choosing a Better Way to Restate the Thesis**

Practice

Following are five clusters. Each cluster consists of a thesis sentence and two sentences that try to restate the thesis. Each restated sentence could be used as part of the conclusion to an essay. Put a *B* next to the sentence in each pair that is a better restatement. Remember that the better choice repeats the same idea as the thesis but does not rely on too many of the same words.

1. thesis: Anyone who is thinking of buying a car should do careful research, plan a realistic budget for car payments, and negotiate intelligently.

restatement 1: __B__ People in the market for a car need to check out choices and prices, set up a practical system of payment, and bargain with know-how.

restatement 2: _____ Careful research, a realistic budget for car payments, and intelligent negotiation are important for anyone who is thinking of buying a car.

2. thesis: One of the best ways to meet people is to take a college class.

restatement 1: _____ Taking a class in college is one of the best ways to meet people.

restatement 2: __B__ College classes can make strangers into friends.

3. thesis: The three household chores I hate the most are cleaning closets, dusting, and folding laundry.

restatement 1: __B__ Taking care of cluttered closets, dusty furniture, and wrinkled laundry makes me crazy.

restatement 2: _____ Cleaning the closets, dusting, and folding the laundry are the three household chores I hate the most.

4. thesis: My first job taught me the importance of being on time.

restatement 1. _____ On my first job, I learned how important it is to be on time.

restatement 2: __B__ Punctuality was the key lesson of my first job.

5. thesis: Saving even a small amount of money each month is better than not saving at all.

restatement 1: _____ Saving a little money every month can be better than not saving at all.

restatement 2: __B__ No matter how small it is, a monthly deposit in a bank account is better than living from paycheck to paycheck.

Revising the Draft

Once you have a rough draft of your essay, you can begin revising it. The following checklist may help you make the necessary changes in your draft.

✔ Checklist

Checklist for Revising the Draft of an Essay

✔ Does the essay have a clear, unifying thesis?

✔ Does the thesis make a point?

✔ Does each body paragraph have a topic sentence?

✔ Is each body paragraph focused on its topic sentence?

✔ Are the body paragraphs roughly the same length?

✔ Do any of the sentences need to be combined?

✔ Do any of the words need to be changed?

✔ Do the ideas seem to be smoothly linked?

✔ Does the introduction catch the reader's interest?

✔ Is there a definite conclusion?

✔ Does the conclusion remind the reader of the thesis?

Transitions Within Paragraphs

In an essay, you can use two kinds of transitions: those within a paragraph and those between paragraphs.

Transitions that link ideas *within a paragraph* are the same kinds you've used earlier. Your choice of words, phrases, or even sentences depends on the kind of connection you want to make. Here is a list of some common transitions and the kind of connection they express:

> **Infobox**
>
> ### Common Transitions Within a Paragraph
>
> **To join two ideas:** again, also, and, another, besides, furthermore, in addition, likewise, moreover, similarly
>
> **To show a contrast or a different opinion:** but, however, in contrast, instead, nevertheless, on the contrary, on the other hand, or, otherwise, still, yet
>
> **To show a cause-and-effect connection:** accordingly, as a result, because, consequently, for, so, therefore, thus
>
> **To give an example:** for example, for instance, in the case of, like, such as, to illustrate
>
> **To show time:** after, at the same time, before, finally, first, meanwhile, next, recently, shortly, soon, subsequently, then, until

Transitions Between Paragraphs

When you write something that is more than one paragraph long, you need transitions that link each paragraph to the others. There are several effective ways to link paragraphs and remind the reader of your main idea and of how the smaller points connect to it. Two ways are restatement and repetition.

    1. Restate an idea from the preceding paragraph at the start of a new paragraph. Look closely at the two paragraphs below and notice how the second paragraph repeats an idea from the first paragraph and provides a link.

> If people were more patient, driving would be less of an ordeal. If, for instance, the driver behind me didn't honk his horn as soon as the traffic light turned green, both he and I would probably have lower blood pressure. He wouldn't be irritating himself by pushing so hard. And I wouldn't be reacting by slowing down, trying to irritate him even more, and getting angry at him. When I get impatient in heavy traffic, I just make a bad situation worse. My hurry doesn't get me to my destination any faster; it just stresses me out.

transition
restating an idea

> The impatient driver doesn't get anywhere; neither does the impatient customer at a restaurant. Impatience at restaurants doesn't pay. I work as a hostess at a restaurant, and I know that the customer who moans and complains about waiting for a table won't get one any faster than the person who makes the best of the wait. In fact, if a customer is too aggressive or obnoxious, the restaurant staff may actually slow down the process of getting that customer a table.

    2. Use synonyms and repetition as a way of reminding the reader of an important point. For example, in the two paragraphs below, notice how certain repeated words, phrases, and synonyms all remind the reader of a point about facing fear. The repeated words and synonyms are underlined.

> Some people just <u>avoid</u> whatever they <u>fear</u>. I have an uncle who is <u>afraid</u> to fly. Whenever he has to go on a trip, he does anything he can to <u>avoid</u> getting on

an airplane. He will drive for days, travel by train, or take a bus trip. Because he is so <u>terrified</u> of flying, he lives with <u>constant anxiety</u> that some day he may have to fly. He is always thinking of the one emergency that could force him to <u>confront what he most dreads</u>. Instead of <u>dealing directly with his fear</u>, he lets it <u>haunt</u> him.

Other people are even worse than my uncle. He will not <u>attack his fear</u> of something external. But there are people who will not <u>deal with their fear</u> of themselves. My friend Sam is a good example of this kind of person. Sam has a serious drinking problem. All Sam's friends know he is an alcoholic. But Sam <u>will not admit</u> his addiction. I think he is <u>afraid to face</u> that part of himself. So he <u>denies</u> his problem, saying he can stop drinking any time he wants to. Of course, until Sam has the courage to <u>admit what he is most afraid of</u>, his alcoholism, he will not be able to change.

A Draft Essay

Below is a draft of the essay on working and going to college. As you read it, you'll notice many changes from the outline on page 242.

TEACHING TIP:
For additional revision practice, ask students to jot down the actual changes. Having them spot examples of transitional words or phrases can help them see the effectiveness of using sentence variety.

Remind students that this draft is not the final version of the essay. The final version is on p. 258.

- An introduction has been added, phrased in the first person, "I," to unify the essay.
- Transitions have been added within and between paragraphs.
- General statements have been replaced by more specific ones.
- Word choice has been improved.
- A conclusion has been added. Some of the ideas added to the conclusion came from the original list of ideas about the topic of work and school. They are ideas that do not fit in the body paragraphs but are useful in the conclusion.

A Draft of an Essay (Thesis and topic sentences are underlined.)

I work thirty hours a week at the front desk of a motel in Riverside. When I first signed up for college classes, I figured college would be fairly easy to fit into my schedule. After all, college students are not in class all day like high school students are. So I thought the twelve hours a week I would spend in class would not be too much of a load. But I was in for a big surprise. <u>My first semester at college showed me that students who work while going to school face problems at school, at work, and at home.</u>

<u>First of all, trying to juggle job and school responsibilities creates problems at school.</u> Early morning classes, for example, are particularly difficult for me. Because I work every weeknight from 6:00 to midnight, I don't get home until 1:00 a.m., and I can't fall asleep until 2:00 a.m. or later. I am too tired to pay attention in my 8:00 a.m. class. Once, I even fell asleep in that class. My work hours create other conflicts. They cut into my study time, so I have little time to do all the assigned reading and papers. I get behind in these assignments, and I never seem to have enough time to catch up. Consequently, my grades are not as good as they could be.

Because I both work and go to school, I have problems doing well at school. <u>But work can also suffer when workers attend college.</u>

Students can bring school into the workplace. One night I tried to study at work, but my boss caught me reading my biology textbook at the front desk. I was reprimanded, and now my boss does not trust me. Sometimes I come to work very tired. When I don't get enough sleep, I can be rude to motel guests who give me a hard time. Then the rudeness can get me into trouble. I remember one particular guest who reported me because I was sarcastic to her. She had spent a half hour complaining about her bill, and I had been too tired to be patient. Once again, my boss reprimanded me. Another time, school interfered with my job when I had to cut work to take a makeup test at school. I know my boss was unhappy with me then, too.

As a working student, I run into trouble on the job and at college. Working students also suffer outside of college and the workplace. Since I work nights during the week, the weekends are the only time I can study. Because I have to use my weekends to do schoolwork, I can't do other things. My apartment is a mess because I have no time to clean it. Worse, my girlfriend is ready to kill me because I have no social life. We never even go to the movies anymore. When she comes over, I am busy studying.

With responsibilities at home, work, and college, I face a cycle of stress. I am constantly racing around, and I can't break the cycle. I want a college education, and I must have a job to pay my tuition. The only way I can manage is to learn to manage my time. I have learned that working students have to be very organized to cope with the responsibilities of college, work, and home.

| **Exercise 10** | ### Identifying the Main Points in the Draft of an Essay |
| Practice | |

Below is the draft of a four-paragraph essay. Read it, reread it, and then underline the thesis and the topic sentences in each body paragraph and in the conclusion.

Discussion Question: This essay is about what one volunteer learned by working with children. Ask students if they have worked with youngsters and what aspects of the ex-perience they find memorable. This discussion could spark ideas for potential essay topics.

Until this year, I had never considered spending my free time helping others in my community. Volunteer work, I thought, was something retired folks and rich people did to fill their days. Just by chance, I became a volunteer for the public library's Classic Connection, a group that arranges read-a-thons and special programs for elementary school children. Although I do not receive a salary, working with some perceptive and entertaining third-graders has been very rewarding in other ways.

Currently, I meet with my small group of four girls and three boys each Saturday morning from ten to eleven o'clock, and they have actually taught me more than I ever thought possible. I usually assign the children various passages in an illustrated children's classic like *The Little Prince,* and I help them with the difficult words as they read aloud. When I occasionally read to them, they follow right along, but when it is their turn, they happily go off track. I have learned that each child has a mind of his or her own, and I now have much more respect for day-care workers and elementary school teachers who must teach, entertain, and discipline thirty rowdy children all day long. I am tired after one hour with just seven children.

<u>I have also learned the value of careful planning</u>. I arrive at each session with a tape recorder and have the children record a sound effect related to the story we will be reading. At certain points during the session, we stop to hear the sound effects. They love to hear themselves, and they seem more focused on reading when I use this method. I feel more relaxed when I am well prepared, and the sessions go smoothly.

<u>I have enjoyed making several new friends and contacts through the Classic Connection</u>. I have become friendly with the parents of the children in my reading group, and one of the fathers has offered me a good-paying job at his printing business. He even mentioned he could be flexible about my schedule. I asked him if he could help me put together a collection of the group's most outrageous original stories, and he said he would be glad to do it in his free time. I have thus learned that the spirit of volunteerism is indeed contagious.

I plan to keep volunteering for the Classic Connection's programs and look forward to a new group that should be starting soon. I don't know if I am ready to graduate to an older group. <u>After all, third graders still have much to teach me.</u>

Exercise 11

Practice

Note: For this exercise, students may want to refer to the infobox on transitions on p. 252.

Adding Transitions to an Essay

The following essay needs transitions. Insert the transitions where indicated. Be sure to add the kind of transition—a word, phrase, or sentence—indicated in parentheses.

When I finished high school, I was determined to go to college. What I hadn't decided was where I would go to college. Most of my friends were planning to go away from home to attend college. They wanted to be responsible for themselves and to be free of their parents' supervision. Like my friends, I thought about going away to college. But I finally decided to go to a college near my home. I chose a college near home for several reasons.

_____ First of all, _____ (add a phrase), I can save money by attending a community college near home. _____Because_____ (add a word) I am still living at home, I do not have to pay for room and board at a college dorm or pay rent at an apartment off campus. I do not have to pay for the transportation costs of visits home. My friends who are away at school tell me about all the money they are spending on the things I get at home for free. These friends are paying for things like doing their laundry or hooking up their cable television. _____In contrast,_____ _____ (add a phrase) my college expenses are basically just tuition, fees, and books. I think I have a better deal than my friends who went away to college.

Saving money is one advantage I gain by staying home to go to school, but there are other good points. _____

_____ (add a sentence). By attending college near home, I have kept a secure home base. I think it would be very hard for me to handle a new school, a new town, a new set of classmates, and a new place to live all at the same time. I have narrowed my challenges to a new school and new classmates.

_____When_____ (add a word) I come home after a stressful day at college, I still have Mom's home cooking and Dad's sympathy to console me. I still sleep in my own comfortable—and comforting—room. Students who go away to school may have more freedom, _____but_____ (add a word) I have more security.

Choosing a nearby college gave me a secure home base. _____

_____

_____ (add a sentence). My decision to stay home for college gave me a secure job base as well. For the past year, I have worked at a job I like very much. My boss is very fair, and she has come to value my work enough to let me set my own work schedule. _____For instance,_____ (add a word or phrase), she lets me plan my work schedule around my class schedule. If I had moved away to attend college, I would have had to find a new job. _____In addition_____ (add a word or phrase) I would have had a hard time finding a boss as understanding as the one I have now.

There are many good reasons to go to a college away from home. <u>On the other hand,</u> (add a word or phrase) there are probably as many good reasons to go to one near home. I know that I am happy with my decision. It has paid off financially and helped me maintain a secure place to live and to work.

Exercise 12
Practice

Recognizing Synonyms and Repetition Used to Link Ideas in an Essay

In the following essay, underline all the synonyms and repetition (of words or phrases) that help remind the reader of the thesis sentence. (To help you, the thesis is underlined.)

Whenever I turn on the TV, I hear the story of an extraordinary act of courage. A firefighter, for example, rushes into a burning building to save an old man. Or a mother risks her own life to save her child from traffic. These are once-in-a-lifetime acts of courage, and they are indeed admirable. But <u>there is another, quiet kind of courage demonstrated all around us every day</u>.

This <u>kind of courage</u> can be the <u>fortitude</u> of the person who has a terminal illness but who still carries on with living. I knew a person like that. He was the father of a family. When he found out he had a year to live, he did not waste much time in misery and despair. Instead, he used every moment to prepare his family for the time when he would no longer be there. He made financial arrangements. He spent time with his children to show them how much he loved them. His <u>bravery</u> in the face of death was <u>not unusual</u>. <u>Every day</u>, there is someone who hears bad news from a doctor and <u>quietly</u> goes on. But because such people are so <u>quiet in their courage</u>, they are not given much credit.

Another example of <u>quiet, everyday courage</u> can be seen in people with the <u>guts</u> to try new and frightening things. The older person who decides to go to college, for instance, must be very scared. But he or she faces that fear and enters the classroom. And any student, of any age, who takes the course that is supposed to be hard, or the teacher who is supposed to be tough, instead of the easier one, shows a certain <u>courage</u>. Equally <u>brave</u> are the people who switch careers in middle age because they have not found satisfaction in the workplace. It is frightening to start over at midlife when starting over means trading job security and money for uncertainty and an entry-level salary. Yet many people make that trade, demonstrating real <u>fortitude</u>.

Sometimes we think that heroes are people who make the news. Granted, there are heroes splashed across the papers and acclaimed on TV. Yet there are other, <u>equally brave people who never make the news</u>. They are the ones whose lives show <u>a less dramatic form of courage.</u> They are <u>all around us,</u> and they deserve our admiration and respect.

Final Lines

Essay
Creating a Title

When you are satisfied with the final version of your essay, you can begin preparing a good copy. Your essay will need a title. Try to think of a short title that is connected to your thesis. Since the title is the reader's first contact with your essay, an imaginative title can create a good first impression. If you can't think of anything clever, try using a key phrase from your essay.

The title is placed at the top of your essay, about an inch above the first paragraph. Always capitalize the first word of the title and all other words *except* "the," "an," "a," or prepositions (like "of," "in," "with") that are under five letters. *Do not* underline or put quotation marks around your title.

The Final Version of an Essay

TEACHING TIP:
Tell students that an essay title should be a phrase and not a sentence. Many students are tempted to reuse their thesis statement for the title.

Following is the final version of the essay on working and going to college. When you compare it to the draft on pages 253–54, you will notice some changes:

- In the first paragraph, the words "I thought" have been added to make it clear that the statement is the writer's opinion.
- One topic sentence, in the second paragraph, has been revised so that it includes the word "students" and the meaning is more precise.
- Words have been changed to sharpen the meaning.
- Transitions have been added.

A Final Version of an Essay (Changes from the draft are underlined.)

Note: Remind students that this sample essay is reduced to fit within a textbook, and the title is thus not one inch above the first paragraph.

Problems of the Working College Student

I work thirty hours a week at the front desk of a motel in Riverside. When I first <u>registered</u> for college classes, I figured college would be fairly easy to fit into my schedule. After all, <u>I thought,</u> college students are not in class all day like high school students are. So I <u>assumed</u> the twelve hours a week I would spend in class would not be too much of a load. But I was in for a big surprise. My first semester at college showed me that students who work while going to college face problems at school, at work, and at home.

First of all, <u>students who try</u> to juggle job and school responsibilities <u>find trouble</u> at school. Early morning classes, for example, are particularly difficult for me. Because I work every weeknight from 6:00 to midnight, I don't get home until 1:00 a.m., and I can't fall asleep until 2:00 a.m. or later. <u>Consequently,</u> I am too tired to pay attention in my 8:00 a.m. class. Once, I even fell asleep in that class. My work hours create other conflicts. They cut into my study time, so I have little time to do all the assigned reading and papers. I get behind in these assignments, and I never seem to have enough time to catch up. <u>As a result,</u> my grades are not as good as they could be.

Because I both work and go to school, I have problems doing well at school. But work can also suffer when workers attend college. Students can bring school into the workplace. <u>I have been guilty of this practice and have paid the price.</u> One night I tried to study at work, but my boss caught me reading my biology textbook at the front desk. I was reprimanded, and now my boss does not trust me. Sometimes I come to work very tired, <u>another problem.</u> When I don't get enough sleep, I can be rude to motel guests who give me a hard time. Then the rudeness can get me into trouble. I remember one particular guest who reported me because I was sarcastic to her. She had spent a half hour complaining about her bill, and I had been too tired to be patient. Once again, my boss reprimanded me. Another time, school interfered with my job when I had to cut work to take a makeup test at school. I know my boss was unhappy with me then, too.

As a working student, I run into trouble on the job and at college. Working students also suffer outside of college and the workplace. <u>My schedule illustrates the conflicts of trying to juggle too many duties.</u> Since I work nights during the week, the weekends are the only time I can study. Because I have to use my weekends to do schoolwork, I can't do other things. My apartment is a mess because I have no time to clean it. Worse, my girlfriend is ready to kill me because I have no social life. We never even go to the movies anymore. When she comes over, I am busy studying.

With responsibilities at home, work, and college, I face a cycle of stress. I am constantly racing around, and I can't break the cycle. I want a college education, and I must have a job to pay my tuition. The only way I can manage is to learn to manage my time. <u>In my first semester at college, I have realized</u> that working students have to be very organized to cope with the responsibilities of college, work, and home.

Before you prepare the final copy of your essay, check your latest draft for errors in spelling and punctuation and for any errors made in typing or copying.

Exercise 13
Practice

Proofreading to Prepare the Final Version

Following is an essay with the kinds of errors that are easy to overlook when you prepare the final version of an assignment. Correct the errors, writing above the lines. There are nineteen errors.

Three Myths About Young People
"Three Myths About Young People"

Today, when a person says the word "teenager" or refers to "college kids," that person may be speaking with a little sneer. Young people have acquired a bad reputation.

reputation
Some of the reputation may be deserved, but some of it may not be. Young people are often judged according to myths, beliefs that are not true. Older people should not

myths
believe in three common myth's about the young.

irresponsible,   there
We are always hearing that young people are irresponsable but their are many teens and people in their early twenties who disprove this statement. In every town, there are young people who hold full-time jobs and support a family. There are even more young people who work and go to school. All of my friends have been working

sophomore   high school
since their sophmore year of High School. The fact that not one of them has ever been fired from a job implies they must be pretty good workers. Furthermore, young people

. They
today are almost forced to be responsible they must learn to work and pay for their clothes and college tuition.

Another foolish belief is that all young people take drugs. Hollywood movies encourage this myth by including a drug-crazed teenager in almost every movie. Whenever television broadcasts a public service advertisement about drugs, the drug user shown is a young person. In reality, many young people have chosen not to take drugs.

probably
For every teen with a problem of abuse, there is probally another teen who has never

school
taken drugs or who has conquered a drug problem. In my high scool, an anonymous student poll showed that more than half of the students had never experimented with drugs.

Some older adults label young people irresponsible and addicted. Even more people are likely to say that the young are apathetic, but such critics are wrong. The young

caring   unconscious
are criticized for not carring about political or social issues, for being unconscience of

Yet
the problems we all face. yet high school and college students are the ones who are out there, cleaning up the litter on the highways or beaches, whenever there is a local clean-up campaign. During the holidays, every school and college collects food,

. Students
clothing, and toys for the needy students organize these drives, and students

distribute
distributes these items. On many weekends, young people are out on the highways,

collecting for charities.

Granted, there are apathetic, addicted, and irresponsible young people. But a
deserves
whole group should not be judged by the actions of a few. Each young person deserve

to be treated as an individual, not as an example of a myth.

Lines of Detail: A Walk-Through Assignment

Choose two radio stations popular with people your age. They can be two stations that broadcast music or two stations that broadcast talk shows. Write a
four-paragraph essay describing who listens to each station. To write the essay,
follow these steps:

Step 1: Begin with some investigation. Listen to two stations, either talk
or music shows, popular with your age group. Before you listen,
prepare a list of at least six questions. The questions will help
you gather details for your essay. For any radio station, you can
ask

What kinds of products or services are advertised?
Does the station offer any contests?
Does the station sponsor any events?

For two music stations, your questions might include

What groups or individuals does the station play?
What kind of music does it play?

For two talk-radio stations, your questions might include

What are the talk-show hosts like? Are they funny or insulting
or serious?
What topics are discussed?
What kinds of people call in?

Listen to the stations you chose, and as you listen, take notes.
Answer your own questions, and write down anything about
each station that catches your interest or that seems relevant.

Step 2: Survey your notes. Mark the related ideas with the same number. Then cluster the information you have gathered, and give
each cluster a title.

Step 3: Focus all your clusters around one point. To find a focus, ask
yourself whether the listeners of the two stations are people of
the same social class, with the same interests, the same educational background, the same ethnic or racial background.

Try to focus your information with a thesis like one of these:

_____ (station name) and _____ (station

name) appeal to the same audience.

_____ (station name) and _____ (station

name) appeal to different audiences.

_____ (station name) and _____ (station name) use different strategies to appeal to the same kind of listeners.

_____ (station name) appeals to young people who _____, but _____ (station name) appeals to young people who _____.

While _____ (station name) is popular with middle-aged listeners interested in_____, _____ (station name) appeals to middle-aged listeners who like _____.

Step 4: Once you have a thesis and clustered details, draft an outline. Revise your draft outline until it is unified, expresses the ideas in a clear order, and has enough supporting details.

Step 5: Write a draft of your essay. Revise the draft, checking it for balanced paragraphs, relevant and specific detail, a strong conclusion, and smooth transitions.

Step 6: Before you prepare the final version of your essay, check for spelling, word choice, punctuation, and mechanical errors. Also, give your essay a title.

Writing Your Own Essay

When you write on any of these topics, be sure to work through the stages of the writing process in preparing your essay.

1. Take any paragraph you wrote for this class and develop it into an essay of four or five paragraphs. If your instructor agrees, read the paragraph to a partner or group, and ask your listener(s) to suggest points inside the paragraph that could be developed into paragraphs of their own.

2. Write an essay using one of the following thesis statements:

   If I won a million dollars, I know what I would do with it.
   Most families waste natural resources every day simply by going through their daily routines.
   Television's coverage of football (or basketball, tennis, or any other sport you choose) could be improved by a few changes.

   The one place I will never visit again is _____ because _____.

   All bad romances share certain characteristics.

   If I could be someone else, I would like to be _____ for several reasons.

3. Write an essay on earliest childhood memories. Interview three class-mates to gather details and to focus your essay. Ask each one to tell you about the earliest memory he or she has of childhood. Before you begin interviewing, make a list of questions like these: What is your earliest memory? How old were you at that time? What were you doing? Do you remember other people or events in that scene? If so, what were the others doing? Were you indoors? Outdoors? Is this a pleasant memory? Why do you think this memory has stayed with you? Use the details collected at the interviews to write a five-paragraph essay with a thesis sentence like one of the following:

> Childhood memories vary a great deal from person to person.
> The childhood memories of different people are surprisingly similar.
> Although some people's first memories are painful, other people remember a happy time.
> Some people claim to remember events from their infancy, but others can't remember anything before their third (fourth, fifth, etc.) birthday.

4. Freewrite for ten minutes on the two best days of your life. After you have completed the freewriting, review it. Do the two days have much in common? Or were they very different? Write a four-paragraph essay based on their similarities or differences, with a thesis like one of these:

> The two best days of my life were both _____. (Focus on similarities.)
>
> While one of the best days of my life was _____, the other great day was _____. (Fill in with differences.)

5. Write an essay on one of the following topics:

Three Careers for Me	The Three Worst Jobs
Three Workplace Hazards	Three Workplace Friends

6. Look closely at the photograph A on page 264. Write a five-paragraph essay in which you describe a situation that the picture may represent. In one body paragraph, you can write about what has already happened; in another paragraph, about what may be happening; and in another paragraph, about what may happen next to the child in this outdoor market.

7. Look closely at the photograph B on page 264. Write a four-paragraph essay in which you describe the personalities of both people in the photograph. You can use your imagination to create personalities, but try to base your imaginings on the facial expressions and body language of the people. You can also describe the relationship between the two: Are they best friends? In love? Brother and sister? Husband and wife?

8. Narrow one of the following topics, and then write an essay on it.

nature	dreams	crime	music	celebrities
fears	family	lies	health	romance

Photograph A

Photograph B

Name: _____   **Section:** _____

Peer Review Form for an Essay

After you have written a draft of your essay, let a writing partner read it. When your partner has completed the form below, discuss the comments. Then repeat the same process for your partner's paragraph.

The thesis of this essay is _____

_____

The topic sentences for the body paragraphs are _____

_____

_____

_____

_____

The topic sentence in the conclusion is _____

_____

The best part of the essay is the _____ (first,

second, third, etc.) paragraph.

I would like to see details added to the part about _____

_____

I would take out the part about _____

The introduction (a) is good or (b) could be better. (Choose one.)

The conclusion (a) is good or (b) could be better. (Choose one.)

I have questions about _____

Additional comments: _____

_____

_____

_____

_____

Reviewer's Name: _____

WRITING FROM READING: The Essay

Eleven
Sandra Cisneros

Sandra Cisneros, the child of a Mexican father and a Mexican-American mother, grew up in Chicago. She has worked as a teacher of high school dropouts and in other areas of education and the arts. A poet and writer of short stories, Cisneros incorporates her ethnic background into her writing. Her story "Eleven" is about a birthday gone wrong.

1   What they don't understand about birthdays and what they never tell you is that when you're eleven, you're also ten, and nine, and eight, and seven, and six, and five, and four, and three, and two, and one. And when you wake up on your eleventh birthday you expect to feel eleven, but you don't. You open your eyes and everything's just like yesterday, only it's today. And you don't feel eleven at all. You feel like you're still ten. And you are—underneath the year that makes you eleven.

2   Like some days you might say something stupid, and that's the part of you that's still ten. Or maybe some days you might need to sit on your mama's lap because you're scared, and that's the part of you that's five. And maybe one day when you're all grown up maybe you will need to cry like if you're three, and that's okay. That's what I tell Mama when she's sad and needs to cry. Maybe she's feeling three.

3   Because the way you grow old is kind of like an onion of like the rings inside a tree trunk or like my little wooden dolls that fit one inside the other, each year inside the next one. That's how being eleven years old is.

4   You don't feel eleven. Not right away. It takes a few days, weeks even, sometimes even months before you say Eleven when they ask you. And you don't feel smart eleven, not until you're almost twelve. That's the way it is.

5   Only today I wish I didn't have only eleven years rattling inside me like pennies in a tin Band-Aid box. Today I wish I was one hundred and two instead of eleven because if I was one hundred and two I'd have known what to say when Mrs. Price put the red sweater on my desk. I would've known how to tell her it wasn't mine instead of just sitting there with that look on my face and nothing coming out of my mouth.

6   "Whose is this?" Mrs. Price says, and she holds the red sweater up in the air for all the class to see. "Whose? It's been sitting in the coatroom for a month."

7   "Not mine," says everybody. "Not me."

8   "It has to belong to somebody," Mrs. Price keeps saying, but nobody can remember. It's an ugly sweater with red plastic buttons and a collar and sleeves all stretched out like you could use it for a jump rope. It's maybe a thousand years old and even if it belonged to me I wouldn't say so.

9   Maybe because I'm skinny, maybe because she doesn't like me, that stupid Sylvia Saldívar says, "I think it belongs to Rachel." An ugly sweater like that, all raggedy and old, but Mrs. Price believes her. Mrs. Price takes the sweater and puts it right on my desk, but when I open my mouth nothing comes out.

10   "That's not. I don't, you're not. . . . Not mine," I finally say in a little voice that was maybe me when I was four.

11   "Of course it's yours," Mrs. Price says. "I remember you wearing it once." Because she's older and the teacher, she's right and I'm not.

12   Not mine, not mine, not mine, but Mrs. Price is already turning to page thirty-two, and math problem number four. I don't know why but all of a sudden I'm feeling sick inside, like the part of me that's three wants to come out of my eyes, only I squeeze them shut tight and bite down on my teeth real hard and try to remember today I am eleven, eleven. Mama is making a cake for me tonight, and when Papa comes home everybody will sing Happy birthday, happy birthday to you.

13   But when the sick feeling goes away and I open my eyes, the red sweater's still sitting there like a big red mountain. I move the red sweater to the corner of my desk with my ruler. I move my pencil and books and eraser as far from it as possible. I even move my chair a little to the right. Not mine, not mine, not mine.

14   In my head I'm thinking how long till lunchtime, how long till I can take the red sweater and throw it over the schoolyard fence, or leave it hanging on a parking meter, or bunch it up into a little ball and toss it in the alley. Except when math period ends Mrs. Price says loud and in front of everybody, "Now, Rachel, that's enough," because she sees I've shoved the red sweater to the tippy-tip corner of my desk and it's hanging all over the edge like a waterfall, but I don't care.

15   "Rachel," Mrs. Price says. She says it like she's getting mad. "You put that sweater on right now and no more nonsense."

16   "But it's not—"

17   "Now!" Mrs. Price says.

18   This is when I wish I wasn't eleven, because all the years inside me—ten, nine, eight, seven, six, five, four, three, two, and one—are pushing at the back of my eyes when I put one arm through one sleeve of the sweater that smells like cottage cheese, and then the other arm through the other and stand there with my arms apart like if the sweater hurts me and it does, all itchy and full of germs that aren't even mine.

19   That's when everything I've been holding in since this morning, since when Mrs. Price put the sweater on my desk, finally lets go, and all of a sudden I'm crying in front of everybody. I wish I was invisible but I'm not. I'm eleven and it's my birthday today and I'm crying like I'm three in front of everybody. I put my head down on the desk and bury my face in my stupid clown-sweater arms. My face all hot and spit coming out of my mouth because I can't stop the little animal noises from coming out of me, until there aren't any more tears left in my eyes, and it's just my body shaking like when you have the hiccups, and my whole head hurts like when you drink milk too fast.

20   But the worst part is right before the bell rings for lunch. That stupid Phyllis Lopez, who is even dumber than Sylvia Saldívar, says she remembers the red sweater is hers! I take it off right away and give it to her, only Mrs. Price pretends like everything's okay.

21   Today I'm eleven. There's a cake Mama's making for tonight, and when Papa comes home from work we'll eat it. There'll be candles and presents and everybody will sing Happy birthday, happy birthday to you, Rachel, only it's too late.

22   I'm eleven today. I'm eleven, ten, nine, eight, seven, six, five, four, three, two, and one, but I wish I was one hundred and two. I wish I was anything but eleven, because I want today to be far away already, far away like a runaway balloon, like a tiny *o* in the sky, so tiny-tiny you have to close your eyes to see it.

WRITING FROM READING: "Eleven"

1. Write about a time when you didn't feel your age. You can call the essay "Seventeen" or "Eleven" or whatever your chronological age was, but write about why you felt you were a different age.

2. Write about a time, or several times, when an older person was wrong and you were right.

3. Write about a teacher you will always remember.

4. Write an essay on three things that children (or teens) fear.

5. You may have heard the saying "You are only as old as you feel." Interview three people. Ask them their age; ask them hold old they feel and why. Use the information you gather to write an essay about people and age.

6. Cisneros writes that "the way you grow old is kind of like an onion or like the rings inside a tree trunk." Write an essay about three memorable "rings," three experiences, when you grew in some significant way.

7. Write an essay about two emotions that Rachel, the girl in "Eleven," feels. Use details from "Eleven" to describe and explain these emotions.

Althea Gibson: Never Give Up
Varla Ventura

Ventura writes about one of the heroes of the sports world, Althea Gibson. Gibson, Ventura writes, changed from " 'bad girl' to tennis sensation" and later became a mentor and coach to a generation of African-American women tennis players.

Words You May Need to Know

sharecropper (paragraph 2): a farmer who rents land and pays the rent with a share of the crop
truant officers (2): officers who check on a child's regular attendance at school
dire (3): terrible, dreadful
naysayers (3): people who make negative comments
patrons (3): people who support others with money or efforts

chafed (4): became irritated and annoyed by
heinous (4): wicked
decrying (4): speaking with disapproval of
Babe Zaharias (5): a famous all-around sportswoman who decided to become a professional golfer in order to make a living
LPGA (5): Ladies' Professional Golf Association

1   From the ghetto to the tennis court, Althea Gibson's story is pure heroism. At a time when tennis was not dominated by whites but by upper-class whites at that, she managed to serve and volley her way to the top.

2   Born in 1927 to a Southern sharecropper family, Althea struggled as a girl with a restless energy that took years for her to channel into positive accomplishments. The family's move to Harlem didn't help. She was bored by school and skipped a lot; teachers and truant officers predicted the worst for Althea, believing that she was a walking attitude problem whose future lay as far as the nearest reform school.

3   Although things looked dire for Althea, she had a thing or two to show the naysayers. Like many heroes, Althea had to bottom out before she could get to the top. She dropped out of school and drifted from job to job until, at a mere fourteen, she found herself a ward of New York City's Welfare Department. This turned out to be the best thing that could have happened to Althea—a wise welfare worker not only helped her find steady work, but also enrolled her into New York's police sports program. Althea fell in love with paddle ball and, upon graduating to real tennis, amazed everyone with her natural ability. The New York Cosmopolitan Club, an interracial sports and social organization, sponsored the teen and arranged for her to have a tennis coach, Fred Johnson. Althea's transformation from "bad girl" to tennis sensation was immediate; she won the New York State Open Championship one year later. She captured the attention of two wealthy patrons who agreed to sponsor her if she finished high school. She did in 1949—and went on to accept a tennis scholarship to Florida Agricultural and Mechanical University.

4 Althea's battles weren't over yet, though. She aced nine straight Negro national chanpionships and chafed at the exclusion from tournaments closed to nonwhite players. Fighting hard to compete with white players, Althea handled herself well, despite being exposed to racism at its most heinous. Her dignified struggle to overcome segregation in tennis won her many supporters of all colors. Finally, one of her biggest fans and admirers, the editor of *American Lawn Tennis* magazine, wrote an article decrying the "color barrier" in tennis. The walls came down. By 1958, Althea Gibson won the singles and doubles at Wimbledon and twice took the U.S. national championships at the U.S. Open as well.

5 Then, citing money woes, she retired; she just couldn't make a living at women's tennis. Like Babe Zaharias, she took up golf, becoming the first black woman to qualify for the LPGA. But she never excelled in golf as she had in tennis, and in the seventies and eighties she returned to the game she truly loved, serving as a mentor and coach to an up-and-coming generation of African American women tennis players.

6 Through sheer excellence and a willingness to work on behalf of her race, Althea Gibson made a huge difference in the sports world for which we are all indebted.

WRITING FROM READING: "Althea Gibson: Never Give Up"

When you write on any of these topics, work through the stages of the writing process in preparing your essay.

1. Write an essay about several obstacles Gibson overcame in her lifetime.

2. As a child and teenager, Gibson did not appear to be headed for success. Write an essay about another person who did not appear to be headed in the right direction but who turned his or her life around. The person does not have to be a celebrity or someone involved in sports.

3. Throughout her struggles and victories, Gibson showed certain strong personal qualities that enabled her to survive and thrive. Write an essay about these qualities; in your details, show how each quality turned up at crucial times in her life. (A personal quality is a trait like dignity or confidence.)

4. Write about a time when you or someone you knew refused to give up.

5. Althea Gibson is credited with helping to break the "color barrier" in tennis. Write an essay about someone who helped to break a barrier. To begin, you can work with a group to brainstorm about barriers. Consider color, gender, or ethnic barriers, and think about people who have helped to break down a barrier. Breaking a barrier does not have to involve a confrontation; it can also mean succeeding at a profession usually closed to certain people or living a life that breaks a stereotype.

Send Your Children to the Libraries
Arthur Ashe

Arthur Ashe was the first African-American Davis Cup participant and the first black man to win the U.S. Open and Wimbledon. Besides being a champion tennis player, he was a graduate of the University of California at Los Angeles, a writer, and a political activist. "Send Your Children to the Libraries," written in 1977, is addressed to African-American parents, but its message can be applied to all parents and children today who dream only of a career in sports.

Words You May Need to Know

pretentious (paragraph 1): showy
dubious (1): doubtful, uncertain
emulate (2): imitate

viable (4): practical, realistic
benchwarmer (7): an athlete who does not get much playing time

1   Since my sophomore year at the University of California, Los Angeles, I have become convinced that we blacks spend too much time on the playing fields and too little time in the libraries. Please don't think of this attitude as being pretentious just because I am a black, single professional athlete. I don't have children, but I can make observations. I strongly believe the black culture expends too much time, energy, and effort raising, praising, and teasing our black children as to the dubious glories of professional sport.

2   All children need models to emulate—parents, relatives, or friends. But when the child starts school, the influence of the parent is shared by teachers and classmates, by the lure of books, movies, ministers, and newspapers, but most of all by television. Which televised events have the greatest number of viewers? Sports—the Olympics, Super Bowl, Masters, World Series, pro basketball playoffs, Forest Hills. ABC-TV even has sports on Monday night prime time from April to December. So your child gets a massive dose of O. J. Simpson, Kareem Abdul-Jabbar, Muhammad Ali, Reggie Jackson, Dr. J. and Lee Elder and other pro athletes. And it is only natural that your child will dream of being a pro athlete himself.

3   But consider these facts: For the major professional sports of hockey, football, basketball, golf, tennis, and boxing, there are roughly only 3,170 major league positions available (attributing 200 positions to golf, 200 to tennis, and 100 to boxing). And the annual turnover is small. We blacks are a subculture of about 28 million. Of the $13\frac{1}{2}$ million men, 5 to 6 million are under 20 years of age, so your son has less than one chance in 1,000 of becoming a pro. Less than one in a thousand. Would you bet your son's future on something with odds of 999 to 1 against you? I wouldn't.

4   Unless a child is exceptionally gifted, you should know by the time he enters high school whether he has a future as an athlete. But what is more impor-

tant is what happens if he doesn't graduate or doesn't land a college scholarship and doesn't have a viable alternative job career. Our high school dropout rate is several times the national average, which contributes to our unemployment rate of roughly twice the national average.

5   And how do you fight the figures in the newspapers every day? Ali has earned more than $30 million boxing, O. J. just signed for $2.5 million, Dr. J. for almost $3 million, Reggie Jackson for $2.8 million, Nate Archibald for $400,000 a year. All that money, recognition, attention, free cars, girls, jobs in the off season—no wonder there is Pop Warner football, Little League baseball, National Junior Tennis League tennis, hockey practice at 5 a.m., and pickup basketball games in any center city at any hour.

6   There must be some way to assure that the 999 who try but don't make it to pro sports don't wind up on the street corners or in the unemployment lines. Unfortunately, our most widely recognized role models are athletes and entertainers—"runnin'" and "jumpin'" and "singin'" and "dancin.'" While we are 60 percent of the National Basketball Association, we are less than 4 percent of the doctors and lawyers. While we are about 35 percent of major league baseball, we are less than 2 percent of the engineers. While we are about 40 percent of the National Football League, we are less than 11 percent of construction workers such as carpenters and bricklayers. Our greatest heroes of the century have been athletes—Jack Johnson, Joe Louis, and Mohammed Ali. Racial and economic discrimination forced us to channel our energies into athletics and entertainment. These were the two ways out of the ghetto, the ways to get that Cadillac, those alligator shoes, that cashmere sport coat.

7   Somehow, parents must instill a desire for learning alongside the desire to be Walt Frazier. Why not start by sending black professional athletes into high schools to explain the facts of life? I have often addressed high school audiences, and my message is always the same. For every hour you spend on the athletic field, spend two in the library. Even if you make it as a pro athlete, your career will be over by the time you are 35. So you will need that diploma. Have these pro athletes explain what happens if you break a leg, get a sore arm, have one bad year or don't make the cut for five or six tournaments. Explain to them the star system, wherein for every O. J. earning millions there are six or seven others making $15,000 or $20,000 or $30,000 a year. But don't just have Walt Frazier or O. J. or Abdul-Jabbar address your class. Invite a benchwarmer or a guy who didn't make it. Ask him if he sleeps every night. Ask him whether he was graduated. Ask him what he would do if he became disabled tomorrow. Ask him where his old high school athletic buddies are.

8   We have been on the same roads—sports and entertainment—too long. We need to pull over, fill up at the library and speed away to Congress and the Supreme Court, the unions and the business world. Don't worry: we will still be able to sing and dance and run and jump better than anybody else.

9   I'll never forget how proud my grandmother was when I graduated from U.C.L.A. in 1966. Never the mind the Davis Cup in 1968, 1969, and 1970. Never mind the Wimbledon title, Forest Hills, etc. To this day, she still doesn't know what those names mean. What mattered to her was that of her more than thirty children and grandchildren, I was the first to be graduated from college, and a famous college at that. Somehow, that made up for all those floors she scrubbed all those years.

WRITING FROM READING: "Send Your Children to the Libraries"

When you write on any of the following topics, be sure to work through the stages of the writing process.

1. Write an essay explaining Ashe's reasons for emphasizing academics over sports.

2. Ashe was a role model in sports, and he is also remembered as a writer and a crusader for equality. Write an essay about another role model who is admirable in more than one area.

3. Ashe asks his readers to consider the realities of a career in professional sports. Write an essay about another career that many people dream of, and explain the difficulties of this career. You can write about the fantasy side of this career, the difficulties of entering this career, and the realities of working in this career.

4. Write a reply to Ashe's essay. In your reply, explain why, in spite of the odds, young people of all races dream of a career in professional athletics.

5. Write an essay about three people who are not athletes but who should be role models for young people.

CHAPTER 11

Writing from Reading

WHAT IS WRITING FROM READING?

TEACHING TIP:

Tell students that summarizing an essay can help them remember its main points. It is a valuable study technique even if they are not doing it for an assignment.

Note: For advice on "Writing for an Essay Test," see pp. 292–93.

One way to find topics for writing is to draw on your ideas, memories, and observations. Another way is to write from reading you have done. You can *react* to it; you can *agree or disagree* with something you have read. In fact, many college assignments or tests ask you to write about an assigned reading: an essay, a chapter in a textbook, an article in a journal. This kind of writing requires an active, involved attitude toward your reading. Such reading is done in steps:

1. Preread.
2. Read.
3. Reread with a pen or pencil.

After you have completed these three steps, you can write from your reading. You can write about what you have read, or you can react to what you have read.

AN APPROACH TO WRITING FROM READING

Attitude

Before you begin the first step of this reading process, you have to have a certain **attitude.** That attitude involves thinking of what you read as half of a conversation. The writer has opinions and ideas; he or she makes points, just like you do when you write or speak. The writer supports his or her points with specific details. If the writer were speaking to you in a conversation, you would respond to his or her opinions or ideas. You would agree, disagree, or question. You would jump into the conversation, linking or contrasting your ideas with those of the other speaker.

The right attitude toward reading demands that you read the way you'd converse: you *become involved.* In doing this, you "talk back" as you read, and later you react in your own writing. Reacting as you read will keep you focused on what you are reading. If you are focused, you will remember more of what you read. With an active, involved attitude, you can begin the step of prereading.

Prereading

Before you actually read an assigned essay, a chapter in a textbook, or an article in a journal, magazine, or newspaper, take a few minutes to look it over, and be ready to answer the questions in the prereading checklist.

✔ Checklist

A Prereading Checklist

✔ How long is this reading?

✔ Will I be able to read it in one sitting, or will I have to schedule several time periods to finish it?

✔ Are there any subheadings in the reading? Do they give any hints about the reading?

✔ Are there any charts? Graphs? Is there any boxed information?

✔ Are there any photographs or illustrations with captions? Do the photos or captions give me any hints about the reading?

✔ Is there any introductory material about the reading or its author? Does the introductory material give me any hints about the reading?

✔ What is the title of the reading? Does the title hint at the point of the reading?

✔ Are any parts of the reading underlined, italicized, or emphasized in some other way? Do the emphasized parts hint at the point of the reading?

Why Preread?

Prereading takes very little time, but it helps you immensely. Some students believe it is a waste of time to scan an assignment; they think they should jump right in and get the reading over with. However, spending just a few minutes on preliminaries can save hours later. Most importantly, prereading helps you to become a *focused reader.*

If you scan the length of an assignment, you can pace yourself. And if you know how long a reading is, you can alert yourself to its plan. A short reading, for example, has to come to its point fairly soon. A longer essay may take more time to develop its point and may use more details and examples.

Subheadings, charts, graphs, illustrations, and boxed or other highlighted materials are important enough that the author wants to emphasize them. Looking over that material *before* you read gives you an overview of the important points the reading will contain.

Introductory material or introductory questions will also help you know what to look for as you read. Background on the author or on the subject may hint at ideas that will come up in the reading. Sometimes even the title of the reading will give you the main idea.

You should preread so that you can start reading the entire assignment with as much knowledge about the writer and the subject as you can get. When you then read the entire assignment, you will be reading *actively* for more knowledge.

Forming Questions Before You Read

If you want to read with a focus, it helps to ask questions before you read. Form questions by using the information you gained from prereading.

Start by noting the title and turning it into a question. If the title of your assigned reading is "Reasons for the Alien and Sedition Acts," you can turn that title into a question: "What were the reasons for the Alien and Sedition Acts?"

You can turn subheadings into questions. If you are reading an article on beach erosion and one subheading is "Artificial Reefs," you can ask, "How are artificial reefs connected to beach erosion?"

You can form questions from graphs and illustrations. If a chapter in your history book includes a photograph of a Gothic cathedral, you can ask, "How are Gothic cathedrals connected to this period in history?" or "Why are Gothic cathedrals important?" or "What is Gothic architecture?"

You can write down these questions, but it's not necessary. Just forming questions and keeping them in the back of your mind helps you read actively and stay focused.

An Example of the Prereading Step

Take a look at the article below. Don't read it; *preread* it.

A Ridiculous Addiction
Gwinn Owens

Gwinn Owens, a retired editor and columnist for the Baltimore Evening Sun, *wrote this essay about his experiences in parking lots, noting that the American search for a good parking space "transcends logic and common sense."*

Words You May Need to Know

preening (paragraph 2): primping, making yourself appear elegant
perusing (2): reading
stymied (3): hindered, blocked, defeated
addiction (5): a compulsive habit
coveted (6): desired, eagerly wished for
transcends (6): rises above, goes beyond the limits of

atavistically (7): primitively
acrimonious (8): bitter, harsh
holy grail (8): a sacred object that the Knights of the Round Table devoted years to finding
ensconced (10): securely sheltered
idiocy (11): foolish behavior
contempt (13): scorn, lack of respect
emporium (14): store

1 Let us follow my friend Frank Bogley as, on the way home from work, he swings into the shopping mall to pick up a liter of Johnny Walker, on sale at the Bottle and Cork. In the vast, herringboned parking area there are, literally, hundreds of empty spaces, but some are perhaps as much as a 40-second walk from the door of the liquor store. So Bogley, a typical American motorist, feels compelled to park as close as possible.

2 He eases down between the rows of parked cars until he notices a blue-haired matron getting into her Mercedes. This is a prime location, not more than

25 steps from the Bottle and Cork. Bogley stops to await her departure so as to slip quickly into the vacated slot. She shuts the door of her car as Bogley's engine surges nervously. But she does not move. She is, in fact, preening her hair and perusing a magazine she just bought.

3   The stymied Bogley is now tying up traffic in that lane. Two more cars with impatient drivers assemble behind him. One driver hits his horn lightly, then angrily. Bogley opens his window and gives him the finger, but reluctantly realizes that the Mercedes isn't about to leave. His arteries harden a little more as, exasperated, he gives up and starts circling the lot in search of another space, passing scores of empty ones which he deems too far from his destination. Predictably, he slips into the space for the handicapped. "Just for a moment," he says to his conscience.

4   The elapsed time of Bogley's search for a convenient parking space is seven minutes. Had he chosen one of the abundant spaces only a few steps farther away, he could have accomplished his mission in less than two minutes, without frazzled nerves or skyrocketing blood pressure—his as well as those who were backed up behind him. He could have enjoyed a little healthful walking to reduce the paunch that is gestating in his middle.

5   Frank Bogley suffers an acute case of parking addiction, which afflicts more Americans than the common cold. We are obsessed with the idea that it is our constitutional right not to have to park more than 10 steps from our destination.

6   Like all addictions, this quest for the coveted spot transcends logic and common sense. Motorists will pursue it without concern over the time it takes, as if a close-in parking space were its own sweet fulfillment. They will park in the fire lane or in the handicapped space or leave the car at the curb, where space is reserved for loading.

7   The quest atavistically transcends politeness and civility. My local paper recently carried a story about two motorists who, seeing a third car about to exit a spot, both lusted for the vacancy. As soon as the departing vehicle was gone, one of the standbys was a little faster and grabbed the coveted prize. The defeated motorist leaped from his car, threw open his rival's door, and punched him in the snoot. He was charged with assault. Hell hath no fury like a motorist who loses the battle for a close-in parking space.

8   The daily obsession to possess the coveted slot probably shortens the life of most Americans by at least 4.2 years. This acrimonious jockeying, waiting, backing, maneuvering for the holy grail of nearness jangles the nerves, constricts the arteries and turns puppylike personalities into snarling mad dogs.

9   I know a few Americans who have actually kicked the habit, and they are extraordinarily happy people. I am one, and I owe my cure to my friend Lou, who is the antithesis of Frank Bogley. One day I recognized Lou's red Escort in the wallflower space of the parking lot of our local supermarket. There was not another vehicle within 80 feet.

10   In the store I asked him why he had ensconced his car in lonely splendor.

His answer made perfect sense: "I pull in and out quickly, nobody else's doors scratch my paint and I get a short walk, which I need." Lou, I might point out, is in his 60s and is built like 25—lean and fit.

11   These days, I do as Lou does, and a great weight has been lifted. Free of the hassle, I am suddenly aware of the collective idiocy of the parking obsession—angry people battling for what is utterly without value. I acquire what does have value: saving of time, fresh air, peace of mind, healthful exercise.

12   The only time I feel the stress now is when I am a passenger with a driver who has not yet taken the cure. On one recent occasion I accepted a ride with my friend Andy to a large banquet at which I was a head-table guest. The banquet hall had its own commodious parking lot, but Andy is another Frank Bogley.

13   He insisted on trying to park near the door "because it is late." He was right, it *was* late, and there being no slots near the door, he then proceeded to thread his way through the labyrinth of the close-in lot, as I pleaded that I didn't mind walking from out where there was plenty of space. He finally used five minutes jockeying his big Lincoln into a Honda-size niche. Thanks to Andy's addiction, I walked late into the banquet hall and stumbled into my conspicuous seat in the midst of the solemn convocation. My attitude toward him was a mixture of pity and contempt, like a recovering alcoholic must feel toward an incipient drunk.

14   These silly parking duels, fought over the right not to walk more than 15 steps, can be found almost anywhere in the 50 states. They reach their ultimate absurdity, however, at my local racquet and fitness club. The battle to park close to the door of the athletic emporium is fought as aggressively as at the shopping mall. Everyone who parks there is intending to engage in tennis, squash, aerobic dancing, muscle building or some other kind of athletic constitutional. But to have to exercise ahead of time by walking from the lot to the door is clearly regarded by most Americans as unconstitutional.

The results of prereading. By prereading the article, you might notice the following:

> The title is "A Ridiculous Addiction."
> The author was a newspaper writer from Baltimore.
> There are many vocabulary words you may need to know.
> The essay is about parking lots.
> The introductory material says Americans' search for a desirable parking
> space goes beyond the limits of common sense.

You might begin reading the article with these questions in mind:

> What is the addiction?
> How can an addiction be ridiculous? An addiction is usually considered
> something very serious, like an addiction to drugs.
> What do parking spaces have to do with addiction?
> What is so illogical about looking for a good parking space?

Reading

The first time you read, try to get a sense of the whole piece you are reading. Reading with questions in mind can help you do this. If you find that you are confused by a certain part of the reading selection, go back and reread that part. If you do not know the meaning of a word, check the vocabulary list to see if the word is defined for you. If it is not defined, try to figure out the meaning from the way the word is used in the sentence.

If you find that you have to read more slowly than you usually do, don't worry. People vary their reading speed according to what they read and why they are reading it. If you are reading for entertainment, for example, you can read quickly; if you are reading a chapter in a textbook, you must read more slowly. The more complicated the reading selection, the more slowly you will read it.

An Example of the Reading Step

Now read "A Ridiculous Addiction." When you have completed your first reading, you will probably have some answers to the prereading questions you formed, like those below:

Answers to Prereading Questions

The author says that the ridiculous addiction is the need to find the best parking space.

He means it's ridiculous because it makes parking a serious issue and because people do silly things to get good parking spots.

People are illogical in getting parking because they'll even be late for an event in order to get a good space. Or they get upset.

Rereading with Pen or Pencil

The second reading is the crucial one. At this point, you begin to *think on paper* as you read. In this step, you take notes or write about what you read. Some students are reluctant to do this, for they are not sure *what* to note or write. Think of taking these notes as a way of learning, thinking, reviewing, and reacting. Reading with a pen or pencil in your hand keeps you alert. With that pen or pencil, you can do the following:

- Mark the main point of the reading.
- Mark other points.
- Define words you don't know.
- Question parts of the reading you're not sure of.
- Evaluate the writer's ideas.
- React to the writer's opinions or examples.
- Add ideas, opinions, or examples of your own.

There is no single system for marking or writing as you read. Some readers like to underline the main idea with two lines and underline other important ideas with one line. Some students like to put an asterisk (a star) next to important ideas while others like to circle key words.

Some people use the margins to write comments like "I agree!" or "Not true!" or "That has happened to me." Sometimes readers put questions in the margin; sometimes they summarize a point in the margin next to its location in the essay. Some people make notes in the white space above the reading and list important points, and others use the space at the end of the reading. Every reader who writes while he or she reads has a personal system; what these systems share is an attitude. *If you write as you read, you concentrate on the reading selection, get to know the writer's ideas, and develop ideas of your own.*

As you reread and write notes, don't worry too much about noticing the "right" ideas. Think of rereading as the time to jump into a conversation with the writer.

An Example of Rereading with Pen or Pencil

For "A Ridiculous Addiction," your marked article might look like the example that follows.

A Ridiculous Addiction
Gwinn Owens

Let us follow my friend Frank Bogley as, on the way home from work, he swings into the shopping mall to pick up a liter of Johnny Walker, on sale at the Bottle and Cork. In the vast, herringboned parking area there are, literally, hundreds of empty spaces, but some are perhaps as much as a 40-second walk from the door of the liquor store. So Bogley, a <u>typical American motorist, feels compelled to park as close as possible.</u>

the bad habit

He eases down between the rows of parked cars until he notices a blue-haired matron getting into her Mercedes. This is a prime location, not more than 25 steps from the Bottle and Cork. Bogley stops to await her departure so as to slip quickly into the vacated slot. She shuts the door of her car as Bogley's engine surges nervously. But she does not move. She is, in fact, preening her hair and perusing a magazine she just bought.

The stymied Bogley is now tying up traffic in that lane. Two more cars with impatient drivers assemble behind him. One driver hits his horn lightly, then angrily. Bogley opens his window and gives him the finger, but reluctantly realizes that the Mercedes isn't about to leave. His arteries harden a little more as, exasperated, he gives up and starts circling the lot in search of another space, passing scores of empty ones which he deems too far from his destination. <u>Predictably, he slips into the space for the handicapped.</u> "Just for a moment," he says to his conscience.

I hate this!

wasted time

<u>The elapsed time of Bogley's search for a convenient parking space is seven minutes.</u> Had he chosen one of the abundant spaces only a few steps farther away, <u>he could have accomplished his mission in less than two minutes</u>, without <u>frazzled nerves</u> or <u>skyrocketing blood pressure</u>—<u>his as well as those who were

irritation backed up behind him.</u> He could have enjoyed a little healthful walking to reduce the paunch that is gestating in his middle.

Frank Bogley suffers an acute case of parking addiction, which afflicts more Americans than the common cold. <u>We are obsessed with the idea that it is our constitutional right not to have to park more than 10 steps from our destination.</u>

<u>Like all addictions, this quest for the coveted spot transcends logic and common sense.</u> Motorists will pursue it without concern over the time it takes, as if a close-in parking space were its own sweet fulfillment. <u>They will park in the fire lane or in the handicapped space or leave the car at the curb, where space is reserved for loading.</u>

example The quest atavistically <u>transcends politeness and civility.</u> My local paper recently carried a story about two motorists who, seeing a third car about to exit a spot, both lusted for the vacancy. As soon as the departing vehicle was gone, one of the standbys was a little faster and grabbed the coveted prize. The defeated motorist leaped from his car, threw open his rival's door, and punched him in the snoot. He was charged with <u>assault.</u> Hell hath no fury like a motorist who loses the battle for a close-in parking space.

The daily obsession to possess the coveted slot probably shortens the life of most Americans by at least 4.2 years. This acrimonious jockeying, waiting, backing, maneuvering for the holy grail of nearness <u>jangles the nerves, constricts the arteries</u> and <u>turns puppylike personalities into snarling mad dogs.</u>

I know a few Americans who have actually kicked the habit, and they are extraordinarily happy people. I am one, and I owe my cure to my friend Lou, who

opposite is the (antithesis) of Frank Bogley. One day I recognized Lou's red Escort in the wallflower space of the parking lot of our local supermarket. There was not another vehicle within 80 feet.

In the store I asked him why he had ensconced his car in lonely splendor. His answer made perfect sense: "<u>I pull in and out quickly, nobody else's doors scratch my paint and I get a short walk, which I need.</u>" Lou, I might point out, is in his 60s and is built like 25—lean and fit.

breaking the habit: advantages

These days, I do as Lou does, and a great weight has been lifted. Free of the hassle, I am suddenly aware of the collective idiocy of the parking obsession—angry people battling for what is utterly without value. I acquire what does have value: <u>saving of time, fresh air, peace of mind, healthful exercise.</u>

more advantages

The only time I feel the stress now is when I am a passenger with a driver who has not yet taken the cure. On one recent occasion I accepted a ride with my friend Andy to a large banquet at which I was a head-table guest. The banquet hall had its own commodious parking lot, but Andy is another Frank Bogley.

back to bad habit

He insisted on trying to park near the door "because it is late." He was right, it *was* late, and there being no slots near the door, he then proceeded to thread his way through the labyrinth of the close-in lot, as I pleaded that I didn't mind walking from out where there was plenty of space. He finally used <u>five minutes jockeying his big Lincoln into a Honda-size niche.</u> Thanks to Andy's addiction, I walked late into the banquet hall and stumbled into my conspicuous seat in the midst of the solemn convocation. My attitude toward him was a mixture of pity and contempt, like a recovering alcoholic must feel toward an incipient drunk.

How true!

<u>These silly parking duels, fought over the right not to walk more than 15 steps, can be found almost anywhere in the 50 states.</u> They reach their ultimate absurdity, however, at my local racquet and fitness club. The battle to park close to the door of the athletic emporium is fought as aggressively as at the shopping mall. Everyone who parks there is intending to engage in tennis, squash, aerobic dancing, muscle building or some other kind of athletic constitutional. But to

more on bad habit

have to exercise ahead of time by walking from the lot to the door is clearly

regarded by most Americans as unconstitutional.

What the Notes Mean

In the sample above, the underlining indicates sentences or phrases that seem important. The words in the margin are often summaries of what is underlined. The words "wasted time" and "irritation" for instance, are like subtitles or labels in the margin.

Some words in the margin are reactions. When Owens describes a man who parked illegally in a handicapped spot, the reader notes, "I hate this!" When the writer talks about a Lincoln trying to fit into a Honda-sized spot, the reader writes, "How true!" One word in the margin is a definition. The word "antithesis" in the selection is defined as "opposite" in the margin.

The marked-up article is a flexible tool. You can go back and mark it further. You may change your mind about your notes and comments and find other, better or more important points in the article.

You write as you read to involve yourself in the reading process. Marking what you read can help you in other ways, too. If you are to be tested on the reading selection or are asked to discuss it, you can scan your markings and notations at a later time for a quick review.

Exercise 1
Practice

Reading and Making Notes

Following is the last paragraph of "A Ridiculous Addiction." First, read it. Then reread it and make notes on the following:

1. Underline the sentence that begins the long example in the paragraph.
2. Circle a word you don't know and define it in the margin.
3. In the margin, add your own example of a place where people fight for parking spaces.
4. At the end of the paragraph, summarize the point of the paragraph.

Paragraph from "A Ridiculous Addiction"

These silly parking duels, fought over the right not to walk more than 15 steps, can be found almost anywhere in the 50 states. They reach their ultimate absurdity, however, at my local racquet and fitness club. The battle to park close to the door of the athletic emporium is fought as aggressively as at the shopping mall. Everyone who parks there is intending to engage in tennis, squash, aerobic dancing, muscle building or some other kind of athletic constitutional. But to have to exercise ahead of time by walking from the lot to the door is clearly regarded by most Americans as unconstitutional.

Answers Will Vary
for numbers 2 and 3.
Possible answer for number 4 shown at right.

Main point of the paragraph: People on their way to a health club show how silly

it is to fight for a parking space.

WRITING A SUMMARY OF A READING

There are a number of ways you can write about what you have read. You may be asked for a summary of an article or chapter, or for a reaction to it, or to write

Note: If you prefer to have students use reading selections as prompts for reacting to key points rather than summarizing them, you can skip to "Writing a Reaction to a Reading" on p. 289.

about it on an essay test. For each of these, this chapter will give you guidelines so you can follow the stages of the writing process.

A **summary** of a reading tells the important ideas in brief form. It includes (1) the writer's main idea, (2) the ideas used to explain the main idea, and (3) some examples used to support the ideas.

When you preread, read, and make notes on the reading selection, you have already begun the thought lines stage for a summary. You can think further, on paper, by listing the points (words, phrases, sentences) you have already marked on the reading selection.

Thought Lines

Marking a List of Ideas

To find the main idea for your summary and the ideas and examples connected to the main idea, you can mark related items on your list. For example, the expanded list below was made from "A Ridiculous Addiction." Four symbols are used:

K marks the **kinds** of close spots people will take.

X marks all **examples** of what can happen when people want a good spot.

– marks the **negative** effects of the close-parking habit.

+ marks the **advantages** of breaking the habit.

A List of Ideas for a Summary of "A Ridiculous Addiction"

K no close spots, takes handicapped
X seven minutes looking for close spot
– wasted time, could have found another in two minutes
X got mad
X made others wait
X they got angry
  Americans obsessed with right to good spot
  transcends logic
  no common sense
K park in fire lane
K leave car at curb
K loading zone
– impolite

X an assault over a spot
– jangles nerves, constricts arteries, and makes people mad dogs kicking the habit
+ get in and out fast
+ no scratched car doors
+ good exercise
+ saving time
+ fresh air
+ peace of mind
+ healthful exercise
X late for big dinner
X fitness clubs the silliest—won't wait

The marked list could be reorganized like this:

kinds of close spots people will take

handicapped
fire lane
curb
loading zone

examples of what can happen when people want a good spot

seven minutes of wasted time

others, waiting behind, get mad
an assault over a spot
late for a big dinner
members of the fitness club won't talk

negative effects of the close-parking habit

wasted time
impolite
jangles nerves, constricts arteries
makes people mad dogs

advantages of breaking the habit

get in and out fast
no scratched car doors
good exercise
saving time
fresh air
peace of mind
healthful exercise

Selecting a Main Idea

The next step in the process is to select the idea you think is the writer's main point. If you look again at the list of ideas, you'll note a cluster of ideas that are unmarked:

Americans obsessed with the right to a good spot
transcends logic
no common sense

You might guess that they are unmarked because they are more general than the other ideas. In fact, these ideas are connected to the title of the essay, "A Ridiculous Addiction," and they are connected to some of the questions in the pre-reading step of reading: "What's the addiction?" and "How can an addiction be ridiculous?"

Linking the ideas may lead you to a main idea for the summary of the reading selection:

Americans' obsession with finding a good parking spot makes no sense.

Once you have a main idea, check that main idea to see if it fits with the other ideas in your organized list. *Do the ideas in the list connect to the main idea?* Yes. "Kinds of close spots people take" explains how silly it is to break the law. "Examples of what can happen" and "negative effects" show why the habit makes no sense, and "advantages of breaking the habit" shows the reasons to conquer the addiction.

Once you have a main point that fits an organized list, you can move to the outlines stage of a summary.

Exercise 2

Practice

Marking a List of Ideas and Finding the Main Idea for a Summary

Below is a list of ideas from an article titled "How to Land the Job You Want." Read the list, and then mark the items on the list with one of these symbols:

X **examples** of people looking for or getting jobs
S **steps** in getting a job
A **advice** from employers

After you've marked all the ideas, survey them, and think of a main idea. Try to focus on an idea that connects to the title, "How to Land the Job You Want."

List of Ideas

<u> X </u> Laid-off engineer used his personality to get a sales job.

<u> A </u> Insurance company manager says applicants can walk in without an appointment.

<u> S </u> Find the hidden job market.

<u> X </u> Unemployed teacher found a job through his insurance agent.

<u> X </u> Bank worker got a job through his club.

<u> S </u> Prepare specifically for each interview.

<u> S </u> Locate hidden openings.

<u> A </u> Company director says a good letter of application is crucial.

<u> S </u> Make résumé strong and polished.

<u> S </u> Put yourself in employer's place when writing a résumé.

<u> X </u> Cabinetmaker checked phone books of nine cities for companies in his field.

<u> S </u> Use the library to research job opportunities.

Answers Will Vary.
Possible answer
shown at right.

Main idea: <u>You can land the job you want if you are willing to work hard at your</u>

<u>job search.</u>

Outlines

Summary

Below is a sample of the kind of outline you could do for a summary of "A Ridiculous Addiction." As you read it, you'll notice that the main idea of the thought lines stage has become the topic sentence of the outline, and the other ideas have become the details.

Outline for a Summary of "A Ridiculous Addiction"

`topic sentence:` Americans' obsession with finding a good parking spot makes no sense.

`details:`

`examples` {
Many bad or silly things can happen when people try for a good spot.
One person wasted seven minutes.
He made other drivers angry.
Someone else got involved in an assault.
Someone else was late for a big dinner.
Silly people, on their way to a fitness club, will avoid the walk in the fitness club parking lot.

```
negative   ⎧ Looking for a close spot can make people impolite or
effects    ⎨ turn them into mad dogs.
           ⎪ It can jangle drivers' nerves or constrict arteries.
           ⎩ Some people will even break the law and take handi-
             capped spots or park in a fire lane or loading zone.

                ⎧ If people can give up the habit, they can gain advan-
advantages      ⎪ tages.
of kicking      ⎨ A faraway spot is not popular, so they can get in and
the habit       ⎪ out of it fast.
                ⎪ Their cars won't be scratched.
                ⎩ They get exercise and fresh air by walking.
```

In the preceding outline, some ideas from the original list have been left out (they were repetitive) and the order of some points has been rearranged. That kind of selecting and rearranging is what you do in the outlines stage of writing a summary.

Rough Lines

Attributing Ideas in a Summary

The draft of your summary paragraph is the place where you combine all the material into one paragraph. This draft is much like the draft of any other paragraph, with one exception: When you summarize another person's ideas, be sure to say whose ideas you are writing. That is, *attribute the ideas to the writer.* Let the reader of your paragraph know

1. the author of the selection you are summarizing, and
2. the title of the selection you are summarizing.

You may wish to do this by giving your summary paragraph a title like this:

```
A Summary of "A Ridiculous Addiction" by Gwinn Owens
```

Note that you put the title of Owens's essay in quotation marks.

Or you may want to put the title and author into the paragraph itself. Following is a draft of a summary of "A Ridiculous Addiction" with the title and the author's name incorporated into the paragraph.

A Draft of a Summary of "A Ridiculous Addiction"

```
     "A Ridiculous Addiction" by Gwinn Owens says that Americans'
obsession with finding a good parking spot makes no sense. Many
bad or silly things can happen when people try for a good spot.
One person wasted seven minutes. He made other drivers angry.
Someone else got involved in an assault. Someone else was late
for a big dinner. Silly people, on their way to a fitness club,
will avoid the walk in the club parking lot. Looking for a close
spot can make people impolite or turn them into mad dogs. It can
be stressful. Some people even break the law and take handicapped
spots or park in a fire lane or loading zone. If people can give
up the habit, they can gain advantages. A faraway spot is not
popular, so they can get in and out of it fast. Their cars won't
be scratched. They get exercise and fresh air by walking.
```

When you look this draft over and read it aloud, you may notice a few problems:

1. It is wordy.
2. In some places, the word choice could be better.
3. Some of the sentences are choppy.
4. It might be a good idea to mention that the examples in the summary were given by Gwinn Owens.

Revising the draft means rewriting it to eliminate some of the wordiness, to combine sentences or smooth out ideas, and to insert the point that the author, Gwinn Owens, gave the examples used in the summary. When you state that Owens created the examples, you are being clear in giving the author credit for his ideas. Giving credit is a way of attributing ideas to the author.

Note: When you refer to an author in something that you write, use the author's first and last name the first time you make a reference. For example, you write "Gwinn Owens" the first time you refer to this author. Later in the paragraph, if you want to refer to the same author, use only his or her last name. Thus, a second reference would be to "Owens."

Final Lines

Summary

Look carefully at the final version of the summary. Notice that sentences have been changed and words have been added or taken out. "Owens" is used to show that the examples given came from the essay.

A Final Version of a Summary of "A Ridiculous Addiction"

"A Ridiculous Addiction" by Gwinn Owens says that Americans' obsession with finding a good parking spot makes no sense. Owens gives many examples of the unpleasant or silly things that can happen when people try for a good spot. One person wasted seven minutes and made the other drivers angry. Someone else got involved in an assault; another person was late for an important dinner. At fitness club parking lots, people coming for exercise are missing out on the exercise of walking through the parking lot. Looking for a good spot can turn polite people into impolite ones or even into mad dogs. The search is not only stressful; it can also lead people to break the law by taking handicapped, fire lane, or loading zone spots. If people broke the habit and took spots farther away from buildings, they would have several advantages. No one wants the faraway spots, so drivers can get in and out fast, without any scratches on their cars. In addition, people who break the habit get exercise and fresh air.

Writing summaries is good writing practice, and it also helps you develop your reading skills. Even if your instructor does not require you to turn in a polished summary of an assigned reading, you may find it helpful to summarize what you have read. In many classes, midterms or other exams cover several assigned readings. If you make a short summary of each reading as it is assigned, you will have a helpful collection of focused, organized material to review.

WRITING A REACTION TO A READING

A summary is one kind of writing you can do after reading, but there are other kinds. You can react to a reading by writing on a topic related to the reading or by agreeing or disagreeing with some idea within the reading.

Writing on a Related Idea

Your instructor might ask you to react by writing about some idea connected to your reading. If you read "A Ridiculous Addiction," for example, your instructor might have asked you to react to it by writing about some practice or habit that irritates you. You can begin to gather ideas by freewriting.

Thought Lines

Freewriting

You can freewrite in a reading journal if you wish. To freewrite, you can

- Write key points made by the author.
- Write about whatever you remember from the reading selection.
- Write down any of the author's ideas that you think you might want to write about someday
- List questions raised by what you have read.
- Connect the reading selection to other things you have read or heard or experienced.
- Write any of the author's exact words that you might like to remember, putting them in quotation marks.

A freewriting that reacts to "A Ridiculous Addiction" might look like this:

Freewriting for a Reaction to a Reading

"A Ridiculous Addiction"—Gwinn Owens

People are silly in fighting for parking spaces. Owens says these are "silly parking duels." They get mean. Take handicapped spots. Angry. They fight over spots. Get angry when people sit in their cars and don't pull out of a spot. They jam big cars in small spaces, cars get damaged. They're "angry people battling for what is utterly without value." Why? To make a quick getaway?

Freewriting helps you review what you've read, and it can give you topics for a paragraph that is different from a summary.

Brainstorming

After you freewrite, you can brainstorm. You can ask yourself questions to lead you toward a topic for your own paragraph. For instance, brainstorming on the idea "angry people battling for what is utterly without value" could look like this:

Brainstorming After Freewriting

Owens says people fighting for spaces are "battling for what is utterly without value." So why do they do it? Is there any other time drivers battle for what has no value?

Sure. On the highway. All the time.

How?
They weave in and out. They cut me off. They tailgate. They speed.

What are they fighting for?
They want to gain a few minutes. They want to get ahead. Driving is some kind of contest to them.

Then, don't they get some kind of satisfaction in the battle?
Not really. I often see them at the same red light I've stopped at. And their driving is very stressful for them. It raises their blood pressure, and it makes them angry and unhappy. They can't really win.

Could you write a paragraph on drivers who think of driving as a contest? If so, your brainstorming, based on your reading and freewriting, has lead you to a topic.

Developing Points of Agreement or Disagreement

Another way to use a reading selection to lead you to a topic is to review the selection and jot down any statements that provoke a strong reaction. You are looking for sentences with which you can agree or disagree. If you already marked "A Ridiculous Addiction" as you read, you might have listed these statements as points of agreement or disagreement:

Points of Agreement or Disagreement

"Hell hath no fury like a motorist who loses the battle for a close-in parking space."—agree

"This quest for the coveted spot transcends logic and common sense."—disagree

Then you might pick one of the statements and agree or disagree with it in writing. If you disagreed with the second statement, "This quest for the coveted spot transcends logic and common sense," you might develop the thought lines part of writing by listing your own ideas. You might focus on why a close parking space is important to you. With a focus and a list of reasons, you could move to the outlines part of writing from reading.

Outlines

Agree or Disagree Paragraph

An outline might look like the one below. As you read it, notice that the topic sentence and ideas are *your opinion*, not the ideas of the author of "A Ridiculous Addiction." You used his ideas to come up with your own thoughts.

An Outline for an Agree or Disagree Paragraph

```
topic sentence: Sometimes a close parking spot is important.

details:

convenience    I may have heavy bags to carry from the store.
             ⎧ Cars can be vandalized.
car safety   ⎨ Vandalism and burglary are more likely if the car
             ⎩ is parked at a distance.
```

```
personal   ⎧  I can be attacked in a parking lot.
safety     ⎨  Attacks are more likely at night.
           ⎩  Muggings are more likely if I am parked far away.
```

Rough Lines

Agree or Disagree Paragraph

If your outline gives you enough good points to develop, you are on your way to a paragraph. If you began with the ideas above, for example, you could develop them into a paragraph like this:

A Draft for an Agree or Disagree Paragraph

```
     Sometimes a close parking spot is important. The short dis-
tance to a store can make a difference if I have heavy bags or
boxes to carry from the store to my car. Convenience is one rea-
son for parking close. A more important reason is safety. In my
neighborhood, cars are often vandalized. Sometimes, cars get bro-
ken into. Cars are more likely to get vandalized or burglarized
if they are parked far from stores. Most of all, I am afraid to
park far from stores or restaurants because I am afraid of being
attacked in a parking lot, especially at night. If I am far away
from buildings and other people, I am more likely to be mugged.
```

Final Lines

Agree or Disagree Paragraph

When you read the paragraph above, you probably noticed some places where it could be revised:

- It could use more specific details.
- It should attribute the original idea about parking to Gwinn Owens, probably in the beginning.
- Some sentences could be combined.

Following is the final version of the same paragraph. As you read it, notice how a new beginning, added details, and combined sentences make it a smoother, clearer, and more developed paragraph.

Final Version for an Agree or Disagree Paragraph

```
     Gwinn Owens says that people who look for close parking spaces
are foolish, but I think that sometimes a close parking spot is
important. The short distance to a store can make a difference
if I have heavy bags or boxes to carry from the store to my car.
Convenience is one reason for parking close, but the more impor-
tant reason is safety. In my neighborhood, cars are often van-
dalized. Antennas get broken off; the paint gets deliberately
scratched. Sometimes, cars get broken into. Radios and CD play-
ers are stolen. Cars are more likely to be vandalized or bur-
glarized if they are parked far from stores. Most of all, I am
```

```
afraid to park far from stores or restaurants because I am afraid
of being attacked in a parking lot, especially at night. If I am
far away from buildings or other people, I am more likely to be
mugged.
```

Reading can give you many ideas for your own writing. Developing those ideas into a polished paragraph requires the same writing process as any good writing, a process that takes you through the stages of thinking, planning, drafting, revising, editing, and proofreading.

WRITING FOR AN ESSAY TEST

Most essay questions require a form of writing from reading. That is, your instructor asks you to write about an assigned reading. Usually, an essay test requires you to write from memory, not from an open book or notes. Such writing can be stressful, but breaking the task into steps can eliminate much of the stress.

Before the Test: The Steps of Reading

If you work through the steps of reading days before the test, you are halfway to your goal. Prereading helps to keep you focused, and your first reading will give you a sense of the whole selection. The third step, rereading with a pen or pencil, can be particularly helpful when you a preparing for a test. Most essay questions will ask you to either summarize or react to a reading selection. In either case, you must be familiar with the reading's main idea, supporting ideas, examples, and details. If you note these by marking the selection, you are teaching yourself about the main point, supporting ideas, and structure of the reading selection.

Shortly before the test, review the marked reading assignment. Your notes will help you to focus on the main point and the supporting ideas.

During the Test: The Stages of Writing

Answering an essay question for a test may seem very different from writing at home. After all, on a test, you must rely on your memory and write within a time limit, and these restrictions can make you feel anxious. However, by following the stages of the writing process, you can meet that challenge calmly and confidently.

Thought Lines Before you begin to write, think about these questions: Is the instructor asking for a summary of a reading selection? Or is he or she asking you to react to a specific idea in the reading by describing or developing that idea with examples or by agreeing or disagreeing? For example, in an essay question about "A Ridiculous Addiction," you might be asked (1) to explain what Gwinn Owens thinks are the advantages and disadvantages of seeking a close parking space (a summary), (2) to explain what he means when he says that fighting for parking turns drivers into mad dogs (a reaction, in which you develop and explain one part of the reading), or (3) to agree or disagree that close spaces are utterly without value (a reaction, so you have to be aware of what Owens said on this point).

Once you have thought about the question, list or freewrite your first ideas about the question. At this time, don't worry about how "right" or "wrong" your writing is; just write your first thoughts.

Outlines Your writing will be clear if you follow a plan. Remember that your audience for this writing is your instructor and that he or she will be evaluating how well you stick to the subject, make a point, and support it. Your plan for making a point about the subject and supporting that point can be written in a brief outline.

First, reread the question. Next, survey your list or freewriting. Does it contain a main point that answers the question? Does it contain supporting ideas and details?

Next, write a main point, and then list supporting ideas and details under the main point. Your main point will be the topic sentence of your answer. If you need more support, try brainstorming.

Rough Lines Write your point and supporting ideas in paragraph form. Remember to use effective transitions and to combine short sentences.

Final Lines You will probably not have time to copy your answer, but you can review it, proofread it, and correct any errors in spelling, punctuation, and word choice. This final check can produce a more polished answer.

Organize Your Time

Some students skip steps: they immediately begin writing their answer to an essay question, without thinking or planning. Sometimes they find themselves stuck in the middle of a paragraph, panicked because they have no more ideas. At other times, they find themselves writing in a circle, repeating the same point over and over. Occasionally, they even forget to include a main idea.

You can avoid these hazards by spending time on each of the stages. Planning is as important as writing. For example, if you have half an hour to write an essay, you can divide your time like this:

5 minutes	thinking, freewriting, listing
10 minutes	planning, outlining
10 minutes	drafting
5 minutes	reviewing and proofreading

Focusing on one stage at a time can make you more confident and your task more manageable.

Lines of Detail: A Walk-Through Assignment

Here are two ideas from "A Ridiculous Addiction":

1. People who want a good parking space often break parking laws.
2. People who search for good parking spots become mean and nasty.

Pick one of the ideas, with which you agree or disagree. Write a paragraph explaining why you agree or disagree. To write your paragraph, follow these steps:

Step 1: Begin by listing at least four reasons why you agree or disagree.

Step 2: Read your list to a partner or group. With the help of your listener(s), you can add reasons or details to explain the reasons.

Step 3: Once you have enough ideas, transform the statement you agree or disagree with into a topic sentence.

Step 4: Write an outline by listing your reasons and details below the topic sentence. Check that your list is in a clear and logical order.

Step 5: Write a draft of your paragraph. Check that you have attributed Gwinn Owens's statement, that you have enough details, and that you have combined any choppy sentences. Revise your draft until the paragraph is smooth and clear.

Step 6: Before you prepare the final copy, check your latest draft for errors in spelling, punctuation, and word choice.

Writing Your Own Paragraph on "A Ridiculous Addiction" by Gwinn Owens

When you write on one of these topics, be sure to work through the stages of the writing process in preparing your paragraph.

1. Gwinn Owens writes about Americans' addiction to the close-in parking space. Write about another addiction that Americans have. Instead of writing about a topic like drug or alcohol addiction, follow Owens's example and write about a social habit that is hard to break. You might, for instance, write about these habits:

   driving while talking on a cell phone   tailgating
   weaving in and out of traffic   speeding
   driving too slowly   pushing in line
   running yellow traffic lights   littering

   Once you've chosen a habit, brainstorm, alone or with a partner, for details. Think about details that could fit these categories:

   why the habit is foolish   where and when people act this way
   why the habit is dangerous   advantages of breaking the habit

   Ask yourself questions, answer them, and let the answers lead to more questions. Once you have collected some good details, work through the stages of writing a paragraph.

2. Gwinn Owens writes about a great invention, the car, and about the parking problems caused by cars. Below are several other recent inventions that can cause problems. Your goal is to write a paragraph about *the problems one of these inventions can cause.*

   To start, pick two of the inventions below. Alone, or with a partner or group, brainstorm both topics: ask questions, answer them, and add details so that each topic can lead you to enough ideas for a paragraph.

   After you have brainstormed, pick the topic you like better and work through the stages of preparing a paragraph.

   Topics to brainstorm: problems that could be caused by telephone answering machines, car alarms, automatic teller machines, cell phones, pagers, or email.

Name: _____   **Section:** _____

Peer Review Form for Writing from Reading

After you have written a draft version of your paragraph, let a writing partner read it. When your partner has completed the form below, discuss the comments. Repeat the same process for your partner's paragraph.

This paragraph (pick one) (1) summarizes, (2) agrees or disagrees, or (3) writes about an idea connected to a reading selection.

I think this paragraph needs/does not need to include the title and author of the reading selection.

The topic sentences of this paragraph is _____

_____

_____

The best part of this paragraph started with the words _____

_____

One suggestion to improve this paragraph is _____

_____

Other comments: _____

_____

_____

_____

_____

_____

_____

_____

_____

_____

_____

Reviewer's Name: _____

Writing from Reading

To practice the skills you have learned in this chapter, follow the steps of pre-reading, reading, and rereading with a pen or pencil as you read the following selection.

Parental Discretion
Dennis Hevesi

Dennis Hevesi is a writer for the New York Times. *In this essay, he writes about how the family structure changes when a parent goes back to school.*

Words You May Need To Know

discretion (title): the right to make your own decision
wrought (paragraph 4): inflicted
havoc (4): disorder, confusion
diehard (4): stubbornly committed, dedicated
feminists (4): people who fight for women's rights
genes (8): a unit in the body that controls the development of hereditary traits

maternal (14): motherly
anthropology (15): a study of the origins and physical and cultural development of mankind
Renaissance (17): a period of European history, roughly from the late 1300s to 1600

1   When the letter came saying that Pamela Stafford, after all her part-time study at night, had been accepted at the age of 34 as a full-time student by the University of California at Berkeley, her two teen-age sons leaped into the air, slapped palms in a high-five and shouted: "We did it! We did it!"

2   "I'm not sure they included me," she said.

3   Several months ago, when Gary Hatfield, also 34, and a sophomore at the Ohio State University, in Columbus, was telling his son, Seth, 11, why he was spending so much time studying, "He patted me on the shoulder and said: 'Dad, I understand. You want to finish school,'" Mr. Hatfield recalled, adding, "Blessed is the child's forgiving nature."

4   In hundreds of homes throughout the nation, as the rolls of those signing up for continuing education courses grow, getting mom or pop off to school has often wrought a kind of joyous havoc on family life and forced the sort of realignment of expectations that would warm the hearts of diehard feminists.

5   Dads or children are doing the shopping, the cooking, the cleaning, the laundry. Teen-agers have become the family chauffeur, or at least make sure the car is available when a parent has to get to class. Schedules have been turned on end. Children have even adopted parental roles—nagging when homework hasn't been done.

6   Mr. Hatfield, an English major, wants to teach high school or college English. "I'll sometimes get jabbed if I make a spelling or grammatical mistake," he said. "Seth will say, 'Hey, English teacher . . .'"

7   What can come through the difficulties and the role reversals is a shared commitment, a strengthened bond and a deepened appreciation for education. "When I went back to school, my older son went from being a C and D student to making honor roll," said Ms. Stafford, who is divorced and lives in Albany, near the university. "The younger guy, well, not as much improvement. But he did develop a more serious attitude toward school. Now, it's sort of a given that what you really do in life is finish school first."

8   And when the boys—Joseph, 18, and Christopher, 14—run into what Ms. Stafford called "the geek mentality" of friends who think doing well in school is totally lame, they are equipped to respond. "Joseph once told his friend," Ms. Stafford said, " 'Hey, my mom is smart. It's in the genes. I can't help being smart.' "

9   Mom is indeed smart. Out of a possible 4.0, Ms. Stafford is maintaining a 3.9 grade-point average as an English major at Berkeley, where she is also on staff as an administrative assistant.

10   "I felt really guilty about taking night courses," she said. "Then, at the end of that first semester, I got an A in ancient Mediterranean literature, and my sons developed an investment in my education. They sort of fired me as a mother and recreated me as a student."

11   Joseph, now a freshman at St. Mary's College in nearby Moraga, said: "I had to cook, wash dishes, pretty much take care of myself and my brother, too. There were times when I wished she was around; when things would happen that I couldn't handle."

12   Joseph said Christopher "was always a hyper kid. So I just had to be real patient. I talked to him about girls, about drugs. He doesn't do the silly stuff he used to do to get attention, like kitchen gymnastics—you know, dancing and flipping around the house like an idiot. Sometimes we fought. But he and I loved each other enough to punch each other and then hug."

13   During midterms and finals, Ms. Stafford said, the boys "would mysteriously disappear" so that she could study. "I like to deejay," Joseph said, "you know, sound-mixing in my room. I had to do this with the headphones the entire time. There could be no noise."

14   Between classes, Ms. Stafford would call home "and try to at least bring a maternal presence into the conversation: 'Have you done your homework? Have you done your chores?' But they would say, 'Hey, we don't need you. Goodness, the things we go through putting a parent through school.' "

15   Sometimes it seemed that Seth Hatfield wasn't so much putting his father through school as accompanying him. "Last quarter, I was taking an anthropology course," Mr. Hatfield said, "and one of the evenings I would take Seth to that class. He would sit and do his homework at the table with me. And the teacher was so nearsighted that she would walk by and give him handouts, just like one of the students."

16   Mr. Hatfield, who is divorced and lives in Columbus, has worked as a landscaper, a salesman, a counselor to juvenile delinquents, and a social worker at a home for the mentally retarded. With a part-time job, a little money in the bank

and a grant from Ohio State, he returned to college in 1987 and is maintaining a grade-point average of 3.2.

17   "I get hit with anxiety attacks," he said, "because here I am plowing through Renaissance literature and wishing I was sitting with my son playing a game."

18   But Seth doesn't complain, and his exposure to college has had benefits. "I found out from his teachers that he speaks proudly of going to Ohio State with his dad," Mr. Hatfield said. "Just walking across campus, with him wearing his Ohio State sweatshirt, give me the opportunity to familiarize him with what the place really is. We go plunder through the library. He knows the computer catalogue search system can lead him to information on Superman."

19   "I might go there when I grow up," Seth said. "When my dad gets his education, if he becomes a teacher, he'll have a larger income and I might even have him as a teacher. Maybe I'll borrow money from him for lunch."

20   Mr. Hatfield realizes that Seth, who lives with his mother about a mile away, is his first priority. "I will cut class to go to his band concert," he said. "Those things are too precious. I can take an incomplete in a course and make it up. I can't take an incomplete as a parent and ever make that up."

WRITING FROM READING: "Parental Discretion"

When you write on any of the following topics, be sure to work through the stages of the writing process in preparing your paragraph.

1. Write a summary paragraph of Hevesi's article. Be sure to include Hevesi's points about the good and bad effects of parents' returning to college.

2. No matter how old you are, attending college presents certain challenges. If you are the "traditional" college age of eighteen or nineteen, you may face the challenge of adjusting to a place that is not like high school. If you are in your twenties, you may be facing other challenges: earning money for college, living at home and going to college, balancing the demands of a family, work, and school. Students in their thirties, forties, fifties, sixties, and seventies all have different problems when they go to college. Write a paragraph about the problems one age group faces in attending college. You may use a topic sentence like this one:

   It's not easy being eighteen (or twenty-five, or thirty, or sixty—you fill in the age) and going to college.

   If your instructor agrees, you might interview a writing partner about the difficulties his or her age group faces in going to college. Then your partner can interview you. By interviewing, each of you can help the other gather details.

3. As an alternative to topic 2, choose a topic sentence that is closer to your experience, like one of these:

   It's not easy working full time and going to college.
   It's not easy being in a wheelchair and going to college.
   It's not easy being a single parent and going to college.

4. Begin this assignment by working with a group. Plan a paragraph with this topic sentence;

Today, the term "college student" can include many kinds of people.

In your group, have each member support the topic sentence by talking about himself or herself. You might mention age, reason for going to college, ethnic background, college major, hobbies, special talents, family background, and so on. As each member describes himself or herself, write down the details. Ask follow-up questions and write down the answers. After you have gathered enough specific examples, write your paragraph.

The Bottom Line
Grammar for Writers

INTRODUCTION

Overview

In this section, you'll be working with "The Bottom Line," the basics of grammar that you need to be a clear writer. If you are willing to memorize certain rules and work through the activities here, you will be able to apply grammatical rules automatically as you write.

Using "The Bottom Line"

Since this portion of the textbook is divided into self-contained segments, it does not have to be read in sequence. Your instructor may suggest you review specific rules and examples, or you may be assigned various segments as either a class or group assignment. Various approaches are possible, and thus you can regard this section as a "user-friendly" grammar handbook for quick reference. Mastering the practical parts of grammar will improve your writing; you will feel more sure of yourself because you will know the bottom line.

CONTENTS

The Bottom Line: Grammar for Writers

CHAPTER 12

The Simple Sentence

Identifying the crucial parts of a sentence is the first step in many writing decisions: how to punctuate, how to avoid sentence fragments, how to be sure that subjects and verbs "agree" (match). To move forward to these decisions requires a few steps back—to basics.

RECOGNIZING A SENTENCE

TEACHING TIP:

Tell students that if a word group has a subject and a verb, is punctuated like a sentence, but makes no sense, it is one type of a fragment.

Note: If your students need help understanding the difference between sentences and fragments, refer to Chapter 15 on sentence fragments.

Let's start with a few basic definitions. A basic unit of language is a **word.**

> **examples:** car, dog, sun

A group of related words can be a **phrase.**

> **examples:** shiny new car; snarling, angry dog; in the bright sun

When the group of words contains a subject and a verb, it is called a **clause.** When the word group has a subject and a verb and makes sense by itself, it is called a **sentence** or an independent clause. When the word group has a subject and a verb but does not make sense by itself, it is called a dependent clause.

If you want to check to see whether you have written a sentence and not just a group of related words, you first have to check for a subject and a verb. It is often easier to locate the verbs first.

RECOGNIZING VERBS

Verbs are words that express some kind of action or being. Verbs about the five senses—sight, touch, smell, taste, sound—are part of the group called **being verbs.** Look at some examples of verbs as they work in sentences:

> **action verbs:**
>
> We *walk* to the store every day.
> The children *ran* to the playground.

> **being verbs:**
>
> My mother *is* a good cook.
> The family *seems* unhappy.
> The soup *smells* delicious.

Exercise 1 **Recognizing Verbs**

Practice Underline the verbs in the following sentences.

1. The truck <u>stalled</u> on the highway.

2. Early in the morning, he <u>jogs</u> around the park.

3. She <u>looks</u> worried about the driving test.

4. My cousin Bill <u>was</u> the best player on the team.

5. The rain <u>floods</u> the street on stormy days.

6. The homemade tortillas <u>taste</u> delicious.

7. Most people <u>love</u> long weekends.

8. Dalmatians <u>are</u> very popular pets today.

9. Single parents <u>face</u> many challenges at home and at work.

10. The old blanket <u>feels</u> rough and scratchy.

More on Verbs

The verb in a sentence can be more than one word. First of all, there can be **helping verbs** in front of the main verb, the action or being verb. Here is a list of some frequently used helping verbs: *is, am, are, was, were, do, must, might, have, shall, will, can, could, may, should, would.*

I *was watching* the Super Bowl. (The helping verb is *was.*)
You *should have called* me. (The helping verbs are *should* and *have.*)
The president *can select* his assistants. (The helping verb is *can.*)
Leroy *will graduate* in May. (The helping verb is *will.*)

Helping verbs can make the verb in a sentence more than one word long. But there can also be more than one main verb:

Andrew *planned* and *practiced* his speech.
I *stumbled* over the rug, *grabbed* a chair, and *fell* on my face.

Exercise 2 **Writing Sentences with Helping Verbs**

Collaborate Complete this exercise with a partner or a group. First, ask one person to add at least one helping verb to the verb given. Then, work together to write two sentences using the main verb and the helping verb(s). Appoint a spokesperson for your group to read all your sentences to the class. Notice how many combinations of main verb and helping verb you hear. The first one is done for you.

1. **verb:** called

   verb with helping verb(s): <u>has called</u>

   sentence 1: <u>Sam has called me twice this week.</u>

   sentence 2: <u>She has called him a hero.</u>

2. verb: moving

verb with helping verb(s): <u>are moving</u>

sentence 1: <u>The tanker trucks are moving cautiously.</u>

sentence 2: <u>Twenty employees are moving to a new branch office.</u>

3. verb: fly

verb with helping verb(s): <u>could fly</u>

sentence 1: <u>The family could fly to Texas.</u>

sentence 2: <u>My parakeet could fly around the room.</u>

4. verb: laughed

verb with helping verb(s): <u>should have laughed</u>

sentence 1: <u>We should have laughed at his jokes.</u>

sentence 2: <u>Jamie should have laughed at his own mistake.</u>

5. verb: spoken

verb with helping verb(s): <u>might have spoken</u>

sentence 1: <u>You might have spoken more kindly.</u>

sentence 2: <u>The officer might have spoken to Tom yesterday.</u>

RECOGNIZING SUBJECTS

TEACHING TIP:
Tell students that an
easy way to spot an
action verb in a sen-
tence is to remember
that it tells what a
subject *does* (present
tense), *did* (past
tense), or *will do*
(future tense). For
example: He cleans
his room; he cleaned
his room; he will
clean his room.

After you can recognize verbs, it is easy to find the subjects of sentences because subjects and verbs are linked. If the verb is an action verb, for example, the subject will be the word or words that answer the question "Who or what is doing that action?"

The truck stalled on the highway.

Step 1: Identify the verb: *stalled*

Step 2: Ask, "Who or what stalled?"

Step 3: The answer is the subject: The *truck* stalled on the highway. The *truck* is the subject.

If your verb expresses being, the same steps apply to finding the subject:

Spike was my best friend.

Step 1: Identify the verb: *was*

Step 2: Ask, "Who or what was my best friend?"

Step 3: The answer is the subject: *Spike* was my best friend. *Spike* is the subject.

Just as there can be more than one word to make up a verb, there can be more than one subject.

examples: *David* and *Leslie* planned the surprise party.
My *father* and *I* worked in the yard yesterday.

Exercise 3	**Recognizing the Subjects in Sentences**
Practice	Underline the subjects in the following sentences.

1. <u>Maggie</u> might have followed the directions more carefully.

2. <u>They</u> were stacking the records in neat piles.

3. Suddenly, a <u>car</u> appeared on the runway.

4. As a matter of fact, <u>houses</u> are not expensive in that neighborhood.

5. <u>Happiness</u> can come in many shapes and forms.

6. <u>Colleges</u> are facing many budget problems.

7. <u>Complaining</u> can sometimes make a situation worse.

8. <u>Joy</u> and <u>excitement</u> filled the locker room.

9. <u>Nothing</u> is wrong with my sister.

10. <u>Somebody</u> took the last piece of cake.

More About Recognizing Subjects and Verbs

When you look for the subject of a sentence, look for the core word or words; don't include descriptive words around the subject. The idea is to look for the subject, not for the words that describe it.

The dark blue *dress* looked lovely on Anita.
Dirty *streets* and grimy *houses* destroy a neighborhood.

The subjects are the core words *dress*, *streets*, and *houses*, not the descriptive words *dark blue*, *dirty*, and *grimy*.

PREPOSITIONS AND PREPOSITIONAL PHRASES

Prepositions are usually small words that often signal a kind of position or possession, as shown in the following list:

Infobox					
Some Common Prepositions					
about	before	during	like	over	upon
above	below	except	near	through	with
across	behind	for	of	to	within
after	beneath	from	off	toward	without
among	beside	in	on	under	
around	between	inside	onto	up	
at	beyond	into			

TEACHING TIP:
Listing prepositional phrases that have become clichés or slang can be an enjoyable way for students to spot prepositional phrases. (For example: under the weather, down on his luck, up in the air.)

Note: ESL students may need help with the prepositions of time and space. See the ESL Appendix.
Non-native speakers often have difficulty understanding the meaning of some colloquial prepositional phrases. Examining literal interpretations of some expressions can be an amusing yet practical examination of prepositions.

A prepositional phrase is made up of a preposition and its object. Here are some prepositional phrases. In each one, the first word is the preposition; the other words are the object of the preposition.

Prepositional Phrases

about the movie	of mice and men
around the corner	off the record
between the lines	on the mark
during recess	up the wall
near my house	with my sister and brother

There is an old memory trick to help you remember prepositions. Think of a chair. Now, think of a series of words you can put *in front of* the chair:

around the chair	*with* the chair
behind the chair	*to* the chair
between the chairs	*near* the chair
by the chairs	*under* the chair
of the chair	*on* the chair
off the chair	*from* the chair

Those words are prepositions.

You need to know about prepositions because they can help you identify the subject of a sentence. There is an important grammar rule about prepositions:

Nothing in a prepositional phrase can ever be the subject of the sentence.

Prepositional phrases describe people, places, or things. They may describe the subject of a sentence, but they never *include* the subject. Whenever you are looking for the subject of a sentence, begin by putting parentheses around all the prepositional phrases:

The restaurant (around the corner) makes the best fried chicken (in town.)

The prepositional phrases are in parentheses. Since *nothing* in them can be the subject, once you have eliminated the prepositional phrases, you can follow the steps to find the subject of the sentence:

What is the verb? *makes*
Who or what makes the best fried chicken? *The restaurant. Restaurant* is the subject of the sentence.

By marking off the prepositional phrases, you are left with the *core* of the sentence. There is less to look at.

(Behind the park), a *carousel* (with gilded horses) delighted children (from all the neighborhoods).
subject: *carousel*

The *dog* (with the ugliest face) was the winner (of the contest).
subject: *dog*

Exercise 4 **Recognizing Prepositional Phrases, Subjects, and Verbs**

Practice

Put parentheses around the prepositional phrases in the following sentences. Then underline the subjects and verbs and put an *S* above each subject and a *V* above each verb.

1. The <u>car</u> in the parking lot near the bank <u>has</u> a huge dent in the rear.

2. <u>Some</u> of the people on my street <u>like</u> sitting on their front steps on a hot night.

3. Several <u>dancers</u> in the play <u>stumbled</u> on the rickety stage.

4. During my lunch hour, <u>I</u> often <u>go</u> to the park across the street from my office.

5. The true <u>story</u> beneath all his lies <u>was</u> a tale with some horrifying twists.

6. <u>She</u> <u>took</u> her credit card from her wallet and <u>handed</u> the card to the clerk behind the counter.

7. The <u>doctor</u> in the emergency room <u>dashed</u> down the hall toward the trauma victim.

8. The little <u>village</u> above the lake <u>gleamed</u> in the sunlight.

9. On sunny days, <u>towns</u> by the beach <u>are</u> usually <u>filled</u> with tourists.

10. Their <u>farm</u> <u>was</u> off the main road between Springfield and Ridgewood.

Exercise 5
👥 Collaborate

Writing Sentences with Prepositional Phrases

Complete this exercise with a partner. First, add one prepositional phrase to the core sentence. Then, ask your partner to add a second prepositional phrase to the same sentence. For the next sentence, let your partner add the first phrase, and you add the second. Keep reversing the process throughout the exercise. When you have completed the exercise, be ready to read the sentences with two prepositional phrases to the class. The first one has been done for you.

1. core sentence: Rain fell.

Add one prepositional phrase: <u>Rain fell on the mountains.</u>

Add another prepositional phrase: <u>From a dark sky, rain fell on the mountains.</u>

2. core sentence: The school was closed.

Answers Will Vary.
Possible answers
shown at right.

Add one prepositional phrase: <u>The school was closed for a week.</u>

Add another prepositional phrase: <u>In January, the school was closed for a week.</u>

3. core sentence: The canoe drifted.

Add one prepositional phrase: <u>The canoe drifted from the shore.</u>

Add another prepositional phrase: <u>The canoe drifted from the shore to the deep water.</u>

4. core sentence: High school seniors are worried.

Add one prepositional phrase: <u>In June, high school seniors are worried.</u>

Add another prepositional phrase: <u>In June, high school seniors are worried about graduation.</u>

5. core sentence: Parents must struggle.

Add one prepositional phrase: <u>Parents of teens must struggle.</u>

Add another prepositional phrase: <u>Parents of teens must struggle with adolescent rebellion.</u>

WORD ORDER

When we speak, we often use a very simple word order: first, the subject; then, the verb. For example, someone might say, "I am going to the store." *I* is the subject that begins the sentence; *am going* is the verb that comes after the subject.

But not all sentences are in such a simple word order. Prepositional phrases, for example, can change the word order:

sentence: Among the contestants was an older man.

Step 1: Mark off the prepositional phrase(s) with parentheses: (Among the contestants) was an older man. Remember that nothing in a prepositional phrase can be the subject of a sentence.

Step 2: Find the verb: *was*

Step 3: Who or what was? An older *man* was. The subject of the sentence is *man*.

After you change the word order of this sentence, you can see the subject (*S*) and verb (*V*) more easily.

$$\text{An older } \overset{S}{man} \overset{V}{was} \text{ among the contestants.}$$

Exercise 6
Practice

Finding Prepositional Phrases, Subjects, and Verbs in Complicated Word Order

Put parentheses around the prepositional phrases in the following sentences. Then underline the subjects and verbs and put an *S* above each subject and a *V* above each verb.

TEACHING TIP:
Tell students to first identify the prepositional phrases, then to pretend the phrases do not appear, so they can more easily spot the subjects and verbs.

1. (Down the street)(from my apartment)^V <u>is</u> an all-night <u>supermarket</u>. ^S

2. (Behind the counter)^V <u>is</u> a <u>cash register</u>. ^S

3. (Inside the student union)^V <u>are</u> video <u>games</u> and vending <u>machines</u>. ^S

4. ( )( ) V S ( )(
 4. Around the outside of the house <u>are</u> tall <u>trees</u> with yellow blossoms on
)
 their spreading branches.

 ( )( ) V S ( )
 5. Above the rooftops of the houses <u>stands</u> the <u>steeple</u> of an old church.

 ( )( ) V S
 6. From the back of the alley <u>came</u> a loud <u>scream</u>.

 ( ) V S ( )(
 7. Between the houses <u>was</u> a <u>fence</u> with a clinging vine of red flowers.

 ( )V S ( )
 8. In my closet <u>is</u> a <u>raincoat</u> with a flannel lining.

 ( )V S ( )( )
 9. Among my fondest memories <u>is</u> a <u>recollection</u> of a day at the park.

 ( )( ) V S ( )
 10. With the man from Wichita <u>came</u> a <u>sheriff</u> in uniform.

More on Word Order

The expected word order of subject first, then verb changes when a sentence
starts with *There is/are, There was/were, Here is/are,* or *Here was/were.* In such
cases, look for the subject after the verb:

> V S S
> There *are* a *bakery* and a *pharmacy* down the street.

> V S
> Here *is* the *man* with the answers.

If it helps you to understand this pattern, change the word order:

> S S V
> A *bakery* and a *pharmacy are* there, down the street.

> S V
> The *man* with the answers *is* here.

You should also note that even if the subject comes after the verb, the verb has
to "match" the subject. For instance, if the subject refers to more than one thing,
the verb must also refer to more than one thing:

> There *are* a *bakery* and a *pharmacy* down the road. (Two things, a bakery
> and a pharmacy, *are* down the road.)

Word Order in Questions

Questions may have a different word order. The main verb and the helping verb
may not be next to each other:

> **question:** Do you like pizza?
> **subject:** *you*
> **verbs:** *do, like*

If it helps you to understand this concept, think of answering the question. If
someone accused you of not liking pizza, you might say, "I *do like* it." You would
use two words as verbs.

> **question:** Will he think about it?
> **subject:** *he*
> **verbs:** *will, think*

> **question:** Is Maria telling the truth?
> **subject:** *Maria*
> **verbs:** *is, telling*

Exercise 7 **Recognizing Subjects and Verbs in Complicated Word Order:**
Practice **A Comprehensive Exercise**

Underline the subjects and verbs and put an *S* above each subject and a *V* above each verb.

1. Beneath all his sarcastic remarks about the contest <u>was</u> a <u>fear</u> of failure.
   (V over "was", S over "fear")
2. <u>Have</u> <u>you</u> <u>seen</u> the latest edition of the local newspaper?
   (V over "Have", S over "you", V over "seen")
3. Near the top of the list <u>was</u> the <u>name</u> of a good friend.
   (V over "was", S over "name")
4. Around the back of the store there <u>were</u> a parking <u>area</u> and a <u>shed</u>.
   (V over "were", S over "area", S over "shed")
5. Inside the mansion <u>was</u> a dark and deadly <u>secret</u>.
   (V over "was", S over "secret")
6. Here <u>are</u> the preliminary <u>designs</u> for the new stadium.
   (V over "are", S over "designs")
7. With him <u>were</u> two of the new <u>managers</u> at the store.
   (V over "were", S over "managers")
8. From three cities <u>came</u> <u>hundreds</u> of applications for the job.
   (V over "came", S over "hundreds")
9. There <u>were</u> good <u>reasons</u> for Tom's choice of career.
   (V over "were", S over "reasons")
10. <u>Is</u> there <u>anything</u> in the box?
   (V over "Is", S over "anything")

Words That Cannot Be Verbs

Sometimes there are words that look like verbs in a sentence, but they are not verbs. Such words include adverbs (words like *always, often, nearly, rarely, never, ever*), which are placed close to the verb but are not verbs. Another word that is placed between a helping verb and a main verb is *not. Not* is not a verb.

When you are looking for verbs in a sentence, be careful to eliminate words like *often* and *not.*

> He will not listen to me. (The verbs are *will listen.*)
> Althea can always find a bargain. (The verbs are *can find.*)

Be careful with contractions:

> They haven't raced in years. (The verbs are *have raced. Not* is not a part
> of the verb, even in contractions.)
> Don't you come from Arizona? (The verbs are *do come.*)
> Won't he ever learn? (The verbs are *will learn. Won't* is a contraction for
> *will not.*)

Recognizing Main Verbs

If you are checking to see if a word is a main verb, try the pronoun test. Combine your word with this simple list of pronouns: *I, you, he, she, it, we, they.* A main verb is a word such as *drive* or *noticed* that can be combined with the words on this list. Now try the pronoun test.

For the word *drive*: I drive, you drive, he drives, she drives, it drives, we drive, they drive

For the word *noticed*: I noticed, you noticed, he noticed, she noticed, it noticed, we noticed, they noticed

But words like *never* cannot be used, alone, with the pronouns:

~~I never, you never, he never, she never, it never, we never, they never~~ (Never did what?)

Never is not a verb. *Not* is not a verb either, as the pronoun test indicates:

~~I not, you not, he not, she not, it not, we not, you not, they not~~ (These combinations do not make sense because *not* is not a verb.)

Verb Forms That Cannot Be Main Verbs

There are forms of verbs that cannot be main verbs by themselves, either. An *-ing* verb, by itself, cannot be the main verb, as the pronoun test shows:

For the word *voting*: ~~I voting, you voting, he voting, she voting, we voting, they voting~~

If you see an *-ing* verb by itself, correct the sentence by adding a helping verb:

Scott ~~riding~~ his motorcycle. (*Riding*, by itself, cannot be a main verb.)
correction: Scott *was riding* his motorcycle.

Another verb form, called an infinitive, also cannot be a main verb. An **infinitive** is the form of the verb that has *to* placed in front of it.

Infobox

Some Common Infinitives

to care	to vote	to repeat
to feel	to play	to stumble
to need	to reject	to view

Try the pronoun test, and you'll see that infinitives cannot be main verbs:

For the infinitive *to vote*: ~~I to vote, you to vote, he to vote, she to vote, we to vote, they to vote~~

So if you see an infinitive being used as a verb, correct the sentence by adding a main verb:

We ~~to vote~~ in the election tomorrow. (There is no verb, just an infinitive.)
correction: We *are going* to vote in the election tomorrow. (Now there is a verb.)

The infinitives and the *-ing* verbs do not work as main verbs. You must put a verb with them to make a correct sentence.

Exercise 8 **Correcting Problems with *-ing* or Infinitive Verb Forms**

Practice　Most—but not all—of the sentences below are faulty; an *-ing* verb or an infinitive may be taking the place of a main verb. Rewrite the sentences that contain errors.

1. Everyone in the senior class to visit the amusement park for a special graduation party.

   rewritten: Everyone in the senior class will visit the amusement park for a special graduation party.

2. My husband paying no attention to the feud between his sisters.

   rewritten: My husband paid no attention to the feud between his sisters.

3. The flashy red sports car ahead of me speeding out of control and into the median.

   rewritten: The flashy red sportscar ahead of me sped out of control and into the median.

4. Sylvia learned to care about her health after her bout with pneumonia.

   rewritten: The sentence is correct.

5. Among his other goals, Jason to win a medal in the 200-meter race.

   rewritten: Among his other goals, Jason wanted to win a medal in the 200 meter race.

6. After all the discussion and deliberation, the committee taking a very conservative position on the question of tenants' rights.

   rewritten: After all the discussion and deliberation, the committee took a very conservative position on the question of tenants' rights.

7. One of the most famous experts in the field of forensic science to speak to my criminal justice class tomorrow.

   rewritten: One of the most famous experts in the field of forensic science will speak to my criminal justice class tomorrow.

8. The dog behind the fence barking uncontrollably for almost two hours.

   rewritten: The dog behind the fence barked uncontrollably for almost two hours.

9. Ever since the accident, I have been picking tiny pieces of glass out of the carpet.

   rewritten: The sentence is correct.

10. In her lectures, the nutritionist emphasizing the importance of fiber in our diet.

rewritten: <u>In her lectures, the nutritionist emphasized the importance of</u>

<u>fiber in our diet.</u>

Exercise 9 **Finding Subjects and Verbs: A Comprehensive Exercise**

Practice

Underline the subjects and verbs in the following sentences and put an *S* above each subject and a *V* above each verb.

1. <u>Do you</u> ever <u>visit</u> your grandmother in Minneapolis?
   (V S   V)

2. <u>They're</u> not <u>playing</u> the game by the rules.
   (S V (are) V)

3. Behind the mall <u>is</u> a huge parking <u>lot</u>.
   (V   S)

4. <u>Robert needs</u> to rehearse for the concert.
   (S V)

5. <u>Won't you consider</u> my suggestion?
   (V (will) S V)

6. Football <u>players are</u> often <u>injured</u> during the season.
   (S V   V)

7. My <u>sister will</u> never <u>repeat</u> that gossip.
   (S V   S)

8. There <u>are</u> three <u>reasons</u> for the price hike.
   (V   S)

9. <u>Jackie should have been thinking</u> about her boyfriend's feelings.
   (S   V)

10. There <u>were</u> a <u>Mazda</u>, a <u>Chrysler</u>, and a <u>Volkswagen</u> in the used car lot.
    (V   S   S   S)

11. <u>Lakeesha paid</u> the bills and <u>balanced</u> her checkbook yesterday.
    (S V   V)

12. Within the fenced yard <u>is</u> a lovely <u>garden</u> of tropical plants.
    (V   S)

13. At the end of the day, <u>he</u> and my <u>father looked</u> tired and dirty.
    (S   S V)

14. Sweet little <u>puppies can develop</u> minds of their own.
    (S   V)

15. <u>Erin has</u> never <u>met</u> her cousin from California.
    (S V   V)

16. <u>I have</u> rarely <u>seen</u> a person with more self-confidence.
    (S V   V)

17. Without his glasses, <u>Nick can't read</u> the road signs.
    (S V (can) V)

18. Here <u>was</u> the <u>solution</u> to the mystery of the locked door.
    (V   S)

19. The <u>neighbors cut</u> the grass, <u>weeded</u> the flower bed, and <u>mended</u> the fence between our houses.
    (S V   V   V)

20. In better times, <u>I might</u> never <u>have taken</u> a job.
    (S V   V)

Exercise 10 Create Your Own Text

Complete this exercise with two partners. Below is a list of the rules you have just studied. Each member of the group should write one example of each rule. When your group has completed three examples for each rule, trade your completed exercise with the members of another group and check their examples while they check yours. The first rule has been done for you.

Rule 1: The verb in a sentence can express some kind of action.

examples: a. Janelle drives to work every day.

b. Last week my cat killed a mouse in the basement.

c. My little sister dyed her hair with Kool-Aid.

Rule 2: The verb in a sentence can express some state of being or one of the five senses.

Answers Will Vary.
Possible answers shown at right.

examples: a. Ricardo is my best friend.

b. This milk tastes sour.

c. My brothers were soccer champions.

Rule 3: The verb in a sentence can consist of more than one word.

examples: a. I could have lost my car keys.

b. The angry motorist yelled and screamed at me.

c. The doctor will see you now.

Rule 4: There can be more than one subject of a sentence.

examples: a. Donique and Terrence are at the movies.

b. My bathroom and kitchen need new cabinets.

c. Drug stores and supermarkets sell cold remedies.

Rule 5: If you take out the prepositional phrases, it is easier to identify the subject of a sentence since nothing in a prepositional phrase can be the subject of a sentence.

examples: (Write sentences containing at least one prepositional phrase and put parentheses around the prepositional phrases.)

a. I heard a noise (from the back) (of the room.)

b. (With a smile,) he took my hand.

c. (Near my apartment) is a Mexican restaurant.

Rule 6: Not all sentences have the simple word order of subject first, then verb.

examples: (Give examples of more complicated word order.)

a. Do you like shrimp and lobster?

b. Here are the assigments.

c. Among the candies was a chocolate cream.

Rule 7: Words like *not, never, often, always, ever* are not verbs.

examples: (Write sentences using those words; then underline the correct verb.)

a. Andrew never visits his mother.

b. I have often wondered about Tiffany's stories.

c. My dog will not learn any tricks.

Rule 8: An *-ing* verb form by itself or an infinitive (*to* preceding the verb) cannot be a main verb.

examples: (Write sentences with *-ing* verb forms or infinitives, and underline the main verbs.)

a. My son wants to be an astronaut.

b. I hate complaining about my job.

c. Mr. Philemon is taking a long vacation.

Beyond the Simple Sentence: Coordination

A group of words containing a subject and verb is called a **clause.** When that group makes sense by itself, it is called a sentence or an independent clause.

The kind of sentence that has one independent clause is called a **simple sentence.** If you rely too heavily on a sentence pattern of simple sentences, you risk writing paragraphs like this:

> I am a college student. I am also a salesperson in a mall. I am always busy. School is time-consuming. Studying is time-consuming. Working makes me tired. Balancing these activities is hard. I work too many hours. Work is important. It pays for school.

Here is a better version:

> I am a college student and a salesperson at a mall, so I am always busy. School and study are time-consuming, and working makes me tired. Balancing these activities is hard. I work too many hours, but that work is important. It pays for school.

OPTIONS FOR COMBINING SIMPLE SENTENCES

Good writing involves sentence variety; it means mixing a simple sentence with a more complicated one, a short sentence with a long one. Sentence variety is easier to achieve if you can combine related, short sentences into one.

Some students avoid such combining because they are not sure how to do it. They do not know how to punctuate the new combinations. It is true that punctuation involves memorizing a few rules, but once you know them, you will be able to use them automatically and write with more confidence. Here are three options for combining simple sentences and the punctuation rules to follow in each case.

OPTION 1: USING A COMMA WITH A COORDINATING CONJUNCTION

You can combine two simple sentences with a comma and a coordinating conjunction. The coordinating conjunctions are *for, and, nor, but, or, yet,* and *so.*

TEACHING TIP:
One easy way for students to remember coordinating conjunctions is to call them, collectively, "fan-boys." (for, and, nor, but, or, yet, so.).

To coordinate means to join equals. When you join two simple sentences with a comma and a coordinating conjunction, each half of the combination remains an independent clause, with its own subject (S) and verb (V).

Here are two simple sentences:

> S   V   S   V
> *He cooked* the dinner. *She washed* the dishes.

Here are the two simple sentences combined with a comma and the word *and*, a coordinating conjunction (CC):

> S   V   , CC S   V
> *He cooked* the dinner, *and she washed* the dishes.

The combined sentences keep the form they had as separate sentences; that is, they are still both independent clauses, with a subject and verb and with the ability to stand alone.

The word that joins them is the **coordinating conjunction.** It is used to join *equals.* Look at some more examples that use coordinating conjunctions to join two simple sentences:

sentences combined with *but*:

> S   V   , CC S V
> *I rushed* to the bank, *but I was* too late.

sentences combined with *or*:

> S   V   , CC S   V
> *She can write* a letter to Jim, *or she can call* him.

sentences combined with *nor*:

> S V   , CC V S V
> *I didn't like* the book, *nor did I like* the movie made from the book.

(Notice what happens to the word order when you use *nor.*)

sentences combined with *for*:

> S   V   , CC S V
> *Sam worried* about the job interview, *for he saw* many qualified applicants in the waiting room.

sentences combined with *yet*:

> S   V   , CC S   V
> *Leo tried* to please his sister, *yet she* never *seemed* appreciative of his efforts.

sentences combined with *so*:

> S V   , CC S V
> *I was* the first in line for the concert tickets, *so I got* the best seats in the stadium.

Where Does the Comma Go?

Notice that the comma comes *before* the coordinating conjunction *(and, but, or, nor, for, yet, so).* It comes before the new idea, the second independent clause. It goes where the first independent clause ends. Try this punctuation check: After you've placed the comma, look at the combined sentences. For example:

> She joined the army, and she traveled overseas.

Split the sentence into two sentences at the comma:

> She joined the army. And she traveled overseas. (The split makes sense.)

If you put the comma in the wrong place, after the coordinating conjunction, your split sentences would be

> She joined the army and. She traveled overseas. (The split doesn't make sense.)

This test helps you see whether the comma has been placed correctly—*where the first independent clause ends.* (Notice that you can begin a sentence with *and.* You can also begin a sentence with *but, or, nor, for, yet,* or *so*—as long as you're writing a complete sentence.)

    Caution: Do *not* use a comma every time you use the words *and, but, or, nor, for, yet* or *so;* use a comma only when the coordinating conjunction joins independent clauses. Do not use a comma when the coordinating conjunction joins words:

> blue and gold   tired but happy   hot or cold

Do not use a comma when a coordinating conjunction joins phrases:

> on the chair or under the table
> in the water and by the shore
> with a smile but without an apology

A comma is used when the coordinating conjunction joins two independent clauses. Another way to say the same rule is to say that the comma is used when the coordinating conjunction joins two simple sentences.

Placing the Comma by Using Subject-Verb (*S-V*) Patterns

An independent clause, or simple sentence, follows one of these basic patterns:

> S V
> He ran.
> S   S V
> He and I ran.
> S V   V
> He ran and swam.
> S   S V   V
> He and I ran and swam.

Study all four patterns for the simple sentence, and you will notice you can draw a line separating the subjects on one side and the verbs on the other:

S	V
SS	V
S	VV
SS	VV

Whether the sentence has one or more subjects and one or more verbs, in the simple sentence the pattern is subject(s) followed by verb(s).

    When you combine two simple sentences, the pattern changes:

two simple sentences:

> S   V   S V
> He swam. I ran.

two simple sentences combined:

S   V   S V
He swam, but I ran.

In the new pattern, *SVSV,* you cannot draw a line separating all the subjects on one side and all the verbs on the other. This new pattern, with two simple sentences (or independent clauses) joined into one, is called a **compound sentence.**

Recognizing the *SVSV* pattern will help you place the comma for compound sentences. Here is another way to remember this rule. If you have this pattern

SV SV

use a comma in front of the coordinating conjunction. Do not use a comma in front of the coordinating conjunction with these patterns:

S	V
SS	V
S	VV
SS	VV

For example, use a comma for this pattern:

S   V   ,   S   V
Jane followed directions, but I rushed ahead.

Do not use a comma for this pattern:

S   V   V
Carol cleans her kitchen every week but never wipes the top of the refrigerator.

AVOIDING RUN-ON SENTENCES

If you run two independent clauses together without the necessary punctuation, you produce an error called a **run-on sentence.** (This error is also called a *fused sentence.*) To avoid this error, you must look at the sentence pattern and check your punctuation.

> **run-on sentence:** Carol cleans her kitchen every week but she never wipes the top of the refrigerator.

> **check the sentence pattern:** Carol cleans her kitchen every
>
> week but *she* never *wipes* the top of the refrigerator.

With the *SVSV* pattern and the coordinating conjunction *but,* you need a comma:

> **run-on corrected:** Carol cleans her kitchen every week, but she never wipes the top of the refrigerator.

You have just studied one way to combine simple sentences. If you are going to take advantage of this method, you have to memorize the coordinating conjunctions—*and, but, or, nor, for, yet, so*—so that your use of them, with the correct punctuation, will become automatic.

Exercise 1   **Recognizing Compound Sentences and Adding Commas**

Practice   Add commas only where they are needed in the following sentences. Do not add any words.

1. I came to see the play, but the theater was closed.

2. The waiter at the crowded restaurant rushed from table to table and tried to pacify the impatient customers.

3. Before my trip I read everything in the library about Puerto Rico, and I took a Spanish class in night school.

4. The young couple are planning to save their money and are hoping to buy a small house in the suburbs.

5. It rained all weekend, so the picnic was postponed.

6. Rosa showed signs of nervousness in her speech, yet her words carried conviction and power.

7. I looked in three stores for the perfect birthday gift for Fred but couldn't find anything at all.

8. You have to prepare for a marathon, or you can do serious damage to your body.

9. She deserved to win first prize, for she had spent years practicing her skills.

10. The customers were not interested in my excuses, nor were they sympathetic with my problems.

Exercise 2   **More on Recognizing Compound Sentences and Adding Commas**

Practice   Add commas only where they are needed in the following sentences.

1. Andrew tried to adjust the television for half an hour, but he couldn't get the fuzz out of the picture.

2. Several of my classmates studied together in the library and shared their notes.

3. The early movie was sold out, so Sarah bought a ticket for a later show.

4. I took my dog to obedience classes, yet he continued barking at strangers.

5. Ricky sang a beautiful ballad, and Mark introduced some new dance music.

6. Ricky and Mark sang a beautiful ballad and introduced some new dance music.

7. Benny pretends to be sympathetic yet is actually bored by other people's problems.

8. Tomorrow Dr. O'Brien will call in a specialist' or she will conduct more tests.

9. James is a good friend and a man with high standards of conduct.

10. The receptionist at the office offered neither information nor advice about applying for a job.

OPTION 2: USING A SEMICOLON BETWEEN TWO SIMPLE SENTENCES

Sometimes you may want to combine two simple sentences (independent clauses) without using a coordinating conjunction. If you want to join two simple sentences that are related in their ideas and you do not use a coordinating conjunction, you can combine them with a semicolon.

two simple sentences:

S V   S V
I cooked the turkey. *She made* the stuffing.

two simple sentences combined with a semicolon:

S V   ; S V
I cooked the turkey; *she made* the stuffing.

Here's another example of this option in use:

S V V   ; S V
Rain can be dangerous; *it makes* the roads slippery.

Notice that when you join two simple sentences with a semicolon, the second sentence begins with a lowercase letter, not a capital letter.

AVOIDING COMMA SPLICES

If you are joining two simple sentences (two independent clauses) without a coordinating conjunction, you must use a semicolon. A comma is not enough. (Joining two simple sentences with a comma and no coordinating conjunction is an error called a **comma splice.**)

comma splice:

S V   S V
The *crowd pushed* forward, *people began* to panic.

correction:

S V   ; S V
The *crowd pushed* forward; *people began* to panic.

You need to memorize the seven coordinating conjunctions (*and, but, or, nor, for, yet, so*) so that you can make a decision about punctuating your combined sentences. Remember these rules:

- If a coordinating conjunction joins the combined sentences, put a comma in front of the coordinating conjunction.

   S V   S V
   Tom had a barbecue in his back yard, and the *food was* delicious

- If there is no coordinating conjunction, put a semicolon in front of the second independent clause.

   S V   ; S V
   Tom had a barbecue in his back yard; the *food was* delicious.

OPTION 3: USING A SEMICOLON AND A CONJUNCTIVE ADVERB

Sometimes you want to join two simple sentences (independent clauses) with a connecting word called a **conjunctive adverb.** This word points out or clarifies a relationship between the sentences.

Infobox			
Some Common Conjunctive Adverbs			
also	furthermore	likewise	otherwise
anyway	however	meanwhile	similarly
as a result	in addition	moreover	still
besides	in fact	nevertheless	then
certainly	incidentally	next	therefore
consequently	indeed	now	thus
finally	instead	on the other hand	undoubtedly

You can put a conjunctive adverb (CA) between simple sentences, but you will still need a semicolon in front of the adverb:

two simple sentences:

    S   V   S V
My *parents checked* my homework every night. *I did* well in math.

two simple sentences joined by a conjunctive adverb and a semicolon:

    S   V   ; CA S V
My *parents checked* my homework every night; *thus I did* well in math.

  S V   ;   CA   S   V
She gave me good advice; *moreover, she helped* me follow it.

Punctuating After a Conjunctive Adverb

Notice the comma after the conjunctive adverb in the preceding example. Here is the generally accepted rule:

Put a comma after the conjunctive adverb if the conjunctive adverb is more than one syllable long.

For example, if the conjunctive adverb is a word like *consequently, furthermore,* or *moreover,* you use a comma. If the conjunctive adverb is one syllable, you do not have to add a comma after it. One-syllable conjunctive adverbs are words like *then* or *thus.*

I saw her cruelty to her staff; *then* I lost respect for her.
We worked on the project all weekend; *consequently,* we finished a week ahead of the deadline.

Exercise 3
Practice

Correcting Run-on (Fused) Sentences

Some of the sentences below are correctly punctuated. Some are run-on (fused) sentences, two simple sentences run together without any punctuation. If a sentence is correctly punctuated, write *OK* in the space provided. If it is a run-on sentence, put an *X* in the space provided and correct the sentence above the lines. To a correct a sentence, add the necessary punctuation. Do not add any words.

1. __X__ Susan gave Sam a clock radio for his birthday; she wanted him to wake up on time for work.

2. __X__ I've never been to Florida, but I hear it has the most beautiful beaches in the world.

3. __X__ Among the wedding presents was a gift certificate for a hardware store; the newlyweds used it to buy a new bathtub.

4. __OK__ Even the most careful people can't avoid accidents or protect themselves from every danger in life.

5. __X__ The book was a real awakening; it opened my eyes to the possibility of a nuclear disaster.

6. __OK__ Movies with lots of blood and gore make me sick and keep me awake at night.

7. __X__ My brother has a car phone; he is constantly worried about theft.

8. __OK__ Mr. Espinoza worked overtime at his laundry yet couldn't seem to make a profit.

9. __X__ Jhoma went to driving school all summer, yet she couldn't learn to parallel park.

10. __OK__ Some families seem to be very close but are putting on act.

Exercise 4
Practice

More on Correcting Run-On (Fused) Sentences

Some of the sentences below are correctly punctuated. Some are run-on (fused) sentences, two simple sentences run together without any punctuation. If a sentence is correctly punctuated, write *OK* in the space provided. If it is a run-on sentence, put an *X* in the space provided and correct the sentence above the lines. To a correct a sentence, add the necessary punctuation. Do not add any words.

1. __X__ Other families argue all the time; then they support each other in a crisis.

2. __X__ Outsiders can't judge a family's relationships; only family members know the truth of the family's connections.

3. __OK__ Actors in television comedies and actors in action films have different schedules and job stresses.

4. __X__ Basketball is the ideal sport for my cousin in Minnesota ; he can play it even in snowy January.

5. __X__ Bernard treated the animal kindly ; thus the stray dog became a loyal and loving pet.

6. __OK__ The two children sneaked out of the house and climbed into the back of the old truck.

7. __X__ The pastry chef covered the cake in whipped cream ; next he placed strawberries over the top.

8. __X__ The driver said he was sorry ; nevertheless , the officer gave the man a speeding ticket.

9. __X__ It's too hot to play baseball ; I'm going inside.

10. __OK__ Alonzo got a room near his job in the city instead of an apartment in the distant suburbs.

Exercise 5 **Correcting Comma Splices**

Practice

Some of the sentences below are correctly punctuated. Some contain comma splices, errors that occur when two simple sentences are joined together with only a comma. If a sentence is correctly punctuated, write *OK* in the space provided. If it contains a comma splice, put an *X* in the space provided and correct the sentence above the lines. To correct a sentence, you do not need to add words; just correct the punctuation.

1. __X__ The people in line for the movie pushed and crowded forward ; some were already late for the show.

2. __X__ Jamie has a pager in her purse ; you can call her and leave a message.

3. __X__ Our neighbors spent a fortune on the latest exercise equipment ; then they got bored with it after a month.

4. __X__ I bought the speakers at a huge sale ; thus I saved nearly a hundred dollars off the list price.

5. __OK__ I was determined to learn conversational Spanish, but I didn't know what class to take.

6. __X__ She sprained her ankle ; nevertheless, she completed the gymnastics exercise.

7. __X__ Our friends helped us move the furniture into our new house ; otherwise, we would have had to rent a truck.

8. __OK__ The man had never taken an art class, yet his talent for drawing was obvious to us all.

9. __X__ Davonia decided to bring her fingerpaints into the living room ; then she decided to decorate the living room walls.

10. __X__ Casita is the best Mexican restaurant in town ; however, it isn't cheap.

Exercise 6
Practice

More on Correcting Comma Splices

Some of the sentences below are correctly punctuated. Some contain comma splices, errors that occur when two simple sentences are joined together with only a comma. If a sentence is correctly punctuated, write *OK* in the space provided. If it contains a comma splice, put an *X* in the space provided and correct the sentence above the lines. To correct a sentence, you do not need to add words; just correct the punctuation.

1. __X__ I hate to throw anything out, as a result, my closets are stuffed with junk.

2. __OK__ James never reminded me about the meeting, so I missed an important vote yesterday.

3. __X__ You have to get there early, the place fills up fast.

4. __OK__ Air conditioning feels good on hot days, but I like to leave the windows open.

5. __X__ One way to meet new people is to join a softball team, another is to do volunteer work.

6. __OK__ One thing I dislike about winter is the rainy days, and another is the melting slush.

7. __X__ Teresa thought she had bought toothpaste, anyway, she meant to get it.

8. __OK__ Michelle drives to work at dawn, so she misses most of the rush-hour traffic.

9. __X__ Michelle drives to work at dawn, therefore she misses most of the rush-hour traffic.

10. __X__ There is a good parking space, you can grab it.

Exercise 7
Practice

Combining Simple Sentences Three Ways

Add a comma, a semicolon, or a semicolon and a comma to the following sentences. Do not add, change, or delete any words; just add the correct punctuation.

1. The cat has been staring at the canary for an hour soon that cat will pounce.

2. All-terrain vehicles are fun to drive but they are not for children.

3. It was the best party of the summer moreover it was the best party of the year.

4. Jeans are popular in all countries U.S.-made jeans cost a fortune in Europe.

5. Renovating a house is a big project furthermore it's an expensive undertaking.

TEACHING TIP:
Tell students not to place a comma between the complete subject and the verb. See if any students were tempted to place a comma between "house" and "is" in item #5.

6. The crowd in the stadium cheered wildly, and the team felt enormously proud.

7. The crowd in the stadium cheered wildly; the team felt enormously proud.

8. You can plan your future carefully; however, you can't avoid surprises.

9. The surfer got up at dawn; then he checked the local weather report.

10. Bill forgot to pack his camera; consequently, he has no pictures of his trip.

Exercise 8
Practice

More on Combining Simple Sentences Three Ways

Add a comma, a semicolon, or a semicolon and a comma to the following sentences. Do not add, change, or delete any words; just add the correct punctuation.

1. Kim was disappointed at the turnout, for she had expected a larger crowd at the last game of the season.

2. We sat in front of the fireplace roasting chestnuts; meanwhile, the snow swirled against the windows.

3. He sat right next to me, yet he ignored me all evening.

4. Driving across the country can be boring; instead, you can look for a cheap airfare.

5. First he showed us the basic scuba equipment; next he stressed the importance of safety.

6. My father never spanked me, nor did he threaten me with a spanking.

7. That restaurant used to be a firehouse; now the antique fire equipment is used for decoration.

8. I am sick of eating fast food; still it beats cooking for myself.

9. The doctor's office kept putting me on hold, so I asked the nurse to call me back.

10. The quarrel was partly his fault; he could have been more tactful in asking for his money back.

Exercise 9
👥 *Collaborate*

Combining Simple Sentences

Below are pairs of simple sentences. Working with a partner or a group, combine each pair into one sentence in two different ways. You have three options: (1) use a comma and a coordinating conjunction, (2) use a semicolon, or (3) use a semicolon and a conjunctive adverb (with a comma, if it is needed). Pick the option that makes the most sense for each sentence. The first one is done for you.

1. Jim missed the beginning of the movie.
   I had to explain the story to him.

combinations:

a. Jim missed the beginning of the movie, so I had to explain the story to him.

b. Jim missed the beginning of the movie; therefore, I had to explain the story to him.

2. The meal was very expensive.
It was worth the price.
combinations:

a. The meal was very expensive, yet it was worth the price.

b. The meal was very expensive; however, it was worth the price.

3. I opened the velvet box.
I saw a beautiful diamond ring.
combinations:

a. I opened the velvet box, and I saw a beautiful diamond ring.

b. I opened the velvet box; then I saw a beautiful diamond ring.

4. He forgot to check the oil regularly.
He had to pay for major car repairs.
combinations:

a. He forgot to check the oil regularly, so he had to pay for major car repairs.

b. He forgot to check the oil regularly; as a result, he had to pay for major car repairs.

5. The bank was closed.
The automatic teller was available.
combinations:

a. The bank was closed, but the automatic teller was available.

b. The bank was closed; however, the automatic teller was available.

CHAPTER **14**

Beyond the Simple Sentence: Subordination

MORE ON COMBINING SIMPLE SENTENCES

Before you go any further, look back. Review the following:

- A clause has a subject and a verb.
- An independent clause is a simple sentence; it is a group of words, with a subject and verb, that makes sense by itself.

There is another kind of clause called a **dependent clause.** It has a subject and a verb, but it does not make sense by itself. It cannot stand alone. It is not complete by itself. That is, it *depends* on the rest of the sentence to give it meaning. You can use a dependent clause in another option for combining simple sentences.

OPTION 4: USING A DEPENDENT CLAUSE TO BEGIN A SENTENCE

Often, you can combine simple sentences by changing an independent clause from one sentence into a dependent clause and placing it at the beginning of the new sentence:

two simple sentences:

S V   S V
I was late for work. My *car had* a flat tire.

changing one simple sentence into a beginning dependent clause:

          S V   S V
Because my *car had* a flat tire, *I was* late for work.

OPTION 5: USING A DEPENDENT CLAUSE TO END A SENTENCE

You can also combine simple sentences by changing an independent clause from one sentence into a dependent clause and placing it at the end of the new sentence:

S V   S V
I was late for work because my *car had* a flat tire.

Notice how one simple sentence can be changed into a dependent clause in two ways:

two simple sentences:

S   S   V   S V
Mother and *Dad wrapped* my presents. *I slept.*

changing one simple sentence into a dependent clause:

S   S   V   S V
Mother and *Dad wrapped* my presents while *I slept.*

or

S V   S   S   V
While *I slept, Mother* and *Dad wrapped* my presents.

Using a Subordinating Conjunction

Changing an independent clause to a dependent one is called subordinating. How do you do it? You add certain words, called **subordinating conjunctions,** to independent clauses, making them dependent—less "important," or subordinate—in the new sentence.

Keep in mind that the subordinate clause is still a clause; it has a subject and a verb, but it does not make sense by itself. For example, let's start with an independent clause:

S   V
Caroline studies.

Somebody (Caroline) does something (studies). The statement makes sense by itself. But if you add a subordinating conjunction to the independent clause, the clause becomes dependent, incomplete, unfinished, like this:

When Caroline studies (When she studies, what happens?)
Unless Caroline studies (Unless she studies, what will happen?)
If Caroline studies (If Caroline studies, what will happen?)

Now, each dependent clause needs an independent clause to finish the idea:

dependent clause   independent clause
When Caroline studies, she gets good grades.

dependent clause   independent clause
Unless Caroline studies, she forgets key ideas.

dependent clause   independent clause
If Caroline studies, she will pass the course.

There are many subordinating conjunctions. When you put any of these words in front of an independent clause, you make that clause dependent. Here is a list of subordinating conjunctions:

Infobox

Some Common Subordinating Conjunctions

after	how	until	whether
although	if	what	which
as	in order that	whatever	whichever
because	since	when	while
before	that	whenever	who
even if	though	where	whoever
even though	unless	whereas	whose

If you pick the right subordinating conjunction, you can effectively combine simple sentences (independent clauses) into a more sophisticated sentence pattern. Such combining helps you add sentence variety to your writing and helps to explain relationships between ideas.

simple sentences:

   S   V   V   S   V
Leo could not *read* music. His *performance was* exciting.

new combination:

dependent clause   independent clause
Although Leo could not read music, his performance was exciting.

simple sentences:

   S   V   S   V
I caught a bad cold last night. *I forgot* to bring a sweater to the baseball
    game.

new combination:

independent clause   dependent clause
I caught a bad cold last night because I forgot to bring a sweater to the
    baseball game.

Punctuating Complex Sentences

A sentence that has one independent clause and one or more dependent clauses is called a **complex sentence.** Complex sentences are very easy to punctuate. See if you can figure out the rule for punctuating by yourself. Look at the following examples. All are punctuated correctly.

dependent clause   independent clause
Whenever the baby smiles, his mother is delighted.

independent clause   dependent clause
His mother is delighted whenever the baby smiles.

dependent clause   independent clause
While you were away, I saved your mail for you.

independent clause   dependent clause
I saved your mail for you while you were away.

TEACHING TIP:
Survey recent magazine and newspaper articles and make copies of articles that incorporate a variety of sentence patterns. Ask students to spot prepositional phrases, subordinating conjunctions, and coordinating conjunctions.

In the examples above, look at the sentences that have a comma. Look at the ones that do not have a comma. Both kinds of sentences are punctuated correctly. Do you see the rule?

If the dependent clause comes at the beginning of the sentence, put a comma after the dependent clause. If the dependent clause comes at the end of the sentence, do not put a comma in front of the dependent clause.

Although we played well, we lost the game.
We lost the game although we played well.

Until he called, I had no date for the dance.
I had no date for the dance until he called.

Exercise 1 Punctuating Complex Sentences

Practice

All the sentences below are complex sentences; that is, they have one independent clause and one or more dependent clauses. Add a comma to each sentence that needs one.

1. Until I tried out for the team, I was overconfident and arrogant.

2. Be careful with that mirror when you take it off the wall.

3. After he bought a microwave oven, he stopped eating at fast-food restaurants.

4. He stopped eating at fast-food restaurants after he bought a microwave oven.

5. He hates to talk to anyone when he wakes up in the morning.

6. Because I was saving money for a vacation, I couldn't splurge on clothes.

7. People will not trust you unless you do something to earn their trust.

8. Carl works out at the gym every day while his brother lifts weights at home.

9. If no one notices my new haircut, I'll be disappointed.

10. Before she goes to her office, she takes her son to his day-care center.

Combining Sentences: A Review of Your Options

As you've seen, there are several ways to combine simple sentences. The following chart will help you review them all:

Infobox

Options for Combining Sentences

Coordination

Option 1 Independent clause	{ , and , but , or , nor , for , yet , so }	independent clause.
Option 2 Independent clause	;	independent clause.
Option 3 Independent clause	{ ; also, ; anyway, ; as a result, ; besides, ; certainly, ; consequently, }	independent clause.

TEACHING TIP:
Remind students that
one-syllable conjunc-
tive adverbs do not
require a comma.

Option 3
Independent clause
{
; finally,
; furthermore,
; however,
; in addition,
; in fact,
; incidentally,
; indeed,
; instead,
; likewise,
; meanwhile,
; moreover,
; nevertheless,
; next
; now
; on the other hand,
; otherwise,
; similarly,
; still
; then
; therefore,
; thus
; undoubtedly,
}
independent
clause.

Subordination

Option 4
Independent clause
{
after
although
as
because
before
even if
even though
how
if
in order that
since
that
though
unless
until
what
whatever
when
whenever
where
whereas
whether
which
whichever
while
who
whoever
whose
}
dependent clause.

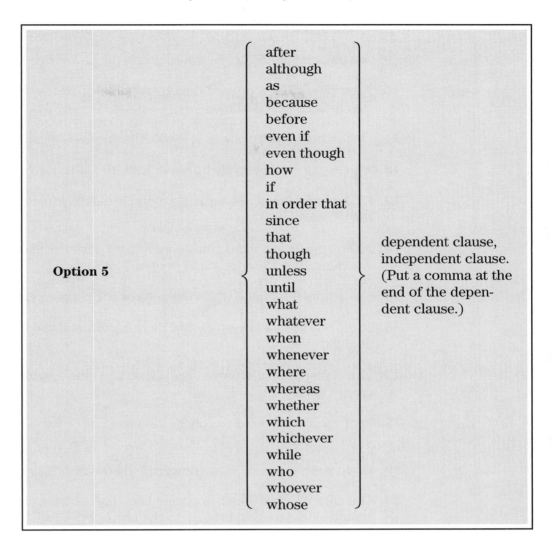

| Option 5 | after
although
as
because
before
even if
even though
how
if
in order that
since
that
though
unless
until
what
whatever
when
whenever
where
whereas
whether
which
whichever
while
who
whoever
whose | dependent clause,
independent clause.
(Put a comma at the
end of the depen-
dent clause.) |

Exercise 2 **Using the Five Options for Combining Sentences**

Practice Add missing commas or semicolons to the following sentences. Some sentences are correct as they are.

1. James can take advantage of a profit-sharing program if he stays with the company for five years.

2. He buys his groceries in bulk, so he saves money on items like cereal and canned vegetables.

3. Janelle called yesterday and invited me to a party; moreover, she told me to bring a friend.

4. Nothing serious happened; we just argued about money.

5. Unless it rains or snows, we will have the carnival on the football field.

6. When the mail comes, my little poodle barks wildly and tries to get outside.

7. Alison's husband quit his job even though he was making a high salary.

8. The tree was hit by lightning and consequently had to be removed.

9. A woman in the crowd began to giggle; then everyone started laughing.

10. After the children opened the presents, their parents took some photographs.

11. One of her favorite places is the desert; she goes there every weekend.

12. It's easy to ride a bicycle; however, it's difficult to ride one in traffic.

13. Dr. Lopez checked the patient's blood pressure while the nurse prepared the bandages.

14. Although she is a demanding supervisor, I have learned a great deal from watching Mrs. Curry relate to people.

15. The actors felt elated when the audience applauded enthusiastically.

16. Maria works in a law office five days a week, and she takes college classes at night.

17. I hate shopping in crowded malls; instead, I get bargains at flea markets and garage sales.

18. My father never went to college, yet he is one of the best-read people in the family.

19. Since you've already made dinner, I'll do the dishes tonight.

20. The edge of the wooden door had been hacked by a chisel or tool; someone had tried to break into the house.

| **Exercise 3** | **Combining Sentences** |

👥 Collaborate

Complete this exercise with a partner or a group. Combine each pair of sentences below into one clear, smooth sentence in two different ways.

TEACHING TIP:
Advise students not to rely too often on the word "and" when it comes to combining sentences. By avoiding "and," they should find more effective ways to combine sentences.

Answers Will Vary.
Possible answers shown at right.

1. I love the music store in the mall.
   The owners let me browse in it for hours.

combination 1: <u>I love the music store in the mall because the owners let me</u>

<u>browse in it for hours.</u>

combination 2: <u>I love the music store in the mall; the owners let me browse</u>

<u>in it for hours.</u>

2. I had never been to the Grand Canyon.
   I wasn't prepared for its beauty.

combination 1: <u>Because I had never been to the Grand Canyon, I wasn't pre-</u>

<u>pared for its beauty.</u>

combination 2: I had never been to the Grand Canyon, so I wasn't prepared for its beauty.

3. Jack was falling asleep at the wheel of his car.
He ran a red light.

combination 1: Jack was falling asleep at the wheel of his car when he ran a red light.

combination 2: Jack was falling asleep at the wheel of his car; consequently, he ran a red light.

4. I fell on the icy sidewalk.
I wasn't injured.

combination 1: I fell on the icy sidewalk, but I wasn't injured.

combination 2: Although I fell on the icy sidewalk, I wasn't injured.

5. Several of my cousins are planning a family reunion.
Not all family members are enthusiastic about the plan.

combination 1: Several of my cousins are planning a family reunion, but not all family members are enthusiastic about the plan.

combination 2: Several of my cousins are planning a family reunion even though not all family members are enthusiastic about the plan.

6. Mario needs a down payment to buy a house.
He is saving money and working overtime.

combination 1: Mario needs a down payment for the house; thus he is saving money and working overtime.

combination 2: Since Mario needs a down payment for the house, he is saving money and working overtime.

7. The air gets damp and chilly in the winter.
I can feel the change in my bones.

combination 1: When the air gets damp and chilly in the winter, I can feel the change in my bones.

combination 2: <u>The air gets damp and chilly in the winter; then I can feel the</u>

<u>change in my bones.</u>

8. He loves the old *Star Trek* series.
He's not impressed with *The Next Generation* of *Star Trek.*

combination 1: <u>He loves the old Star Trek series; on the other hand, he's not</u>

<u>impressed with The Next Generation of Star Trek.</u>

combination 2: <u>He loves the old Star Trek series, but he's not impressed with</u>

<u>The Next Generation of Star Trek.</u>

9. My father and brother watch football together.
They always argue about the fine points of the game.

combination 1: <u>When my father and brother watch football together, they</u>

<u>always argue about the fine points of the game.</u>

combination 2: <u>My father and brother watch football together, and they</u>

<u>always argue about the fine points of the game.</u>

10. I love Japanese food.
I've never tried to cook it.

combination 1: <u>I love Japanese food, yet I've never tried to cook it.</u>

combination 2: <u>While I love Japanese food, I've never tried to cook it.</u>

Exercise 4 **Create Your Own Text on Combining Sentences**

 Collaborate

Below is a list of rules for coordinating and subordinating sentences. Working
with a group, write two examples for each rule.

Option 1: You can join two simple sentences (two independent clauses)
into a compound sentence with a coordinating conjunction
and a comma in front of it. (The coordinating conjunctions are
and, but, or, nor, for, yet, and *so.*)

Answers Will Vary.
Possible answers
shown at right.

example 1: <u>I woke up early, so I made breakfast for my family.</u>

example 2: <u>Chrissie could speak Portuguese, and she could also read it.</u>

Option 2: You can combine two simple sentences (two independent clauses) into a compound sentence with a semicolon between independent clauses.

example 1: Seafood can be expensive; Maine lobster is particularly expensive.

example 2: My grandfather taught me about fishing; he took me on some wonderful fishing trips.

Option 3: You can combine two simple sentences (independent clauses) into a compound sentence with a semicolon and a conjunctive adverb between independent clauses. (Some conjunctive adverbs are *also, anyway, as a result, besides, certainly, consequently, finally, furthermore, however, incidentally, in addition, indeed, in fact, instead, likewise, meanwhile, moreover, nevertheless, next, now, on the other hand, otherwise, similarly, still, then, therefore, thus,* and *undoubtedly.*)

example 1: Lev is a champion runner; undoubtedly, he will win the race.

example 2: I used to love chocolate; now I rarely crave it.

Option 4: You can combine two simple sentences (two independent clauses) into a complex sentence by making one clause dependent. The dependent clause starts with a subordinating conjunction. Then, if the dependent clause begins the sentence, the clause ends with a comma. (Some common subordinating conjunctions are *after, although, as, because, before, even if, even though, how, if, in order that, since, that, though, unless, until, what, whatever, when, whenever, where, whereas, whether, which, whichever, while, who, whoever,* and *whose.*)

example 1: Before I started college, I worked at a supermarket.

example 2: As the boys argued loudly, a crowd formed aound them.

Option 5: You can combine two simple sentences (independent clauses) into a complex sentence by making one clause independent. Then, if the dependent clause comes after the independent clause, no comma is needed.

example 1: <u>Lorraine will fix the pipes whenever she can get a free weekend.</u>

_____

example 2: <u>It's an honor to be nominated even if I do not win.</u>

_____

CHAPTER 15

Avoiding Sentence Fragments

A **sentence fragment** is a group of words that looks like a sentence and is punctuated like a sentence but is not a sentence. Writing a sentence fragment is a major error because it reveals that the writer is not sure what a sentence is.

The following groups of words are all fragments:

> Because customers are often in a hurry and have little time to look for bargains.
> My job being very stressful and fast-paced.
> For example, the introduction of salad bars into fast-food restaurants.

There are two easy steps to help you check your writing for sentence fragments:

Infobox

Two Steps in Recognizing Sentence Fragments

Step 1: Check each group of words punctuated like a sentence, looking for a subject and a verb.

Step 2: If you find a subject and a verb, check that the group of words makes a complete statement.

RECOGNIZING FRAGMENTS: STEP 1

Step 1: Check for a subject and a verb. Some groups of words that look like sentences may have a subject but no verb, or they may have a verb but no subject, or they may have no subject *or* verb.

> The puppy in the pet store window. (*Puppy* could be the subject of a sentence, but there is no verb.)
> Doesn't matter to me one way or the other. (There is a verb, *Does matter*, but there is no subject.)
> In the back of my mind. (There are two prepositional phrases, *In the back* and *of my mind*, but there is no subject or verb.)

Remember that an *-ing* verb by itself cannot be the main verb in a sentence. Therefore, groups of words like the ones on the following page may look like sentences, but they lack a verb and are really fragments:

343

Your sister having all the skills required of a good salesperson.

The two top tennis players struggling with exhaustion and the stress of a highly competitive tournament.

Jack being the only one in the room with a piece of paper.

An infinitive (*to* plus a verb) cannot be a main verb in a sentence, either. The following groups of words are also fragments:

The manager of the store to attend the meeting of regional managers next month in Philadelphia.

The purpose to explain the fine points of the game to new players.

Groups of words beginning with words like *also, especially, except, for example, in addition,* and *such as* need subjects and verbs, too. Without subjects and verbs, these groups can be fragments, like the ones below:

Also a good place to grow up.

Especially the youngest member of the family.

For example, a person without a high school diploma.

| **Exercise 1** | **Checking Groups of Words for Subjects and Verbs** |
| Practice | |

Some of the following groups of words have subjects and verbs; these are sentences. Some groups are missing subjects, verbs, or both; these are fragments. Put an *S* by each sentence and an *F* by each fragment.

1. __S__ For example, candy wrappers and soda cans litter the park.

2. __F__ For instance, another tie for my father on his birthday.

3. __F__ The rock musician strutting across the stage, rhythmically swinging the microphone toward the audience and back again.

4. __F__ Can't possibly be the person with the best chance of getting the job.

5. __F__ Especially a small child afraid of the water.

6. __S__ The child was skipping across the sidewalk and trying hard not to step on a crack.

7. __F__ In the darkest part of the forest with no flashlight.

8. __S__ In addition, the pizza was stale and soggy.

9. __F__ Spike being the brightest of the boys in the family.

10. __S__ Across the street from her house was an empty lot.

| **Exercise 2** | **More on Checking Groups of Words for Subjects and Verbs** |
| Practice | |

Some of the following groups of words have subjects and verbs; these are sentences. Some groups are missing subjects, verbs, or both; these are fragments. Put an *S* by each sentence and an *F* by each fragment.

1. __F__ My best friend Jaime to go with me to the tournament.

2. __F__ Someone without a hope of passing the driving exam.

3. __F__ The reason being the lack of good schools in that area.

4. __S__ My cousin Christina wanted to see a city with nightlife.

5. __F__ Could have been an accident instead of a crime.

6. __F__ Ivan doing all the work and Luisa calling in sick.

7. __F__ Rushing from one place to another in a search of the perfect gift.

8. __F__ Especially a child in a large and loving family.

9. __S__ From the back came a small voice.

10. __F__ Might take as long as a month.

RECOGNIZING FRAGMENTS: STEP 2

Step 2: If a group of words has both a subject and a verb, check that it makes a complete statement. Many groups of words that have both a subject and a verb do not make sense by themselves. They are **dependent clauses.** How can you tell if a clause is dependent? After you have checked each group of words for a subject and verb, check to see if it begins with one of the subordinating conjunctions that start dependent clauses. (Here are some common subordinating conjunctions: *after, although, as, because, before, even if, even though, how, if, in order that, since, that, though, unless, until, what, whatever, when, whenever, where, whereas, whether, which, whichever, while, who, whoever,* and *whose.*)

A clause that begins with a subordinating conjunction is a dependent clause. When you punctuate a dependent clause as if it were a sentence, you have a kind of fragment called a **dependent clause fragment:**

After I woke up this morning.
Because he liked football better than soccer.
Unless it stops raining by lunchtime.

It is important to remember both steps in checking for fragments:

Step 1: Check for a subject and a verb.
Step 2: If you find a subject and a verb, check that the group of words makes a complete statement.

Exercise 3 **Checking for Dependent-Clause Fragments**

Practice Some of the following groups of words are sentences. Some are dependent clauses punctuated like sentences; these are sentence fragments. Put an *S* by each sentence and an *F* by each fragment.

1. __F__ As he carefully washed the outside of the car and polished the chrome trim with a special cloth.

2. __S__ Commuters rushed past the ticket windows and slipped into the train at the last possible minute.

3. __F__ Because no one in the class had been able to buy a copy of the required text in the campus bookstore.

4. __F__ Even though many people expect to own their own home and to be able to meet the mortgage payments.

5. __S__ Most of the movies were sequels to the popular movies of last summer.

6. __F__ While I wanted to go to a place in the desert with dry air and bright sunshine.

7. __F__ Although defendants in some countries are considered guilty until they prove their innocence.

8. __F__ If people in our community were more serious about conserving water.

9. __F__ Ever since Ron began taking martial arts classes.

10. __F__ When women are afraid to leave their homes at night.

Exercise 4 **More on Checking for Dependent-Clause Fragments**

Practice

Some of the following groups of words are sentences. Some are dependent clauses punctuated like sentences; these are sentence fragments. Put an *S* by each sentence and an *F* by each fragment.

1. __F__ After a long and dreary ride on an old, creaky plane.

2. __S__ Down the hill came the red wagon.

3. __F__ Since the day I first saw him in the street.

4. __S__ Near the store stands a huge elm tree.

5. __S__ Suddenly a siren began to blare.

6. __F__ Because no seems to have an answer to the question.

7. __F__ While Sergei worried about being late for class.

8. __F__ Before the doctor told him about the new medication.

9. __F__ Unless the movie is lighthearted and funny.

10. __F__ Whenever my car needs an oil change.

Exercise 5 **Using Two Steps to Recognize Sentence Fragments**

Practice

Some of the following are complete sentences; some are sentence fragments. To recognize the fragments, check each group of words by using the two-step process:

> **Step 1:** Check for a subject and a verb.

> **Step 2:** If you find a subject and a verb, check that the group of words makes a complete statement.

Then put an *S* by each sentence and an *F* by each fragment.

1. __F__ The reason being a computer error on the bill from the telephone company.

2. __F__ As the graduates lined up for their march into the auditorium.

3. __S__ Christopher was being very stubborn about apologizing to his uncle.

4. __F__ Whenever it is cold and dreary outside and my bed seems warm and cozy.

5. __F__ Without a single word of explanation for her rude behavior.

6. __S__ Around the border of the yard was a thick hedge of holly bushes.

7. __S__ Without a comfortable pair of shoes, you'll have trouble walking that distance.

8. __F__ Because of their lack of education and inability to compete with others in the workforce.

9. __S__ Expensive cars representing the height of success to him.

10. __F__ Which was precisely the wrong thing to say to her.

11. __F__ Armand feeling lost and alone without his family.

12. __F__ For example, a child with no self-esteem or self-confidence.

13. __F__ Although I'd never thought much about it, one way or another.

14. __F__ The expensive gift to be sent by overnight air freight to the girl from California.

15. __F__ Oranges providing a good source of vitamin C in the winter.

16. __F__ While he did all the paperwork and paid all the bills.

17. __S__ From the first day of school to the last, she enjoyed her math class.

18. __F__ When I'd spent hours pleading with her to keep it a secret.

19. __S__ The answer came to me all of a sudden.

20. __F__ The reason being a resistance to facing the truth about herself.

CORRECTING FRAGMENTS

You can correct fragments easily if you follow the two steps for identifying them.

Step 1: Check for a subject and a verb. If a group of words is a fragment because it lacks a subject, a verb, or both, *add what is missing.*

> **fragment:** My father being a very strong person. (This fragment lacks a main verb.)
> **corrected:** My father is a very strong person. (The main verb *is* replaces *being*, which is not a main verb.)

      fragment: Doesn't care about the party. (This fragment lacks a subject.)
      corrected: Alicia doesn't care about the party. (A subject, *Alicia*, is added.)

      fragment: Especially on dark winter days. (This fragment has neither a subject nor a verb.)
      corrected: I love a bonfire, especially on dark winter days. (A subject, *I*, and a verb, *love*, are added.)

Step 2: If you find a subject and a verb, check that the group of words makes a complete statement. To correct the fragment, you can turn a dependent clause into an independent clause by removing the subordinating conjunction, *or* you can add an independent clause to the dependent one to create a sentence.

      fragment: When the rain beat against the windows. (The statement does not make sense by itself. The subordinating conjunction *when* leads the reader to ask, "What happened when the rain beat against the windows?" The subordinating conjunction makes this a dependent clause, not a sentence.)
      corrected: The rain beat against the windows. (Removing the subordinating conjunction makes this an independent clause, a sentence.)
      corrected: When the rain beat against the windows, I reconsidered my plans for the picnic. (Adding an independent clause makes this a sentence.)

Note: Sometimes you can correct a fragment by linking it to the sentence before it or after it.

      fragment (underlined): I have always enjoyed outdoor concerts. <u>Like the ones at Pioneer Park.</u>
      corrected: I have always enjoyed outdoor concerts like the ones at Pioneer Park.

      fragment (underlined): <u>Even if she apologizes for that nasty remark.</u> I will never trust her again.
      corrected: Even if she apologizes for that nasty remark, I will never trust her again.

You have several choices for correcting fragments: you can add words, phrases, or clauses; you can take words out; or you can combine independent and dependent clauses. You can transform fragments into simple sentences or create compound or complex sentences. To punctuate your new sentences, remember the rules for combining sentences.

Exercise 6   Correcting Fragments

Practice   Correct each sentence fragment below in the most appropriate way.

1. Once a year, I brighten up my room with some inexpensive decoration. Such as new curtains, a plant, or fresh paint.

Answers Will Vary.
Possible answers
shown at right.

    corrected: <u>Once a year, I brighten up my room with some inexpensive decora-</u>

    <u>tion such as new curtains, a plant, or fresh paint.</u>

2. If Michael asks his boss for the day off. His boss will probably say yes.

corrected: If Michael asks his boss for the day off, his boss will probably say yes.

3. Exploring the city without a map. We ended up walking in a circle.

corrected: Because we were exploring the city without a map, we ended up walking in a circle.

4. Everyone was fascinated by the "get rich quick" scheme. Especially Ned.

corrected: Everyone was fascinated by the get-rich-quick scheme, especially Ned.

5. The toddler learning to drink milk from a cup instead of a baby bottle.

corrected: The toddler learned to drink from a cup instead of a baby bottle.

6. Whoever borrowed my camera without my permission.

corrected: I want whoever borrowed my camera without my permission to give it back.

7. Because we ran out of staples. We were forced to use paper clips.

corrected: Because we ran out of staples, we were forced to use paper clips.

8. The dancers demanded more music. As the band packed up for the night.

corrected: The dancers demanded more music as the band packed up for the night.

9. He was eager to meet his co-workers. To get to know their habits and to learn their routines.

corrected: He was eager to meet his co-workers, to get to know their habits and to learn their routines.

10. Anyone can learn to ski. If he or she is willing to keep trying.

corrected: Anyone can learn to ski if he or she is willing to keep trying.

Exercise 7 **Correcting Fragments**

Collaborate

Working with a partner or a group, correct each sentence fragment below in two ways. The first one is done for you.

1. Whenever I am waiting for an important phone call.

   corrected: I am waiting for an important phone call.

   _____

   corrected: Whenever I am waiting for an important phone call, I am extremely impatient and nervous.

2. Christina took the customers' orders. While Robert worked in the kitchen.

   corrected: Christina took the customers' orders while Robert worked in the kitchen.

   corrected: Christina took the customers' orders; meanwhile, Robert worked in the kitchen.

3. When we get together on Sundays. We have an enormous dinner.

   corrected: When we get together on Sundays, we have an enormous dinner.

   _____

   corrected: We have an enormous dinner when we get together on Sundays.

   _____

4. Jason being more talented than any of the professional hockey players.

   corrected: Jason is more talented than any of the professional hockey players.

   corrected: Jason may be more talented than any of the professional hockey players.

5. With a great deal of enthusiasm for his subject. He began his lecture.

   corrected: With a great deal of enthusiasm for his subject, he began his lecture.

   corrected: He began his lecture with a great deal of enthusiasm for his subject.

6. Although no one could tell him how to get to the mall.

corrected: <u>Although no one could tell him how to get to the mall, he eventual-</u>
<u>ly found it.</u>

corrected: <u>No one could tell him how to get to the mall.</u>

_____

7. In the forest, where the fighting had originally broken out.

corrected: <u>In the forest, where the fighting had originally broken out, was an</u>
<u>old army campsite.</u>

corrected: <u>The fighting had originally broken out in the forest.</u>

_____

8. He'll never make friends. Unless he learns to control his temper.

corrected: <u>He'll never make friends unless he learns to control his temper.</u>

_____

corrected: <u>Unless he learns to control his temper, he'll never make friends.</u>

_____

9. I was beginning to feel sick. As the boat rocked from side to side.

corrected: <u>I was beginning to feel sick as the boat rocked from side to side.</u>

_____

corrected: <u>As the boat rocked from side to side, I was beginning to feel sick.</u>

_____

10. Which is one place I'd like to visit.

corrected: <u>Disney World is one place I'd like to visit.</u>

_____

corrected: <u>My brother is going to Barbados, which is one place I'd like to visit.</u>

_____

Using Parallelism in Sentences

Parallelism means balance in a sentence. To create sentences with parallelism, remember this rule:

Similar points should get a similar structure.

Often, you will include two or three (or more) related ideas, examples, or details in one sentence. If you express these ideas in a parallel structure, they will be clearer, smoother, and more convincing.

Here are some pairs of sentences with and without parallelism:

not parallel: Of all the sports I've played, I prefer tennis, handball, and playing golf.

parallel: Of all the sports I've played, I prefer *tennis*, *handball*, and *golf*. (Three words are parallel.)

not parallel: If you're looking for the car keys, you should look under the table, the kitchen counter, and behind the refrigerator.

parallel: If you're looking for the car keys, you should look *under the table*, *on the kitchen counter*, and *behind the refrigerator*. (Three prepositional phrases are parallel.)

not parallel: He is a good choice for manager because he works hard, he keeps calm, and well-liked.

parallel: He is a good choice for manager because *he works hard*, *he keeps calm*, and *he is well-liked*. (Three clauses are parallel.)

From these examples, you can see that parallelism involves matching the structures of parts of your sentence. There are two steps that can help you check your writing for parallelism:

Infobox

Two Steps in Checking a Sentence for Parallel Structure

Step 1: Look for the list in the sentence.

Step 2: Put the parts of the list into a similar structure. (You may have to change or add something to get a parallel structure.)

ACHIEVING PARALLELISM

Let's correct the parallelism of the following sentence:

>**sample sentence:** The committee for neighborhood safety met to set up a schedule for patrols, coordinating teams of volunteers, and also for the purpose of creating new rules.

To correct this sentence, we'll follow the steps:

>**Step 1:** Look for the list. The committee met to do three things. Here's the list:
>
>1. to set up a schedule for patrols
>2. coordinating teams of volunteers
>3. for the purpose of creating new rules

>**Step 2:** Put the parts of the list into a similar structure:
>
>1. *to set up* a schedule for patrols
>2. *to coordinate* teams of volunteers
>3. *to create* new rules

Now revise to get a parallel sentence:

>**parallel:** The committee for neighborhood safety met *to set up* a schedule for patrols, *to coordinate* teams of volunteers, and *to create* new rules.

If you follow steps 1 and 2, you can also write the sentence like this:

>**parallel:** The committee for neighborhood safety met to *set up* a schedule for patrols, *coordinate* teams of volunteers, and *create* new rules.

But you cannot write a sentence like this:

>**not parallel:** The committee for neighborhood safety met to set up a schedule for patrols, coordinate teams, and to create new rules.

Think of the list again. You can have

The committee met
1. to set up
2. to coordinate   } parallel
3. to create

Or you can have

The committee met to
1. set up
2. coordinate   } parallel
3. create

But your list cannot be

The committee met to
1. set up
2. coordinate   } not parallel
3. to create

In other words, either use *to* once (if it fits every part of the list), or use it with every part of the list.

Caution: Sometimes making ideas parallel means adding something to a sentence because all the parts of the list cannot match exactly.

sample sentence: In his pocket the little boy had a ruler, rubber band, baseball card, and apple.

Step 1: Look for the list. In his pocket the little boy had a

1. ruler
2. rubber band
3. baseball card
4. apple

Note: If non-native speakers need additional work on articles, see the ESL Appendix.

As the sentence is written, *a* goes with *a ruler, a rubber band, a baseball card,* and *a apple*. But *a* isn't the right word to put in front of apple. Words that begin with a vowel *(a, e, i, o,* or *u)* need *an* in front of them: *an apple*. So to make the sentence parallel, you have to change something in the sentence.

Step 2: Put the parts of the list into a parallel structure.

parallel: In his pocket the little boy had *a ruler, a rubber band, a base-ball card,* and *an apple.*

Here's another example:

sample sentence: She was amused and interested in the silly plot of the movie.

Step 1: Look for the list. She was

1. amused
2. interested in

the silly plot of the movie.

Check the sense of that sentence by looking at each part of the list and how it works in the sentence: "She was *interested in* the silly plot of the movie." That part of the list seems clear. But "She was *amused* the silly plot of the movie"? Or "She was *amused in* the silly plot of the movie"? Neither sentence is right. People are not *amused in.*

Step 2: The sentence needs a word added to make the structure parallel.

parallel: She was *amused by* and *interested in* the silly plot of the movie.

When you follow the two steps to check for parallelism, you can write clear sentences and improve your style.

TEACHING TIP:
Ask students what they plan to do on their next school vacation or on a day off from work. List some responses on the board or on an overhead projector. Have students compose several sentences in parallel structure that incorporate information from the list.

| **Exercise 1** | **Revising Sentences for Parallelism** |

Practice

Some of the following sentences need to be revised so that they have parallel structures. Revise the ones that need parallelism.

1. The road begins at the beach; the city center is where it ends.

Answers Will Vary.
Possible answers shown at right.

revised: The road begins at the beach and ends at the city center.

2. The restaurant is very popular and has crowds.

revised: The restaurant is very popular and crowded.

3. My workday is so crowded with activities that I have to shop for groceries, washing and ironing my clothes, and clean my room at night.

   revised: My workday is so crowded with activities that I have to shop for gro-

   ceries, wash and iron my clothes, and clean my room at night.

4. You can get to the carnival by a bus or by a special train.

   revised: OK

5. He is a player with great energy and who is ambitious.

   revised: He is player with great energy and ambition.

6. When we meet tomorrow, I'd like to discuss your job description, explaining your health benefits, and describe the package of retirement options you will have also.

   revised: When we meet tomorrow, I'd like to discuss your job description,

   health benefits, and retirement package.

7. The location of the house, its size, and how much it cost made it the best choice for the family.

   revised: The location, size, and cost of the house made it the best choice for

   the family.

8. Going to college is not the same as when you go to high school.

   revised: Going to college is not the same as going to high school.

9. Jim was the friendliest person she met at school, also the most helpful person and the most funny.

   revised: Jim was the friendliest, most helpful, and funniest person she met

   at school.

10. Ramona would rather sew her own wedding gown than paying a fortune to buy one.

    revised: Ramona would rather sew her own wedding gown than pay a

    fortune to buy one.

Writing Sentences with Parallelism

Complete this exercise with a partner or a group. First, brainstorm a draft list; then, revise the list for parallelism. Finally, complete the sentence in parallel structure. You may want to assign one step (brainstorming a draft list, revising it, etc.) to each group member, then switch steps on the next sentence. The first one is done for you.

1. Three habits I'd like to break are
   draft list: revised list:

   a. worry too much   a. worrying too much

   b. talking on the phone for hours   b. talking on the phone for hours

   c. lose my temper   c. losing my temper

   sentence: Three habits I'd like to break are worrying too much, talking on the phone for hours, and losing my temper.

Answers Will Vary.
Possible answers shown at right.

2. Three ways to spend a rainy Sunday are
   draft list: revised list:

   a. take a nap   a. taking a nap

   b. TV   b. watching TV

   c. reading a book   c. reading a book

   sentence: Three ways to spend a rainy Sunday are taking a nap, watching TV, and reading a book.

3. Two reasons to stop smoking are
   draft list: revised list:

   a. it is expensive   a. cost

   b. health dangers   b. health dangers

   sentence: Two reasons to stop smoking are the cost and the health dangers.

4. Three irritations in my daily life are
   draft list: revised list:

   a. slow drivers   a. slow drivers

   b. customers who are rude   b. rude customers

   c. my boss nags me   c. a nagging boss

sentence: <u>Three irritations in my daily life are slow drivers, rude customers,</u>

<u>and a nagging boss.</u>

5. Exercise is good for you because (add three reasons)

draft list:	revised list:
a. <u>calories are burned</u>	a. <u>burns calories</u>
b. <u>relieves stress</u>	b. <u>relieves stress</u>
c. <u>helps your heart</u>	c. <u>helps your heart</u>

sentence: <u>Exercise is good for you because it burns calories, relieves stress,</u>

<u>and helps your heart.</u>

6. Driving in traffic can be stressful because (add three reasons)

draft list:	revised list:
a. <u>traffic jams</u>	a. <u>traffic jams</u>
b. <u>some drivers are aggressive</u>	b. <u>aggressive drivers</u>
c. <u>construction creates delays</u>	c. <u>construction delays</u>

sentence: <u>Driving in traffic can be stressful because of traffic jams, aggres-</u>

<u>sive drivers, and construction delays.</u>

7. My goals in attending college are (add two goals)

draft list:	revised list:
a. <u>preparing for a career</u>	a. <u>to prepare for a career</u>
b. <u>to develop confidence</u>	b. <u>to develop confidence</u>

sentence: <u>My goals in attending college are to prepare for a career and to</u>

<u>develop confidence.</u>

8. I am happiest when (add three times or occasions)

draft list:	revised list:
a. <u>with friends</u>	a. <u>socializing with friends</u>
b. <u>playing with my dog</u>	b. <u>playing with my dog</u>
c. <u>at a party, dancing</u>	c. <u>dancing at a party</u>

sentence: <u>I am happiest when I am socializing with friends, playing with my</u>

<u>dog, or dancing at a party.</u>

9. Three characteristics of a good leader are
   draft list: revised list:

   a. <u>he or she is strong</u>   a. <u>strength</u>

   b. <u>someone you can depend on</u>   b. <u>dependability</u>

   c. <u>has determination</u>   c. <u>determination</u>

   sentence: <u>Three characteristics of a good leader are strength, dependability,</u>

   <u>and determination.</u>

10. Two experiences I'd like to avoid are
    draft list: revised list:

    a. <u>not having a job</u>   a. <u>unemployment</u>

    b. <u>divorcing</u>   b. <u>divorce</u>

    sentence: <u>Two experiences I'd like to avoid are unemployment and divorce.</u>

Exercise 3
Practice

Combining Sentences and Creating a Parallel Structure

Combine each cluster of sentences below into one clear, smooth sentence that includes some parallel structure. The first one is done for you.

1. Before you buy a used car, you should research what similar models are selling for.
   It would be a good idea to have a mechanic examine the car.
   Also, how much mileage it has racked up is a consideration.

   combination: <u>Before you buy a used car, you should compare prices of similar</u>

   <u>models, get a mechanic to examine the car, and think carefully about the mileage.</u>

2. The dinner was delicious.
   The dinner was full of nutritional value.
   It was priced inexpensively.

   combination: <u>The dinner was delicious, nutritious, and inexpensive.</u>

Answers Will Vary.
Possible answers shown at right.

3. If you want to lose weight, you should limit the amount of fat in your diet.
   Cutting back on junk food is also a good idea.
   Regular exercise is important, too.

   combination: <u>If you want to lose weight, you should limit the amount of fat</u>

   <u>in your diet, cut back on junk food, and exercise regularly.</u>

4. Businesspeople advertise by computer.
   Children use computers to play video games.

Computers are used by teachers to teach basic skills.

combination: Business people use computers to advertise, children use them to play video games, and teachers use them to teach basic skills.

5. He was a dynamic salesman.
He had energy.
He had enthusiasm.

combination: He was a dynamic, energetic, and enthusiastic salesman.

6. As a friend, he was extremely loyal.
As a friend, he also told the truth.
He was also a compassionate friend.

combination: As a friend, he was loyal, honest, and compassionate.

7. Richard joined the bicycle club.
Richard rode with club members every weekend.
Richard soon became a strong competitive cyclist.

combination: Richard joined the bicycle club, rode with club members every weekend, and soon became a strong competitive cyclist.

8. The demonstrators came from small towns.
The demonstrators came from major cities.
The demonstrators came from farms.
The demonstrators came from factories.
The demonstrators came to express their concern about the environment.

combination: The demonstrators came from small towns, major cities, farms, and factories to express their concern about the environment.

9. People crowded the entrances to the department store.
They hoped to be the first inside the store.
Their goal was to find a bargain at the sale.

combination: People crowded the entrances to the department store; they hoped to be the first inside and to find a bargain at the sale.

10. The house was old.
It had a spiral staircase.
It had elaborately carved woodwork.
It had bay windows.
The house was beautiful.

combination: The beautiful old house had a spiral staircase, elaborately carved woodwork, and bay windows.

Using Adjectives and Adverbs

WHAT ARE ADJECTIVES?

Adjectives describe nouns (persons, places, or things) or pronouns (words that substitute for nouns).

TEACHING TIP:
This chapter is a good place to remind students about sensory (sight, sound, smell, taste, touch) details. Ask students to describe an extremely messy kitchen, a hospital waiting room, a liquid cold medicine, etc. Some amusing descriptions should emerge, and students will see that adjectives often relate to one of the five senses.

adjectives:

She stood in a *dark* corner. (*Dark* describes the noun *corner.*)
I need a *little* help. (*Little* describes the noun *help.*)
She looked *happy.* (*Happy* describes the pronoun *she.*)

An adjective usually comes before the word it describes.

He gave me a *beautiful* ring. (*Beautiful* describes *ring.*)
A *small* horse pulled the cart. (*Small* describes *horse.*)

Sometimes it comes after a being verb, a verb that tells what something is. Being verbs are words like *is, are, was, am,* and *has been.* Words like *feels, looks, seems, smells, sounds,* and *tastes* are part of the group called being verbs.

He seems *unhappy.* (*Unhappy* describes *he* and follows the being verb *seems.*)
Alan was *confident.* (*Confident* describes *Alan* and follows the being verb *was.*)

Exercise 1 **Recognizing Adjectives**

Practice

Circle the adjectives in the following sentences.

1. I swallowed the (bitter) medicine.

2. We are (optimistic) about the future.

3. Susanna wanted a (loud) horn.

4. The casserole tastes (delicious)

5. The (angry) bear began to growl.

6. A (large) envelope arrived in the mail.

7. Callie looks (pretty) in her uniform.

8. The bedroom has a (large) closet.

9. Mike and Jack were (kind) neighbors.

10. I ran into the (dark) alley.

ADJECTIVES: COMPARATIVE AND SUPERLATIVE FORMS

The **comparative** form of an adjective compares two persons or things. The **superlative** form compares three or more persons or things.

> **comparative:** Your car is *cleaner* than mine.
> **superlative:** Your car is the *cleanest* one in the parking lot.

> **comparative:** Hamburger is *cheaper* than steak.
> **superlative:** Hamburger is the *cheapest* meat on the menu.

> **comparative:** Lisa is *friendlier* than her sister.
> **superlative:** Lisa is the *friendliest* of the three sisters.

For most adjectives of one syllable, add *-er* to form the comparative, and add *-est* to form the superlative:

> The weather is *colder* than it was yesterday, but Friday was the *coldest* day of the year.
> Orange juice is *sweeter* than grapefruit juice, but the *sweetest* juice is grape juice.

For longer adjectives, use *more* to form the comparative, and use *most* to form the superlative:

> I thought Intermediate Algebra was *more difficult* than English Composition; however, Introductory Physics was the *most difficult* course I ever took.
> My brother is *more outgoing* than my sister, but my father is the *most outgoing* member of the family.

The three forms of adjectives usually look like this:

Adjective	Comparative (two)	Superlative (three or more)
sweet	sweeter	sweetest
fast	faster	fastest
short	shorter	shortest
quick	quicker	quickest
old	older	oldest

They may look like this instead:

Adjective	Comparative (two)	Superlative (three or more)
confused	more confused	most confused
specific	more specific	most specific
dangerous	more dangerous	most dangerous

confident   more confident   most confident
beautiful   more beautiful   most beautiful

However, there are some irregular forms of adjectives:

Adjective	Comparative (two)	Superlative (three or more)
good	better	best
bad	worse	worst
little	less	least
many, much	more	most

Exercise 2   **Selecting the Correct Adjective Form**

Practice   Write the correct form of each adjective in parentheses in the following sentences.

1. Theo was the _____ best _____ (good) friend I've ever had.

2. I saw *The Phantom Menace* and *The Matrix*; *The Matrix* was the

   _____ better _____ (good) movie.

3. My sister believes modern dance is _____ harder _____ (hard) than intermediate swimming, but she is convinced that bowling is the _____ most difficult _____ (difficult) physical education course at her school.

4. Of the two brothers, John is the _____ more responsible _____ (responsible).

5. I've had three meals at the Coffee Café, and lunch was the

   _____ worst _____ (bad) of the three.

6. Taking vitamins can be _____ good _____ (good) for you; however, eating

   a balanced diet can be _____ better _____ (good) than getting all your vitamins from pills.

7. Which one of these three blankets feels the _____ softest _____ (soft)?

8. At the car auction, we saw two cars we wanted; the Mazda cost

   _____ less _____ (little) money than the Ford.

9. Cable television gives me _____ many _____ (many) channels, but Steve's

   new satellite dish gives him _____ more _____ (many) channels than I get.

10. Losing your keys is worse _____ worse _____ (bad) than losing your

    umbrella.

Exercise 3 **Writing Sentences with Adjectives**

 Collaborate

Working with a partner or a group, write a sentence that correctly uses each of the following adjectives. Be prepared to share your answers with another group or with the class.

Answers Will Vary. Possible answers shown at right.

1. best   The car is the best buy in the used car lot.

2. more honest   Subash was more honest than Camille.

3. happiest   Monday was the happiest day of my life.

4. thickest   I want the thickest steak on the menu.

5. worse   The second operation was worse than the first.

6. most loving   Fluffy is the most loving kitten I've ever seen.

7. brighter   The sun is brighter today than it was yesterday.

8. better   My sister is a better driver than my brother.

9. older   James is the older of the two cousins.

10. good   Dr. Gonzalez will give you good advice.

WHAT ARE ADVERBS?

Adverbs describe verbs, adjectives, or other adverbs.

adverbs:

As she spoke, Steve listened *thoughtfully*. (*Thoughtfully* describes the verb *listened*.)

I said I was *really* sorry for my error. (*Really* describes the adjective *sorry*.)

The cook worked *very* quickly. (*Very* describes the adverb *quickly*.)

Adverbs answer questions like "How?" "How much?" "How often?" "When?" "Why?" and "Where?"

Exercise 4 **Recognizing Adverbs**

Practice

Circle the adverbs in the following sentences.

1. Ralph tapped his fingers (impatiently) as he waited for the traffic light to change.

2. On my birthday, my brother began act (very strangely)

3. Aunt Inez is not (really) angry about the broken window.

4. My son made a (brightly) painted mask in his kindergarten class.

5. The manager said she was (sincerely) sorry about the delay.

6. Computer programmers are (fully) involved in their work.

7. The (highly) polished bowl gleamed under the dazzling light.

8. I was (often) angry when my boss treated me (unfairly)

9. An inexpensive, sturdy suitcase is (sometimes) hard to find.

10. By noon, we had (nearly) finished the job.

Exercise 5
👥 Collaborate

Writing Sentences with Adverbs

Working with a partner or a group, write a sentence that correctly uses each of the following adverbs. Be prepared to share your answers with another group or with the class.

Answers Will Vary.
Possible answers shown at right.

TEACHING TIP:

Group Work. Distribute copies of a recent local newspaper article about a prominent person or issue. Ask one group to find adjectives and the words they modify; ask the other group to find adverbs and the words they modify. Then ask each group to find the most descriptive sentences. Discuss why some sentences are more descriptive than others.

1. unkindly The superintendent spoke to me unkindly.

2. rarely I rarely drink orange juice.

3. often Jerry often takes a shortcut to school.

4. truly It was a truly beautiful wedding.

5. sweetly The little girl smiled sweetly.

6. proudly The new recruit saluted proudly.

7. clearly The candidate spoke clearly.

8. mildly The show was mildly entertaining.

9. joyfully The chorus sang joyfully.

10. very You are not very enthusiastic about the project.

HINTS ABOUT ADJECTIVES AND ADVERBS

Do not use an adjective when you need an adverb. Some writers make the mistake of using an adjective when they need an adverb.

not this: Talk to me ~~honest~~.
but this: Talk to me honestly.

not this: You can say it ~~simple~~.
but this: You can say it simply.

not this: He was breathing ~~deep~~.
but this: He was breathing deeply.

Exercise 6
Practice

Changing Adjectives to Adverbs

In each pair of sentences below, change the italicized adjective in the first sentence to an adverb in the second sentence. The first one is done for you.

1. a. She is a *graceful* dancer.

   b. She dances ___gracefully___.

2. a. His answer was *kind.*

b. He answered ____kindly____.

3. a. The customer made a *bitter* complaint.

b. The customer complained ____bitterly____.

4. a. The driver made a *careless* turn.

b. The driver turned ____carelessly____.

5. a. The sculptor made a *crude* model of the figure.

b. The sculptor's model of the figure was ____crudely____ made.

6. a. His response seemed *intelligent.*

b. He answered ____intelligently____.

7. a. Malcolm nevers gives a *direct* answer.

b. Malcolm never answers ____directly____.

8. a. Kyle had a *violent* reaction to his new medication.

b. When he took his new medication, Kyle reacted ____violently____.

9. a. His question had a *suspicious* tone.

b. He questioned me ____suspiciously____.

10. a. Mr. Chang gave a *generous* donation.

b. Mr. Chang donated ____generously____.

Do Not Confuse *Good* and *Well* or *Bad* and *Badly*

Remember that *good* is an adjective; it describes nouns. *Well* is an adverb; it describes verbs. (The only time *well* can be used as an adjective is when it means "healthy": *I feel well today.*

not this: You ran that race ~~good~~.
but this: You ran that race well.

not this: I cook eggs ~~good~~.
but this: I cook eggs well.

not this: How ~~good~~ do you understand grammar?
but this: How well do you understand grammar?

Bad is an adjective; it describes nouns. It also follows being verbs like *is, are, was, am,* and *has been.* Words like *feels, looks, seems, smells, sounds,* and *tastes* are part of the group called being verbs. *Badly* is an adverb; it describes action verbs.

not this: He feels ~~badly~~ about his mistake.
but this: He feels bad about his mistake. (*Feels* is a being verb; it is described by the adjective *bad.*)

> **not this:** That soup smells ~~badly~~.
> **but this:** That soup smells bad. (*Smells* is a being verb; it is described by the adjective *bad*.)

> **not this:** He dances ~~bad~~.
> **but this:** He dances badly.

Exercise 7 **Using *Good* and *Well*, *Bad* and *Badly***

Practice Write the appropriate word in each of the following sentences.

1. It isn't easy to move from one apartment to another, but you managed the job _____well_____ (good, well).

2. Crystal missed the picnic because she wasn't feeling _____well_____ (good, well).

3. That letter was sloppy and _____badly_____ (bad, badly) written.

4. Al was sure he had done _____well_____ (good, well) on his physiology test.

5. My cat and dog get along _____well_____ (good, well) together.

6. Bertrand shouldn't feel _____bad_____ (bad, badly) about the accident; it wasn't his fault.

7. Mrs. Ibarra needed a job _____badly_____ (bad, badly).

8. When you hear it on the radio, the song sounds _____bad_____ (bad, badly).

9. That new suit looks _____good_____ (good, well) on you.

10. The driver of the wrecked bus was hurt _____badly_____ (bad, badly).

Not *More* + -er or *Most* + -est

Be careful. Never write both an *-er* ending and *more* or an *-est* ending and *most*.

> **not this:** I want to work with someone ~~more smarter~~.
> **but this:** I want to work with someone smarter.

> **not this:** Alan is the ~~most richest~~ man in town.
> **but this:** Alan is the richest man in town.

Use *Than*, not *Then*, in Comparisons

When you compare things, use *than*. *Then* means "at a later time."

> **not this:** You are taller ~~then~~ I am.
> **but this:** You are taller than I am.

> **not this:** I'd like a car that is faster ~~then~~ my old one.
> **but this:** I'd like a car that is faster than my old one.

When Do I Need a Comma Between Adjectives?

Sometimes you use more than one adjective to describe a noun.

> I visited a cold, dark cave.
> The cat had pale blue eyes.

If you look at the preceding examples, one has a comma between the adjectives *cold* and *dark*, but the other does not have a comma between the adjectives *pale* and *blue*. Both sentences are correctly punctuated. To decide whether you need a comma, try one of these tests:

Test 1: Try to put *and* between the adjectives. If the sentence still makes sense, put a comma between the adjectives.

> **check for comma:** I visited a cold, dark cave. (Do you need the comma? Add *and* between the adjectives.)
> **add and:** I visited a cold *and* dark cave. (Does the sentence still make sense? Yes. You need the comma.)
> **correct sentence:** I visited a cold, dark cave.

> **check for comma:** The cat had pale blue eyes. (Do you need the comma? Add *and* between the adjectives.)
> **add and:** The cat had pale *and* blue eyes. (Does the sentence still make sense? No. You do not need the comma.)
> **correct sentence:** The cat had pale blue eyes.

Test 2: Try to reverse the order of the adjectives. If the sentence still makes sense, put a comma between the adjectives.

> **check for comma:** I visited a cold, dark cave. (Do you need the comma? Reverse the order of the adjectives.)
> **reversed order:** I visited a dark, cold cave. (Does the sentence still make sense? Yes. You need the comma.)
> **correct sentence:** I visited a cold, dark cave.

> **check for comma:** The cat had pale blue eyes. (Do you need the comma? Reverse the order of the adjectives.)
> **reversed order:** The cat had blue pale eyes. (Does the sentence still make sense? No. You don't need a comma.)
> **correct sentence:** The cat had pale blue eyes.

You can use test 1 or test 2 to determine whether you need a comma between adjectives.

Exercise 8

Practice

Editing for Errors in Adjectives and Adverbs

Edit the following paragraph, correcting all the errors in the use of adjectives and adverbs. Write your corrections above the errors. There are eight errors.

tough little (no comma)
When I was a tough, little teenager, I learned a lesson about taking risks.

One evening, my friends Mike and Andre and I sneaked out to skateboard at a

forbidden place—the courthouse steps. Those thirty-two concrete steps were

worst
a very big temptation for bold skateboarders like us. Twilight was the worse

time of day for skateboarding stunts. We thought we could see, but we really

more

couldn't. The fading light was most dangerous than total darkness because in

the dark, the streetlights would have been on. Mike started the competition by

braver (omit "more.")

jumping eight steps. Andre felt more braver and jumped ten steps. It was get-

ting darker. I knew I had to beat them both and took a leap down fifteen steps.

badly

I was hurt bad. I broke my ankle, split my front tooth, and cut my mouth. Yet I

less   *than*

felt least pain from my physical injuries then from the damage to my pride. Try-

foolishly

ing to show off, I had behaved foolish, and my actions brought me deep shame.

CHAPTER 18

Correcting Problems with Modifiers

Modifiers are words, phrases, or clauses that describe (modify) something in a sentence. All the italicized words, phrases, and clauses below are modifiers:

> the *blue* van (word)
> the van *in the garage* (phrase)
> the van *that she bought* (clause)

> *foreign* tourists (word)
> tourists *coming to Florida* (phrase)
> tourists *who visit the state* (clause)

Sometimes modifiers limit another word. They make another word (or words) more specific.

> the girl *in the corner* (tells which girl)
> *fifty* acres (tells how many acres)
> the movie *that I liked best* (tells which movie)
> He *never* calls. (tells how often)

Exercise 1 **Recognizing Modifiers**

Practice

In each sentence below, underline the modifiers (words, phrases, or clauses) that describe the italicized word or phrase.

1. *The kitten* <u>with the gray and white stripes</u> has the sweetest disposition.

2. I saw *a girl* <u>driving a beautifully restored Corvette</u>.

3. *The people* <u>standing in the long lines</u> showed great patience.

4. The fisherman reeled in *the fish*, <u>fighting for its life</u>.

5. Julie and Kate always write <u>thank-you</u> *notes*.

6. I found <u>my neighbor's lost</u> *parakeet*.

7. <u>Flashing its pink neon message</u>, *the sign* attracted many new customers.

8. *The* <u>little</u> *boy* <u>dressed in a sailor suit</u> saluted the troops.

9. <u>Jumping across the sidewalk</u>, *the frog* startled me.

10. *The* <u>battered old jean</u> *jacket*, <u>with its frayed sleeves and torn pocket</u>, finally had to be thrown out.

CORRECTING MODIFIER PROBLEMS

Modifiers can make your writing more specific and more concrete. Used effectively and correctly, modifiers give the reader a clear, exact picture of what you want to say, and they help you to say it precisely. But modifiers have to be used correctly. You can check for errors with modifers as you revise your sentences.

Infobox

Three Steps in Checking for Sentence Errors with Modifiers

Step 1: Find the modifier.

Step 2: Ask, "Does the modifier have something to modify?"

Step 3: Ask, "Is the modifier in the right place, as close as possible to the word, phrase, or clause it modifies?"

If you answer no in either step 2 or step 3, you need to revise your sentence. Let's use the steps in the following example:

sample sentence: I saw a girl driving a Porsche wearing a bikini.

Step 1: Find the modifier. The modifiers are *driving a Porsche* and *wearing a bikini.*

Step 2: Ask, "Does the modifier have something to modify?" The answer is yes. The girl is driving a Porsche. The girl is wearing a bikini. Both modifiers go with *a girl.*

Step 3: Ask, "Is the modifier in the right place?" The answer is yes and no. One modifier is in the right place:

I saw a *girl driving a Porsche*

The other modifier is *not* in the right place:

a *Porsche wearing a bikini*

The Porsche is not wearing a bikini.

revised: I saw a girl *wearing a bikini and driving a Porsche.*

Let's work through the steps once more:

sample sentence: Scampering through the forest, the hunters saw two rabbits.

Step 1: Find the modifier. The modifiers are *scampering through the forest* and *two.*

Step 2: Ask, "Does the modifier have something to modify?"

The answer is yes. There are *two* rabbits. The rabbits are *scampering through the forest.*

Step 3: Ask, "Is the modifier in the right place?" The answer is yes and no. The word *two* is in the right place:

two rabbits

But *scampering through the forest* is in the wrong place:

Scampering through the forest, the hunters

The hunters are not scampering through the forest. The rabbits are.

revised: The hunters saw two rabbits *scampering through the forest.*

Caution: Be sure to put words like *almost, even, exactly, hardly, just, merely, nearly, only, scarcely,* and *simply* as close as possible to what they modify. If you put them in the wrong place, you may write a confusing sentence.

sample sentence: Etienne only wants to grow carrots and zucchini. (The modifier that creates confusion here is *only.* Does Etienne have only one goal in life—to grow carrots and zucchini? Or are these the only vegetables he wants to grow? To create a clearer sentence, move the modifier.)

revised: Etienne wants to grow *only* carrots and zucchini.

The examples you have just worked with show one common error in using modifiers. This error involves **misplaced modifiers,** words that describe something but are not where they should be in the sentence. Here is the rule to remember:

Put a modifier as close as possible to the word, phrase, or clause it modifies.

| **Exercise 2** | **Correcting Sentences with Misplaced Modifiers** |
| Practice | |

Some of the following sentences contain misplaced modifiers. Revise any sentence that has a misplaced modifier by putting the modifier as close as possible to whatever it modifies.

1. Falling from the top of my refrigerator, I saw my best glass dish.

   revised: <u>I saw my best glass dish falling from the top of the refrigerator.</u>

2. When we criticized her performance, the actress was ready to nearly cry.

   revised: <u>When we criticized her performance, the actress was nearly ready to cry.</u>

3. When she goes to the supermarket, she only wants to buy necessary items.

   revised: <u>When she goes to the supermarket, she wants to buy only necessary items.</u>

4. Wrapped in shiny paper, I accepted the tiny gift.

   revised: <u>I accepted the tiny gift wrapped in shiny paper.</u>

5. The doctor gave the prescription for sedatives to the nervous patient.

    revised: <u>OK</u>

    _____

6. When he starts college next fall, he wants to take only business courses.

    revised: <u>OK</u>

    _____

7. Cracked in two places, she was sure the window would have to be replaced.

    revised: <u>She was sure the window, cracked in two places, would have to be</u>

    <u>replaced.</u>

8. The team doesn't like the umpire that lost the game.

    revised: <u>The team that lost the game doesn't like the umpire.</u>

    _____

9. Soaked in brandy, she tasted the fruitcake.

    revised: <u>She tasted the fruitcake soaked in brandy.</u>

    _____

10. Straining against the leash, Jim pulled back his bulldog.

    revised: <u>Jim pulled back his bulldog, straining against the leash.</u>

    _____

Correcting Dangling Modifiers

The three steps for correcting modifier problems can help you recognize another kind of error. Let's use the steps to check the following sentence:

> **sample sentence:** Strolling through the tropical paradise, many colorful birds could be seen.
>
> **Step 1:** Find the modifier. The modifiers are *Strolling through the tropical paradise* and *many colorful*.
>
> **Step 2:** Ask, "Does the modifer have something to modify?" The answer is yes and no. The words *many* and *colorful* modify birds. But who or what is *strolling through the tropical paradise*? There is no person mentioned in this sentence. The birds are not strolling.

This kind of error is called a **dangling modifier.** The modifier does not have anything to modify; it just dangles in the sentence. To correct this kind of error, you cannot just move the modifier:

still incorrect: Many colorful birds could be seen strolling through the tropical paradise. (There is still no person strolling.)

The way to correct this kind of error is to add something to the sentence. If you gave the modifer something to modify, you might come up with several different revised sentences:

As I strolled through the tropical paradise, I saw many colorful birds.

or

Many colorful birds could be seen *when we were strolling through the tropical paradise.*

or

While the tourists strolled through the tropical paradise, they saw many colorful birds.

Try the process for correcting dangling modifiers once more:

sample sentence: Ascending in the glass elevator, the hotel lobby glittered in the light.

Step 1: Find the modifier. The modifiers are *Ascending in the glass elevator* and *hotel*.

Step 2: Ask, "Does the modifier have anything to modify?" The answer is yes and no. The word *hotel* modifies lobby, but *ascending in the glass elevator* doesn't modify anything. Who is ascending in the elevator? There is nobody mentioned in the sentence.

To revise this sentence, put somebody or something in it for the modifier to describe:

As the guests ascended in the glass elevator, the hotel lobby glittered in the light.

or

Ascending in the glass elevator, she saw the hotel lobby *glitter* in the light.

Remember that you cannot correct a dangling modifier just by moving the modifier. You have to give the modifier something to modify; you have to add something to the sentence.

Exercise 3

Practice

Correcting Sentences with Dangling Modifiers

Some of the following sentences use modifiers correctly, but some have dangling modifiers. Revise the sentences with dangling modifiers by adding words or changing words.

Answers Will Vary.
Possible answers
shown at right.

1. Racing across the station, the train was reached before the doors closed.

   revised: <u>Racing across the station, I reached the train before the doors</u>

   <u>closed.</u>

2. Breaking into the house at night, the homeowners lost their most valuable possessions.

revised: When thieves broke into the house at night, the homeowners lost their most valuable possessions.

3. At the age of five, my family moved to Pennsylvania.

revised: My family moved to Pennsylvania when I was five.

4. Lost in the fog, the lighthouse could not be seen.

revised: Lost in the fog, the sailors could not see the lighthouse.

5. Stumbling across the finish line, the runner gasped for breath.

revised: OK

6. When taking the geometry exam, an argument began between the teacher and a student.

revised: When the class was taking the geometry exam, an argument between the teacher and a student began.

7. While mowing the lawn, a wasp stung him.

revised: While he was mowing the lawn, a wasp stung him.

8. Tired and irritable, the work day seemed endless.

revised: Because I was tired and irritable, the work day seemed endless.

9. Visiting Mexico for the first time, I thought the country was exciting.

revised: OK

10. To enter that contest, a fee of $50.00 is needed.

revised: To enter that contest, you have to pay a $50.00 entry fee.

REVIEWING THE STEPS AND THE SOLUTIONS

It is important to recognize problems with modifiers and to correct these problems. Modifier problems can result in confusing or even silly sentences. And when you confuse or unintentionally amuse your reader, you are not making your point.

Remember to check for modifier problems in three steps, then correct each kind of problem in the appropriate way.

Infobox

A Summary of Modifier Problems

Checking for Modifier Problems

Step 1: Find the modifier.

Step 2: Ask, "Does the modifier have something to modify?"

Step 3: Ask, "Is the modifier in the right place?"

Correcting Modifier Problems

If the modifier is in the wrong place (a misplaced modifier), put it as close as possible to the word, phrase, or clause it modifies.

If the modifier has nothing to modify (a dangling modifier), add or change words so that it has something to modify.

Exercise 4   **Revising Sentences with Modifier Problems**

Practice

The following sentences have modifier problems. Write a new, correct sentence for each one. You may move words, add words, change words, or remove words. The first one is done for you.

1. Stopping suddenly, the box with the cake in it fell from the seat of the car.

   revised: When I had to stop suddenly, the box with the cake in it fell from the

   seat of the car.

Answers Will Vary.
Possible answers
shown at right.

2. Without a trace of bitterness, the argument between the neighbors was settled.

   revised: The neighbors settled the argument without a trace of bitterness.

3. Staring into space, the teacher scolded the student.

   revised: The teacher scolded the student who was staring into space.

4. After considering the alternatives, a compromise was reached by the two sides.

   revised: After considering the alternatives, the two sides reached a compro-

   mise.

5. After drag racing down the street until 3:00 a.m., the neighbors decided to complain to the teenager's parents.

   revised: After the teenager drag raced down the street until 3:00 a.m., the neighbors decided to complain to the teen's parents.

6. Inflated to huge dimensions, he dragged the inner tube across the stream.

   revised: He dragged the inner tube, inflated to huge dimensions, across the stream.

7. Susan nearly missed all the multiple-choice questions on the test.

   revised: Susan missed nearly all the multiple-choice questions on the test.

8. Covered in mud, I doubted if the shoes could ever be clean again.

   revised: I doubted if the shoes, covered in mud, could ever be clean again.

9. To make friends at school, an outgoing personality is necessary.

   revised: To make friends at school, you need an outgoing personality.

10. When packing a suitcase for a trip, a little ingenuity and planning go a long way.

    revised: When you pack a suitcase for a long trip, a little ingenuity and planning go a long way.

CHAPTER **19**

Using Verbs Correctly

Verbs are words that show some kind of action or being. These verbs show action or being:

> **verb**
> He *runs* to the park.

> **verb**
> Melanie *is* my best friend.

> **verb**
> The pizza *tastes* delicious.

Verbs also tell about time.

> He *will run* to the park. (The time is future.)
> Melanie *was* my best friend. (The time is past.)
> The pizza *tastes* delicious. (The time is present.)

The time of a verb is called its *tense*. You can say a verb is in the *present tense, future tense,* or many other tenses.

Using verbs correctly involves knowing which form of the verb to use, choosing the right verb tense, and being consistent in verb tense.

USING STANDARD VERB FORMS

Many people use nonstandard verb forms in everyday conversation. But everyone who wants to write and speak effectively should know different levels of language, from the slang and dialect of everyday conversation to the **standard English** of college, business, and professional environments.

In everyday conversation, you may use **nonstandard forms** like these:

I goes	he don't	we was
you was	it don't	she smile
you be	I be	they walks

But these are not correct forms in standard English.

THE PRESENT TENSE

Look at the standard verb forms for the present tense of the word *listen:*

verb: listen

I listen	we listen
you listen	you listen
he, she, it listens	they listen

Take a closer look at the standard verb forms. Only one form is different:

he, she, it *listens*

This is the only form that ends in *s* in the present tense.

Infobox

In the present tense, use an *-s* or *-es* ending on the verb only when the subject is *he, she,* or *it* or the equivalent.

He calls his mother every day.
She chases the cat away from the birdcage.
It runs like a new car.

Jim calls his mother every day.
Samantha chases the cat away from the birdcage.
The jalopy runs like a new car.

Take another look at the present tense. If the verb is a standard verb, it will follow this form in the present tense:

I attend every lecture.
You care about the truth.
He visits his grandfather regularly.
She drives a new car.
The new *album sounds* great.
We follow that team.
You work well together.
They buy the store brand of cereal.

Exercise 1   **Picking the Correct Verb in the Present Tense**

Practice   Underline the subject and circle the correct form of the verb in parentheses in each sentence below.

1. The <u>dress</u> in the discount store (look, (looks)) better to me than the one in the boutique.

2. <u>I</u> ((work), works) in a dirty part of the city.

3. <u>Grocery shopping</u> (take, (takes)) a good part of the morning.

4. The <u>snake</u> in the yard (frighten, (frightens)) my sister.

5. <u>She</u> sometimes (travel, (travels)) for three days without calling home.

6. <u>Jimmie</u> (concentrate, (concentrates)) better with the radio on.

7. Down the street by the bank (stand,(stands)) a statue of Thomas Jefferson.

8. With great determination, Carla and Leon ((exercise), exercises) every day.

9. A meal in a restaurant (cost,(costs)) more than a meal at home.

10. It (seem,(seems)) like a good idea.

Exercise 2	**More on Picking the Correct Verb in the Present Tense**
Practice	Underline the subject and circle the correct form of the verb in parentheses in each sentence below.

Note: For more on using the correct verb form in sentences with prepositional phrases, see Chapter 21, "Making Subjects and Verbs Agree."

1. In cold weather, the pond (freeze,(freezes)) over for days at a time.

2. You ((want), wants) more money than I can give you.

3. The vice president (carry,(carries)) a lot of weight in the club.

4. A rich dessert (add,(adds)) empty calories.

5. Behind the wall (live,(lives)) a tiny grey mouse.

6. The car with the antilock brakes (appeal,(appeals)) to my wife.

7. Sometimes the customers ((wait), waits) for hours.

8. Cookies ((taste), tastes) better with milk.

9. My grandfather (walk,(walks)) two miles to his job.

10. Every weekend, they ((explore), explores) a new part of the city.

THE PAST TENSE

The past tense of most verbs is formed by adding *-d* or *-ed* to the verb.

TEACHING TIP:
An easy rule for students to remember is that if a verb ends in "e," they can just add a "d" for the past tense. If it ends in "y," they can change the "y" to "i" and add "ed." (For example: "tried.")

verb: listen

I listened	we listened
you listened	you listened
he, she, it listened	they listened

Add *-ed* to *listen* to form the past tense. For some other verbs, you may add *-d*.

The sun *faded* from the sky.
He *quaked* with fear.
She *crumpled* the paper into a ball.

Exercise 3	**Writing the Correct Form of Past Tense**
Practice	Write the correct past tense form of the verb in parentheses in each setence below.

1. Last week, he and I ____removed____ (remove) the stain from the counter.

2. The coach in high school ____warned____ (warn) some players to pay attention to the game.

3. As a child, Lucille ___performed___ (perform) in a children's theater troupe.

4. After doing some research on the company, I ___rejected___ (reject) its offer of a job.

5. Last night, we ___compromised___ (compromise) on the issue of where to build the park.

6. Yesterday, Christine ___called___ (call) me about driving to the party.

7. Reporters at the scene of last night's train accident ___interviewed___ (interview) a witness.

8. Ten years ago, Arnold and Bruce ___started___ (start) a climb to success in Hollywood.

9. The girl at the desk ___waved___ (wave) at me.

10. You ___wasted___ (waste) too much time on it yesterday.

THE FOUR MAIN FORMS OF A VERB: PRESENT, PAST, PRESENT PARTICIPLE, AND PAST PARTICIPLE

When you are deciding what form of a verb to use, you will probably rely on one of four forms: the present tense, the past tense, the present participle, and the past participle. Most of the time, you will use one of these forms or add a helping verb to it. Look at the four main forms of the verb *listen:*

Present	Past	Present Participle	Past Participle
listen	listened	listening	listened

You use the four verb forms—present, past, present participle, and past participle—alone or with helping verbs, to express time (tense). Forms of regular verbs like *listen* are very easy to remember. Use the present form for the present tense:

> We *listen* to the news on the radio.

The past form expresses past tense:

> I *listened* to language tapes for three hours yesterday.

The present participle or *-ing* form is used with helping verbs:

> He *was listening* to me.
> I *am listening* to you.
> You *should have been listening* more carefully.

The past participle is the form used with the helping verbs *have, has,* or *had:*

Note: Non-native speakers may have trouble remembering the *-ed* on the past participle form. See the ESL Appendix.

> I *have listened* for hours.
> She *has listened* to the tape.
> We *had listened* to the tape before we bought it.

Of course, you can add many helping verbs to the present tense:

present tense:

> We *listen* to the news on the car radio.

TEACHING TIP:
Remind students that by reading a draft aloud, they may find a missing -d in some past tense forms. (For example: "He used to play basketball; he was supposed to coach us.")

add helping verbs:

We *will* listen to the news on the car radio.
We *should* listen to the news on the car radio.
We *can* listen to the news on the car radio.

When a verb is regular, the past form is created by adding *-d* or *-ed* to the present form. The present participle is formed by adding *-ing* to the present form, and the past particple form is the same as the past form.

IRREGULAR VERBS

Irregular verbs do not follow the same rules for creating verb forms that regular verbs do. Three verbs that we use all the time—*be, have, do*—are irregular verbs. You need to study them closely. Look at the present tense forms for all three, and compare the standard present tense forms to the nonstandard ones. *Remember to use the standard forms for college or professional writing.*

verb: be

Nonstandard	Standard
I be or I is	I am
you be	you are
he, she, it be	he, she, it is
we be	we are
you be	you are
they be	they are

verb: have

Nonstandard	Standard
I has	I have
you has	you have
he, she, it have	he, she, it has
we has	we have
you has	you have
they has	they have

verb: do

Nonstandard	Standard
I does	I do
you does	you do
he, she, it do	he, she, it does
we does	we do
you does	you do
they does	they do

Caution: Be careful when you add *not* to *does*. If you are writing a contraction of *does not*, be sure you write *doesn't*, not *don't*.

> **not this:** The light don't work.
> **but this:** The light doesn't work.

Exercise 4 **Choosing the Correct Form of *be, have,* or *do* in the Present Tense**

Practice Circle the correct form of the verb in parentheses in each sentence below.

1. Two of the salesmen (is, (are)) meeting at the branch office.

2. I am sure the dancers (has, (have)) the ability to reach the top.

3. My mother (don't, (doesn't)) need another set of towels for her birthday.

4. The winner of the contest (do, (does)) whatever he or she wants with the money.

5. Without an excuse, he ((has), have) no choice but to apologize.

6. Every weekend, I ((do), does) the laundry for the whole family.

7. The musicians (has, (have)) a huge bus equipped for traveling long distances.

8. I (is, (am)) very embarrassed.

9. They know he (do, (does)) his exercises early in the morning.

10. Rose and Lee (be, (are)) coming over in half an hour.

Exercise 5
Practice

More on Choosing the Correct Form of *be*, *have*, or *do* in the Present Tense

Circle the correct form of the verb in parentheses in each sentence below.

1. Unfortunately, Lisa ((has), have) no excuse for her behavior.

2. Today I (be, (am)) the only one of the cousins still living at home.

3. I told her it ((has), have) nothing to do with her.

4. Spelling is important; it (do, (does)) count in your grade.

5. On Saturday mornings, you ((do), does) the yard work too early for me to help.

6. Cleo ((doesn't), don't) gossip about her friends.

7. Once a year, we (has, (have)) a family reunion.

8. Emilio and his cousin ((do), does) yard work for Mrs. Chen.

9. Our new house ((has), have) a big basement.

10. Unless you (has, (have)) proof, you shouldn't make accusations.

The Past Tense of *be, have, do*

The past forms of the irregular verbs *be*, *have*, and *do* can be confusing. Again, compare the nonstandard forms to the standard forms. *Remember to use the standard forms for college or professional writing.*

verb: be

Nonstandard	Standard
~~I were~~	I was
~~you was~~	you were
~~he, she, it were~~	he, she, it was
~~we was~~	we were
~~you was~~	you were
~~they was~~	they were

verb: have

Nonstandard	Standard
~~I has~~	I had
~~you has~~	you had
~~he, she, it have~~	he, she, it had
~~we has~~	we had
~~you has~~	you had
~~they has~~	they had

verb: do

Nonstandard	Standard
~~I done~~	I did
~~you done~~	you did
~~he, she, it done~~	he, she, it did
~~we done~~	we did
~~you done~~	you did
~~they done~~	they did

Exercise 6 **Choosing the Correct Form of** *be, have* **or** *do* **in the Past Tense**

Practice Circle the correct form of the verb in parentheses in each sentence below.

1. The people next door (was, (were)) mysterious in their habits.

2. Last night, Alonzo (done, (did)) the decorating for the Super Bowl party.

3. In spite of the rain, the club ((had) have) a large turnout for the picnic.

4. Three hours after the deadline, we (was, (were)) still busy.

5. Yesterday, at that intersection, I (have, (had)) a minor car accident.

6. As a little girl, Dora ((was), were) quiet and shy around strangers.

7. Believing in helping others, the volunteers ((did), done) a good deed for two lost people.

8. I ((was), were) unhappy with the grade on my math test.

9. Two years ago, you ((were), was) the most valuable player on the team.

10. Her class in music appreciation ((did), done) the most to interest her in music.

Exercise 7 **More on Choosing the Correct Form of** *be,* ***have*** **or** *do* **in the Past Tense**

Practice Circle the correct form of the verb in parentheses in each sentence below.

1. James and I (was, were) best friends in middle school.

2. Last night he (had, have) a meeting with a lawyer.

3. When I (was, were) a child, I took piano lessons.

4. At least you (did, done) the best you could on the exam.

5. We (was, were) just standing around when the fight started.

6. My brother Armand (has, have) a bad habit of expecting the worst.

7. Two weeks ago, you and I (was, were) unhappy and unemployed.

8. After the burgulary, Sheila (had, have) to get an alarm system.

9. I can relax because I (did, done) my assignment yesterday.

10. Gilda's job at the bank (has, have) its advantages.

More Irregular Verb Forms

Be, have, and *do* are not the only verbs with irregular forms. There are many such verbs, and everybody who writes uses some form of an irregular verb. When you write and you are not certain if you are using the correct form of a verb, check the list of irregular verbs below.

For each irregular verb listed, the *present,* the *past,* and the *past participle* forms are given. The present participle isn't included because it is always formed by adding *-ing* to the present form.

TEACHING TIP:
Ask students to spend a few minutes reviewing the list. Have them circle any verb form that seems "strange." Then discuss some of their choices and what form they would have been tempted to use instead of the correct one. They should see that conversational verb forms may differ from standard verb forms.

Irregular Verb Forms

Present	Past	Past Participle
(Today I *arise.*)	(Yesterday I *arose.*)	(I have/had *arisen.*)
arise	arose	arisen
awake	awoke, awaked	awoken, awaked
bear	bore	borne, born
beat	beat	beaten
become	became	become
begin	began	begun
bend	bent	bent
bite	bit	bitten
bleed	bled	bled
blow	blew	blown
break	broke	broken
bring	brought	brought
build	built	built
burst	burst	burst
buy	bought	bought
catch	caught	caught
choose	chose	chosen
come	came	come

Present	Past	Past Participle
cling	clung	clung
cost	cost	cost
creep	crept	crept
cut	cut	cut
deal	dealt	dealt
draw	drew	drawn
dream	dreamed	dreamed
drink	drank	drunk
drive	drove	driven
eat	ate	eaten
fall	fell	fallen
feed	fed	fed
feel	felt	felt
fight	fought	fought
find	found	found
fling	flung	flung
fly	flew	flown
forget	forgot	forgotten, forgot
freeze	froze	frozen
get	got	got, gotten
give	gave	given
go	went	gone
grow	grew	grown
hear	heard	heard
hide	hid	hidden
hit	hit	hit
hold	held	held
hurt	hurt	hurt
keep	kept	kept
know	knew	known
lay (put)	laid	laid
lead	led	led
leave	left	left
lend	lent	lent
let	let	let
lie (recline)	lay	lain
light	lit, lighted	lit, lighted
lose	lost	lost
make	made	made
mean	meant	meant
meet	met	met
pay	paid	paid
prove	proved	proved, proven
ride	rode	ridden
ring	rang	rung
rise	rose	risen
run	ran	run
say	said	said
see	saw	seen
sell	sold	sold
send	sent	sent
sew	sewed	sewn, sewed

Present	Past	Past Participle
shake	shook	shaken
shine	shone, shined	shone, shined
shrink	shrank	shrunk
shut	shut	shut
sing	sang	sung
sit	sat	sat
sleep	slept	slept
slide	slid	slid
sling	slung	slung
speak	spoke	spoken
spend	spent	spent
stand	stood	stood
steal	stole	stolen
stick	stuck	stuck
sting	stung	stung
stink	stank, stunk	stunk
string	strung	strung
swear	swore	sworn
swim	swam	swum
teach	taught	taught
tear	tore	torn
tell	told	told
think	thought	thought
throw	threw	thrown
wake	woke, waked	woken, waked
wear	wore	worn
win	won	won
write	wrote	written

Exercise 8 Choosing the Correct Form of Irregular Verbs

Practice Write the correct form of the verb in parentheses in each sentence below. Be sure to check the list of irregular verbs.

1. I bought a huge bag of potato chips last night, and by midnight, I had

   _____ eaten _____ (eat) the whole thing.

2. Patty and Tom should have _____ known _____ (know) how to get to the store; they've been there before.

3. We separated the glass beads into three colorful piles and then

   _____ strung _____ (string) the beads, alternating the colors.

4. I bought my five-year-old a new pair of blue jeans yesterday, but she has

   _____ torn _____ (tear) them already.

5. I don't know what he _____ meant _____ (mean) when he said, "I'm not interested."

6. Virginia asked Jack if he had ever _____ lent _____ (lend) money to a friend.

7. I went to the beach yesterday, and I _____lay_____ (lie) in the sun too long.

8. For years, that pawnbroker has _____dealt_____ (deal) in stolen merchandise, but now he is being investigated.

9. The children have _____drunk_____ (drink) all the milk in the refrigerator.

10. The child was hoping to get toys for his birthday, but instead his uncle _____brought_____ (bring) a sweater.

11. My brother has never _____spoken_____ (speak) to me like that before.

12. My first employer _____taught_____ (teach) me the value of a good attitude.

13. Michelle has _____driven_____ (drive) to Cleveland many times.

14. This morning I _____slept_____ (sleep) right through the sound of my alarm clock.

15. The cowboys had _____ridden_____ (ride) all the way to the creek.

16. The accused man _____swore_____ (swear) he was innocent.

17. Martin suffered, but he _____bore_____ (bear) his troubles patiently.

18. My toddler had _____stuck_____ (stick) a peanut butter sandwich in the VCR.

19. In a fit of temper, Tom _____flung_____ (fling) the paper across the room.

20. Yesterday I _____thought_____ (think) about calling my sister.

Exercise 9
Collaborate

Writing Sentences with Correct Verb Forms

Working with a partner or a group, write two sentences that correctly use each of the verb forms below. In writing these sentences, you may add helping verbs to the verb forms, but do not change the verb form itself. The first one is done for you.

1. sent

   a. He sent her a dozen roses on Valentine's Day.

   b. I have sent him all the information he needs.

2. bitten

Answers Will Vary.
Possible answers
shown at right.

   a. My dog has bitten a hole in my shoe.

   b. Squirrels have bitten through the cord on the bird feeder.

3. cost

    a. Jack's rudeness cost him a good position at the bank.

    b. The apples cost more today than they did yesterday.

4. drew

    a. The artist drew a pastel portrait of my mother.

    b. The smell of popcorn drew the children closer to the tent.

5. run

    a. I run two miles every day.

    b. I have run in that marathon for years.

6. felt

    a. Yesterday, Sammy felt tired.

    b. Susan has felt tired all week.

7. hurt

    a. You have hurt my feelings.

    b. Yesterday, I hurt my arm playing softball.

8. froze

    a. Ricardo froze the leftovers in a plastic container.

    b. During the cold weather, the oranges froze on the tree.

9. gotten

    a. I have gotten many compliments on my cooking.

    b. Marisol has gotten a bad cold.

10. eaten

    a. The ducks had eaten all the pieces of bread.

    b. I have eaten too much dinner.

CHAPTER 20

More on Verbs: Consistency and Voice

Remember that your choice of verb form indicates the time (tense) of your statements. Be careful not to shift from one tense to another unless you have a reason to change the time.

CONSISTENT VERB TENSES

Staying in one tense (unless you have a reason to change tenses) is called **consistency of verb tense.**

> **incorrect shifts in tense:**
>
> The waitress *ran* to the kitchen with the order in her hand, *raced* back to her customers with glasses of water, and *smiles* calmly.
> He *grins* at me from the ticket booth and *closed* the ticket window.

You can correct these errors by putting all the verbs in the same tense:

TEACHING TIP:

This is a good time to review parallel structure. See Chapter 16 on parallelism in sentences.

> **consistent present tense:**
>
> The waitress *runs* to the kitchen with the order in her hand, *races* back to her customers with glasses of water, and *smiles* calmly.
> He *grins* at me from the ticket booth and *closes* the ticket window.

> **consistent past tense:**
>
> The waitress *ran* to the kitchen with the order in her hand, *raced* back to her customers with glasses of water, and *smiled* calmly.
> He *grinned* at me from the ticket booth and *closed* the ticket window.

Whether you correct by changing all the verbs to the present tense or by changing them to the past tense, you are making the tenses consistent. Consistency of tense is important when you describe events because it helps the reader understand what happened and when it happened.

Exercise 1 **Correcting Sentences That Are Inconsistent in Tense**

Practice

In each sentence below, one verb is inconsistent in tense. Cross it out and write the correct tense above it.

1. Every month I stack all the household bills in a pile and get out my checkbook; then I ~~paid~~ *pay* all the bills at one time.

2. On the news, the reporter described the scene of the accident and interviewed a witness, but the reporter never ~~explains~~ *explained* how the accident happened.

3. When my father comes home from work, he sits in his recliner and turns
on the televsion because he ~~was~~ *is* too tired to talk.

4. Hundreds of pieces of junk mail come to our house every year and ~~offered~~ *offer*
us magazine subscriptions, gifts, clothes, and fabulous prizes, but I throw
all that junk mail in the garbage.

5. They were the top athletes in their class because they trained rigorously
and ~~follow~~ *followed* a strict exercise routine.

6. In the kitchen, Adam struggled with the pipes under the sink and swore
loudly; meanwhile, Jason ~~calls~~ *called* a plumber.

7. Whenever she is depressed, she buys something chocolate and ~~devoured~~ *devours* it.

8. Because the parking lot at the supermarket is always crowded, people
~~parked~~ *park* next door and walk the extra distance.

9. Working nights is hard for me because I ~~had~~ *have* to get up early for classes,
and I have to find time for my family.

10. Although my friend says he's not afraid of heights, he ~~shrank~~ *shrinks* back
whenever he is at the edge of a balcony or apartment railing.

Exercise 2 **Editing Paragraphs for Consistency of Verb Tense**

Practice

Read the following paragraphs. Then cross out any verbs that are inconsistent in
tense and write the corrections above.

1. The rain came suddenly and pelted the holiday crowd. The storm trans-
formed the scene. People grabbed their blankets and picnic baskets and
~~run~~ *ran* for cover. Several people congregated under nearby trees, but the
lightning flashed nearby and worried them. Others ~~sit~~ *sat* under a picnic

table while some raced to their cars. Everyone was soaking wet, and the

picnic area ~~becomes~~ *became* a scene of sopping paper plates and waterlogged

barbecue grills.

2. The alarm clock blasted into my ear. I cringed, crawled out from under

the covers, and reached my arm across the nightstand. I ~~fling~~ *flung* the stupid

clock across the room and burrowed back under the covers. The bed felt

warm and cozy. I tried to fall back into my dream. But soon my dog leaped

into the room, jumped onto the bed, and ~~plants~~ *planted* kisses all over my face. In

spite of all my attempts to go back to sleep, all the signs told me it was

time to get up.

Exercise 3
Collaborate

Writing a Paragraph with Consistent Verb Tense

The paragraph below shifts between past and present tenses. Working with a group, write two versions of the paragraph, one in the present tense and one in the past tense. Half the group may write the paragraph in one tense while the other half writes it in the other tense. After both rewrites are complete, read the new paragraph aloud to the whole group.

The day starts off well, but it doesn't end that way. At first, I am confident about taking my driving test and getting my driver's license. Then I got into the car with the examiner and wait for him to tell me to start. When he does, I turned the key in the ignition and slowly pull out of the parking lot. For some reason, I am sweating with fear, but I tried not to show it. I managed to drive without hitting another car. I remember to stop at a stop sign. But when it came to parallel parking, I knocked down all those orange markers! My driving examiner never cracks a smile or even talked to me. He just gives instructions. But I knew what he was thinking, and I know I won't get a license. I feel like the worst driver in the world.

paragraph revised for consistent tenses:

The day starts off well, but it doesn't end that way. At first, I am confident about taking my driving test and getting my driver's license. Then I *get* into the car with the examiner and wait for him to tell me to start. When he does, I *turn* the key in the ignition and slowly pull out of the parking lot. For some reason, I am sweating with fear, but I *try* not to show it. I *manage* to drive without hitting another car. I remember to stop at a stop sign. But when it *comes* to parallel parking, I *knock* down all those orange markers! My driving examiner never cracks a smile or even *talks* to me. He just gives instructions. But I *know* what he *is* thinking, and I know I won't *get* a license. I feel like the worst driver in the world.

The day *started* off well, but it *didn't* end that way. At first, I *was* confident about taking my driving test and getting my driver's license. Then I *got* into the car with the examiner and *waited* for him to tell me to start. When he *did*, I turned the key in the ignition and slowly *pulled* out of the parking lot. For some reason, I *was* sweating with fear, but I tried not to show it. I managed to drive without hitting another car. I *remembered* to stop at a stop sign. But when it came to parallel parking, I knocked down all those orange markers! My driving examiner never *cracked* a smile or even talked to me. He just *gave* instructions. But I knew what he was thinking, and I knew I *wouldn't* get a license. I *felt* like the worst driver in the world.

THE PRESENT PERFECT TENSE

When you are choosing the right verb tense, you should know about two verb tenses, the present perfect and the past perfect, that can make your meaning clear.

The **present perfect tense** is made up of the past participle form of the verb plus *have* or *has* as a helping verb. Use this tense to show an action that started in the past but is still going on in the present.

> **past tense:** My father *drove* a truck for five months. (He doesn't drive a truck any more, but he did drive one in the past.)
> **present perfect tense:** My father *has driven* a truck for five months. (He started driving a truck five months ago; he is still driving a truck.)
>
> **past tense:** For years, I *studied* ballet. (I don't study ballet now; I used to.)
> **present perfect tense:** For years, I *have studied* ballet. (I still study ballet.)

Remember, use the present perfect tense to show that an action started in the past and is still going on.

Exercise 4   **Distinguishing Between Past and Present Perfect Tenses**

Practice   Circle the correct verb in parentheses in each sentence below. Be sure to look carefully at the meaning of the sentences.

1. Jason (has borrowed, (borrowed)) a book from the library last night.

2. William (sang, (has sung)) in the choir for many years now.

3. The old car (was, (has been)) having mechanical problems, but no one wants to get rid of it.

4. I called the office and (have asked, (asked)) for the supervisor.

5. The comedians (performed, (have performed)) together for two years and are now appearing at our campus theater.

6. Two of my best friends ((were), have been) musicians but gave up music for business careers.

7. MTV (was, (has been)) influencing teenagers for years now.

8. While he was in basic training, he (has written, (wrote)) many letters home.

9. He ((sent) has sent) his résumé to fifty companies and accepted a job from the first company that responded.

10. Melissa ((lost) has lost) that bracelet three weeks ago.

THE PAST PERFECT TENSE

The **past perfect tense** is made up of the past participle form of the verb and *had* as a helping verb. You can use the past perfect tense to show more than one event in the past—that is, when two or more things happened in the past but at different times.

> **past tense:** He *washed* the dishes.
> **past perfect tense:** He *had washed* the dishes by the time I came home. (He washed the dishes before I came home. Both actions happened in the past, but one happened earlier than the other.)
>
> **past tense:** Susan *waited* for an hour.
> **past perfect tense:** Susan *had waited* for an hour when she gave up on him. (Waiting came first; giving up came second. Both actions are in the past.)

Note: Past perfect tense is difficult for most students, especially for non-native speakers.

The past perfect tense is especially useful because you write most of your essays in the past tense, and you often need to get further back into the past. Remember, to form the past perfect tense, use *had* with the past participle of the verb.

| **Exercise 5** | **Distinguishing Between the Past and the Past Perfect Tense** |

Practice Circle the correct verb in parentheses in each sentence below. Be sure to look carefully at the meaning of the sentences.

1. The child ((had hidden), hid) the shattered vase just minutes before his aunt entered the living room.

2. My father drove a rental car last week because he (had wrecked, wrecked) his own car last month.

3. Bernie bought a set of drums yesterday; he (had saved, saved) for that set for years.

4. Every weekend, (I had run, ran) errands and ironed my clothes.

5. The salesman asked whether we (had received, received) the merchandise yet.

6. As I (had cut, cut) the pattern for another dress, I thought about becoming a dress designer.

7. They (had left, left) for the party by the time we came to pick them up.

8. She (threw, had thrown) the candy wrapper on the grass and ignored a nearby trash bin.

9. I was not sure whether he (had returned, returned) my tools earlier in the day.

10. When the little boy screamed, his mother (had jumped, jumped) up with a worried look on her face.

PASSIVE AND ACTIVE VOICE

Verbs not only have tenses; they also have voices. When the subject in the sentence is doing something, the verb is in the **active voice.** When something is done to the subject—that is, when the subject receives the action of the verb—the verb is in the **passive voice.**

> **active voice:**
>
> I painted the house. (*I*, the subject, did it.)
> The people on the corner made a donation to the emergency fund. (The *people*, the subject, did it.)
>
> **passive voice:**
>
> The house was painted by me. (The *house*, the subject, didn't do anything. It received the action—it was painted.)
> A donation to the emergency fund was made by the people on the corner. (The *donation*, the subject, didn't do anything. It received the action—it was given.)

Notice what happens when you use the passive voice instead of the active:

> **active voice:** I painted the house.
> **passive voice:** The house was painted by me.

The sentence in the passive voice is two words longer than the one in the active voice. Yet the sentence that uses the passive voice does not say anything different, and it does not say anything more clearly than the one in the active voice.

Using the passive voice can make your sentences wordy, it can slow them down, and it can make them boring. The passive voice can also confuse readers. When the subject of the sentence is not doing anything, readers may have to look carefully to see who or what *is* doing something. Look at this sentence:

A decision to fire you was reached.

Who made the decision? In this sentence, it is hard to find the answer to that question.

Of course, there will be times when you have to use the passive voice. For example, you may have to use it when you do not know who did something:

Our house was broken into last night.
A leather jacket was left behind in the classroom.

But in general, you should avoid using the passive voice and rewrite sentences so they are in the active voice.

TEACHING TIP:
Stress that the passive voice is easily overused. Remind students that using the active voice whenever possible leads to stronger and more precise writing.

| **Exercise 6** Practice | **Rewriting Sentences, Changing the Passive Voice to the Active Voice** |

In the following sentences, change the passive voice to the active voice. If the original sentence does not tell you who or what performed the action, add words that tell who or what did it. An example is done for you.

example: Sandy Adams was appointed chief negotiator last night.

rewritten: The union leaders appointed Sandy Adams chief negotiator last night.

Answers Will Vary.
Possible answers shown at right.

1. My favorite actor was arrested in Hollywood yesterday.

rewritten: Hollywood police arrested my favorite actor yesterday.

2. A compromise has been reached by the lawyers on both sides.

rewritten: The lawyers on both sides reached a compromise.

3. The wrong number was called several times.

rewritten: He called the wrong number several times.

4. Finally, a restaurant was decided on by the hungry family.

rewritten: The hungry family finally decided on a restaurant.

5. Great care was taken to protect the fragile package.

rewritten: She took great care to protect the fragile package.

6. The dolls were placed in a row by the little girl.

rewritten: <u>The little girl placed the dolls in a row.</u>

_____

7. Every day, the park is patrolled by a security guard.

rewritten: <u>A security guard patrols the park every day.</u>

_____

8. Last week, my car was hit by a careless driver.

rewritten: <u>Last week, a careless driver hit my car.</u>

_____

9. The real reason for his tardiness was not known by his teacher.

rewritten: <u>His teacher didn't know the real reason for his tardiness.</u>

_____

10. The murder is being investigated by the police.

rewritten: <u>The police are investigating the murder.</u>

_____

Avoiding Unnecessary Shifts in Voice

Just as you should be consistent in the tense of verbs, you should be consistent in the voice of verbs. Do not shift from active voice to passive voice, or vice versa, without some good reason to do so.

>   **active**   **passive**
> **shift:** _I designed_ the decorations for the dance; _they were put up_ by Chuck.
>
>   **active**   **passive**
> **rewritten:** _I designed_ the decorations for the dance; _Chuck put them up._
>
>   **passive**
> **shift:** Many _problems were discussed_ by the council members,
>
>   **active**
> but _they found_ no easy answers.
>
>   **active**
> **rewritten:** The council _members discussed_ many problems, but
>
>   **active**
> _they found_ no easy answers.

Being consistent in voice can help you write clearly and smoothly.

Exercise 7 **Rewriting Sentences to Correct Shifts in Voice**

Practice   Rewrite the sentences below so that all the verbs are in the active voice. You may change the wording to make the sentences clear, smooth, and consistent in voice.

Answers Will Vary.
Possible answers
shown at right.

1. Christine called Jack yesterday, but I was called by Tom today.

rewritten: Christine called Jack yesterday, but Tom called me today.

2. A revised set of rules is being written by the disciplinary committee; the committee is also writing a list of penalties.

rewritten: The disciplinary committee is writing a revised set of rules; the committee is also writing a list of penalties.

3. That girl can be helped by your advice because you know her problems.

rewritten: Your advice can help that girl because you know her problems.

4. The windows were opened by the office workers as the temperature soared above ninety degrees.

rewritten: The office workers opened the windows as the temperature soared above ninety degrees.

5. It was decided by a team of experts that the water contains harmful bacteria.

rewritten: A team of experts decided that the water contains harmful bacteria.

6. My sister has been chosen by the senior class to speak at graduation; she will deliver the welcoming address.

rewritten: The senior class has chosen my sister to speak at graduation; she will deliver the welcome address.

7. Some people worship celebrities; musicians, actors, and athletes are regarded as superhuman.

rewritten: Some people worship celebrities; they regard musicians, athletes, and actors as superhuman.

8. Michael showed his dismay when his brother Chris was rejected by the admissions committee.

rewritten: Michael showed his dismay when the admissions committee rejected his brother Chris.

9. If a deal was made by the officers, I never knew about it.

rewritten: <u>If the officers made a deal, I never knew about it.</u>

_____

10. People didn't worry about protecting their homes until South Florida was hit by a monster hurricane.

rewritten: <u>People didn't worry about protecting their homes until a monster hurri-</u>

<u>cane hit South Florida.</u>

Small Reminders About Verbs

There are a few errors that people tend to make with verbs. If you are aware of these errors, you'll be on the lookout for them as you edit your writing.

**Used to:** Be careful when you write that someone _used to_ do, say, or feel something. It is incorrect to write _use to._

> **not this:** Janine ~~use to~~ visit her mother every week.
> They ~~use to~~ like Thai food.
> **but this:** Janine _used to_ visit her mother every week.
> They _used to_ like Thai food.

**Could Have, Should Have, Would Have:** Using _of_ instead of _have_ is another error with verbs.

> **not this:** I ~~could of~~ done better on the test.
> **but this:** I _could have_ done better on the test.

> **not this:** He ~~should of~~ been paying attention.
> **but this:** He _should have_ been paying attention.

> **not this:** The girls ~~would of~~ liked to visit Washington.
> **but this:** The girls _would have_ liked to visit Washington.

**Would Have/Had:** If you are writing about something that might have been possible but that did not happen, use _had_ as the helping verb.

> **not this:** If I ~~would have~~ taken a foreign language in high school, I wouldn't have to take one now.
> **but this:** If I _had_ taken a foreign language in high school, I wouldn't have to take one now.

> **not this:** I wish they ~~would have~~ won the game.
> **but this:** I wish they _had_ won the game.

> **not this:** If she ~~would have~~ been smart, she would have called a plumber.
> **but this:** If she _had_ been smart, she would have called a plumber.

 **Exercise 8** Collaborate **Writing Sentences with the Correct Verb Forms**

Complete this exercise with a partner or a group. Follow the directions to write or complete each sentence below.

Answers Will Vary.
Possible answers
shown at right.

1. Complete this sentence and add a verb in the correct tense:
I had cleaned the whole house by the time

I had cleaned the whole house by the time my wife arrived.

2. Write a sentence more than six words long that includes the words *has studied karate* in the middle of it.

Sheila has studied karate for six years.

3. Write a sentence that uses the past tense form of both these words: *run, stumble.*

As the toddler ran to his sister, he stumbled in the grass.

4. Write a sentence in the passive voice.

A diamond ring was stolen from the jewelry store window.

5. Write a sentence in the active voice.

Someone stole a diamond from the jewelry store window.

6. Write a sentence that uses *would have* and *had.*

I would have been more understanding if I had known about Teresa's family

problems.

7. Write a sentence more than six words long that uses the words *had called* and *before.*

Vincent had called 911 on his cell phone just before he ran to help the accident

victims.

8. Write a sentence more than six words long that uses the words *used to.*

For years, I used to dream of being an astronaut.

9. Write a sentence that contains two verbs in the same tense.

Bettina sneezed as she grabbed a tissue.

10. Write a sentence that uses the words *should have.*

I should have left the house earlier.

CHAPTER 21

Making Subjects and Verbs Agree

Subjects and verbs have to agree in number. That means a singular subject must be matched to a singular verb form, and a plural subject must be matched to a plural verb form.

> singular subject, singular verb
> My *sister walks* to work every morning.

> plural subject, plural verb
> *Mary, David, and Sam believe* in ghosts.

> singular subject, singular verb
> That *movie is* too violent for me.

> plural subject, plural verb
> Bulky *packages are* difficult to carry.

Caution: Remember that a regular verb has an *-s* ending in one singular form in the present tense—the form that goes with *he, she, it,* or their equivalents:

> He *makes* me feel confident.
> She *appreciates* intelligent conversation.
> It *seems* like a good buy.
> Bo *runs* every day.
> That girl *swims* well.
> That machine *jams* too often.

Exercise 1	**Correcting Errors in Subject-Verb Agreement in a Paragraph**
Practice	

There are errors in subject-verb agreement in the paragraph below. If a verb does not agree with its subject, change the verb form. Cross out the incorrect verb form and write the correct one above it. There are four errors in agreement in the paragraph.

Every night, my sister follows the same routine. She pours a big glass

sits

of diet cola, ~~sit~~ in an old easy chair, and settles down for a night on the

calls

telephone. My sister always ~~call~~ the same person, her best friend, Irene.

talk

She and Irene ~~talks~~ for hours about the most trivial subjects. The two girls

gossip about their friends, about their enemies, about what happened that

day, and about what will happen the next day. My brother says men never

says

spend so much time on the phone. But he always ~~say~~ that while he is try-

ing to get the phone from my sister so he can make his evening calls!

PRONOUNS AS SUBJECTS

Pronouns can be used as subjects. Pronouns are words that take the place of nouns. When pronouns are used as subjects, they must agree in number with verbs.

Here is a list of the subjective pronouns and the regular verb forms that agree with them, in the present tense:

Infobox

Subjective Pronouns and a Present Tense Verb

Pronoun	Verb	
I	listen	
you	listen	all singular forms
he, she, it	listens	
we	listen	
you	listen	all plural forms
they	listen	

In the sentences below, the pronoun used as the subject of the sentence agrees in number with the verb:

singular pronoun, singular verb
I make the best omelet in town.

singular pronoun, singular verb
You dance very well.

singular pronoun, singular verb
She performs like a trained athlete.

plural pronoun, plural verb
We need a new refrigerator.

plural pronoun, plural verb
They understand the situation.

SPECIAL PROBLEMS WITH AGREEMENT

Agreement seems fairly simple: If a subject is singular, you use a singular verb form, and if a subject is plural, you use a plural verb form. However, there are special problems with agreement that will come up in your writing. Sometimes, it is hard to find the subject of a sentence; at other times, it is hard to determine whether a subject is singular or plural.

Finding the Subject

When you are checking for subject-verb agreement, you can find the real subject of the sentence by first eliminating the prepositional phrases. To find the real subject, put parentheses around the prepositional phrases. Then it is easy to find the subject because nothing in a prepositional phrase can be the subject of a sentence.

prepositional phrases in parentheses:

S   V
One (of my oldest friends) *is* a social worker.

      S   V
A *student* (from one)(of the nearby school districts) *is* the winner.

      S   V
The *store* (across the street) (from my house) *is* open all night.

    S   V
Jim, (with all his silly jokes), *is* a nice person.

Note: Words and phrases such as *along with, as well as, except, in addition to, including, plus,* and *together with* introduce prepositional phrases. The words that follow them are part of the prepositional phrase and cannot be part of the subject.

         S   V
My *sister,* (along with her husband), *is* planning a trip to Bolivia.

         S   V
Tom's *house,* (as well as his apartment), *is* part of a family inheritance.

Exercise 2 **Finding the Real Subject by Recognizing Prepositional Phrases**

Practice Put parentheses around the prepositional phrases in the sentences below. Put an *S* above each subject and a *V* above each verb.

     S (   ) V   (
1. Two of my favorite television shows are comedies with African-American
)
stars.

         S   (   )( )V
2. The toothpaste with fluoride in it is the best choice.

    S (   )(   )V
3. One of the three people on the decorations committee is a professional

artist.

       S (   )(   )V
4. The clerk behind the counter at the bakery is a new employee.

        S   (   )(   )(
5. A representative of the company, in addition to an architect with experi-
)(   )   V
ence in urban planning, has presented a convincing proposal.

S (   )V
6. The cat behind the curtains is my sister's pet.

S   (   ) V (   )(
7. The middle school with the modern architecture is down the road from

)
my house.

(   ) S   V   (
8. With a great deal of poise, she took the termination notice from her

)
employer's hand.

S (   )(   )V   (   )
9. The coat with the keys in it is the one in the downstairs closet.

S   (   ) V   (   )
10. My best friend, as well as her younger sister, takes a course in yoga

(   )
for beginners.

Exercise 3 **Selecting the Correct Verb Form by Identifying Prepositional Phrases**

Practice

Put parentheses around the prepositional phrases in the sentences below. Then circle the correct verb in parentheses in each sentence.

(   )   (
1. A speaker from the Council of Cities (is, are) lecturing in our anthropology

)
class today.

(   )(   )(
2. Several of the biggest bargains in the antique shop, plus a great wicker

)
chair, (is, are) stashed in the back room.

(   )(   )
3. One of the contestants from the semifinal rounds (face, faces) the winner

(   )
of this round.

(   )(   )
4. The consequences of her argument with her father (seem, seems) severe.

(   )(   )
5. A salesperson with a background in communications (has, have) a com-

petitive advantage.

(   )(   )   (   )
6. With a velvet ribbon in her hair, the girl in the cereal advertisements

(   )
(look, looks) like a little angel.

(   )(   )   (   )
7. A friend of mine from the boondocks (is, are) dazzled by the big mall

(   )
at the edge of town.

(   )   (   )(   )
8. A change of plans (is, are) no reason for a change in your attitude.

(   )(   )(
9. An honest statement of the facts, together with a talent for

) (   )(   )
compromise, (is, are) behind the mayor's popularity in this city.

(   )
10. A person with energy, intelligence, and drive (is, are) needed for this job.

Changed Word Order

You are probably used to looking for the subject of a sentence in front of the verb, but not all sentences follow this pattern. Questions, sentences beginning with words like *here* or *there*, and other sentences change the word order, making subjects harder to find. So you have to look carefully to check for subject-verb agreement.

          V   S
Where *are* my *friends*?

        V S   V
When *is he going* to work?

                          V   S
Behind the elm trees *stands* a huge *statue*.

         V   S
There *are potholes* in the road.

         V   S
There *is* a *reason* for his impatience.

Exercise 4
Practice

TEACHING TIP:
Before students begin this exercise, remind them that a verb must always agree with its subject and that subjects are not always found at the beginning of a sentence.

Making Subjects and Verbs Agree in Sentences with Changed Word Order

In each sentence below, underline the subject and circle the correct verb in parentheses.

1. Included in the package of coupons (**was**, were) a <u>coupon</u> for a free breakfast.

2. Among my happiest memories (**is**, are) the <u>memory</u> of a day at the beach.

3. <u>Along</u> the side of the road (is, **are**) a flower <u>stand</u> and an old-fashioned diner.

4. There (is, **are**) several <u>explanations</u> for his tantrum.

5. There (was, **were**) my <u>brother</u> and <u>sister</u>, in the midst of an argument about my birthday party.

6. Behind the fence (lurk, **lurks**) a fierce and evil <u>dog</u>.

7. There (**was**, were) a sudden <u>increase</u> in the price of groceries.

8. Under the porch (sit, **sits**) an enormous <u>frog</u>.

9. Where (is, **are**) the <u>photographs</u> of your trip to Mexico?

10. Here (**is**, are) the insurance <u>policy</u> for the car.

11. Apart from Sal's money troubles, there (is, **are**) his legal and family <u>problems</u>.

12. Outside Boston (is, **are**) a historic <u>house</u> and a famous <u>church</u>.

13. Suddenly, there (**was**, were) the <u>sound</u> of six huge dogs barking fiercely.

14. Deep in her heart (is, **are**) a <u>commitment</u> to the poor and a <u>love</u> of her fellow man.

15. Where in the world (is, are) my driver's <u>license</u>?

16. Riding in the back seat of the car (was, were) a beautiful golden <u>retriever</u> and two excited <u>poodles</u>.

17. In the package from my sister in Idaho (was, were) homemade <u>fudge</u> and chocolate chip <u>cookies</u>.

18. Underneath all the lies (is, are) a <u>bit</u> of truth.

19. Recently there (has, have) been several <u>burglaries</u> in the Oakville district.

20. Within walking distance (is, are) a movie <u>theater</u> with stadium seating.

COMPOUND SUBJECTS

A compound subject is two or more subjects joined by *and, or,* or *nor.*
When subjects are joined by *and,* they are usually plural:

> S   S   V
> *Jermaine* and *Lisa are* bargain hunters.

> S   S   V
> The *house* and the *garden need* attention.

> S   S   V
> A *bakery* and a *pharmacy are* down the street.

Caution: Be careful to check for a compound subject when the word order changes.

> V   S   S
> There *are* a *bakery* and a *pharmacy* down the street. (Two things, a *bakery* and a *pharmacy, are* down the street.)

> V   S   S
> Here *are* a *picture* of your father and a *copy* of his birth certificate. (A *picture* and a *copy,* two things, *are* here.)

When subjects are joined by *or, either . . . or, neither . . . nor,* or *not only . . . but also,* the verb form agrees with the subject closer to the verb:

>   singular S   plural S, plural V
> Not only the restaurant *manager* but also the *waiters were* pleased with the new policy.

>   plural S   singular S, singular V
> Not only the *waiters* but also the restaurant *manager was* pleased with the new policy.

>   plural S   singular S, singular V
> Either the *parents* or the *boy walks* the dog every morning.

>   singular S   plural S, plural V
> Either the *boy* or the *parents walk* the dog every morning.

Exercise 5   **Making Subjects and Verbs Agree: Compound Subjects**

Practice   Circle the correct form of the verb in parentheses in each sentence below.

1. Neither my sister nor my cousin (is, are) good at sports.

2. When they came to this country, Stephen and Richard (was, were) eager to find employment.

3. Here (is, are) the guest of honor and her husband.

4. Either Jaime or his sisters (is, are) supposed to take out the garbage on Saturdays.

5. Either his sisters or Jaime (is, are) supposed to take out the garbage on Saturdays.

6. Doughnuts and a coffee cake (was, were) in the bag.

7. Under the sofa there (is, are) a ragged slipper and a shriveled apple.

8. Either Christopher or Ted (is, are) going to play first base.

9. Not only the teacher but also the students (like, likes) the new classroom.

10. Hanging out with my friends and complaining about my parents

(was, were) my principal activities in high school.

INDEFINITE PRONOUNS

Certain pronouns called **indefinite pronouns** always take singular verbs.

Infobox			
Indefinite Pronouns			
one	nobody	nothing	each
anyone	anybody	anything	either
someone	somebody	something	neither
everyone	everybody	everything	

If you want to write clearly and correctly, you must memorize these words and remember that they always take a singular verb. Using your common sense is not enough because some of these words seem plural: for example, *everybody* seems to mean more than one person, but in grammatically correct English, it takes a singular verb. Here are some examples of the pronouns used with singular verbs:

singular S   singular V
Everyone in town *is talking* about the scandal.

singular S   singular V
Each of the boys *is* talented.

singular S   singular V
One of their biggest concerns *is* crime in the streets.

singular S   singular V
Neither of the cats *is* mine.

TEACHING TIP:
Emphasize that indefinite pronouns often end in the words "one," "body," or "thing," and since these words are singular, students can then remember to use the singular verb form.

Hint: You can memorize the indefinite pronouns as the *-one*, *-thing*, and *-body* words (*everyone, everything, everybody,* and so forth) plus *each, either,* and *neither*.

Exercise 6   **Making Subjects and Verbs Agree: Using Indefinite Pronouns**

Practice   Circle the correct verb in parentheses in each sentence below.

1. Anybody in the suburbs (know, knows) the way to that turnpike exit.

2. Nothing in the sales racks (is, are) marked down.

3. Somebody (has, have) painted graffiti all over the walls.

4. Everything in the closet and in the hallways (is, are) neatly packed in cardboard boxes.

5. (Is, Are) anyone coming over for birthday cake?

6. Everybody in both schools (listen, listens) to the same radio station.

7. Nobody from the service clubs (was, were) interested in volunteering for this project.

8. Anything in light shades of pink or green (match, matches) my new dress.

9. One of my most foolish decisions (was, were) to call in sick last week.

10. Here (is, are) someone to see you.

11. (Has, Have) anybody seen my car keys?

12. Either of the restaurants (is, are) a fine place for lunch.

13. Someone (leaves, leave) trash in the empty lot every weekend.

14. Each of my aunts (visits, visit) Jamaica at least once a year.

15. Neither of the cars (has, have) antilock brakes.

16. On certain days, everyone in my math class (seem, seems) energetic and interested.

17. Something about the decoration of the four rooms (need, needs) improvement.

18. Under the pile of old blankets, there (was, were) nothing to be found.

19. At that time of night, (was, were) anyone awake?

20. Everything about horror movies (frighten, frightens) my brother.

COLLECTIVE NOUNS

Collective nouns refer to more than one person or thing:

team	company	council
class	corporation	government
committee	family	group
audience	jury	crowd

Collective nouns usually take a singular verb:

> **singular S, singular V**
> The *committee is sponsoring* a fund-raiser.

> **singular S, singular V**
> The *audience was* impatient.

> **singular S. singular V**
> The *jury has reached* a verdict.

The singular verb is used because the group is sponsoring, or getting impatient, or reaching a verdict, *as one unit.* Collective nouns take a plural verb only when the members of the group are acting individually, not as a unit:

> The sophomore *class are fighting* among themselves. (The phrase *among themselves* shows that the class is not acting as one unit.)

Exercise 7
Practice

Making Subjects and Verbs Agree: Using Collective Nouns

Circle the correct verb in parentheses in each sentence below.

1. My family (is, are) moving to another state next month.

2. The company with the safest work environment (is, are) receiving an award tomorrow.

3. Our class (has, have) less school spirit than other classes.

4. The student council (meet, meets) every Tuesday afternoon.

5. My group of friends (is, are) as close as friends can be.

6. A team from the Phillipines (was, were) competing in the international contest.

7. After Labor Day, the crowd at the beach (isn't, aren't) so large.

8. A truly enthusiastic audience (help, helps) the performers.

9. The governing board (vote, votes) on the annual budget tomorrow night.

10. The men's club (has, have) never endorsed candidates for political office.

MAKING SUBJECTS AND VERBS AGREE: THE BOTTOM LINE

As you have probably realized, making subjects and verbs agree is not as simple as it first appears. But if you can remember the basic ideas in this section, you will be able to apply them automatically as you edit your own writing. Below is a quick summary of subject-verb agreement.

Infobox

Making Subjects and Verbs Agree: A Summary

1. Subjects and verbs should agree in number: singular subjects get singular verb forms, and plural subjects get plural verb forms.

2. When pronouns are used as subjects, they must agree in number with verbs.

(continued)

Infobox

3. Nothing in a prepositional phrase can be the subject of a sentence.

4. Questions, sentences beginning with *here* or *there*, and other sentences can change word order, making subjects harder to find.

5. Compound subjects joined by *and* are usually plural.

6. When subjects are joined by *or, either . . . or, neither . . . nor,* or *not only . . . but also,* the verb form agrees with the subject closest to the verb.

7. Indefinite pronouns always take singular verbs.

8. Collective nouns usually take singular verbs.

Exercise 8 **A Comprehensive Exercise on Subject-Verb Agreement**

Practice Circle the correct verb in parentheses in each sentence below.

1. One of the cooks at the restaurant (**was**, were) in my math class last year.

2. Anybody from Arizona (know, **knows**) how to stay cool in the summer.

3. When (was, **were**) the packages delivered?

4. Each of the cars on the showroom floor (**was**, were) polished to a dazzling brightness.

5. Within the circle of diamonds (**was**, were) a deep red stone.

6. Neither my cousin nor his parents ever (**think**, thinks) about home security.

7. Every day, apathy and pessimism (**grow**, grows) stronger.

8. Nothing in ten years (**has**, have) pleased her more than that party.

9. The candidate with a strong background in liberal arts and good leadership skills (remain, **remains**) my first choice for the position.

10. Not only the parents but also their son (enjoy, **enjoys**) a visit to the museum.

11. Everything in the botanical gardens (**is**, are) rare and exotic.

12. Down the street from the bank there (is, **are**) a Chinese restaurant and an Italian deli.

13. Because of the lateness of the hour, the jury (**is**, are) adjourning until tomorrow.

14. The company (**was**, were) not eager to recruit college graduates.

15. Clearly defined steps and a realistic schedule (**help**, helps) you complete a difficult project.

16. If the city doesn't fix that road soon, someone (**is**, are) going to have an accident.

17. Last year there (was, (were)) a shooting and two muggings in the parking lot by the club.

18. Neither of my parents ((is), are) anxious about my decision.

19. The most popular nightclubs ((look), looks) shabby in daylight.

20. Jacqueline, as well as Alberto, ((studies), study) anatomy and physiology.

Exercise 9

👥 Collaborate

Writing Sentences with Subject-Verb Agreement

Working with a partner or a group, turn each of the following phrases into a pair of sentences. In each case, use a verb that fits, and put the verb in the present tense. Be sure that the verb agrees with the subject.

Answers Will Vary.
Possible answers shown at right.

1. A crate of oranges _arrives at my house in the winter._

   A crate of oranges _is a gift from my aunt in Florida._

2. Either Superman or Batman _appeals to children._

   Either Superman or Batman _saves the day._

3. The committee _decides on the annual budget._

   The committee _is used to handling complaints._

4. Thelma and Louise _are adventurous women._

   Thelma and Louise _often drive recklessly._

5. Everything in my closet _is at least a year old._

   Everything in my closet _needs to be washed._

6. Someone from the suburbs _wants to rent my apartment._

Someone from the suburbs <u>knows directions to the theater.</u>

_____

7. Not only the child but also his parents <u>like to watch cartoons.</u>

_____

Not only the child but also his parents <u>are interested in the martial arts.</u>

_____

8. Anybody in town <u>is a suspect in the crime.</u>

_____

Anybody in town <u>has a chance to win the contest.</u>

_____

9. One of my greatest fears <u>is of snakes.</u>

_____

One of my greatest fears <u>has to do with flying.</u>

_____

10. Everyone in the office <u>takes a coffee break in the morning.</u>

_____

Everyone in the office <u>likes the new supervisor.</u>

_____

Exercise 10 | Editing a Paragraph for Subject-Verb Agreement

Practice

Edit the following paragraph by correcting any verbs that do not agree with their subjects. Write your corrections above the lines. There are five errors.

                                  has

    I wonder if anybody in the restaurant business have ever studied the effect of customers' rudeness on restaurant staff. Since I am a waiter myself, I know that nothing is more stressful to me than unhappy customers. Some customers enter the restaurant in a bad mood, and neither

                            is

friendly words nor a warm smile are enough to make them happy. When I seat them at a table, they want a different table. After I move them to another table, they become irritated at having to wait for a menu. Then

                                     displeases

everything on the menu, including the prices, displease them. After they

have gobbled up their meal, they start complaining again. They say there
was too many onions in the onion soup, and there were something wrong

_{were}

_{was}

with the cole slaw. By now, they are so loud that everyone at the tables

nearby is listening, and I am biting my tongue, trying to stay calm. I have

to be diplomatic until these customers depart, leaving me with a small tip

and a big load of stress.

Exercise 11

👥 Collaborate

Create Your Own Text on Subject-Verb Agreement

Complete this exercise with a partner or a group. Below is a list of rules on subject-verb agreement. Write one sentence that is an example of each rule. The first one is done for you.

Answers Will Vary.
Possible answers
shown at right.

Rule 1: Subjects and verbs should agree in number: singular subjects get singular verb forms, and plural subjects get plural verb forms.

example: A battered old car stands in the front yard.

Rule 2: When pronouns are used as subjects, they must agree in number with verbs.

example: We practice our dance routine on Friday afternoons.

Rule 3: Nothing in a prepositional phrase can be the subject of a sentence.

example: One of my brothers is a volunteer at the animal shelter.

Rule 4: Questions, sentences beginning with *here* or *there*, and other sentences can change word order, making subjects harder to find.

example: Here are the answers to your questions about the loan.

Rule 5: Compound subjects joined by *and* are usually plural.

example: The car and the truck need washing.

Rule 6: When subjects are joined by *or, either . . . or, neither . . . nor,* or *not only . . . but also,* the verb form agrees with the subject closest to the verb.

example: Neither the girls nor their brother is at home today.

Rule 7: Indefinite pronouns always take singular verbs.

example: At that restaurant, everything is expensive.

Rule 8: Collective nouns usually take singular verbs.

example: The company is recruiting at our college.

Using Pronouns Correctly: Agreement and Reference

NOUNS AND PRONOUNS

Nouns are the names of persons, places, or things.

> The band is from *Orlando*. (*Orlando* is the name of a place.)
> *Jack* is a good friend. (*Jack* is the name of a person.)
> I hated the *movie*. (*Movie* is the name of a thing.)

Pronouns are words that substitute for nouns. A pronoun's **antecedent** is the word or words it replaces.

> antecedent   pronoun
> *Jack* is a good friend; *he* is very loyal.

> antecdent   pronoun
> I hated the *movie* because *it* was too violent.

> antecedent   pronoun
> *Playing tennis* was fun, but *it* started to take up too much of my time.

> antecedent   pronoun
> *Mike and Michelle* are sure *they* are in love.

> antecedent   pronoun
> *Sharon* gave away *her* old clothes.

> antecedent   pronoun
> The *dog* rattled *its* dish, begging for dinner.

Exercise 1 **Identifying the Antecedents of Pronouns**

Practice Underline the word or words that are the antecedent of the italicized pronoun in each of the following sentences.

1. <u>Kim and I</u> are quitting tomorrow because *we* can't make enough money at the job.

2. <u>Riding a stationary bike</u> is good exercise because *it* strengthens leg muscles.

3. <u>My parents</u> said *they* couldn't afford to send me to college.

4. <u>The museum</u> presented *its* best collection last week.

5. <u>David</u>, can *you* ever forgive me?

6. <u>A small boy</u> learns a great deal by observing *his* father.

7. Alan loves <u>swimming</u>, but I am not fond of *it*.

8. We told <u>the security guard</u> we had lost our tickets, but *he* wouldn't let us in.

9. <u>The musicians</u> at the club play *their* last set at midnight.

10. <u>Constant criticism</u> is dangerous; in fact, *it* can destroy a person's confidence.

AGREEMENT OF A PRONOUN AND ITS ANTECEDENT

A pronoun must agree in number with its antecedent. If the antecedent is singular, the pronoun must be singular. If the antecedent is plural, the pronoun must be plural.

singular antecedent   **singular pronoun**
Susan tried to arrive on time, but *she* got caught in traffic.

plural antecedent   **plural pronoun**
Susan and Ray tried to arrive on time, but *they* got caught in traffic.

plural antecedent   **plural pronoun**
The visitors tried to arrive on time, but *they* got caught in traffic.

Agreement of pronoun and antecedent seems fairly simple. If an antecedent is singular, you use a singular pronoun. If an antecedent is plural, you use a plural pronoun. There are, however, some special problems with agreement of pronouns, and these problems will come up in your writing. If you become familiar with the explanations, examples, and exercises that follow, you will be ready to handle the special problems.

INDEFINITE PRONOUNS

Certain words called **indefinite pronouns** are always singular. Therefore, if an indefinite pronoun is the antecedent, the pronoun that replaces it must be singular.

Infobox			
Indefinite Pronouns			
one	nobody	nothing	each
anyone	anybody	anything	either
someone	somebody	something	neither
everyone	everybody	everything	

You may think that *everybody* is plural, but in grammatically correct English, *everybody* is a singular word. Therefore, if you want to write clearly and correctly, memorize the *-one*, *-thing*, and *-body* words: every*one*, every*thing*, every*body*, and so on, plus *each*, *either*, and *neither*. If any of these words is an antecedent, the pronoun that refers to it is singular.

singular antecedent   **singular pronoun**
Each of the Boy Scouts received *his* merit badge.

TEACHING TIP:
Most students will
want to use "their"
with "everyone."
Tell students to
look at the ending.
The word "one" is
singular, and it is thus
a reminder to use the
singular "his or her."

singular antecedent   singular pronoun
Everyone in the sorority donated *her* time to the project.

Avoiding Sexism

Consider this sentence:

Everybody in the math class brought _____ own calculator.

How do you choose the correct pronoun to fill in the blank? If everybody in the class is male, you can write

Everybody in the math class brought *his* own calculator.

Or if everybody in the class is female, you can write

Everybody in the math class brought *her* own calculator.

If the class has students of both sexes, you can write

Everybody in the math class brought *his or her* own calculator.

In the past, most writers used the pronoun *his* to refer to both men and women. Today, many writers try to use *his or her* to avoid sexism. If you find using *his or her* is getting awkward or repetitive, you can rewrite the sentence and make the antecedent plural:

correct: *The students* in the math class brought *their* own calculators.

But you cannot shift from singular to plural. You *cannot* write

incorrect: ~~Everybody in the math class brought their own calculators.~~

Exercise 2
Practice

Making Pronouns and Antecedents Agree

Write the appropriate pronoun in the blank in each sentence below. Look carefully for the antecedent before you choose the pronoun.

1. The hall closet is disorganized and messy; I really should clean ___it___.

2. Years ago, most people were careful with their cash; ___they___ were taught to save money, not to spend it.

3. I noticed that a woman was advertising a reward for the return of ___her___ engagement ring.

4. Some of the customers at the store use ___their___ credit cards whenever there is a sale.

5. When the little girl had a birthday party, ___she___ wanted to invite the whole neighborhood.

6. A boy with nothing to do all summer may wind up getting into trouble with

   ___his___ friends because he's bored.

7. Neither of the men chosen to lead the campaign wanted to devote ___his___ time to fund-raising.

8. Everyone named an Outstanding Mother of the Year had ___her___ own opinion about the ceremony.

9. Each of the brothers has won an athletic scholarship to the college of

    _____his_____ choice.

10. I am beginning to enjoy my exercise class; _____it_____ helps me relax.

11. You can give me anything from the sale book racks; _____it_____ will make a
    fine gift.

12. In the bleachers, somebody from the girls' club yelled _____her_____ loudest
    yell.

13. On Tuesdays, Mark and Larry take _____their_____ sons to school.

14. One of the cars costs too much; I could never afford _____it_____.

15. All the sisters at the reunion brought _____their_____ family pictures.

16. Everyone at the meeting of the American Association of University Women

    gave _____her_____ opinion of the speech.

17. My brother is very neat; he wants everthing on his shelves to be in

    _____its_____ place.

18. I think somebody from the Girl Scouts lost _____her_____ badge.

19. Nothing in the catalogs looked as if _____it_____ would fit in a small
    apartment.

20. Either of the boys can bring _____his_____ soccer ball to the field.

COLLECTIVE NOUNS

Collective nouns refer to more than one person or thing:

Some Collective Nouns

team	company	council
class	corporation	government
committee	family	group
audience	jury	crowd

Collective nouns usually take a singular pronoun:

collective noun   **singular pronoun**
The *team* that was ahead in the playoffs lost *its* home game.

collective noun   **singular pronoun**
The *corporation* changed *its* policy on parental leave.

Collective nouns are usually singular: the group as a whole is losing a game or
changing a policy. Collective nouns take a plural pronoun only when the members of the group are acting individually, not as a unit:

The *class* picked up *their* class rings this morning. (The members of the
class picked up their rings individually.)

Exercise 3 **Making Pronouns and Antecedents Agree: Collective Nouns**

Practice Circle the correct pronoun in parentheses in each sentence below.

1. The computer company has a reputation for being extremely generous to (their, *its*) employees.

2. Skyward Airlines was involved in a campaign to change (their, *its*) image.

3. The hiring committee deliberated for hours and then told the applicant (their, *its*) decision.

4. After the singer left the stage, the audience expressed (their, *its*) disappointment with boos and shouts.

5. Two of the teams were selling candy to raise money for (*their*, its) equipment.

6. The family lost (their, *its*) home in a fire last week.

7. I loved working at the Castle Company because (*it*, they) gave me such a generous package of benefits.

8. The club divided the responsibilities among (itself, *themselves*).

9. The general was worried that the army would not be able to hold (their, *its*) position.

10. The gang began to fall apart when the members quarreled among (*themselves*, itself).

Exercise 4 **Correcting Errors of Pronoun-Antecedent Agreement Within**

Practice **a Paragraph**

Read the following paragraph carefully, looking for errors in agreement of pronouns and their antecedents. Cross out each pronoun that does not agree with its antecedent and write the correct pronoun above it. There are five pronouns that need correcting.

The Paper Company is a great place to work. The managers are firm

but friendly in their relations with the employees, and working conditions

                                         its

are pleasant. The company has designed ~~their~~ policies to motivate

employees, not to intimidate them. Everybody in the workplace knows

he or she

~~they~~ will be treated fairly. The Paper Company is not only considerate of

workers; it is concerned for the environment. All the products are made

                                                its

of recyled paper. Thus, each of the items made for sale contributes ~~their~~

part to conservation. Workers and managers can feel good, knowing that

they
~~he or she~~ can help the planet. I wish everyone in this country would do
his or her
~~their~~ part, just as the Paper Company does.

Exercise 5

👥 Collaborate

Writing Sentences with Pronoun-Antecedent Agreement

Complete this exercise with a partner or a group. Write a sentence for each pair of words below, using each pair as a pronoun and its antecedent. The first pair is done for you.

1. women . . . their

   sentence: Women who work outside the home have to plan their time

   carefully.

2. council . . . its

   sentence: The homeowners' council prepared its annual report.

Answers Will Vary.
Possible answers
shown at right.

3. anyone . . . his or her

   sentence: Anyone in the neighborhood can bring his or her items to the

   garage sale.

4. celebrities . . . they

   sentence: When sports celebrities appear in public, they are often asked for

   autographs.

5. complaining . . . it

   sentence: Complaining is foolish; it rarely improves a situation.

6. neither . . . her

   sentence: Neither of the women has lost her sense of humor.

7. each . . . his or her

   sentence: Each of the contestants did his or her best to answer the

   questions.

8. Puerto Rico . . . it

   sentence: I grew up in Puerto Rico, and sometimes I am homesick for it.

9. television and video games . . . they

    sentence: <u>Television and video games can help children pass the time, but</u>

    <u>they can also help children waste time.</u>

10. daily exercise . . . it

    sentence: <u>My doctor told me to get some daily exercise because it would be</u>

    <u>good for my heart.</u>

PRONOUNS AND THEIR ANTECEDENTS: BEING CLEAR

Remember that pronouns are words that replace or refer to other words, and the words that are replaced or referred to are antecedents.

Make sure that a pronoun has one clear antecedent. Your writing will be vague and confusing if a pronoun appears to refer to more than one antecdent or if it doesn't have any specific antecedent to refer to. In grammar, such confusing language is called a problem with *reference of pronouns.*

When a pronoun refers to more than one thing, the sentence becomes confusing or silly. The following are examples of unclear reference:

Jim told his father his bike had been stolen. (Whose bike was stolen? Jim's? His father's?)

She put the cake on the table, took off her apron, pulled up a chair, and began to eat it. (What did she eat? The cake? The table? Her apron? The chair?)

If there is not a clear antecedent, you must rewrite the sentence to make the reference clear. Sometimes the rewritten sentence may seem repetitive, but a little repetition is better than a lot of confusion.

unclear: Jim told his father his bike had been stolen.
clear: Jim told his father Jim's bike had been stolen.
clear: Jim told his father his father's bike had been stolen.
clear: Jim told his father, "My bike has been stolen."

unclear: She put the cake on the table, took off her apron, pulled up a chair, and began to eat it.
clear: She put the cake on the table, took off her apron, pulled up a chair, and began to eat the cake.

Sometimes the problem is a little more tricky. Can you spot what's wrong with this sentence?

unclear: Bill decided to take a part-time job, which worried his parents. (What worried Bill's parents? His decision to work part time? Or the job itself?)

Be very careful with the pronoun *which.* If there is any chance that using *which* will confuse the reader, rewrite the sentence and get rid of *which.*

clear: Bill's parents were worried about the kind of part-time job he chose.
clear: Bill's decision to work part time worried his parents.

Sometimes, a pronoun has nothing to refer to; it has no antecedent.

> When Bill got to the train station, they said the train was going to be late. (Who said the train was going to be late? The ticket agents? Strangers Bill met on the tracks?)
>
> Maria has always loved medicine and has decided that's what she wants to be. (What does the word *that* refer to? The only word it could refer to is *medicine*, but Maria certainly doesn't want to be a medicine. She doesn't want to be an aspirin or a cough drop.)

If a pronoun lacks an antecedent, add an antecedent or get rid of the pronoun.

> **add an antecedent:** When Bill got to the train station and asked the ticket agents about the schedule, they said the train was going to be late.
>
> **drop the pronoun:** Maria has always loved medicine and has decided she wants to be a physician.

Note: To check for clear reference of pronouns, underline any pronoun that may not be clear. Then try to draw a line from that pronoun to its antecedent. Are there two or more possible antecedents? Is there no antecedent? In either case, you need to rewrite.

Exercise 6
Practice

Rewriting Sentences for Clear Reference of Pronouns

Rewrite the following sentences so that the pronouns have clear references. You may add, take out, or change words.

Answers Will Vary. Possible answers shown at right.

1. Ashley told Laura ~~she~~ *that Laura* had the messiest room in the dormitory.
2. Every time I go to Quick Mart, ~~they~~ *the clerks* are too busy gossiping on the phone to help me.
3. ~~I was offered a position at Express Service which pleased me.~~ *I was pleased to be offered a position at Express Service.*
4. I loved my visit to Mexico City; ~~they~~ *the Mexicans* are so friendly and warm.
5. My father is a successful salesman, but I am not interested in ~~it~~ *sales*.
6. Parents often fight with adolescent children because ~~they~~ *the children* are stubborn and inflexible.
7. The supervisor told the assistant ~~that his~~ *,"Your office will be moved to a new location."* ~~would~~ be moved to a new location.
8. The car crossed the median and hit a truck, but ~~it~~ *the truck* wasn't badly damaged.
9. ~~They~~ *The apartment manager* never told me about the fine print when I signed a lease for my apartment.
10. Ray accused Diane of starting the argument~~, which was silly~~ *the silly argument.*

23 Using Pronouns Correctly: Consistency and Case

When you write, you write from a point of view, and each point of view gets its own form. If you write from the first person point of view, your pronouns are in the *I* (singular) or *we* (plural) forms. If you write from the second person point of view, your pronouns are in the *you* form, whether they are singular or plural. If you write from the third person point of view, your pronouns are in the *he*, *she*, or *it* (singular) or *they* (plural) forms.

Different kinds of writing may require different points of view. When you are writing a set of directions, for example, you may use the second person *(you)* point of view. An essay about your childhood may use the first person *(I)* point of view.

Whatever point of view you use, be consistent in using pronouns. That is, you should not shift the form of your pronouns without some good reason.

> **not consistent:** Every time *I* go to that mall, the parking lot is so crowded *you* have to drive around for hours, looking for a parking space.
> **consistent:** Every time *I* go to that mall, the parking lot is so crowded *I* have to drive around for hours, looking for a parking space.

Exercise 1 Consistency in Pronouns

Practice

Correct any inconsistency in point of view in each sentence below. Cross out each incorrect pronoun and write the correct pronoun above it.

1. Birthdays, for me, are times when I can look back at what I've accomplished
   and plan ~~your~~ goals for the year ahead. *[my]*

2. When passengers board the plane, the flight attendant greets ~~you~~ with a *[them]*
   friendly smile.

3. Beginners should be careful when they cook soufflés; if ~~you~~ open the oven *[they]*
   at the wrong time, they will destroy the soufflé.

4. At my doctor's office, patients can wait for an hour before the doctor is
   them
   ready to see ~~you~~.

5. The law students filed into the auditorium, nervously waiting for the
   them
   proctors to enter and give ~~you~~ the three-hour exam.
   they
6. They were irritated by his conversation because ~~you~~ couldn't get a word

   into his endless chatter.
   we
7. Although we have our tires checked before a trip, ~~you~~ have to remember

   to have the belts checked also.
   she
8. As she drove her jeep through through the valley, the fog was so thick ~~you~~

   couldn't see the lights of the village.
   I
9. Every time I visit my sister's house, ~~you~~ know she's been cleaning and

   polishing all day.

10. The last time I ate at Billy's Barbecue, I thought the staff was so rude to
    me
    ~~you~~ that I swore I'd never eat there again.

Exercise 2   **Correcting Sentences with Consistency Problems**

Practice   Rewrite the following sentences, correcting any errors in consistency of pronouns. To make the corrections, you may have to change, add, or take out words.

1. You could smell autumn in the air when we walked through the woods.

   Answers Will Vary.
   Possible answers
   shown at right.

   rewrite: _I could smell autumn in the air when we walked through the woods._

   _____

2. My grandmother's house was a favorite with all the grandchildren; you
   knew you would always have fun there.

   rewrite: _My grandmother's house was a favorite with all the grandchildren;_

   they knew they would always have fun there.

3. A supervisor can gain respect if you treat all the workers fairly.

   rewrite: _A supervisor can gain respect if he or she treats all the workers_

   fairly.

4. Students who are just starting college can be overwhelmed by the reading
   assignments; you are not used to reading so much so quickly.

rewrite: Students who are just starting college can be overwhelmed by the reading assignments; they are not used to reading so much so quickly.

5. Public speaking was my favorite course; I enjoyed planning my presentation, the audience responding to you, and the feedback from my peers.

rewrite: Public speaking was my favorite course; I enjoyed planning my presentation, the audience responding to me, and the feedback from my peers.

6. I can't ask Miguel to help me because he'll talk your ear off about self-reliance.

rewrite: I can't ask Miguel to help me because he'll talk my ear off about self-reliance.

7. It doesn't matter how politely I try to explain my situation; she'll get angry with you every time.

rewrite: It doesn't matter how politely I try to explain my situation; she'll get angry with me every time.

8. Students who miss the test can take a makeup test only after the instructor decides you have a valid excuse.

rewrite: Students who miss the test can take a make-up test only after the instructor decides they have a valid excuse.

9. The worst thing about my job at the market is that you have to spend hours on your feet.

rewrite: The worst thing about my job at the market is that I have to spend hours on my feet.

10. If a worker genuinely cares about a pleasant work environment, you shouldn't gossip with co-workers.

rewrite: If a worker genuinely cares about a pleasant work environment, he or she shouldn't gossip with co-workers.

CHOOSING THE CASE OF PRONOUNS

Pronouns have forms that show number and person, and they also have forms that show **case**.

Singular Pronouns	Subjective Case	Objective Case	Possessive Case
1st person	I	me	my
2nd person	you	you	your
3rd person	he, she, it	him, her, it	his, her, its

Plural Pronouns

1st person	we	us	our
2nd person	you	you	your
3rd person	they	them	their

The rules for choosing the case of pronouns are simple:

1. When a pronoun is used as a subject, use the subjective case.
2. When a pronoun is used as the object of a verb or the object of a preposition, use the objective case.
3. When a pronoun is used to show ownership, use the possessive case.

pronouns used as subjects:

He practices his pitching every day.
Bill painted the walls, and *we* polished the floors.

pronouns used as objects:

Ernestine called *him* yesterday.
He gave all his money to *me*.

pronouns used to show possession:

I'm worried about *my* grade in Spanish.
The nightclub has lost *its* popularity.

Problems Choosing Pronoun Case

One time you need to be careful in choosing case is when the pronoun is part of a related group of words. If the pronoun is part of a related group of words, isolate the pronoun. Next, try out the pronoun choices. Then decide which pronoun is correct and write the correct sentence. For example, which of these sentences is correct?

Aunt Sophie planned a big dinner for Tom and *I*.

or

Aunt Sophie planned a big dinner for Tom and *me*.

Step 1: Isolate the pronoun. Eliminate the related words *Tom and*.

Step 2: Try each case:

Aunt Sophie planned a big dinner for *I*.

or

Aunt Sophie planned a big dinner for *me*.

Step 3: The correct sentence is

Aunt Sophie planned a big dinner for Tom and me.

The pronoun acts as an object, so it takes the objective case.

Try working through the steps once more, to be sure that you understand this principle. Which of the following sentences is correct?

Last week, *me* and my friend took a ride on the new commuter train.

or

Last week, *I* and my friend took a ride on the new commuter train.

Step 1: Isolate the pronoun. Eliminate the related words *and my friend*.

Step 2: Try each case:

Last week, *me* took a ride on the new commuter train.

or

Last week, *I* took a ride on the new commuter train.

Step 3: The correct sentence is

Last week, *I and my friend* took a ride on the new commuter train.

The pronoun acts as a subject, so it takes the subjective case.
Note: You can also write the sentence this way:

Last week *my friend and I* took a ride on the new commuter train.

COMMON ERRORS WITH CASE OF PRONOUNS

Be careful to avoid these common errors:

1. *Between* is a preposition, so the pronouns that follow it are objects of the preposition: between *us*, between *them*, between *you and me*. It is never correct to write *between you and I:*

   not this: ~~The plans for the surprise party must be kept secret between you and I.~~
   but this: The plans for the surprise party must be kept secret between you and me.

2. Never use *myself* as a replacement for *I* or *me:*

   not this: ~~My father and myself want to thank you for this honor.~~
   but this: My father and I want to thank you for this honor.

   not this: ~~She thought the prize should be awarded to Arthur and myself.~~
   but this: She thought the prize should be awarded to Arthur and me.

3. The possessive pronoun *its* has no apostrophe:

   not this: ~~The car held it's value.~~
   but this: The car held its value.

   not this: ~~The baby bird had fallen from it's nest.~~
   but this: The baby bird had fallen from its nest.

4. Pronouns that complete comparisons can be in the subjective, objective, or possessive case:

   subjective: Christa speaks better than *I.*
   objective: The storm hurt Manny more than *her.*
   possessive: My car is as fast as *his.*

To decide on the correct pronoun, add the words that complete the comparison and say them aloud:

Christa speaks better than I *speak.*
The storm hurt Manny more than *the storm hurt* her.
My car is as fast as his *car.*

Exercise 3 **Choosing the Right Case of Pronoun**

Practice Circle the correct pronoun in parentheses in each sentence below.

1. The elephant escaped when the trainer left (its, it's) cage open.

2. My co-workers and (I, myself) would like to arrange a formal meeting with the management.

3. When the neighbors couldn't get an answer, he kept calling Carla and (they, them) all night.

4. I like to cook, but Peter cooks better than (I, me).

5. Without a guidebook, Mr. Martinez and (she, her) were lost in the big city.

6. I promise not to mention what we discussed; our conversation will be strictly between you and (I, me).

7. The nominating committee selected two applicants from out of town and (me, myself) as finalists for the position.

8. My pickup truck is twelve years old; it's on (it's, its) last legs.

9. His comments about the proposal were unfairly critical of my staff and (myself, me).

10. The security officer and (we, us) looked all over for the missing car.

Exercise 4   **More on Choosing the Right Case of Pronouns**

Practice

Circle the correct pronoun in parentheses in each sentence below.

1. The job was a wonderful opportunity; it was a new beginning for (me, I) and him.

2. After dinner, Eliza and (her, she) went out for a walk.

3. Ms. Delgado was strict; however, my new boss is just as strict as (her, she).

4. Daniel is a more understanding person than (he, him).

5. My father gave a graduation party for my sisters and (I, me).

6. Although you look alike, your eyes are much darker than (him, his).

7. It's too bad that the investment has not held (its, it's) value.

8. I have an extra television, so I thought I would give it to my brother and (she, her).

9. I don't think the money was fairly distributed between Brian and (me, myself).

10. The girls and (I, me) visited a country store last weekend.

Exercise 5   **Write Your Own Text on Pronoun Case**

Working with a partner or a group, write two sentences that could be used as examples for each of the following rules. The first one is done for you.

> **Rule 1:** When a pronoun is used as a subject, use the subjective case.
>
> examples: He complained about the noise in the street.
>
> _____ Tired and hungry, they stopped for lunch. _____
>
> **Rule 2:** When a pronoun is used as the object of a verb or the object of a preposition, use the objective case.

Answers Will Vary.
Possible answers
shown at right.

> examples: Damien gave the tickets to me.
>
> The train took them to Philadelphia.
>
> **Rule 3:** When a pronoun is used to show ownership, use the possessive case.
>
> examples: The restaurant has changed its menu.
>
> Her mother is a state legislator.
>
> **Rule 4:** When a pronoun is part of a related group of words, isolate the pronoun to choose the case. (For examples, write two sentences in which the pronoun is part of a related group of words.)
>
> examples: He and Doug worked on the car all weekend.
>
> The new rule makes driving difficult for my father and me.

CHAPTER 24

Punctuation

You probably know a good deal about punctuating. In fact, you probably know most rules so well that you punctuate automatically, without having to think about the rules. Nevertheless, there are times when every writer has to stop and think, "Do I put a comma here?" or "Should I capitalize this word?" The following review of the basic rules of punctuation can help you answer such questions.

THE PERIOD

Periods are used in two ways:

1. Use a period to mark the end of a sentence that makes a statement:

   We invited him to dinner at our house.
   When Richard spoke, no one paid attention.

2. Use a period after an abbreviation:

   Mr. Ryan
   James Wing, Sr.
   10:00 p.m.

THE QUESTION MARK

Use a question mark after a direct question:

   Isn't my grandchild adorable?
   Do you have car insurance?

If a question is not a direct question, it does not get a question mark:

   They asked whether I thought their grandchild was adorable.
   She questioned whether I had car insurance.

THE SEMICOLON

There are two ways to use semicolons:

1. Use a semicolon to join two independent clauses.

Michael loved his old Camaro; he worked on it every weekend.
The situation was hopeless; I couldn't do anything.

Note: If the independent clauses are joined by a conjunctive adverb, you still need a semicolon. You will also need a comma after any conjunctive adverb that is more than one syllable long.

He was fluent in Spanish; consequently, he was the perfect companion for our trip to Venezuela.
I called the hotline for twenty minutes; then I called another number.

Independent clauses joined by coordinating conjunctions (the words *and, but, or, nor, for, yet, so*) do not need semicolons. Use a comma in front of the coordinating conjunction:

Michael loved his old Camaro, and he worked on it every weekend.
He was fluent in Spanish, so he was the perfect companion for our trip to Venezuela.

2. If a list contains commas, you may need semicolons to separate the items on the list, making the list easier to read.

examples:

The contestants came from Rochester, New York; Pittsburgh, Pennsylvania; Trenton, New Jersey; and Boston, Massachusetts. (The semicolons show that Rochester is a city in the state of New York, Pittsburgh is a city in the state of Pennsylvania, and so forth.)
The new officers of the club will be Althea Bethell, president; François Rivière, vice-president; Ricardo Perez, secretary; and Lou Phillips, treasurer. (The semicolons link the person Althea Bethell with the office of president, and so forth.)

Exercise 1 **Punctuating with Periods, Question Marks, and Semicolons**

Practice

Add any missing periods, question marks, and semicolons to the following sentences. Do not change or take out any existing punctuation marks; do not change small letters to capital letters. Some sentences do not need any additional punctuation.

1. *OK*
   The house needed cleaning and repair, and the back yard needed work, too.

2. Has John ever told you about his college days *?*

3. Linda asked me to stay with her *;* she was afraid to be alone in the house.

4. I am sure Dr *.* Welch is a reasonable man.

5. I don't know whether they are arriving tomorrow *.*

6. The day was cloudy and cool *;* nevertheless, we had a wonderful time at the beach.

7. Are they arriving tomorrow *?*

8. Sarah thinks they are coming in at around 4:00 p *.* m *.*, but I'm not sure.

9. You can have that dress; it doesn't fit me any more.

10. Julia asked me if I was going to the festival.

THE COMMA

There are four main ways to use a comma, as well as other, less important ways. *Memorize the four main ways.* If you can learn and understand these four rules, you will be more confident and correct in your punctuation. That is, you will use a comma only when you have a reason to do so; you will not be scattering commas in your sentences simply because you think a comma might fit, as many writers do.

The four main ways to use a comma are as a lister, a linker, an introducer, or an inserter (use two commas).

1. **Use a comma as a lister.** Commas support items in a series. These items can be words, phrases, or clauses:

   comma between words in a list: Her bedroom was decorated in shades of blue, green, and gold.
   comma between phrases in a list: I looked for my ring under the coffee table, between the sofa cushions, and behind the chairs.
   comma between clauses in a list: Last week he graduated from college, he found the woman of his dreams, and he won the lottery.

Note: In a list, the comma before *and* is optional, but most writers use it.

2. **Use a comma as a linker.** A comma and a coordinating conjunction link two independent clauses. The coordinating conjunctions are *and, but, or, nor, for, yet,* and *so.* The comma goes in front of the coordinating conjunction:

   I have to get to work on time, or I'll get into trouble with my boss.
   My mother gave me a beautiful card, and she wrote a note on it.

3. **Use a comma as an introducer.** Put a comma after introductory words, phrases, or clauses in a sentence:

   Yes, I agree with you on that issue.
   In the long run, you'll be better off without him.
   If you call home, your parents will be pleased.

4. **Use a comma as an inserter.** When words or phrases that are *not* necessary are inserted into a sentence, put a comma on *both* sides of the inserted material.

   The game, unfortunately, was rained out.
   My test score, believe it or not, was the highest in the class.
   Potato chips, my favorite snack food, are better tasting when they're fresh.
   James, caught in the middle of the argument, tried to keep the peace.

Using commas as inserters requires that you decide what is essential to the meaning of the sentence and what is nonessential. Here is the rule:

> **If you do not need material in a sentence, put commas around the material. If you need material in a sentence, do not put commas around the material.**

For example, consider this sentence:

> The girl who called me was selling magazine subscriptions.

Do you need the words *who called me* to understand the meaning of the sentence? To answer that question, write the sentence without those words:

> The girl was selling magazine subscriptions.

Reading the shorter sentence, you might ask, "Which girl?" The words *who called me* are essential to the sentence. Therefore you do not put commas around them.

> **correct:** The girl who called me was selling magazine subscriptions.

Remember that the proper name of a person, place, or thing is always sufficient to identify it. Therefore any information that follows a proper name is inserted material; it gets commas on both sides.

> Video Views, which is nearby, has the best prices for video rentals.
> Sam Harris, the man who won the marathon, lives on my block.

Remember the four main ways to use a comma—as a lister, linker, introducer, or inserter—and you'll solve many of your problems with punctuation.

TEACHING TIP:
To emphasize the difference between essential and nonessential information, write the following sentence on the board: "My grandmother who rides a motorcycle is eighty." Inserting commas implies the writer has one grandmother; omitting commas implies the writer has two grandmothers.

Exercise 2
Practice

Punctuating with Commas: The Four Main Ways

Add commas only where they are needed in the following sentences. Do not add any other punctuation, and do not change any existing punctuation. Some of the sentences do not need commas.

1. Whether you like it or not, you have to get up early tomorrow.

2. Nancy and I decorated our dorm room with pillows, curtains, posters, and rugs.

3. I was forced to call the emergency towing service and wait two hours for help. OK

4. The two-story house by the lake is the most attractive one in the neighborhood. OK

5. Chicken Delights, the only restaurant in my neighborhood, is always crowded on a Saturday night.

6. No, you can't get a bus to the city on Saturdays unless you are prepared to leave early.

7. Dripping wet and miserable, I crouched under a huge tree until the rain stopped.

8. Nick got a job right after college, for he had spent his senior year making contacts and sending applications.

9. I wanted to look professional for my job interview, so I wore a conservative suit.

10. Cleaning the kitchen is a chore because I have to scrub the sink, wipe the counters, empty the trash, and wash the floor.

Other Ways to Use a Comma

There are other places to use a comma. Reviewing these uses will help you feel more confident as a writer.

1. **Use commas with quotations.** Use a comma to set off a direct quotation from the rest of the sentence:

   My father told me, "Money doesn't grow on trees."
   "Let's split the bill," Raymond said.

Note that the comma that introduces the quotation goes before the quotation marks. But once the quotation has begun, commas or periods go inside the quotation marks.

2. **Use commas with dates and addresses.** Use commas between the items in dates and addresses:

   August 5, 1950, is Chip's date of birth.
   We lived at 133 Emerson Road, Lake Park, Pennsylvania, before we
       moved to Florida.

Notice the comma after the year in the date and the comma after the state in the address. These commas are needed when you write a date or address within a sentence.

3. **Use commas in numbers.** Use commas in numbers of one thousand or larger.

   The price of equipment was $1,293.

4. **Use commas for clarity.** Add a comma when you need it to make something clear.

   Whoever it is, is about to be punished.
   While hunting, the eagle is swift and strong.
   I don't like to dress up, but in this job I have to, to get ahead.

Exercise 3   **Punctuation: Other Ways to Use a Comma**

Practice   Add commas only where they are needed in the following sentences. Do not add any other punctuation, and do not change any existing punctuation.

1. Mr. Chen used to say "Every cloud has a silver lining."

2. My best friend was born on January 29 1976 in Philadelphia Pennsylvania.

3. "I would never borrow your car without asking first" my little brother asserted.

4. She bit into the apple and mumbled "This is the best apple I've ever tasted."

5. I graduated from Deerfield High School on June 19 1995 and started my

   first real job on June 19 1996 in the same town.

6. The repairs on my truck cost me $2392.

7. The Reilly mansion across town is selling for $359000.

8. The first graders dressed as trees danced in in leotards covered with paper leaves.

9. On April 14, 1999, my father warned me, "Don't forget to mail your income tax forms."

10. "Nothing exciting ever happens around here," my cousin complained.

Exercise 4 **Punctuating with Commas: A Comprehensive Exercise**

Practice

Add commas only where they are needed in the following sentences. Do not add any other punctuation, and do not change any existing punctuation. Some of the sentences do not need commas.

1. I wanted a fabric with gray, white, and navy in it, but I had to settle for one with gray and white.

2. He was born on July 15, 1970, in a small town in Ohio.

3. I am sure, Jeffrey, that you are not telling me the whole story.

4. The family wanted to spend a quiet weekend at home but ended up doing errands all over town. OK

5. My miniature poodle, a truly crazy dog, is afraid of the vacuum cleaner.

6. She devoted an entire day to cleaning the kitchen cabinets, reorganizing the pantry shelves, and scrubbing the hall floor.

7. The man who wrote you is a friend of mine. OK

8. Whether David likes it or not, he has to work overtime again.

9. "Get out your notebooks," the teacher said.

10. Honestly, I can't say which is a better buy.

11. I tried to reason with her, I tried to warn her, and I even tried to frighten her, but she was determined to proceed with her plans.

12. Pizza Pronto, my favorite restaurant, is going out of business.

13. We can call him tomorrow or stop by his house. OK

14. For the third time, the child whispered, "Mommy, I want to go home now."

15. People who have never seen the ocean are not prepared for its beauty. OK

16. My sister is in two important ways the opposite of my mother. OK

17. In two important ways, my sister is the opposite of my mother.

18. The visitors were friendly and polite, yet they seemed a little shy.

19. If you lose, lose with style and class.

20. The car in the garage doesn't belong to me, nor do I have permission to borrow it.

THE APOSTROPHE

Note: This is a good place to tell students that contractions are usually omitted in formal writing such as research papers, business letters, and legal documents. Remind students that they should always check with their instructors to see whether contractions are acceptable in their writing assignments.

Note: Non-native speakers may have difficulty recognizing the verb in a contraction. See the ESL Appendix.

Note: Some students have learned that the proper way to indicate possession for proper names ending in "s" is to add "'s." You can assure students that either James' or James's, for example, is correct. However, you can also note that newspapers and magazines have their own style sheets and preferences for writers to follow.

Use the apostrophe in the following ways:

1. Use an apostrophe in contractions to show that letters have been omitted:

do not = don't
I will = I'll
is not = isn't
she would = she'd
will not = won't

Use an apostrophe to show that numbers have been omitted:

the summer of 1998 = the summer of '98

2. Use an apostrophe to show possession. If a word does not end in *s,* show ownership by adding an apostrophe and *-s.*

the ring belongs to Jill = Jill's ring
the wallet belongs to somebody = somebody's wallet
the books are owned by my father = my father's books

If two people jointly own something, put the *-'s* on the last person's name.

Ann and Mike own a house = Ann and Mike's house

If a word already ends in *s* and you want to show ownership, just add an apostrophe:

the ring belongs to Frances = Frances' ring
two boys own a dog = the boys' dog
the house belongs to Ms. Jones = Ms. Jones' house

3. Use the apostrophe for special uses of time and to create a plural of numbers mentioned as numbers, letters mentioned as letters, and words that normally do not have plurals:

special uses of time: It will take a week's work.
numbers mentioned as numbers: Take out the 5's.
letters mentioned as letters: Cross your *t*'s.
words that normally do not have plurals: I want no more *maybe*'s.

Caution: Be careful with apostrophes. These words, the possessive pronouns, do not take apostrophes: *his, hers, theirs, ours, yours, its.*

not this: ~~The pencils were their's.~~
but this: The pencils were theirs.

not this: ~~The steak lost it's flavor.~~
but this: The steak lost its flavor.

Do not add an apostrophe to a simple plural.

not this: ~~He lost three suitcase's.~~
but this: He lost three suitcases.

Exercise 5 **Using Apostrophes**

Practice

Circle the correct form in parentheses in each sentence below.

1. Carmen will never forget the blizzard of (94, **'94**).

2. The television lost (**its**, it's) picture.

3. My dog found (someones, someone's) cap.

4. I worked at a hotel for three (summers, summer's).

5. My town (doesnt, doesn't) have a movie theater.

6. Ernie borrowed (Bill's and David's, Bill and David's) lawn mower.

7. The hospital has (its, it's) own cafeteria.

8. I had a (months, month's) vacation saved up.

9. Someone stole the two (boy's, boys') backpacks, and the boys were left stranded.

10. I do not want to hear any more (nos, no's) from you.

11. The ladder belongs to (Charles, Charle's).

12. The police are checking (everyones, everyone's) identification.

13. We are going to the (men's, mens') tennis tournament.

14. Sarah is a wonderful painter; I wish I had half that (womans, woman's) talent.

15. I must have had thirty phone (calls, call's) yesterday.

16. My sister was disappointed by the (apartments, apartment's) small kitchen.

17. The attorney needs to interview (Mr. Harris, Mr. Harris') wife.

18. The beautiful green parrot was (her's, hers).

19. The city never loses (its, it's) charm.

20. Several (residents, resident's) patrol the neighborhood.

Exercise 6	**Punctuating with Apostrophes**

Practice

Add apostrophes where they are needed in the following sentences. Some sentences do not need apostrophes.

1. I'm sure Morris' intentions were good.

2. That movie sure doesn't live up to its reputation.

3. I love my cousins, but I disagree with their political views. OK

4. I was sure that the items recovered in the police raid would turn out to be ours. OK

5. I was surprised by Dallas' glass buildings and its network of highways.

6. Professor Lyons is an expert in the field of children's rights.

7. She had lost the women's tickets.

8. I know shes not interested in aerobics.

9. Theyll take the train to Jim and Davids house.

10. I can give the boys advice, but the problem is still theirs. OK

11. Sean writes his 7s with a line through the middle, so his numbers are difficult to read.

12. It's hard to know when somethings wrong with my car because it always makes strange noises.

13. Toms sister has a precise way of pronouncing her *b*s.

14. The casserole dishes were ours; the salad plates were theirs. OK

15. Leon cant make it to Sylvia and Richards party; its on the same day as his fathers birthday.

16. Whos making the arrangements for the conference on womens sports?

17. You have too many *ands* in your sentence.

18. Elvis Presley was a famous singer for the 50s generation.

19. In a years time, I will have finished my education and started my career.

20. Flowers make good gifts for holidays. OK

THE COLON

A colon is used at the end of a complete statement. It introduces a list or an explanation:

> **colon introduces a list:** When I went grocery shopping, I picked up a few things: milk, eggs, and coffee.
> **colon introduces an explanation:** The room was a mess: dirty clothes were piled on the chairs, wet towels were thrown on the floor, and an empty pizza box was tossed in the closet.

Remember that the colon comes after a complete statement. What comes after the colon explains or describes what came before the colon. Look once more at the two examples, and you'll see the point:

> When I went grocery shopping, I picked up a few things: milk, eggs, and coffee. (The words after the colon—*milk, eggs, and coffee*—explain what few things I picked up.)

> The room was a mess: dirty clothes were piled on the chairs, wet towels were thrown on the floor, and an empty pizza box was tossed in the closet. (In this sentence, all the words after the colon describe what the mess was like.)

Some people use a colon every time they put a list in a sentence, but this is not a good rule to follow. Instead, remember that a colon, even one that introduces a list, must come after a complete statement:

> **not this:** ~~When I go to the beach, I always bring: suntan lotion, a big towel, and a cooler with iced tea.~~
> **but this:** When I go to the beach, I always bring my supplies: suntan lotion, a big towel, and a cooler with iced tea.

A colon may also introduce long quotations:

> In a letter to a woman who had lost several sons in the Civil War, Abraham Lincoln said: "I feel how weak and fruitless must be any words of mine which should attempt to beguile you from the grief of a loss so overwhelming. But I cannot refrain from tendering to you the consolation that may be found in the thanks of the Republic they died to save."

THE EXCLAMATION MARK

The exclamation mark is used at the end of sentences that express strong emotion:

> **appropriate:** You've won the lottery!
> **inappropriate:** We had a great time! (*Great* already implies excitement.)

Be careful not to overuse the exclamation mark. If your choice of words is descriptive, you should not have to rely on the exclamation point for emphasis. Use it sparingly, for it is easy to rely on exclamations instead of using better vocabulary.

THE DASH

Use a dash to interrupt a sentence. It usually indicates a dramatic shift in tone or thought:

> I picked up the crystal bowl carefully, cradled it in my arms, walked softy—and tripped, sending the bowl flying.

Two dashes set off dramatic words that interrupt a sentence:

> Ramon took the life preserver—our only one—and tossed it far out to sea.

Since dashes are somewhat dramatic, use them sparingly.

PARENTHESES

Use parentheses to enclose extra material and afterthoughts:

> I was sure that Ridgefield (the town I'd just visited) was not the place for me.
> Her name (which I have just remembered) was Celestine.

Note: Commas in pairs, dashes in pairs, and parentheses are all used as inserters. They set off material that interrupts the flow of the sentence. The least dramatic and smoothest way to insert material is to use commas.

THE HYPHEN

A hyphen joins two or more descriptive words that act as a single word:

> The old car had a souped-up engine.
> Bill was a smooth-talking charmer.

Exercise 7 **Punctuating with Colons, Exclamation Marks, Dashes, Parentheses,**
Practice **and Hyphens**

In the sentences below, add any missing colons, exclamation marks, dashes, parentheses, and hyphens.

1. His plan for making a million dollars was the most lame-brained scheme I'd ever heard.

2. The Carlton Gallery of Fine Art (the place where I had my first job) is located east of the river. (*or dashes*)

3. My nephew can't go anywhere without his collection of stuffed animals: two panda bears, a purple dinosaur, and a pink alligator.

4. Rosa could tell that the speaker was nervous: he fidgeted with his notes, stumbled over his words, and blushed beet red.

5. I am so angry I could just scream!

6. The man in the tuxedo approached the princess, bowed gracefully, kissed her hand — then smashed a cream pie in her face.

7. Cocoa Forest (the smallest town in Midland County) is best known for its Victorian houses and restored town square. (*or dashes*)

8. Don't you ever speak to me like that again!

9. There are two kinds of desserts: desserts that are good for you and desserts that taste good.

10. She grabbed the gun — her only hope — and fired.

QUOTATION MARKS

Use quotation marks for direct quotations, for the titles of short works, and for other special uses.

1. Put quotation marks around direct quotations that repeat a speaker's or writer's exact words:

   My mother told me, "There are plenty of fish in the sea."
   "I'm never going there again," said Irene.
   "I'd like to buy you dinner," Peter said, "but I'm out of cash."
   My best friend warned me, "Stay away from that guy. He will break your heart."

Look carefully at the preceding examples. Notice that a comma is used to introduce a direct quotation and that at the end of the quotation, the comma or period goes inside the quotation marks:

   My mother told me, "There are plenty of fish in the sea."

Notice how direct quotations of more than one sentence are punctuated. If the quotation is written in one unit, quotation marks go before the first quoted word and after the last quoted word:

   My best friend warned me, "Stay away from that guy. He will break your heart."

But if the quotation is not written as one unit, the punctuation changes:

"Stay away from that guy," my best friend warned me. "He will break your heart."

Caution: Do *not* put quotation marks around indirect quotations:

indirect quotation: He asked if he could come with us.
direct quotation: He asked, "May I come with you?"

indirect quotation: She said that she wanted more time.
direct quotation: "I want more time," she said.

2. Put quotation marks around the titles of short works. If you are writing the title of a short work like a short story, an essay, a newspaper or magazine article, a poem, or a song, put quotation marks around the title:

In middle school, we read Robert Frost's poem "The Road Not Taken."
My little sister has learned to sing "Itsby Bitsy Spider."

If you are writing the title of a longer work like a book, movie, magazine, play, television show, or CD, underline the title:

Last night I saw an old movie, <u>Stand By Me.</u>
I read an article called "Campus Crime" in <u>Newsweek.</u>

In printed publications such as books or magazines, titles of long works are put in italics. But when you are handwriting, typing, or using a word processor, underline the titles of long works.

3. There are other, special uses of quotation marks. You may use quotation marks around words mentioned as words in a sentence:

When you said "never," did you mean it?
People from the Midwest pronounce "water" differently than I do.

If you are using a quotation within a quotation, use single quotation marks:

My brother complained, "Every time we get in trouble, Mom has to say 'I told you so.' "
Kyle said, "Linda has a way of saying 'Excuse me' that is really very rude."

CAPITAL LETTERS

There are ten main situations in which you capitalize.

1. Capitalize the first word of every sentence:

Yesterday we saw our first soccer game.

2. Capitalize the first word in a direct quotation if the word begins a sentence:

My aunt said, "This is a gift for your birthday."
"Have some birthday cake," my aunt said," and have some more ice cream." (Notice that the second section of this quotation does not begin with a capital letter because it does not begin a sentence.)

3. Capitalize the names of persons:

Nancy Perez and Frank Murray came to see me at the store.
I asked Mother to feed my cat.

Do not capitalize words like *mother*, *father*, or *aunt* if you put a possessive in front of them:

> I asked my mother to feed my cat.

4. Capitalize the titles of persons:

> I was a patient of Dr. Wilson.
> He has to see Dean Johnston.

Do not capitalize when the title is not connected to a name:

> I was a patient of that doctor.
> He has to see the dean.

5. Always capitalize nationalities, religions, races, months, days of the week, documents, organizations, holidays, and historical events or periods:

> In high school, we never studied the Vietnam War, just the Civil War.
> The Polish-American Club will hold a picnic on Labor Day.

Use small letters for the seasons:

> I love fall because I love to watch the leaves change color.

6. Capitalize the names of particular places:

> We used to hold our annual meetings at Northside Auditorium in Springfield, Iowa, but this year we are meeting at Riverview Theater in Langton, Missouri.

Use small letters if a particular place is not given:

> We are looking for an auditorium we can rent for our meeting.

7. Use capital letters for geographic locations:

> Jim was determined to find a good job in the West.

But use small letters for geographic directions:

> To get to my house, you have to drive west on the turnpike.

8. Capitalize the names of specific products:

> I always drink Diet Pepsi for breakfast.

But use small letters for a kind of product:

> I always drink a diet cola for breakfast.

9. Capitalize the names of specific school courses:

> I have to take Child Psychology 101 next term.

But use small letters for a general academic subject:

> My advisor told me to take a child psychology course.

10. Capitalize the first and last words in the titles of long or short works, and capitalize all other significant words in the titles:

> I've always wanted to read <u>The Old Man and the Sea.</u>
> Whenever we go to see the team play, my uncle sings "Take Me Out to the Ballgame."

(Remember that the titles of long works, like books, are underlined; the titles of short ones, like songs, are quoted.)

Exercise 8 **Punctuating with Quotation Marks, Underlining, and Capital Letters**

Practice In the sentences below, add any missing quotation marks, underlining, and capital letters.

1. "Don't ever call me again," the repairman said, "unless it's an emergency."

2. No one expected <u>Home Alone</u> to be such a popular movie, but it broke all box office records at the Sunset ~~mall~~ M ~~theaters~~ T.

3. "James, you should be careful what you wish for," my aunt said, "because you may get it."

4. That old word "jock" is mistakenly applied to anyone who likes sports.

5. My sisters all attended Broward Community ~~college~~ C, but I'm going to a community college in the ~~midwest~~ M.

6. When I was a growing up, my favorite television show was <u>Charles in Charge</u>, but now I love to watch old movies like <u>Rocky</u> or <u>The Breakfast Club</u>.

7. Yesterday I tried to buy tickets for the concert at the ~~coral~~ C ~~beach~~ B ~~amphitheater~~ A, but the man at the ticket office said, ~~we're~~ W sold out.

8. "You always say 'I'm sorry' but you never mean it," my boyfriend complained.

9. I told ~~uncle~~ U Phil to be on time, but my uncle is a procrastinator.

10. Next semester I'm taking courses in speech, business, and economics. OK

NUMBERS

Spell out numbers that take one or two words:

> Alice mailed two hundred brochures.
> I spent ninety dollars on car repairs.

Use the numbers themselves if it takes more than two words to spell them out:

> We looked through 243 old photographs.
> The sticker price was $10,397.99.

Also use numbers to write dates, times, and addresses:

> We live at 24 Cambridge Street.
> They were married on April 3, 1993.

ABBREVIATIONS

Although you should spell out most words rather than abbreviate them, you may abbreviate *Mr.*, *Mrs.*, *Ms.*, *Jr.*, *Sr.*, and *Dr.* when they are used with a proper name. You should abbreviate references to time and to organizations widely known by initials.

The moderator asked Ms. Steinem to comment.
The bus left at 5:00 p.m., and the trip took two hours.
He works for the FBI.

You should spell out the names of places, months, days of the week, courses of study, and words referring to parts of a book:

> **not this:** ~~I missed the last class, so I never got the notes for Chap. Three.~~
> **but this:** I missed the last class, so I never got the notes for Chapter Three.

> **not this:** ~~He lives on Chestnut Street in Boston, Mass.~~
> **but this:** He lives on Chestnut Street in Boston, Massachusetts.

> **not this:** ~~Pete missed his trig. test~~.
> **but this:** Pete missed his trigonometry test.

Exercise 9
Practice

A Comprehensive Exercise on Punctuation

Add any missing punctuation to the following sentences. Correct any errors in capitalization and in use of numbers or abbreviations.

1. My sister had a hard time meeting her three boys' demands for attention' but she did her best.

2. The people at the store were extremely helpful' furthermore' they were willing to handle special orders.

3. Turquoise blue' which is my favorite color' is being used to decorate many restaurants.

4. " Every time I study with you' she said' I get good grades on my tests. "

5. Parents should be willing to listen' children should be willing to talk' and both groups should be open to new ideas if families are going to live in harmony.

6. Repairing the damages caused by the fire cost $357. ~~three hundred and fifty-seven dollars~~.

7. Most people have trouble hitting the high notes in "The Star-Spangled B " ~~b~~anner. "

8. Don't forget to pick up the food we need for the picnic' hamburgers' hot dogs' potato salad' and corn.

9. No one told Jose about the job opening' so he didn't apply for the position.

10. Leo was born in Philadelphia Penn. , Pennsylvania, on June 3' 1968' and he grew up in a nearby town.

11. Christina Ruggiero' who always sends me a birthday card' is a considerate and thoughtful person.

12. We were sure that' rain or shine' he would be there.

13. I'm sorry, Dad, that I was late for James' farewell dinner.

14. Unless you replace those worn-out tires, you can't drive safely on rain-slicked roads.

15. Philip asked, "Is there a shortcut to the warehouse?"

16. Philip asked if there was a shortcut to the warehouse.

17. When he was in high school he took English courses but at Jackson College he is taking communications courses.

18. The girl running across the ice slipped and fell; then she grabbed at a fence post and pulled herself up.

19. Bolton Furniture has kept its reputation for quality merchandise at a reasonable price; thus it's been able to survive in hard times.

20. I'm thinking of writing a book called How To Manage Your Time, but I never seem to have time to write it.

CHAPTER 25

Spelling

No one is a perfect speller, but there are ways to become a better speller. If you can learn a few spelling rules, you can answer many of your spelling questions.

VOWELS AND CONSONANTS

To understand the spelling rules, you need to know the difference between vowels and consonants. **Vowels** are the letters *a, e, i, o, u,* and sometimes *y.* **Consonants** are all the other letters.

The letter *y* is a vowel when it has a vowel sound:

silly	(The *y* sounds like *ee,* a vowel sound.)
cry	(The *y* sounds like *i,* a vowel sound.)

The letter *y* is a consonant when it has a consonant sound:

yellow	(The *y* has a consonant sound.)
yesterday	(The *y* has a consonant sound.)

SPELLING RULE 1: DOUBLING A FINAL CONSONANT

Double the final consonant of a word if all three of the following are true:

1. The word is one syllable, or the accent is on the last syllable,
2. The word ends in a single consonant preceded by a single vowel, and
3. The ending you are adding starts with a vowel.

begin	+	ing	=	beginning
shop	+	er	=	shopper
stir	+	ed	=	stirred
occur	+	ed	=	occurred
fat	+	est	=	fattest
pin	+	ing	=	pinning

Exercise 1 **Doubling a Final Consonant**

Practice Add -*ed* to the following words, applying the rule for doubling a final consonant.

1. murmur	murmured	6. repel	repelled
2. pet	petted	7. repeal	repealed
3. wait	waited	8. bat	batted
4. order	ordered	9. compel	compelled
5. commit	committed	10. confer	conferred

SPELLING RULE 2: DROPPING THE FINAL *e*

Drop the final *e* before you add an ending that starts with a vowel:

observe	+	ing	=	observing
excite	+	able	=	excitable
fame	+	ous	=	famous
create	+	ive	=	creative

Keep the final *e* before an ending that starts with a consonant:

love	+	ly	=	lovely
hope	+	ful	=	hopeful
excite	+	ment	=	excitement
life	+	less	=	lifeless

Exercise 2
Practice

Dropping the Final *e*

Combine the following words and endings, following the rules for dropping the final *e*.

1. exterminate	+	tion	extermination
2. forgive	+	able	forgivable
3. advise	+	ment	advisement
4. grace	+	ful	graceful
5. place	+	ing	placing
6. blame	+	less	blameless
7. offense	+	ive	offensive
8. definite	+	ly	definitely
9. adore	+	able	adorable
10. refuse	+	ing	refusing

SPELLING RULE 3: CHANGING THE FINAL *y* TO *i*

When a word ends in a consonant plus *y*, change the *y* to *i* when you add an ending:

try	+	es	=	tries
silly	+	er	=	sillier

rely	+	ance	=	reliance
tardy	+	ness	=	tardiness

Note: When you add *-ing* to words ending in *y*, always keep the *y*:

cry	+	ing	=	crying
rely	+	ing	=	relying

Exercise 3 **Changing the Final *y* to *i***

Practice

Combine the following words and endings, applying the rules for changing the final *y* to *i*.

1. happy   +   er   <u>happier</u>

2. betray   +   ing   <u>betraying</u>

3. play   +   er   <u>player</u>

4. pity   +   less   <u>pitiless</u>

5. marry   +   ed   <u>married</u>

6. sky   +   es   <u>skies</u>

7. defy   +   ance   <u>defiance</u>

8. comply   +   ant   <u>compliant</u>

9. hearty   +   ness   <u>heartiness</u>

10. supply   +   ing   <u>supplying</u>

SPELLING RULE 4: ADDING -s OR -es

Add *-es* instead of *-s* to a word if the word ends in *ch*, *sh*, *ss*, *x*, or *z*. The *-es* ending adds an extra syllable to the word.

box	+	es	=	boxes
witch	+	es	=	witches
class	+	es	=	classes
clash	+	es	=	clashes

Exercise 4 **Adding *-s* or *-es***

Practice

Apply the rule for adding *-s* or *-es* to the following words.

1. banish   <u>banishes</u>   6. tax   <u>taxes</u>

2. defeat   <u>defeats</u>   7. pass   <u>passes</u>

3. lurch   <u>lurches</u>   8. rash   <u>rashes</u>

4. stock   <u>stocks</u>   9. relax   <u>relaxes</u>

5. express   <u>expresses</u>   10. catch   <u>catches</u>

SPELLING RULE 5: USING *ie* OR *ei*

Use *i* before *e*, except after *c*, or when the sound is like *a*, as in *neighbor* and *weigh*.

i before e:

relief   conscience   friend   piece

e before i:

conceive   sleigh   weight   receive

Exercise 5 **Using *ie* or *ei***

Practice

Apply the rule for using *ie* or *ei* in the following words.

1. conc_e__i_t

2. _e__i_ghty

3. profic_i__e_nt

4. bel_i__e_f

5. cash_i__e_r

6. gr_i__e_f

7. c_e__i_ling

8. p_i__e_ce

9. rel_i__e_ve

10. dec_e__i_ve

Exercise 6 **Spelling Rules: A Comprehensive Exercise**

Practice

Combine the following words and endings, applying the spelling rules.

1. occur   +   ed   occurred

2. carry   +   ed   carried

3. fizz   +   s *or* es   fizzes

4. snappy   +   er   snappier

5. flash   +   s *or* es   flashes

6. glass   +   s *or* es   glasses

7. trip   +   ed   tripped

8. ready   +   ness   readiness

9. rely   +   able   reliable

10. concur   +   ed   concurred

11. render   +   ed   rendered

12. ignite   +   ion   ignition

13. shame   +   ful   shameful

14. relate   +   ive   relative

15.	encourage	+	ment	encouragement
16.	cry	+	es	cries
17.	annoy	+	ance	annoyance
19.	match	+	s _or_ es	matches
20.	prefer	+	ed	preferred

Exercise 7 **Editing a Paragraph for Spelling**

Practice

Correct the spelling errors in the following paragraph. Write your correction above each error. There are eleven errors.

                                               relieved

When I took my first college math class, I was releived to discover that I could handle the material and the teaching method. I had expected
boxes
to have so much homework that I would have to carry it home in boxs. I
assignments   _easier_
do have regular assignmentes, but they are easyer than I thought, and I
carrying
am not carring home crates of math problems. In class, my teacher is
famous
patient, clear, and very funny. He is fameous for his sense of humor, and
excitement
his energy brings excitment to the classroom. In addition, he never
vanishes
vanishs after class; he goes to his office where he gives extra help to students. With my instructor's help and my own consistent effort, I am doing
hopeful   _experience_
better than I had expected. I am hopful that my expereince in this class is
beginning
the begining of a wonderful college career.

DO YOU SPELL IT AS ONE WORD OR TWO?

Sometimes you can be confused about certain words. You are not sure whether to combine them to make one word or to spell them as two words.

Words That Should Not Be Combined

a lot	each other	high school	every time
even though	good night	in front	no one
living room	dining room	all right	

Words That Should Be Combined

another	newspapers	bathroom
bedroom	playroom	good-bye, goodbye, or good-by
bookkeeper	roommate	cannot
schoolteacher	downstairs	southeast, northwest, etc.
grandmother	throughout	nearby
worthwhile	nevertheless	yourself, himself, etc.

Words Whose Spelling Depends on Their Meaning

TEACHING TIP:
Emphasize that computer spell-checks will not be able to distinguish whether one-word or two-word spellings are correct. Students who say that the spelling is fine since "I ran it through my spell-check program" are usually surprised when the instructor finds several spelling errors.

one word: *Already* means "before."
  He offered to do the dishes, but I had *already* done them.
two words: *All ready* means "ready."
  My dog was *all ready* to play Frisbee.

one word: *Altogether* means "entirely."
  That movie was *altogether* too confusing.
two words: *All together* means "in a group."
  My sisters were *all together* in the kitchen.

one word: *Always* means "every time."
  My grandfather is *always* right about baseball statistics.
two words: *All ways* means "every path" or "every aspect."
  We tried *all ways* to get to the beach house.
  He is a gentleman in *all ways*.

one word: *Anymore* means "any longer."
  I do not want to exercise *anymore*.
two words: *Any more* means "additional."
  Are there *any more* pickles?

one word: *Anyone* means "any person at all."
  Is *anyone* home?
two words: *Any one* means "one person or thing in a special group."
  I'll take *any one* of the chairs on sale.

one word: *Apart* means "separate."
  Liam stood *apart* from his friends.
two words: *A part* is a piece or section.
  I read *a part* of the chapter.

one word: *Everyday* means "ordinary."
  Tim was wearing his *everyday* clothes.
two words: *Every day* means "each day."
  Sam jogs *every day*.

one word: *Everyone* means "all the people."
  Everyone has bad days.
two words: *Every one* means "all the people or things in a specific group."
  My father asked *every one* of the neighbors for a donation to the Red Cross.

Exercise 8 **Do You Spell It as One Word or Two?**

Practice

Circle the correct word in parentheses in each sentence below.

1. I haven't been back to Sterling Court since I finished (high school, highschool).

2. When friends quarrel, they can hurt (each other, eachother) with cruel comments.

3. As Sarah left, she said (good bye, goodbye) in a sad voice.

4. Be careful with that ladder; you may fall and hurt (your self, (yourself)).

5. My grandmother stuffs me with food ((every time), everytime) I visit.

6. The traffic cop was ((all ready) already) to give me a lecture.

7. ((Any one), Anyone) of the contestants could have become a professional singer.

8. It wasn't a migraine; it was a common, (every day, (everyday)) headache.

9. Brandon gets up early ((every day) everyday).

10. I ((cannot) can not) stay with you.

Exercise 9   **Do You Spell It as One Word or Two? Correcting Errors in a Paragraph**

Practice   The following paragraph contains errors in word combinations. Correct the errors above the lines. There are eight errors.

        altogether
My daughter is an all together charming baby. LaShonda sits in her bed
        playroom
room, which is decorated like a play room, and she acts like a happy little
        every time
princess. She giggles and smiles everytime the bunny mobile dances over
        in front
her crib, and she cannot keep still when I dangle her teddy bear infront of
        already
her. At ten months, she is all ready crawling, and I have already watched
        cannot   *Everyone*
her try to push herself to her feet. I can not wait to see her walk. Every

one tells me how beautiful she is, and I am a proud father, telling all my

friends about every one of her "firsts": her first smile, her first visit to
grandmother's
grand mother's house, her first ride in her stroller. I am sure I am not bor-

ing people with my stories because anyone would fall in love with my

daughter.

COMMONLY MISSPELLED WORDS

Following is a list of words you use often in your writing. Study this list and use it as a reference.

1. absence
2. absent
3. accept
4. accommodate
5. achieve
6. ache
7. acquire
8. across
9. actually
10. advertise
11. again
12. a lot
13. all right
14. almost
15. always
16. amateur
17. American
18. answer
19. anxious
20. apparent
21. appetite
22. apology
23. appreciate
24. argue

TEACHING TIP:

Ask students to circle any word that does not seem right to them. Such words can go on their personal spelling list. Also remind students to use a dictionary whenever possible; too many students prefer to jot down several versions of a word to see which one "looks correct," but such habits only reinforce poor spelling.

25. argument
26. asked
27. athlete
28. attempt
29. August
30. aunt
31. author
32. automobile
33. autumn
34. avenue
35. awful
36. awkward
37. balance
38. basically
39. because
40. becoming
41. beginning
42. behavior
43. belief
44. believe
45. benefit
46. bicycle
47. bought
48. breakfast
49. breathe
50. brilliant
51. brother
52. brought
53. bruise
54. build
55. bulletin
56. bureau
57. buried
58. business
59. busy
60. calendar
61. cannot
62. career
63. careful
64. catch
65. category
66. caught
67. cemetery
68. cereal
69. certain
70. chair
71. cheat
72. chief
73. chicken
74. children
75. cigarette
76. citizen
77. city

78. college
79. color
80. comfortable
81. committee
82. competition
83. conscience
84. convenient
85. conversation
86. copy
87. cough
88. cousin
89. criticism
90. criticize
91. crowded
92. daily
93. daughter
94. deceive
95. decide
96. definite
97. dentist
98. dependent
99. deposit
100. describe
101. desperate
102. development
103. different
104. dilemma
105. dining
106. direction
107. disappearance
108. disappoint
109. discipline
110. disease
111. divide
112. doctor
113. doesn't
114. don't
115. doubt
116. during
117. dying
118. early
119. earth
120. eighth
121. eligible
122. embarrass
123. encouragement
124. enough
125. environment
126. especially
127. etc. (et cetera)
128. every
129. exact
130. exaggeration

131. excellent
132. except
133. exercise
134. excite
135. existence
136. expect
137. experience
138. explanation
139. factory
140. familiar
141. family
142. fascinating
143. February
144. finally
145. forehead
146. foreign
147. forty
148. fourteen
149. friend
150. fundamental
151. general
152. generally
153. goes
154. going
155. government
156. grammar
157. grateful
158. grocery
159. guarantee
160. guard
161. guess
162. guidance
163. guide
164. half
165. happiness
166. handkerchief
167. heavy
168. height
169. heroes
170. holiday
171. hospital
172. humorous
173. identity
174. illegal
175. imaginary
176. immediately
177. important
178. independent
179. integration
180. intelligent
181. interest
182. interfere
183. interpretation

184. interrupt	230. operate	275. sandwich
185. irrelevant	231. opinion	276. Saturday
186. irritable	232. optimist	277. scene
187. iron	233. original	278. schedule
188. island	234. parallel	279. scissors
189. January	235. particular	280. secretary
190. jewelry	236. peculiar	281. seize
191. judgment	237. perform	282. several
192. kindergarten	238. perhaps	283. severely
193. kitchen	239. permanent	284. significant
194. knowledge	240. persevere	285. similar
195. laboratory	241. personnel	286. since
196. language	242. persuade	287. sincerely
197. laugh	243. physically	288. soldier
198. leisure	244. pleasant	289. sophomore
199. length	245. possess	290. strength
200. library	246. possible	291. studying
201. loneliness	247. potato	292. success
202. listen	248. practical	293. surely
203. lying	249. prefer	294. surprise
204. maintain	250. prejudice	295. taught
205. maintenance	251. prescription	296. temperature
206. marriage	252. presence	297. theater
207. mathematics	253. president	298. thorough
208. meant	254. privilege	299. thousand
209. measure	255. probably	300. tied
210. medicine	256. professor	301. tomorrow
211. millennium	257. psychology	302. tongue
212. million	258. punctuation	303. tragedy
213. miniature	259. pursue	304. trouble
214. minute	260. quart	305. truly
215. muscle	261. really	306. twelfth
216. mysterious	262. receipt	307. unfortunately
217. naturally	263. receive	308. unknown
218. necessary	264. recognize	309. until
219. neighbor	265. recommend	310. unusual
220. nervous	266. reference	311. using
221. nickel	267. religious	312. variety
222. niece	268. reluctantly	313. vegetable
223. ninety	269. remember	314. Wednesday
224. ninth	270. resource	315. weird
225. occasion	271. restaurant	316. which
226. o'clock	272. ridiculous	317. writing
227. often	273. right	318. written
228. omission	274. rhythm	319. yesterday
229. once		

26 Words That Sound Alike/Look Alike

WORDS THAT SOUND ALIKE/LOOK ALIKE

Words that sound alike or look alike can be confusing. Here is a list of some of the confusing words. Study this list, and make a note of any words that give you trouble.

a, an, and *A* is used before a word beginning with a consonant or consonant sound:

> Jason bought *a* car.

An is used before a word beginning with a vowel or vowel sound:

> Nancy took *an* apple to work.

And joins words or ideas:

> Pudding *and* cake are my favorite desserts.
> Fresh vegetables taste delicious, *and* they are nutritious.

accept, except *Accept* means "to receive":

> I *accept* your apology.

Except means "excluding":

> I'll give you all my books *except* my dictionary.

addition, edition An *addition* is something that is added:

> My father built an *addition* to our house in the form of a porch.

An *edition* is an issue of a newspaper or one of a series of printings of a book:

> I checked the latest *edition* of the *Daily News* to see if my advertisement is in it.

advice, advise *Advice* is an opinion offered as a guide; it is what you give someone:

> Betty asked for my *advice* about finding a job.

Advise is what you do when you give an opinion offered as a guide:

> I couldn't *advise* Betty about finding a job.

affect, effect *Affect* means "to influence something":

> Getting a bad grade will *affect* my chances for a scholarship.

Effect means "a result" or "to cause something to happen":

> Your kindness had a great *effect* on me.
> The committee struggled to *effect* a compromise.

allowed, aloud *Allowed* means "permitted":
> I'm not *allowed* to skateboard on those steps.

Aloud means "out loud":
> The teacher read the story *aloud*.

all ready, already *All ready* means "ready":
> The dog was *all ready* to go for a walk.

Already means "before":
> David had *already* made the salad.

altar, alter An *altar* is a table or place in a church:
> They were married in front of the *altar*.

Alter means "to change":
> My plane was delayed, so I had to *alter* my plans for the evening.

angel, angle An *angel* is a heavenly being:
> That night, I felt an *angel* guiding me.

An *angle* is the space within two lines:
> The road turned at a sharp *angle*.

are, our *Are* is a verb, the plural of *is:*
> We *are* friends of the mayor.

Our means "belonging to us":
> We have *our* family quarrels.

beside, besides *Beside* means "next to":
> He sat *beside* me at the concert.

Besides means "in addition":
> I would never lie to you; *besides*, I have no reason to lie.

brake, break *Brake* means "to stop" or "a device for stopping":
> That truck *brakes* at railroad crossings.
> When he saw the animal on the road, he hit the *brakes*.

Break means "to come apart" or "to make something come apart":
> The eggs are likely to *break*.
> I can *break* the seal on that package.

breath, breathe *Breath* is the air you take in, and it rhymes with *death:*
> I was running so fast, I lost my *breath*.

Breathe means "to take in air":
> He found it hard to *breathe* in high altitudes.

buy, by *Buy* means "to purchase something":
> Sylvia wants to *buy* a shovel.

By means "near," "by means of," or "before":
> He sat *by* his sister.
> I learn *by* taking good notes in class.
> *By* ten o'clock, Nick was tired.

capital, capitol *Capital* means "city" or "wealth":
> Albany is the *capital* of New York.
> Jack invested his *capital* in real estate.

A *capitol* is a building:
> The city has a famous *capitol* building.

cereal, serial A *cereal* is a breakfast food or a type of grain:
> My favorite *cereal* is Cheerios.

Serial means "in a series":
> Look for the *serial* number on the appliance.

choose, chose *Choose* means "to select." It rhymes with *snooze:*
> Today I am going to *choose* a new sofa.

Chose is the past tense of *choose:*
> Yesterday I *chose* a new rug.

close, clothes, cloths *Close* means "near" or "intimate." It can also mean "to end or shut something":
> We live *close* to the train station.
> James and Margie are *close* friends.
> Noreen wants to *close* her eyes for ten minutes.

Clothes are wearing apparel:
> Eduardo has new *clothes.*

Cloths are pieces of fabric:
> I clean the silver with damp *cloths* and a special polish.

coarse, course *Coarse* means "rough" or "crude":
> The top of the table had a *coarse* texture.
> His language was *coarse.*

A *course* is a direction or path. It is also a subject in school:
> The hurricane took a northern *course.*
> In my freshman year, I took a *course* in drama.

complement, compliment *Complement* means "complete" or "make better":
> The colors in that room *complement* the style of the furniture.

A *compliment* is praise:
> Trevor gave me a *compliment* about my cooking.

conscience, conscious Your *conscience* is your inner, moral guide:
> His *conscience* bothered him when he told a lie.

Conscious means "aware" or "awake":
> The accident victim was not fully *conscious.*

council, counsel A *council* is a group of people:
> The city *council* meets tonight.

Counsel means "advice" or "to give advice":
> I need your *counsel* about my investments.
> My father always *counsels* me about my career.

decent, descent *Decent* means "suitable or proper":
> I hope Mike gets a *decent* job.

Descent means "going down, falling, or sinking":
> The plane began its *descent* to the airport.

desert, dessert A *desert* is dry land. To *desert* means "to abandon":
> To survive a trip across the *desert*, people need water.
> He will never *desert* a friend.

Dessert is the sweet food we eat at the end of a meal:
> I want ice cream for *dessert.*

do, due *Do* means "to perform":
> I have to stop complaining; I *do* it constantly.

Due means "owing" or "because of":
> The rent is *due* tomorrow.
> The game was canceled *due* to rain.

does, dose *Does* is a form of *do:*
> My father *does* the laundry.

A *dose* is a quantity of medicine:

> Whenever I had a cold, my mother gave me a *dose* of cough syrup.

fair, fare *Fair* means "unbiased." It can also mean "promising" or "good":

> The judge's decision was *fair*.
> Jose has a *fair* chance of winning the title.

A *fare* is the amount of money a passenger must pay:

> I couldn't afford the plane *fare* to Miami.

farther, further *Farther* means "a greater physical distance":

> His house is a few blocks *farther* down the street.

Further means "greater" or "additional." Use it when you are not describing a physical distance:

> My second French class gave me *further* training in French conversation.

flour, flower *Flour* is ground-up grain, an ingredient used in cooking:

> I use whole-wheat *flour* in my muffins.

A *flower* is a blossom:

> She wore a *flower* in her hair.

forth, fourth *Forth* means "forward":

> The pendulum on the clock swung back and *forth*.

Fourth means number four in a sequence:

> I was *fourth* in line for tickets.

hear, here *Hear* means "to receive sounds in the ear":

> I can *hear* the music.

Here is a place:

> We can have the meeting *here*.

heard, herd *Heard* is the past tense of *hear:*

> I *heard* you talk in your sleep last night.

A *herd* is a group of animals:

> The farmer has a fine *herd* of cows.

hole, whole A *hole* is an empty place or opening:

> I see a *hole* in the wall.

Whole means "complete" or "entire":

> Silvio gave me the *whole* steak.

its, it's *Its* means "belonging to it":

> The car lost *its* rear bumper.

It's is a shortened form of *it is* or *it has:*

> *It's* a beautiful day.
> *It's* been a pleasure to meet you.

knew, new *Knew* is the past tense of *know:*

> I *knew* Teresa in high school.

New means "fresh, recent, not old":

> I want some *new* shoes.

know, no *Know* means "to understand":

> They *know* how to play soccer.

No is a negative:

> Carla has *no* fear of heights.

Exercise 1
Practice

Words That Sound Alike/Look Alike

Circle the correct words in parentheses in each sentence below.

1. All the (angels, angles) in heaven couldn't get me any (farther, further) in my physics studies.

2. Carlos will not (accept, except) Samantha's (advice, advise) about fixing the sink.

3. Quincy is not sure how the award will (affect, effect) his job evaluation, but he knows the award has had a great (affect, effect) on his confidence.

4. When I was a child, I was not (aloud, allowed) to pick a (flour, flower) in my grandmother's garden without asking her permission.

5. Danielle could not (breath, breathe) in the tiny apartment on the (forth, fourth) floor.

6. Every Saturday, Ibette (does, dose) her laundry and irons her (close, clothes, cloths).

7. (Are, Our) pastor gave us a (complement, compliment) for decorating the (altar, alter) so beautifully.

8. (Its, It's) difficult to keep a dog from gobbling (its, it's) food.

9. The (hole, whole) school (knew, new) about the graduation party.

10. Sara is a welcome (addition, edition) to our team; she is very (conscience, conscious) of the team's philosophy.

Exercise 2
👤👤 Collaborate

Words That Sound Alike/Look Alike

Working with a partner or a group, write a sentence for each word below.

Answers Will Vary.
Possible answers
shown at right.

1. a. hear — Everyone can hear the noise.

   b. here — Daniella said we could meet here.

2. a. fair — Simon won in a fair contest.

   b. fare — The city has raised the subway fare.

3. a. do — I do a series of exercises each day.

   b. due — Due to road construction, I took a detour.

4. a. beside — The puppy fell asleep beside me.

   b. besides — Don has other reasons besides money worries.

5. a. brake   The car needed new brakes.

     b. break   If you fall, you can break your leg.

6. a. desert   Ralph will never desert the team.

     b. dessert   Dessert is Julie's favorite part of dinner.

7. a. coarse   The stranger made a coarse remark.

     b. course   The sailors carefully planned their course.

8. a. heard   Carmella heard the soft music.

     b. herd   On the ranch, I saw a herd of cattle.

9. a. cereal   Hot cereal is a nutritious breakfast food.

     b. serial   The movie was about a serial killer.

10. a. council   My mother works for the housing council.

     b. counsel   My advisor gave me good counsel.

Exercise 3

Practice

Editing a Paragraph for Words That Sound Alike/Look Alike

The following paragraph has errors in words that sound alike/look alike. Correct each error in the space above it. There are ten errors.

> The most difficult part of my job is commuting. My job is a twenty-
> *farther*
> minute drive from my apartment, but some days it seems much further
> *it's*   *breaking*
> away. I have a car, but its old, and it's always braking down. I have had the
> *addition*   *buy*
> car repaired twice this month; in edition, I have had to by new tires. I
> *already*
> have all ready spent $700 on car repairs, and I just don't have that kind of
> money. I also face other commuting problems. Whenever the car is in the
> *fare it's*
> shop, I take the bus to work. I don't mind paying bus fair; its cheaper than
> maintaining a car. However, the bus stop has no shelter, so many days I
> wait in the rain. By the time I have waited in the rain at one end and then
> run half a mile from the bus to my workplace at the other end, I am soak-
> *decently*
> ing wet. I am not descently dressed for my job. I know that my appear-
> *effect*
> ance has an affect on my co-workers' opinion of me. I wish I could arrive
> at work looking better, but I consider it a victory that I have arrived at all.

MORE WORDS THAT SOUND ALIKE/LOOK ALIKE

lead, led When *lead* rhymes with *need*, it means "to give directions, to take charge." When *lead* rhymes with *bed*, it is a metal:

The marching band will *lead* the parade.

Your bookbag is a heavy as *lead*.

Led is the past form of *lead* when it means "to give direction, to take charge":

The cheerleaders *led* the parade last year.

loan, lone A *loan* is something you give on the condition that it be returned:

When I was broke, I got a *loan* of fifty dollars from my aunt.

Lone means "solitary, alone":

A *lone* shopper stood in the checkout line.

loose, lose *Loose* means "not tight":

In the summer, *loose* clothing keeps me cool.

To *lose* something means "to be unable to keep it":

I'm afraid I will *lose* my car keys.

moral, morale *Moral* means "upright, honorable, connected to ethical standards":

I have a *moral* obligation to care for my children.

Morale is confidence or spirit:

After the game, the team's *morale* was low.

pain, pane *Pain* means "suffering":

I had very little *pain* after the surgery.

A *pane* is a piece of glass:

The girl's wild throw broke a window *pane*.

pair, pear A *pair* is a set of two:

Mark has a *pair* of antique swords.

A *pear* is a fruit:

In the autumn, I like a *pear* for a snack.

passed, past *Passed* means "went by." It can also mean "handed to":

The happy days *passed* too quickly.

Janice *passed* me the mustard.

Past means "the time that has gone by":

Let's leave the *past* behind us.

patience, patients *Patience* is calm endurance:

When I am caught in a traffic jam, I should have more *patience*.

Patients are people under medical care:

There are too many *patients* in the doctor's waiting room.

peace, piece *Peace* is calmness:

Looking at the ocean brings me a sense of *peace*.

A *piece* is a part of something:

Norman took a *piece* of coconut cake.

personal, personnel *Personal* means "connected to a person." It can also mean "intimate":

Whether to lease or own a car is a *personal* choice.

That information is too *personal* to share.

Personnel are the staff in an office:

The Digby Electronics Company is developing a new health plan for its *personnel*.

plain, plane *Plain* means "simple, clear, or ordinary." It can also mean "flat land":

> The restaurant serves *plain* but tasty food.
> Her house was in the center of a windy *plain*.

A *plane* is an aircraft:

> We took a small *plane* to the island.

presence, presents Your *presence* is your attendance, your being somewhere:

> We request your *presence* at our wedding.

Presents are gifts:

> My daughter got too many birthday *presents*.

principal, principle *Principal* means "most important." It also means "the head of a school":

> My *principal* reason for quitting is the low salary.
> The *principal* of Crestview Elementary School is popular with students.

A *principle* is a guiding rule:

> Betraying a friend is against my *principles*.

quiet, quit, quite *Quiet* means "without noise":

> The library has many *quiet* corners.

Quit means "stop":

> Will you *quit* complaining?

Quite means "truly or exactly":

> Victor's speech was *quite* convincing.

rain, reign, rein *Rain* is wet weather:

> We have had a week of *rain*.

To *reign* is to rule; *reign* is royal rule:

> King Arthur's *reign* in Camelot is the subject of many poems.

A *rein* is a leather strap in an animal's harness:

> When Charlie got on the horse, he held the *reins* very tight.

right, rite, write *Right* is a direction (the opposite of left). It can also mean "correct":

> To get to the gas station, turn *right* at the corner.
> On my sociology test, I got nineteen out of twenty questions *right*.

A *rite* is a ceremony:

> I am interested in the funeral *rites* of other cultures.

To *write* is to set down in words:

> Brian has to *write* a book report.

sight, site, cite A *sight* is something you can see:

> The truck stop was a welcome *sight*.

A *site* is a location:

> The city is building a courthouse on the *site* of my old school.

Cite means "to quote an authority." It can also mean "to give an example":

> In her term paper, Christina wanted to *cite* several computer experts.
> When my father lectured me on speeding, he *cited* the story of my best friend's car accident.

sole, soul A *sole* is the bottom of a foot or shoe:

> My left boot needs a new *sole*.

A *soul* is the spiritual part of a person:

> Some people say meditation is good for the *soul*.

stair, stare A *stair* is a step:
> The toddler carefully climbed each *stair*.

A *stare* is a long, fixed look:
> I wish that woman wouldn't *stare* at me.

stake, steak A *stake* is a stick driven into the ground:
> The gardener put *stakes* around the tomato plants.

A *steak* is a piece of meat or fish:
> I like my *steak* cooked medium rare.

stationary, stationery *Stationary* means "standing still":
> As the speaker presented his speech, he remained *stationary*.

Stationery is writing paper:
> For my birthday, my uncle gave me some *stationery* with my name printed on it.

than, then *Than* is used to compare things:
> My dog is more intelligent *than* many people.

Then means "at that time":
> I lived in Buffalo for two years; *then* I moved to Albany.

their, there, they're *Their* means "belonging to them":
> My grandparents donated *their* old television to a women's shelter.

There means "at that place." It can also be used as an introductory word:
> Sit *there*, next to Simone.
> *There* is a reason for his happiness.

They're is a contraction of *they are*:
> Jaime and Sandra are visiting; *they're* my cousins.

thorough, through, threw *Thorough* means "complete":
> I did a *thorough* cleaning of my closet.

Through means "from one side to the other." It can also mean "finished":
> We drove *through* Greenview on our way to Lake Western.
> I'm *through* with my studies.

to, too, two *To* means "in a direction toward." It is also a word that can go in front of a verb:
> I am driving *to* Miami.
> Selena loves *to* write poems.

Too means "also." It also means "very":
> Anita played great golf; Adam did well, *too*.
> It is *too* kind of you to visit.

Two is the number:
> Mr. Almeida owns *two* clothing stores.

vain, vane, vein *Vain* means "conceited." It also means "unsuccessful":
> Victor is *vain* about his dark, curly hair.
> The doctor made a *vain* attempt to revive the patient.

A *vane* is a device that moves to indicate the direction of the wind:
> There was an old weather *vane* on the barn roof.

A *vein* is a blood vessel:
> I could see the *veins* in his hands.

waist, waste The *waist* is the middle part of the body:
> He had a leather belt around his *waist*.

Waste means "to use carelessly." It also means "thrown away because it is useless":

I can't *waste* my time watching trashy television shows.
That manufacturing plant has many *waste* products.

wait, weight *Wait* means "to hold oneself ready for something":
I can't *wait* until my check arrives.
Weight means "heaviness":
He tested the *weight* of the bat.

weather, whether *Weather* refers to conditions outside:
If the *weather* is warm, I'll go swimming.
Whether means "if":
Whether you help me or not, I'll paint the hallway.

were, we're, where *Were* is the past form of *are*:
Only last year, we *were* scared to start college.
We're is the shortened form of *we are*:
Today *we're* confident sophomores.
Where refers to a place:
Show me *where* you used to play basketball.

whined, wind, wined *Whined* means "complained":
Polly *whined* about the weather because the rain kept her indoors.
Wind (if it rhymes with *find*) means "to coil or wrap something" or "to turn a key":
Wind that extension cord, or you'll trip on it.
Wind (if it rhymes with *sinned*) is air in motion:
The *wind* blew my cap off.
If someone *wined* you, he or she treated you to some wine:
My brother *wined* and dined his boss.

who's, whose *Who's* is a short form of *who is* or *who has*:
Who's driving?
Whose means "belonging to whom":
I wonder *whose* dog this is.

woman, women *Woman* means "one adult female person":
A *woman* in the supermarket gave me her extra coupons.
Women means "more than one woman":
Three *women* from Missouri joined the management team.

wood, would *Wood* is a hard substance made from trees:
I have a table made of a polished *wood*.
Would is the past form of *will*:
Albert said he *would* think about the offer.

your, you're *Your* means "belonging to you":
I think you dropped *your* wallet.
You're is the short form of *you are*:
You're not telling the truth.

Exercise 4 **More Words That Sound Alike/Look Alike**

Practice   Circle the correct words in parentheses in each sentence below.

1. A (woman, women) from Scotland gave a lecture about the (rain, reign, rein) of Mary, Queen of Scots.

2. You were (right, rite, write) about the movie; it is (quiet, quite) exciting.

3. My (principal, principle) objection to your proposal is that the salary cut will hurt the (personal, personnel) at the office.

4. Although they were wrapped in (plain, plane) brown paper, the (presence, presents) Nadia sent were wonderful.

5. When the boss fails to (lead, led), employee (moral, morale) is low.

6. If you don't study, Professor Caruso will (loose, lose) his (patience, patients) with you.

7. First make a list of your goals; (than, then) it will be easier to see if your ambitions are greater (than, then) your abilities.

8. Luisa's cousins gave (their, there, they're) mother a trip to Colombia; (their, there, they're) very generous.

9. The (to, too, two) boys were moving to Sacramento, and Gary was moving, (to, too, two).

10. Professor Salzman gave a (thorough, through, threw) explanation of how (wood, would) becomes paper.

Exercise 5
Collaborate

More Words That Sound Alike/Look Alike

Working with a partner or a group, write a sentence for each word below. When you have completed this exercise, exchange work with another group for evaluation.

Answers Will Vary.
Possible answers
shown at right.

1. a. stationary   One actor was stationary during the scene.

   b. stationery   The company's address is on its stationery.

2. a. loan   The bank gave Jeffrey a small loan.

   b. lone   A lone skier came down the slope.

3. a. passed   Because I was busy, the time passed quickly.

   b. past   No one can change the past.

4. a. weather   The weather in Arizona was hot and dry.

   b. whether   I wonder whether Mrs. Chan will call.

5. a. were   The visitors were scientists from India.

   b. we're   We're friends of the team manager.

6. a. who's   I know who's going to win.

    b. whose   The officer asked whose car had been stolen.

7. a. pain   Running too fast, I felt a pain in my leg.

    b. pane   Rain splattered against the window pane.

8. a. sight   The sunset was a spectacular sight.

    b. site   The old farm is the site of a new mall.

    c. cite   The debater cited facts and authorities.

9. a. pair   She wore a pair of silver earrings.

    b. pear   On the table was a bowl of apples and pears.

10. a. stair   The burglar paused on the top stair.

    b. stare   The dog had an unfriendly stare.

Exercise 6
Practice

Editing a Paragraph for Errors in More Words That Sound Alike/Look Alike

The following paragraph has errors in words that sound alike/look alike. Correct each error in the space above it. There are eleven errors.

           rite
    A wedding ceremony should be a right of commitment and love, but

some people turn it into a time to display their wealth. Rather than plan a
         personal
small and personnel ceremony for family and friends, some people invite
                principal
everyone they've ever known. The principle goal of these brides and

grooms is to impress everyone with the size of the wedding and the

amount of money spent. Such wedding couples also seem more con-
        their
cerned with there guests' presents rather than their presence. Or perhaps

the families of the bride and groom insist on an extravagant wedding.
                      Whose
Such parents should remember one question: Who's wedding is it, any-
             quiet
way? For many engaged couples, a quite, simple wedding would be a
     sight   *vain*
beautiful cite. Unfortunately, too many brides and grooms stage a vane
         waste
fight against the waist of energy, time, and money of a big wedding.
Whether
Weather the parents or the wedding couple themselves choose a lavish
                                     through
wedding, they should not forget the love that must shine threw any

ceremony, big or small.

Exercise 7   **Words That Sound Alike/Look Alike: A Comprehensive Exercise**

Practice   Circle the correct words in parentheses in each sentence below.

1. Larry said he (wood, **would**) fix the creaking (**stairs**, stares) on Wednesday.

2. The dancer exercises on a (**stationary**, stationery) bike in (**addition**, edition) to practicing her dance movements.

3. The detective has (all ready, **already**) discovered (who's, **whose**) finger-prints are on the gun.

4. I (**knew**, new) the roof was slanted at a steep (angel, **angle**).

5. Bill was (conscience, **conscious**) of a (loan, **lone**) figure following him.

6. Henry tied the rope in a (**loose**, lose) knot and tested (**its**, it's) strength.

7. Knowing she would never (**desert**, dessert) me gave me a sense of (**peace**, piece).

8. Some (woman, **women**) say they are looking for a (**decent**, descent) man with sound (**moral**, morale) values.

9. The forecaster said tomorrow's (**weather**, whether) would be (**fair**, fare) and cool.

10. (Do, **Due**) to the blister on my foot, I was unable to walk any (**farther**, further).

11. The tablecloths were made of three (**coarse**, course) cotton (close, clothes, **cloths**) in bright colors.

12. My dog Daisy is (quiet, quit, **quite**) happy to walk in the snow but hates the (**rain**, reign, rein).

13. Carl has no patience with fancy food; he likes (**plain**, plane) old (stake, **steak**) and potatoes.

14. (**Their**, There, They're) new crayons pleased the children more (**than**, then) any other new toy.

15. Anthony has a trim (**waist**, waste), but you can't see it since he wears (**loose**, lose) (close, **clothes**, cloths).

16. Al is (**vain**, vein) about all his talents (accept, **except**) his ability to imitate a pig.

17. Mrs. Portrusky gave me some good (advice, advise) about how to (choose, chose) a college.

18. I'd like to (buy, by) a (cereal, serial) without too much sugar in it.

19. We had to (wait, weight) three hours for (are, our) (plain, plane) to arrive.

20. The (pain, pane) was so bad he could hardly (breath, breathe).

Exercise 8	**Editing a Paragraph for Errors in Words That Sound Alike/Look Alike:**
Practice	**A Comprehensive Exercise**

The following paragraph has errors in words that sound alike or look alike. Correct each error in the space above it. There are eleven errors.

                                  pair
Carmen lives by a pear of principles: stay strong, and help others.

What she means by "strong" includes her body, mind, and heart. She eats
right   *beside*
rite, and every morning she runs besides her golden retriever. Although
                                      course
she has finished college, she is always taking a new coarse in science or

computers to keep her mind active. She tries to stay emotionally strong by
                                   past
staying close to those who have cared for her in the passed. Carmen uses
                       whose
her strength to help those who's lives have taken a sad turn. Sometimes
                                        counsels
she volunteers at a soup kitchen, and at other times she councils callers
                           hears
to a mental health hotline. She often heres sad stories, but she always
does   *their*
dose her best to help her callers solve there problems. Carmen is a
woman
women who cares, and her strength and kindness make her a role model

in her community.

Word Choice

One way to improve your writing is to pay attention to your choice of words. As you revise and edit, be careful to use precise language and to avoid wordiness and clichés.

PRECISE LANGUAGE

Try to be as specific as you can in explaining or describing. Replace vague, general words or phrases with more precise language.

> **not this:** Last night, I made ~~a lot~~ of money in tips.
> **but this:** Last night, I made *$50* in tips.

> **not this:** He gave me a ~~nice~~ smile.
> **but this:** He gave me a *friendly* smile.
> **or this:** He gave me a *reassuring* smile.
> **or this:** He gave me a *welcoming* smile.

> **not this:** Maggie is a ~~good~~ friend.
> **but this:** Maggie is a *loyal* friend.
> **or this:** Maggie is a *devoted* friend.

Exercise 1 **Using Precise Language**

Practice

In each sentence below, replace the italicized word or phrase with a more precise word or phrase. Write your revisions above the lines.

Answers Will Vary.
Possible answers
shown at right.

1. Sylvia and Aaron live in a *nice* house.
   ^{handsome brick}
2. Charlie drinks *a lot* of coffee in the morning.
   ^{four cups}
3. I visit San Antonio *often*.
   ^{twice a month.}
4. Mrs. Lin has a *nice* personality.
   ^{warm}
5. Chris was caught in a *bad* situation.
   ^{dangerous}

6. The movie had several *interesting* scenes.
   suspenseful

7. I spent *a lot* of time studying for the geography test.
   six hours

8. Mr. Zaccarelli is a *bad* driver.
   careless

9. The ice cream smelled *funny.*
   sour.

10. The party was *great.*
   filled with music and friends.

WORDINESS

As you revise and edit your work, check for **wordiness,** the use of extra words. If you can say the same thing in fewer words, do so. You can be precise *and* direct.

> **not this:** After the accident, ~~I thought in my mind that~~ I was to blame.
> **but this:** After the accident, *I thought* I was to blame.

> **not this:** ~~In my opinion,~~ I think children should exercise daily.
> **but this:** *I think* children should exercise daily.

> **not this:** Jorge bought a CD ~~for the price of~~ $10.95.
> **but this:** Jorge bought a CD *for* $10.95.

Here is a list of some wordy expressions and possible substitutes:

Wordy Expressions	Possible Substitutes
attach together	attach
at that time	then
at the present time	now
basic essentials	essentials
blend together	blend
by means of	by
by the fact that	because
day in and day out	daily
deep down inside he believed	he believed
due to the fact that	because
for the reason that	because
have a need for	need
have a realization of	realize
I felt inside	I felt
I personally feel	I feel
I thought in my head	I thought
I thought to myself	I thought
in the field of art (music, etc.)	in art (music, etc.)
in the near future	soon
in this day and age	today
in this modern world	today
in my mind, I think	I think
in my opinion, I think	I think
in order to	to
in today's society	today
maximum amount	maximum
of a remarkable kind	remarkable

on a daily basis	daily
on a regular basis	regularly
past experience	experience
refer back	refer
repeat again	repeat
short in stature	short
small in size	small
the reason being	because
top priority	priority
two different kinds	two kinds
very unique	unique

Exercise 2 **Revising for Wordiness**

Practice

Revise the following sentences, eliminating wordiness. Write your revisions above the lines.

1. ~~Due to the fact that~~ (Because) their lives are stressful, people ~~have a need for~~ (need) exercise ~~on a daily basis~~ (daily exercise).

2. ~~In today's society~~ (Today), many ~~different kinds of~~ mothers work outside the home.

3. ~~For the reason that~~ (Because) the crate was ~~large in size~~ (large), two men had to carry it.

4. I cannot ~~refer back~~ (refer) to that ~~point in time~~ (time) unless I consult my notes.

5. You can't camp in the woods unless you have the ~~basic essentials~~ (essentials).

6. I quit my receptionist job ~~for the reason that~~ (because) I was sick of repeating "How can I help you?" ~~again and again~~.

7. ~~In the near future~~ (Soon), we can expect to receive email ~~on a regular basis~~ (regularly).

8. Simon spent weeks combining the two systems ~~in order~~ to be sure they would blend ~~together~~ efficiently.

9. My parents' ~~past~~ experience with technology was limited, but ~~in this day and age~~ (today), everyone needs to be an expert in ~~the field of~~ technology.

10. The salesperson promised that the car would provide ~~a maxiumum amount of~~ (maximum) satisfaction at a reasonable price.

CLICHÉS

Clichés are worn-out expressions. Once they were a new way of making a point, but now they are old and tired. You should avoid them in your writing.

> **not this:** I know that Monica will always ~~be there for me~~.
> **but this:** I know that Monica will always *support me*.

TEACHING TIP:
If you have non-native speakers, ask them to list some commonly used clichés from their native language. Ask them to give the common meaning of the cliché, and then ask them for the literal translation. This may be an amusing way for all students to spot clichés in their own writing. (For example: "Me estas tomando el pelo" is a Spanish cliché that means "You're kidding me." However, the literal translation is "You're drinking my hair." The expression is analogous to "You're pulling my leg."

not this: Alan experienced the ~~trials and tribulations~~ of late registration.
but this: Alan experienced the *difficulties* of late registration.

Following are some common clichés. If you spot clichés in your writing, replace them with more direct or thoughtful statements of your own.

Some Common Clichés

all in all	I wouldn't be where I am today
beat around the bush	information superhighway
between a rock and a hard place	last but not least
break new ground	let bygones be bygones
break the ice	light as a feather
climb the ladder of success	make ends meet
cry my eyes out	on top of the world
cutting edge	quick as a wink
dead as a doornail	shoulder to cry on
a drop in the bucket	sick as a dog
few and far between	state of the art
free as a bird	tried and true
go the distance	up at the crack of dawn
grass is always greener	when all is said and done
hard as a rock	without a shadow of a doubt
hit the nail on the head	worked and slaved
hustle and bustle	work like a dog

Exercise 3   **Revising Clichés**

👥 Collaborate

The following sentences contain clichés (italicized). Working with a partner or a group, rewrite the sentences, replacing the clichés with more direct or thoughtful words or phrases. Write your revisions above the lines.

Answers Will Vary.
Possible answers shown at right.

1. My new quilt was *as light as a feather*. [as light as foam.]

2. Don't *beat around the bush;* just tell me what is wrong with my engine. [hesitate]

3. Two excellent singers performed, and then a magician pulled a rabbit out of a hat; *last but not least*, a ventriloquist entertained the crowd. [finally]

4. When I lost the contest, I was ready to *cry my eyes out*. [cry.]

5. Antwan got a *state-of-the-art* sound system for his car. [new]

6. Many people are stressed by the *hustle and bustle* of city life. [hurried pace]

7. When her daughter needed expensive medical care, Maureen had difficulty *making ends meet*. [paying the bills.]

8. The locksmith opened the door *as quick as a wink*. [quickly]

9. When I worked at a bakery, I had to be *up at the crack of dawn*. [up at 5:00 a.m.]

10. Reynaldo *worked and slaved* to finance his college education. [worked hard]

Exercise 4 **Identifying Clichés**

Practice Underline all the clichés in the following paragraph. There are ten clichés.

My father really <u>hit the nail on the head</u> when he said I would have to

<u>work and slave</u> to <u>climb the ladder of success</u>. In my first year at

Freemont Foods, I had to <u>work like a dog</u>. My typical workday began at

8:00 a.m. and ended at 7:00 p.m. Sometimes I worked overtime to earn

extra money and to impress my manager, so I wouldn't leave work until

10:00 p.m. Finally, in my second year, I was placed in a mangement train-

ing program. I felt <u>on top of the world</u> because management opportunities

are <u>few and far between</u>. The program was challenging, and I began to

doubt whether I could <u>go the distance</u>. There were times when I felt

exhausted and longed <u>for a shoulder to cry on</u>. Somehow I persevered

through the dark moments and completed management training. Today I

am an assistant manager in the customer relations department at

Freemont Foods. <u>When all is said and done</u>, I am grateful for the early

years of hard work and tough training because <u>I wouldn't be where I am</u>

<u>today</u> without them.

Exercise 5 **Editing for Precise Language, Wordiness, and Clichés**

Practice Edit the following paragraph for precise language, wordiness, and clichés. Write
your revisions above the lines. There are eight places that need editing.

Answers Will Vary.
Possible answers
shown at right.

One of my co-workers makes my job unpleasant. She constantly com-

plains about our customers, our boss, and our working conditions. When I

try to change the subject, she repeats her complaint ~~again~~. I have to listen

to her ~~bad~~ *nasty* comments ~~on a daily basis~~ *daily*, and they make my job difficult ~~due~~

~~to the fact that~~ *because* she poisons the atmosphere. The woman has never come

to work smiling, yet I am sure that ~~deep down inside~~ she feels she is a

realistic and honest person. She probably thinks of herself as a person

who doesn't ~~beat around the bush~~ *avoid the truth*, but I ~~personally~~ feel she enjoys being

nasty. I don't care if she isn't ~~nice~~ *pleasant* on her days off, but when she's at work,

she should leave her negativity at home.

CHAPTER 28 Sentence Variety

One way to polish your writing is to work on **sentence variety,** the use of different lengths and kinds of sentences. You can become skilled in sentence variety by (1) revising your writing for a balance of short and long sentences and for a mix of sentence types and (2) being aware of the kinds of sentences you can use.

BALANCING LONG AND SHORT SENTENCES

There are no grammar errors in the following paragraph, but it needs revision for sentence variety:

> I have a routine for waking up. First, I grab a can of Diet Pepsi. I gulp it down. I turn on the TV at the same time. I watch cartoons. I sit for about half an hour. Then the caffeine in the Pepsi starts working. I move to the shower. I make the water temperature very hot. Steam fills the bathroom. My muscles come alive. I begin to feel fully awake.

The paragraph is filled with short sentences. Read it aloud, and you will notice the choppy, boring style of the writing. Compare it to the following revised paragraph, which contains a variety of short and long sentences:

> I have a routine for waking up. First, I grab a can of Diet Pepsi and gulp it down while I turn on the TV. Then I watch cartoons for about half an hour. When the caffeine in the Pepsi starts working, I move to the shower. I make the water temperature so hot that steam fills the bathroom. My muscles come alive as I begin to feel fully awake.

The revised paragraph balances short and long sentences. Read it aloud, and you will notice the way the varied lengths create a more flowing, interesting style.

Some writers rely too heavily on short sentences; others use too many long sentences. The following paragraph contains too many long sentences:

> Randall wanted to make new friends because his old friends had become a bad influence. Randall loved his old friends, especially Michael, but they had begun to be involved in some dangerous activities, and Randall didn't want to be part of these crimes because Randall wanted to apply to

the police academy, and he knew that having a record would destroy his chances of admission. Consequently, Randall was honest with Michael, and Randall told him that Randall couldn't risk his future by mixing with people who liked to joyride in stolen cars or steal from neighborhood stores. The rest of Randall's friends sensed he was distancing himself from them, and they stopped asking him to go out with them. For a while, Randall felt lonely and isolated, but eventually, Randall formed some new friendships, and he was happy to be part of a new group and happy it was one that didn't break the law.

Read the previous paragraph aloud, and you will notice that the sentences are so long and complicated that part of their meaning is lost. Piling on one long sentence after another can make a paragraph boring and difficult to follow. Compare the previous paragraph to the following revised version:

Randall wanted to make new friends because his old friends had become a bad influence. Randall loved his old friends, especially Michael. However, they had begun to be involved in some dangerous activities, and Randall didn't want to be a part of these crimes. He wanted to apply to the police academy and knew that having a record would destroy his chances of admission. Consequently, Randall spoke honestly to Michael. Randall explained that he couldn't risk his future by mixing with people who liked to joyride in stolen cars or steal from neighborhood stores. Sensing that he was distancing himself from them, the rest of Randall's friends soon stopped asking him to go with them. For a while, Randall felt lonely and isolated. Eventually, Randall formed some new friendships and was happy to be part of a new, law-abiding group.

Read the revised paragraph aloud, and you will notice that the combination of long and short sentences makes the paragraph clearer and smoother. Careful revision helps you achieve such a mix.

Exercise 1   **Revising Short Sentences**

Practice

The following paragraph is composed entirely of short sentences. Rewrite it so that it contains a mix of short and long sentences. Write your revisions above the lines.

Answers Will Vary. Possible answers shown at right.

Revision (handwritten above the lines):

My sister Alicia knows how to save money. She bought a used car, and she changes the oil and replaces the belts herself. After she researched car insurance on the Internet, she found the best deal and got a safe driver discount. Another way Alicia saves is by automatically putting 10% of her salary into savings each week, through payroll deduction. Alicia also saves when she shops. She watches for sales on clothes and buys them at discount stores and outlet malls. At the supermarket, she clips

Original short-sentence paragraph:

My sister Alicia knows how to save money. She bought a used car. She changes the oil herself. She replaces the belts herself. She researched car insurance on the Internet. She found the best deal. She got a safe driver discount on her insurance. Another way Alica saves is by putting ten percent of her salary into savings. She does this automatically. She does it each week. She does it through payroll deduction. Alicia also saves when she shops. She watches for sales on clothes. She buys clothes at discount stores. She buys them at outlet malls. She saves at the supermarket. She

coupons and buys store brands, which are cheaper than national brands
clips coupons. She buys store brands. Store brands are cheaper than

like Nabisco, Kellogg's or Kraft.
national brands. National brands are brands like Nabisco or Kellogg's or

My sister rarely worries about money. She feels secure because she is
Kraft. My sister rarely worries about money. She feels secure. She is wise

wise about spending and saving.
about spending and saving.

Exercise 2   **Revising Long Sentences**

Practice   The following paragraph is composed entirely of long sentences. Rewrite it so that it contains a mix of short and long sentences. Write your revisions above the lines.

Answers Will Vary.
Possible answers
shown at right.

I had a frustrating experience at the doctor's office yesterday; it was
I had a frustrating experience at the doctor's office yesterday; it was

made more frustrating because no one was really to blame.   First of all, I
made more frustrating because no one was really to blame. First of all, I

arrived at the office an hour early. I had lost my note with the appointment
arrived at the office an hour early because I had lost my note with the

time on it and got so busy at work that I forgot to call the doctor's office to
appointment time on it, and I got so busy at work that I forgot to call the

check the time. Instead, I just guessed at the appointment time. I guessed
doctor's office to check the time, so I just guessed at the appointment

wrong and wound up arriving during the doctor's lunch break. I was forced to
time. I guessed wrong and arrived during the doctor's lunch break and

sit there, looking through a bunch of old Road and Track and Golf Digest
was forced to wait, looking through a bunch of old *Road and Track* and

magazines.   Soon the waiting room began to fill up with mothers
Golf Digest magazines. Soon the waiting room began to fill up with moth-

and small children and people in walkers while the nurse didn't call anyone in
ers and small children and older people with walkers, but the nurse didn't

to see the doctor.   The patients soon discovered the doctor
call anyone in to see the doctor. The patients soon discovered the doctor

was late getting back to the office. He had been involved in a minor car acci-
was late getting back to the office because he had been involved in a

dent and had to wait for the police to arrive to fill out an accident report.
minor car accident and had to wait for the police to arrive to fill out an

Consequently, all the patients waited an extra hour.   When my turn to
accident report, so all the patients waited an extra hour. When my turn to

see the doctor finally came, the nurse put me in an examining room where I
see the doctor finally came, the nurse put me in an examining room where

waited for another half hour, but the doctor never came. I was stuck reading
I waited for another half hour, but the doctor never came, and I was stuck

more issues of Road and Track.   At last the nurse returned, looking
reading more issues of *Road and Track*. At last the nurse returned, but

unhappy.   Apologetically, she told me that the doc-
her face didn't look too happy, and her tone was apologetic when she told

tor had been called away on an emergency and I would have to reschedule my
me that the doctor had been called away on an emergency and I would

appointment.
have to reschedule my appointment.

USING DIFFERENT WAYS TO BEGIN SENTENCES

Most of the time, writers begin sentences with the subject. However, if you change the word order, you can break the monotony of using the same pattern over and over.

Begin with an Adverb

One way to change the word order is to begin with an **adverb,** a word that describes verbs, adjectives, or other adverbs. (For more on adverbs, see Chapter 17.) You can move adverbs from the middle to the beginning of the sentence as long as the meaning is clear:

> **adverb in middle:** Ricky opened the package *carefully* and checked the contents.
> **adverb at beginning:** *Carefully*, Ricky opened the package and checked the contents.
>
> **adverb in middle:** The police officer *calmly* issued a ticket to the aggressive driver.
> **adverb at beginning:** *Calmly*, the police officer issued a ticket to the aggressive driver.

Exercise 3

Practice

Writing Sentences That Begin with an Adverb

Rewrite each sentence below so that it begins with an adverb. Write your revisions above the lines.

Quietly, the thief pried open the window.
1. The thief quietly pried open the window.

Suddenly, Alicia's racing car skidded across the tracks.
2. Alicia's racing car suddenly skidded across the tracks.

Angrily, the teacher glared at the noisy student.
3. The teacher glared angrily at the noisy student.

Carefully, the master chef prepared the roast chicken.
4. The master chef carefully prepared the roast chicken.

Desperately, the convicted criminal pleaded for a light sentence.
5. The convicted criminal pleaded desperately for a light sentence.

Remorsefully, my brother cried over his thoughtless behavior.
6. My brother cried remorsefully over his thoughtless behavior.

Gracefully, the little ballerina performed the Dance of the Flowers.
7. The little ballerina gracefully performed the Dance of the Flowers.

Frequently, our boss offers us overtime.
8. Our boss frequently offers us overtime work.

Cheerfully, her mother handed Carla the keys to the Lexus.
9. Her mother cheerfully handed Carla the keys to the Lexus.

Rudely, the angry man pushed his way through the crowd.
10. The angry man rudely pushed his way through the crowd.

Begin with a Prepositional Phrase

A **prepositional phrase** contains a preposition and its object. (For more on prepositions, see Chapter 12.) You can change the usual word order by moving a prepositional phrase from the end of a sentence to the beginning. You can do this as long as the meaning of the sentence remains clear.

> **prepositional phrase at end:** A gleaming silver convertible suddenly passed me *in the left lane.*

prepositional phrase at beginning: *In the left lane,* a gleaming silver convertible suddenly passed me.

prepositional phrase at end: The bulldog growled and snarled *with fierce intensity.*

prepositional phrase at beginning: *With fierce intensity,* the bulldog growled and snarled.

Note: Most of the time, you put a comma after a prepositional phrase that begins a sentence. However, you do not need a comma if the prepositional phrase is short.

Exercise 4
Practice

Writing Sentences That Begin with a Prepositional Phrase

Rewrite the following sentences, moving a prepositional phrase to the beginning of each sentence. Write your revisions above the lines.

For no good reason, Arthur cut class and missed a quiz.
1. Arthur cut class and missed a quiz for no good reason.

In the third quarter, the home team was losing.
2. The home team was losing in the third quarter.

Near the giant pile of cash, the lottery winner stood smiling.
3. The lottery winner stood smiling near the giant pile of cash.

At the Discovery Center, you can study dinosaurs and fossils.
4. You can study dinosaurs and fossils at the Discovery Center.

Beside the old man, a white dog waited patiently.
5. A white dog waited patiently beside the old man.

After your family dinner, we can see a movie.
6. We can see a late movie after your family dinner.

Behind the clouds, you can see a pink glow.
7. You can see a pink glow behind the clouds.

Beneath his rough manner, Mr. Stelios is a kind man.
8. Mr. Stelios is a kind man beneath his rough manner.

With style and grace, Rachel will deliver her speech.
9. Rachel will deliver her speech with style and grace.

Before dawn, the heavy rain had subsided.
10. The heavy rain had subsided before dawn.

Exercise 5
Collaborate

Creating Sentences That Begin with Prepositional Phrases

Working with a partner or a group, write sentences that begin with the following prepositional phrases.

1. With a broad grin, Jack shook my hand.

2. At the funeral, the family greeted all the mourners.

3. Between the houses was a grove of orange trees.

4. Near the shore, two children splashed water at each other.

5. Before midnight, I heard the strange noise again.

6. Under the bed, a hissing snake uncoiled.

7. After the long plane trip, we were ready to explore the city.

8. For days, I waited for the letter to arrive.

9. Without a ticket, <u>I had no chance of seeing the show.</u>

10. In the summer, <u>the days are long and leisurely.</u>

USING DIFFERENT WAYS TO JOIN IDEAS

Another way to create sentence variety is to try different methods of combining ideas. Among these methods are (1) using an *-ing* modifier, (2) using an *-ed* modifier, (3) using an appositive, and (4) using a *who, which,* or *that* clause.

Use an *-ing* Modifier

You can avoid short, choppy sentences by using an *-ing* modifier. This way, one of the short sentences becomes a phrase. (For more on modifiers, see Chapter 18.)

>   **two short sentences:** Sarah was talking on her cell phone. She drove into a tree.
>   **combined with *-ing* modifier:** *Talking on her cell phone,* Sarah drove into a tree.

Note: If the modifier begins the sentence, be sure that the next word is the one the modifier describes.

>   **two short sentences:** Mr. Martinez loves to read travel books. He plans his next vacation.
>   **combined with *-ing* modifier:** Mr. Martinez loves to read travel books, *planning his next vacation.*

Exercise 6   **Using *-ing* Modifiers**

Practice

Following are pairs of sentences. Combine each pair, using an *-ing* modifier.

Answers Will Vary.
Possible answers
shown at right.

1. My cat dug her claws into the curtain. My cat climbed to the top of the window.

    combined: <u>Digging her claws into the curtain, my cat climbed to the top of</u>

    <u>the window.</u>

2. The children played until dark. The children enjoyed the new swing set.

    combined: <u>The children, enjoying the new swing set, played until dark.</u>

    _____

3. Alfredo studied for hours. Alfredo concentrated on the most difficult concepts.

    combined: <u>Concentrating on the most difficult concepts, Alfredo studied for</u>

    <u>hours.</u>

4. The ambulance raced through the intersection. The ambulance blasted its siren.

combined: <u>Racing through the intersection, the ambulance blasted its siren.</u>

5. Some teenagers buy expensive clothes. They want to make an impression.

   combined: <u>Wanting to make an impression, some teenagers buy expensive</u>

   <u>clothes.</u>

6. Three men waited in the ticket line for six hours. The men hoped to get the best seats.

   combined: <u>Hoping to get the best seats, three men waited in the ticket line</u>

   <u>for six hours.</u>

7. My sister called me last night. She cried about her divorce.

   combined: <u>My sister called me last night, crying about her divorce.</u>

8. Dawn ran down the stairs. Dawn announced her good news.

   combined: <u>Dawn ran down the stairs, announcing her good news.</u>

9. Mark criticized the government. Mark blamed it for crime in the streets.

   combined: <u>Mark criticized the government, blaming it for crime in streets.</u>

10. The casserole bubbled on the stove. The casserole tempted me to taste it.

    combined: <u>Bubbling on the stove, the casserole tempted me to taste it.</u>

Use an *-ed* Modifier

You can also avoid short, choppy sentences by using an *-ed* modifier. This way, one of the short sentences becomes a phrase. (For more on modifiers, see Chapter 18.)

> **two short sentences:** The fish was broiled with lemon and butter. The fish was delicious.
>
> **combined with *-ed* modifier:** *Broiled with lemon and butter*, the fish was delicious.

Note: If the modifier begins the sentence, be sure that the next word is the one the modifier describes.

two short sentences: Sam gave me a jewelry box. It was painted with silver and blue flowers.

combined with *-ed* modifier: Sam gave me a jewelry box *painted with silver and blue flowers.*

Exercise 7 **Using *-ed* Modifiers**

Practice

Following are pairs of sentences. Combine each pair, using an *-ed* modifier.

Answers Will Vary.
Possible answers
shown at right.

1. The brass bowl was wrapped in tissue paper. The brass bowl was protected from scratches.

   combined: Wrapped in tissue paper, the brass bowl was protected from scratches.

2. The walls of our house are constructed of stone. Our house has thick walls.

   combined: Our house has thick walls constructed of stone.

3. Inez was praised by her coach. Inez found a reason to keep practicing.

   combined: Praised by her coach, Inez found a reason to keep practicing.

4. Professor Swenson found an old letter. The letter was hidden in a secret panel.

   combined: Professor Swenson found an old letter hidden in a secret panel.

5. The instructions were printed in tiny letters. The instructions were difficult to read.

   combined: Printed in tiny letters, the instructions were difficult to read.

6. Mr. and Mrs. Goldstein were honored as heroes. They saved a child from drowning.

   combined: Honored as heroes, Mr. and Mrs. Goldstein saved a child from drowning.

7. Our terrier was wrapped in a big blue blanket. He looked adorable.

   combined: Wrapped in a big blue blanket, our terrier looked adorable.

8. Ian was educated in England. He spelled some words differently than Americans do.

combined: <u>Educated in England, Ian spelled some words differently than</u>

<u>Americans do.</u>

9. Adam was invited to a formal dance. He had to rent a tuxedo.

combined: <u>Invited to a formal dance, Adam had to rent a tuxedo.</u>

_____

10. Jeanette ordered a chocolate wedding cake. The cake was covered in creamy white icing.

combined: <u>Jeanette ordered a chocolate wedding cake covered in creamy</u>

<u>white icing.</u>

Exercise 8   **Completing Sentences with *-ing* or *-ed* Modifiers**

 Collaborate   Working with a partner or a group, complete each sentence below.

Answers Will Vary.
Possible answers
shown at right.

1. Trapped by the flood, <u>the residents climbed to higher ground.</u>

2. Dangling from the frayed rope, <u>the heavy bell was a menace.</u>

3. Speaking in a strange voice, <u>the caller uttered a warning.</u>

4. Persuaded to tell the truth, <u>the suspect finally confessed.</u>

5. Attracted by his charming smile, <u>she smiled back.</u>

6. Driving in a strange city, <u>the tourists consulted their map.</u>

7. Running through the crowd, <u>I tried to catch the thief.</u>

8. Infuriated by their rude behavior, <u>Mary turned away from them.</u>

9. Exhausted by the workout, <u>the team stretched out on the lawn.</u>

10. Slowly climbing the stairs, <u>she struggled with the heavy bag.</u>

Use an Appositive

Another way to combine short, choppy sentences is to use an appositive. An **appositive** is a phrase that renames or describes a noun. Appositives can go in the beginning, middle, or end of a sentence. Use commas to set off the appositive.

> **two short sentences:** Chocolate milk contains calcium and vitamins. It is a favorite of children.
> **combined with appositive:** Chocolate milk, *a favorite of children*, contains calcium and vitamins.

TEACHING TIP:
If you remind students that an appositive gives "extra information" about a noun, they should easily see why commas are used to separate the additional material from the core sentence.

two short sentences: Richard is my best friend. He has been a wrestler for several years.
combined with appositive: Richard, *my best friend*, has been a wrestler for several years.

two short sentences: I am looking forward to Thanksgiving. It is my favorite holiday.
combined with appositive: I am looking forward to Thanksgiving, *my favorite holiday*.

Exercise 9 **Using Appositives**

Practice

Following are pairs of sentences. Combine each pair, using an appositive.

Answers Will Vary.
Possible answers shown at right.

1. Colton is an accomplished musician. He is on tour in South America.

   combined: Colton, an accomplished musician, is on tour in South America.

2. Springsdale Mall is the oldest mall in the county. It is being renovated and expanded.

   combined: Springsdale Mall, the oldest mall in the county, is being renovated and expanded.

3. Never buy Carlotta's cookies. They are the worst cookies on earth.

   combined: Never buy Carlotta's cookies, the worst cookies on earth.

4. My father offered me a trip to Cozumel. It is a good place for diving.

   combined: My father offered me a trip to Cozumel, a good place for diving.

5. Michael was the most responsible son. He took care of the younger children.

   combined: Michael, the most responsible son, took care of the younger children.

6. Cereal is a cheap meal. It was my dinner for years.

   combined: Cereal, a cheap meal, was my dinner for years.

7. Tom wants a happy marriage. He is a child of divorce.

   combined: Tom, a child of divorce, wants a happy marriage.

8. Aspirin has many medical uses. It is an over-the-counter drug.

   combined: <u>Aspirin, an over-the-counter drug, has many medical uses.</u>

   _____

9. Alexandra is the youngest in her calculus class. Alexandra is the best student.

   combined: <u>Alexandra, the youngest in her calculus class, is the best student</u>

   _____

10. Arlene Gerhard is a highly respected physician. She is a specialist in tropical diseases.

    combined: <u>Arlene Gerhard, a specialist in tropical diseases, is a highly</u>

    <u>respected physician.</u> _____

Use a *Who, Which,* or *That* Clause

Clauses beginning with *who, which,* or *that* can combine short sentences:

> **two short sentences:** Jacob is my favorite cousin. He won the golf tournament.
> **combined with *who* clause:** Jacob, *who is my favorite cousin,* won the golf tournament.

> **two short sentences:** Good running shoes can be expensive. They make running easier.
> **combined with *which* clause:** Good running shoes, *which can be expensive,* make running easier.

> **two short sentences:** The cinnamon buns were delicious. I tasted them.
> **combined with *that* clause:** The cinnamon buns *that I tasted* were delicious.

Punctuating *who, which,* or *that* clauses requires some thought. Decide whether the information in the clause is *essential* or *nonessential.* If the information is essential, do not put commas around it:

> **essential clause:** Mel is the person *who deserves to win.* (Without the clause *who deserves to win,* the sentence would not have the same meaning. Therefore, the clause is essential, and it is not set off by commas.)
> **nonessential clause:** Mel, *who has been singing for years,* deserves to win. (The clause *who has been singing for years* is not essential to the meaning of the sentence. Therefore, it is set off by commas.)

If you have to choose between *which* and *that, which* usually begins a nonessential clause, and *that* usually begins an essential clause:

> **essential clause:** The car *that he was driving* is expensive.
> **nonessential clause:** The car, *which I've had for years,* needs a new muffler.

For more on punctuating essential and nonessential clauses, see Chapter 24.

	Exercise 10	Using *Who, Which,* or *That* Clauses

Practice   Following are pairs of sentences. Combine each pair, using a *who, which,* or *that* clause.

Answers Will Vary.
Possible answers
shown at right.

1. Adrienne gave me some advice. I'll never forget the advice.

combined: Adrienne gave me some advice that I'll never forget.

2. Rattlesnake tastes like chicken. Rattlesnake is a delicacy in some fancy restaurants.

combined: Rattlesnake, which tastes like chicken, is a delicacy in some fancy restaurants.

3. The Chevrolet Malibu is a classic. It has been in our family for twenty years.

combined: The Chevrolet Malibu that has been in our family for twenty years is a classic.

4. Selena speaks fluent Portugese. She had a wonderful time in Brazil.

combined: Selena, who speaks fluent Portugese, had a wonderful time in Brazil.

5. People are desperate for cash. They should beware of "get rich quick" schemes.

combined: People who are desperate for cash should beware of "get rich quick" schemes.

6. Dr. Barthelmy is a renowned heart surgeon. He saved my mother's life.

combined: Dr. Barthelmy, who is a renowned heart surgeon, saved my mother's life.

7. Happy Face potato chips come in a bright yellow bag. They are popular with children.

combined: Happy Face potato chips, which come in a bright yellow bag, are popular with children.

8. I want a new knapsack. It must be kinder to my shoulders and back.

combined: I want a new knapsack that is kinder to my shoulders and back.

9. Alonso is grateful to his oldest sister. She tutored him through his biology class.

combined: <u>Alonso is grateful to his oldest sister, who tutored him through</u>

<u>his biology class.</u>

10. Horror movies used to be my favorite films. They don't interest me anymore.

combined: <u>Horror movies, which used to be my favorite films, don't interest</u>

<u>me anymore.</u>

| **Exercise 11** | **Revising for Sentence Variety: A Comprehensive Exercise** |

Connect

Rewrite the following paragraph, combining each pair of italicized sentences by using one of the following: an *-ing* modifier, an *-ed* modifier, an appositive, or a *who*, *which*, or *that* clause. Write your revisions above the lines.

Answers Will Vary.
Possible answers
shown at right.

When I was six, I had an imaginary friend who helped me through some

When I was six, I had an imaginary friend. He helped me through

lonely times.

some lonely times. My family had just moved to a new city, and I was

So I created an imaginary buddy named Super

having a hard time fitting in. *So I created an imaginary buddy. He was*

Jeff.   Always leaping over buildings and

named Super Jeff. Jeff was my hero. *He was always leaping over build-*

crashing through walls, he came to my rescue when I felt sad or afraid.

ings and crashing through walls. He came to my rescue when I felt sad

or afraid. At night, I had long conversations with Jeff; we discussed the

best way to handle the bullies at school or the stuck-up girls in my class.

Bolstered by his presence, I could

Jeff gave me confidence and strength. *I was bolstered by his presence. I*

face each day with confidence.

could face each day with confidence. As I grew more secure, Jeff gradu-

By the time I had made real friends, my imaginary friend

ally disappeared. *By the time I had made real friends, my imaginary*

was gone, moving on to another person who needed him.

friend was gone. He was moving on to another person who needed him.

APPENDIX

Grammar for ESL Students

NOUNS AND ARTICLES

A **noun** names a person, place, or thing. There are count nouns and noncount nouns.

Count nouns refer to persons, places, or things that can be counted:

three *doughnuts*, two *kittens*, five *pencils*

Noncount nouns refer to things that can't be counted:

medicine, housework, mail

Here are some more examples of count and noncount nouns:

Count	Noncount
rumor	gossip
violin	music
school	intelligence
suitcase	luggage

One way to remember the difference between count and noncount nouns is to put the word *much* in front of the noun. For example, if you can say *much luggage*, then *luggage* is a noncount noun.

Exercise 1 **Identifying Count and Noncount Nouns**

Practice Write *count* or *noncount* next to each word below.

1. _count_ automobile

2. _noncount_ water

3. _noncount_ furniture

4. _count_ bed

5. _count_ clock

6. _noncount_ honesty

7. _noncount_ research

8. _noncount_ milk

9. _count_ banana

10. _count_ tree

Using Articles with Nouns

Articles point out nouns. Articles are either **indefinite** *(a, an)* or **definite** *(the)*. There are several rules for using these articles:

- Use *a* in front of consonant sounds, and use *an* before vowel sounds:

a card	an orange
a radio	an answer
a button	an entrance
a thread	an invitation
a nightmare	an uncle

- Use *a* or *an* in front of singular count nouns. (*A* and *an* both mean "any one.")

  I ate *an* egg.
  James planted *a* tree.

- Do not use *a* or *an* with noncount nouns:

  not this: Selena filled the tank with ~~a~~ gasoline.
  but this: Selena filled the tank with gasoline.

  not this: I am studying ~~an~~ algebra.
  but this: I am studying algebra.

- Use *the* before both singular and plural count nouns whose specific identity is known to the reader:

  The dress with the sequins on it is my party dress.
  Most of *the* movies I rent are science fiction films.

- Use *the* before noncount nouns only when they are specifically identified:

  not this: I need ~~the~~ help. (Whose help? What help? The noncount noun *help* is not specifically identified.)
  but this: I need *the help of a good plumber.* (Now *help* is specifically identified.)

  not this: ~~Kindness~~ of the people who took me in was remarkable. (The nouncount noun *kindness* is specifically identifed, so you need *the*.)
  but this: *The kindness of the people who took me in* was remarkable.

Exercise 2   **Using *a* or *an***

Practice

Write *a* or *an* in each space where it is needed. Some sentences are correct as they are.

1. The doctor gave me __a__ prescription.

2. My counselor gave me _____ advice.

3. Sometimes __an__ insult can hurt you.

4. Christina went to the market to buy _____ fruit.

5. She bought __an__ apple and __a__ pear.

6. Alan is doing very well in _____ biology.

7. Patel doesn't like to drive in _____ traffic.

8. I'm looking for _**a**_ book and _**an**_ album.

9. My brother was driving _**a**_ truck.

10. That child needs _____ attention.

Exercise 3 Using *the*

Practice

Write *the* in the spaces where it is needed. Some sentences are correct as they are.

1. My nephew reached for _**the**_ toy his mother offered him.

2. He has _____ faith in _**the**_ future of the corporation.

3. Nancy likes to gaze at _**the**_ sky.

4. With _**the**_ assistance of my neighbors, I was able to repair my home.

5. My cousin was _**the**_ first member of _**the**_ family to study at _**the**_ University of Michigan.

6. _**The**_ books I like most are thrillers.

7. _**The**_ job interview at Microsoft taught me about answering hard questions.

8. Renald has _**the**_ athletic ability of a much older boy.

9. Amy needed _**the**_ house keys she had left behind.

10. Almost every day, Emily eats _____ ice cream.

Exercise 4 Correcting a Paragraph with Errors in Articles

Practice

Correct the errors with *a*, *an*, or *the* in the following paragraph. You may need to add, change, or eliminate articles. Write the corrections above the errors. There are twelve errors.

Sometimes ~~the~~ *a* book can make a dream come true. Last week I was looking for ~~the~~ *a* book about colleges and universities. I wanted the book my sister had used to help her find ~~a~~ *the* right college for her. I needed a college that stressed ~~the~~ technology and offered ~~a~~ good financial aid. *A (good)* Good financial aid package was most important *the* factor in my college choice. My sister had found *a* guide that covered ~~the~~ technical colleges and universities and listed available financial aid. I finally found the book I wanted, ~~a~~ *the* one that had helped my sister. With that book, I was able to locate ~~a~~ *the* best school for me, one that would save me ~~the~~ money and teach me about

technology.

NOUNS OR PRONOUNS USED AS SUBJECTS

A noun or a pronoun (a word that takes the place of a noun) is the subject of each sentence or dependent clause. Be sure that all sentences or dependent clauses have a subject:

> **not this:** Drives to work every day.
> **but this:** *He* drives to work every day.

> **not this:** My sister is pleased when gets a compliment.
> **but this:** My sister is pleased when *she* gets a compliment.

Be careful not to repeat the subject:

> **not this:** The police officer ~~she~~ said I was speeding.
> **but this:** The police officer said I was speeding.

> **not this:** The car that I needed ~~it~~ was a sports car.
> **but this:** The car that I needed was a sports car.

Exercise 5   **Correcting Errors with Subjects**

Practice

Correct any errors with subjects in the sentences below. Write your corrections above the lines.

My uncle Reynaldo never stops complaining.
1. My uncle Reynaldo he never stops complaining.

After dinner, my dog began to beg for a walk.
2. After dinner, my dog she began to beg for a walk.

Cars with dents in them rust quickly.
3. Cars with dents in them they rust quickly.

Sometimes in winter, it is hard to get out of a warm bed.
4. Sometimes in winter, is hard to get out of a warm bed.

Vegetables are good for you; they can also be delicious.
5. Vegetables are good for you; can also be delicious.

My daughter Briana is cranky after she wakes up from her nap.
6. My daughter Briana she is cranky after wakes up from her nap.

Last week, the cash register at my counter was broken.
7. Last week, the cash register at my counter it was broken.

Ann needs to save money by watching for bargains.
8. Needs to save money by watching for bargains.

When Bill gets his paycheck, he cashes it right away.
9. When gets his paycheck, he cashes it right away.

The most beautiful place in Jamaica was a quiet beach.
10. The most beautiful place in Jamaica it was a quiet beach.

VERBS

Necessary Verbs

Be sure that a main verb is not missing from your sentences or dependent clauses:

> **not this:** My boyfriend very ambitious.
> **but this:** My boyfriend *is* very ambitious.

not this: Sylvia brought her calculator when came over.
but this: Sylvia brought her calculator when *she* came over.

-s Endings

Be sure to put the -*s* on present tense verbs in the third person singular:

not this: He ~~run~~ in the park every morning.
but this: He *runs* in the park every morning.

not this: The concert ~~start~~ at 9:00 p.m.
but this: The concert *starts* at 9:00 p.m.

-ed Endings

Be sure to put an -*ed* ending when it is needed on the past participle form of a verb. There are three main forms of a verb:

present: Today I walk.
past: Yesterday I walked.
past participle: I *have* walked. He *has* talked.

The past particple form is also used after *were, was, had,* and *has:*

not this: He has ~~call~~ me every day this week.
but this: He has *called* me every day this week.

not this: My neighbor was ~~surprise~~ by the sudden storm.
but this: My neighbor was *surprised* by the sudden storm.

Do not add -*ed* endings to infinitives. An infinitive is the verb form that uses *to* plus the present form of the verb:

infinitives: to consider   to obey

not this: Dean wanted me to ~~considered~~ the proposal.
but this: Dean wanted me to *consider* the proposal.

not this: I taught my dog to ~~obeyed~~ commands.
but this: I taught my dog to *obey* commands.

Exercise 6
Practice

Correcting Errors in Verbs: Necessary Verbs, Third Person Present Tense, Past Participles, and Infinitives

Correct any errors in verbs in the sentences below. Write your corrections above the lines. Some sentences do not need any corrections.

1. The cake was ~~bake~~ (baked) at a pastry shop where my sister works part time.

2. When I started my job at the restaurant, I tried to ~~listened~~ (listen) to directions, but my boss talked very fast.

3. The children were amused by the puppets and the clown.

4. Every Saturday afternoon, Jasmine buys a lottery ticket and dreams of great wealth.

5. My Ford Explorer ~~run~~ (runs) well, but I need to get the oil changed.

6. By the time his parents arrived, Michael had ~~clean~~ (cleaned) up the mess from the party.

                 is
7. One of the closest malls in this area Midlakes Center Mall.

                                    prepared
8. I am not worried about the test because I have ~~prepare~~ for it.

       is
9. Honesty important in any true friendship.

               forgets shop   calls   orders
10. If David ~~forget~~ to ~~shopped~~ for dinner, he ~~call~~ a pizza place and ~~order~~ a large pepperoni pizza.

Exercise 7
Practice **Correcting a Paragraph with Errors in Necessary Verbs, Third Person Present Tense, Past Participles, and Infinitives**

Correct the verb errors in the following paragraph. Write your corrections above the lines. There are eight errors.

                      interviewed
     Simon was ~~interview~~ at three places before he found a job that he

wanted. At the first place, a furniture store, the manager said Simon was

                      trained   qualify
not sufficiently ~~train~~ in sales to ~~qualified~~ for the job. The second interview,

                  was
for a job as a waiter, more promising. The restaurant owner wanted to

                     work
hire Simon, but she wanted him to ~~worked~~ eight hours a day, from 8:00

a.m. to 4:00 p.m. Simon couldn't work those hours and still attend his

                        called
daytime college classes. After he had ~~call~~ six more stores and restaurants,

Simon finally got an interview at a deli. The interview was so successful

               offered
that Simon was ~~offer~~ a chance to work at the deli at night. Simon now

takes
~~take~~ his college classes in the daytime and earns money at night.

Two-Word Verbs

Two-word verbs contain a verb plus another word, either a preposition or adverb. The meaning of each word by itself is different from the meaning of the two words together. Look at this example:

    Sometimes Consuelo *runs across* her sister at the park.

You might check *run* in the dictionary and find that it means "to move quickly." *Across* means "from one side to the other." But *run across* means something different:

    not this: Sometimes Consuelo ~~moves quickly from one side to the other of~~ her sister at the park.
    but this: Sometimes Consuelo *encounters* her sister at the park.

Sometimes a word or words come between the words of a two-word verb:

    On Friday night, I *put* the garbage *out*; the sanitation department collects it early Saturday morning.

Here are some common two-word verbs:

ask out	Jamal wants to *ask* Teresa *out* for dinner.
break down	I hope my car doesn't *break down*.
call off	You can *call* the party *off*.
call on	I need to *call on* you for help.
call up	Jim will *call* Ken *up* tomorrow.
come across	I often *come across* bargains at thrift shops.
drop in	Let's *drop in* on Claude.
drop off	My father will *drop* the package *off*.
fill in	You can *fill in* your name.
fill out	Danny has to *fill out* a complaint form.
hand in	We have to *hand in* our assignments.
hand out	I hope the theater *hands out* free passes.
keep on	You must *keep on* practicing your speech.
look into	Jonelle will *look into* the situation.
look over	Jake needs to *look* the plans *over*.
look up	I had to *look* the word *up* in the dictionary.
pick up	Tomorrow I *pick up* my first paycheck.
quiet down	The teacher told the class to *quiet down*.
run into	Nancy will *run into* Alan at the gym.
run out	The family has *run out* of money.
think over	I like your idea; let me *think* it *over*.
try on	Before you buy the shirt, *try* it *on*.
try out	She wants to *try* the lawnmower *out*.
turn on	*Turn* the television *on*.
turn down	Sal thinks Wayne should *turn* the job *down*.
turn up	Nick is sure to *turn up* at the party.

Exercise 8 **Writing Sentences with Two-Word Verbs**

Practice

Write a sentence for each of the following two-word verbs. Use the examples above as a guide, but consult a dictionary if you are not sure what the verbs mean.

Answers Will Vary.
Possible answers
shown on the right.

1. think over — Tim made an offer, but I will think the deal over.

2. call up — Steve wants to call up an old friend.

3. look into — You need to look into the man's background.

4. run out — I have run out of ideas for my report.

5. run across — I often run across old boyfriends at church.

6. turn up — The lost wallet will surely turn up somewhere.

7. drop in — You can drop in to see me any weekend.

8. come across — Did you come across any spare change in the purse?

9. keep on — Sylvia said she will keep on trying to reach Liz.

10. try out — I want to try the treadmill out before I buy it.

Contractions and Verbs

Contractions often contain verbs you may not recognize in their shortened forms:

contraction: *I'm* losing weight.
long form: *I am* losing weight.

contraction: *She's* been my best friend for years.
long form: *She has* been my best friend for years.

contraction: *He's* leaving tomorrow.
long form: *He is* leaving tomorrow.

contraction: *They'll* never know.
long form: *They will* never know.

contraction: The *truck's* in the garage.
long form: The *truck is* in the garage.

Exercise 9   **Contractions and Verbs**

Practice   In the space above each italicized contraction, write its long form. The first one is done for you.

He would
1. *He'd* lend me the money if he had it.

Jack is
2. *Jack's* taking a class in architecture.

Jack has
3. *Jack's* taken a class in architecture.

We will
4. *We'll* miss the movie.

clock is
5. The *clock's* ten minutes fast.

I am
6. On weekends, *I'm* too busy to exercise.

You are
7. *You're* not listening to me at all.

You would
8. *You'd* like that, wouldn't you?

she will
9. I know *she'll* always be happy.

will not
10. That dog *won't* stop barking.

PREPOSITIONS

Prepositions are little words such as *with, for, of, around,* or *near.* Some prepositions can be confusing; these are the ones that show time and place.

Prepositions That Show Time

Use *at* to show a specific or precise time:

I will call you *at* 7:30 p.m.
The movie starts *at* midnight.

Use *on* with a specific day or date:

The meeting is *on* Friday.
Frances begins basic training *on* June 23.

Use *by* when you mean "no later than that time":

Jean has to be at work *by* 8:00 a.m.
We should be finished with the cleaning *by* 5:00 p.m.

Use *until* when you mean "continuing up to a time":

Yesterday I slept *until* 10:00 a.m.
The dentist cannot see me *until* tomorrow.

Use *in* when you refer to a specific time period (minutes, hours, days, months, years):

I'll be with you *in* a minute.
Nikela works *in* the morning. (You can also say *in* the afternoon, *in* the morning, or *in* the evening, but you must say *at* night.)

Use *during* when you refer to a continuing time period or within the time period:

I fell asleep *during* his speech.
My sister will study management *during* the summer.

Use *for* to tell the length of a period of time:

We have been married *for* two years.
Wanda and Max cleaned the attic *for* three hours.

Use *since* to tell the starting time of an action:

He has been calling *since* 9:00 a.m.
We have been best friends *since* third grade.

Prepositions That Show Place

Use *in* to refer to a country, area, state, city, or neighborhood:

He studied *in* Ecuador.
Mr. Etienne lives *in* Houston.

Use *in* to refer to an enclosed space:

He put the money *in* his wallet.
Delia waited for me *in* the dining room.

Use *at* to refer to a specific adddress:

The repair shop is *at* 7330 Glades Road.
I live *at* 7520 Maple Lane.

Use *at* to refer to a corner or an intersection:

We went to a garage sale *at* the corner of Spring Street and Lincoln Avenue.
The accident occured *at* the intersection of Madison Boulevard and Temple Road.

Use *on* to refer to a street or a block:

Dr. Lopez lives *on* Hawthorne Street.
Malcolm bought the biggest house *on* the block.

Use *on* to refer to a surface:

Put the sandwiches *on* the table.
There was a bright rug *on* the floor.

Use *off* to refer to a surface:

> Take the sandwiches *off* the table.
> She wiped the mud *off* the floor.

Use *into* and *out of* for small vehicles such as cars:

> Our dog leaped *into* the convertible.
> The children climbed *out of* the car.

Use *on* and *off* for large vehicles like planes, trains, buses, and boats:

> I was so seasick, I couldn't wait to get *off* the ship.
> I like to ride *on* the bus.

Exercise 10   **Correcting Errors in Prepositions**

Practice

Correct any errors in prepositions in the following sentences. Write your corrections above the lines.

1. The concert starts ~~in~~ _at_ 8:00 p.m. and will be over by 11:00 p.m.

2. When Patricia visited her cousins in Mexico City, she learned a great deal of Spanish ~~on~~ _in_ three weeks.

3. ~~By~~ _In_ ten minutes, I will collect the papers and put them ~~on~~ _in_ a sealed envelope.

4. At noon, we will get off the bus and start our ride ~~in~~ _on_ the train.

5. The flowers ~~in~~ _on_ the counter have lasted for five days.

6. I will see you on Wednesday, and then we can talk about old times ~~at~~ _on_ Cedar Street.

7. We used to live ~~on~~ _at_ 195 Clark Street, but now we live on Riverdale Lane.

8. My painting is hanging ~~in~~ _on_ the wall; it has been on display since last year.

9. We discovered a great seafood restaurant ~~in~~ _at_ the corner of Olive Street and Palm Avenue.

10. Although I am not a citizen, I have lived ~~at~~ _in_ this country for seven years.

Text Credits

Page 36: Janice Castro, with Dan Cook and Cristina Garcia, "Spanglish" from "Spanish Spoken Here." *Time.* July 11, 1988. Copyright © 1988 by Time Inc. Reprinted with permission.

Page 62: Elizabeth Wong, "A Present for Popo" from the *Los Angeles Times* (December 30, 1992). Copyright © 1992 by Elizabeth Wong. Reprinted with permission.

Page 87: Edna Buchanan, "Rocky Rowf" from *The Corpse Had a Familiar Face.* Copyright © 1987 by Edna Buchanan. Reprinted with the permission of Random House, Inc.

Page 108: Davidyne Mayleas, "How to Land the Job You Want" from *Empire Journal* (May 23, 1976)/*Reader's Digest* (June 1976). Copyright © 1976 by Reader's Digest Association. Reprinted with the permission of Reader's Digest.

Page 138: Brad Wackerlin, "Against All Odds, I'm Just Fine" from *Newsweek* 65, no. 27 (June 1990). Copyright © 1990 by Brad Wackerlin. Reprinted with the permission of the author.

Page 157: John Holt, "Three Disciplines for Children" from *Freedom and Beyond* (New York: E. P. Dutton, 1972). Copyright © 1972 by John Holt. Reprinted with the permission of Holt Associates; Heinemann, A Division of Reed Elsevier Inc, Portsmouth, NH.

Page 179: Virak Khiev, "Breaking the Bonds of Hate" from *Newsweek* (April 27, 1992). Copyright © 1992. Reprinted with permission.

Page 203: John Kellmayer, "Students in Shock" from David I. Daniels, Janet M. Goldstein, and Christopher G. Hayes, *A Basic Reader for College Writers.* Reprinted with the permission of the author.

Page 225: James Beekman, "Athletic Heroes" from *Newsweek "My Turn" Essays: More Student Opinion*, Newsweek Educational Programs. Copyright © 1996. Reprinted with permission.

Page 228: Julianne Malveaux, "Afrocentric Education Pointless if Girls Are Excluded" (1991). Reprinted with the permission of Julianne Malveaux/Last Word Publications.

Page 266: Sandra Cisneros, "Eleven" from *Woman Hollering Creek and Other Stories* (New York: Random House, 1991). Copyright © 1991 by Sandra Cisneros. Reprinted with the permission of Susan Bergholz Literary Services, New York. All rights reserved.

Page 269: Varla Ventura, "Althea Gibson: Never Give Up." Excerpted from *Sheroes* by Varla Ventura. Copyright © 1998 by Varla Ventura. Reprinted with the permission of Conari Press.

Page 271: Arthur Ashe, "Send Your Children to the Libraries" from the *New York Times* (February 6, 1977). Copyright © 1977 by The New York Times Company. Reprinted with permission.

Page 280: Gwinn Owens, "A Ridiculous Addiction" from *Newsweek* (December 4,1989). Copyright © 1989 by Gwinn Owens. Reprinted with permission.

Page 296: Dennis Hevesi, "Parental Discretion" from the *New York Times* (April 8, 1990), Educational Supplement. Copyright © 1990 by The New York Times Company. Reprinted with permission.

Photograph Credits

Page 60 **A**, Bruce Heinemann/PhotoDisc, Inc.; **page 60 B**, Doug Menuez/PhotoDisc, Inc.; **page 85 A**, Jeremy Woodhouse/PhotoDisc, Inc.; **page 85 B**, Doug Menuez/PhotoDisc, Inc.; **page 264 A**, Mark Downey/PhotoDisc, Inc.; **page 264 B**, Barbara Penoya/PhotoDisc, Inc.

Index